Routledge Revivals

Corporate Financial Disclosure, 1900–1933

This book, first published in 1986, is a close analysis into management's financial disclosure practices of the first half of the twentieth century. With criticisms of existing financial disclosure practices continuing to today, this study aims to make sense of the present through an examination of past practices, difficulties and solutions.

Corporate Financial Disclosure, 1900–1933

A Study of Management Inertia Within a Rapidly Changing Environment

David F. Hawkins

Routledge
Taylor & Francis Group

First published in 1986
by Garland Publishing, Inc.

This edition first published in 2021 by Routledge
2 Park Square, Milton Park, Abingdon, Oxon, OX14 4RN
and by Routledge
605 Third Avenue, New York, NY 10017

Routledge is an imprint of the Taylor & Francis Group, an informa business

Publisher's Note

The publisher has gone to great lengths to ensure the quality of this reprint but points out that some imperfections in the original copies may be apparent.

Disclaimer

The publisher has made every effort to trace copyright holders and welcomes correspondence from those they have been unable to contact.

A Library of Congress record exists under LCCN: 86014961

ISBN 13: 978-0-367-77019-8 (hbk)
ISBN 13: 978-1-003-16942-0 (ebk)
ISBN 13: 978-0-367-77021-1 (pbk)

DOI: 10.4324/9781003169420

CORPORATE FINANCIAL DISCLOSURE, 1900–1933

A Study of Management Inertia Within a Rapidly Changing Environment

David F. Hawkins

Garland Publishing, Inc.
New York and London
1986

For a complete list of Garland's publications in accounting, please see the final pages of this volume.

Library of Congress Cataloging-in-Publication Data

Hawkins, David F.
Corporate financial disclosure, 1900–1933.

(Accounting thought and practice through the years)
Bibliography: p.
Thesis (doctoral)—Harvard, 1962.
1. Disclosure of information (Securities law)—United States—History. 2 Corporations—Accounting—Law and legislation—United States—History. I. Title.
KF1449 H39 1986 346.73'0666 86-14961
347.306666
ISBN 0-8240-7851-9 (alk. paper)

Design by Bonnie Goldsmith

The volumes in this series are printed on acid-free, 250-year-life paper.

Printed in the United States of America

CORPORATE FINANCIAL DISCLOSURE, 1900-1933

A Study of Management Inertia Within a Rapidly Changing Environment

A thesis presented

by

DAVID FREDERICK HAWKINS

to

The Graduate School of Business Administration

in partial fulfillment of the requirements

for the degree of

Doctor of Business Administration

Harvard University

Cambridge, Massachusetts

April 1962

ACKNOWLEDGEMENTS

This thesis was prepared under the direction of three members of the faculty of the Harvard Graduate School of Business Administration: Professors Walter F. Frese, Ralph W. Hidy and John R. Yeager. To each of these men goes my heartfelt thanks for their constructive comments, good cheer and patience--all of which was needed to get the thesis to its final stage. Two others, Professor Vincent P. Carosso and Miss Marian V. Sears, while not officially connected with the thesis project, were kind enough to read critically an earlier draft. A number of their suggestions, which were most welcome, were incorporated in the final product. None of these people, of course, can be held responsible for the thesis itself. That responsibility must rest solely with the author.

TABLE OF CONTENTS

CHAPTER | Page

CHAPTER Page

LIST OF ILLUSTRATIONS

INTRODUCTION

In recent years a number of those who rely upon published corporate financial statements, especially for security investment decision purposes, have expressed dissatisfaction with the existing financial disclosure practices of corporate management. Out of a concern with this contemporary criticism of corporate life there grew a desire, on the part of the author, to further examine and appraise this criticism, particularly from the point of view of corporate management. Therefore, as a preliminary step, it was decided to look first into history to see if an analogous situation involving criticism of management's financial disclosure practices had previously existed. Hopefully, through the study of such a situation, if one had ever existed, the present would be made more comprehensible.

Accordingly, after some preliminary research, the history from about 1900 to the passage of the 1933 Securities Act, of three topics--management's prospectus disclosure practices, the demands of those external to the firm for greater corporate publicity and the state and federal regulation of corporate securities--showed enough promise to warrant further research. All three areas, as the thesis illustrates, were relevant to the enactment of the Securities Act of 1933: the first attempt by the federal government to regulate the financial disclosure practices of those corporations approaching the public money markets. Thus, the following historical material touching upon these three topics and the concluding observations are presented primarily with one goal in mind: to assist today's management to understand better the opportunities and dangers inherent in the existing discrepancy between management practices and the articulated user needs in the area of corporate financial disclosure.

The thesis itself is an historical survey beginning in 1900 of those economic, social and political events, trends, attitudes and practices which culminated in the passage of the 1933 Securities Act. In particular, the study seeks to identify, analyze and interpret--in both the historical and predictive sense--the factors--internal and external to the firm--which led to the need to create minimum standards of corporate financial disclosure through federal legislation. This analysis, the author believes, provides a number of insights into the relationship of the management function to corporate financial disclosure practices to investors. In addition, the study clearly illustrates some of the problems, pressures and dangers created when management's financial disclosure practices persistently fall short of the standards against which these practices are evaluated by those external to the firm.

More specifically, the thesis examines the relationship, between 1900 and 1933, of corporate financial disclosure practices, as revealed in prospectuses and the standards of certain public groups against which such practices were evaluated. Other topics covered included management's statements and practices pertaining to financial disclosure to investors; the expressed needs related to financial disclosure of the numerous users of financial statements; and the attitudes and practices of public accountants and investment bankers toward corporate disclosure. Also discussed is the influence of the New York Stock Exchange upon financial disclosure; the demands for greater corporate publicity of the so-called critics of big business; the securities regulation, proposed and enacted, involving the federal and various state governments; and, finally, the changing social, political and economic framework within which each of these numerous and diverse groups existed, interacted and developed.

Hopefully, this study of the period 1900-1933, as noted above, will lead to a better appreciation by today's management of some present trends, practices and conditions related to corporate financial disclosure which, unless checked or modified, may well result in further limitations upon the flexibility now enjoyed by management in the preparation of periodic reports to stockholders. Currently a number of persons--accountants, politicians, security analysts and "professional minority" stockholders--are highly critical of management's "inadequate" financial statements included in annual reports to stockholders. In fact, one observer has labelled the whole area of corporate financial disclosure as "financial fantasy." Disturbed by this situation, over three years ago, the American Institute of Certified Public Accountants set up a group, the Accounting Principles Board, to review the field of financial accounting and, if possible, establish authoritative accounting principles to govern the drawing up of financial reports to the public.

To date, the Accounting Principles Board has jealously excluded corporate executives from its deliberations and, in addition, made little progress. Most corporate executives have shown but a passing interest in these proceedings and few companies have improved their financial disclosure practices so as to satisfy management's critics. And in the background the Securities and Exchange Commission waits, patiently, for either the accountants or corporate management to bring about the asked for reforms in the area of financial disclosure. Eventually, in the absence of reform, the Securities and Exchange Commission must bring about the asked for improvements through regulation--and uninvited regulation of corporate activity has seldom proved acceptable to management. A few comments on this matter are presented toward the end of the thesis.

Finally, the author must admit to three assumptions which guided him in the development of his research plan. Namely, corporate financial disclosure was a management responsibility; the ultimate determinant of corporate financial disclosure practices was management's attitude toward corporate publicity; and management wished to avoid uninvited government regulation. Subsequently, each of these assumptions was, hopefully without undue effort on the part of the researcher, shown to have been reasonable and appropriate to the period covered.

Definitions

Defined below are a number of the terms used repeatedly throughout the thesis.

The term "investor", for the purposes of this study, unless stated otherwise, encompassed the great variety of individuals and institutions who purchased--

for investment or speculation--corporate securities in the open market. In particular, the study looked at those investors interested in the securities of nonregulated nonfinancial industries, especially industrial corporations, for it was this group of investors who were most directly touched by the Securities Act of 1933.

"Corporate disclosure" and "corporate publicity", as used below, are synonomous terms which embraced all management inspired published information--quantitative and qualitative--related to corporate activities. This information pertained to such things as financial position, operating results, managerial pricing policy, labor relations, ownership and pension schemes. Part of the material included within this broad category is also covered by the term "financial disclosure" which, when used separately, referred to either the financial or accounting information made public by corporate management. The particular term "prospectus financial disclosure" is used to cover financial disclosure as revealed in prospectuses.

A "prospectus", broadly defined, included all written material used to offer corporate securities to the public. Prospectuses, for the purposes of analysis, were classified in two ways: first, according to who was principally responsible for those statements reproduced in the prospectus; and, second, according to the amount of material disclosed. The first method led to the establishment of two classes: "bankers prospectuses" and "management prospectuses". The second method resulted in three types of prospectus: "full prospectus", "abridged prospectus" and "circular." Any one prospectus could, of course, be classified according to both systems of classification.

In general, the prospectuses issued during much of the period studied consisted of four or fewer pages of written material and were either the representations of the investment banker marketing the issue, in which case the prospectus was labelled "bankers prospectus"; or the representation of an officer of the corporation issuing the securities, in which case the prospectus was classed as a "management prospectus." The latter type, of course, was of particular interest to this study. Since, in practice, the number of pages provided a rough index of the amount of material disclosed in prospectuses, the "full prospectus" class, in general, included prospectuses of three or more pages in length; the "abridged prospectus" group included most two-page prospectuses; and the "circular" class included nearly all of the one page prospectuses. In practice, of course, the classification problem was more complex and, the author suggests, the reader not concern himself with the various sub-groups of prospectuses until chapter seven--the first chapter to examine these sub-classes. In chapter seven a fuller discussion of the various categories of prospectuses is presented.

Finally, the term "corporate management", in general, refers to the management group at the top of the corporate pyramid, especially the management organizations of the large publicly owned industrial corporations.

Why 1900-1933 and Prospectuses?

The decision to focus the study on the period 1900-1933 and to limit the analysis of management disclosure practices to prospectuses, particularly of industrial corporations, was made for the variety of reasons discussed below.

1900-1933

The historical analysis was confined to 1900-1933 since this was a period of great change in a number of the factors which, the author believed, were relevant to corporate financial disclosure. The year 1900 was chosen as the starting point as it marked the beginning of the era during which industrial corporations sought, on an ever increasing scale, capital from external sources on a nation-wide basis. The year 1933 was selected as the cut-off date since the impact of the Securities Act of 1933 so greatly affected later prospectus disclosure standards, almost to the exclusion of all other factors, that the period after 1933 is not comparable to the earlier years. Also, the Securities Act, and the years subsequent to 1933, raise a number of extremely complex questions related to prospectus disclosure which, within the suggested time limits for writing a Harvard Business School doctoral thesis, were unmanageable.

During the thirty-three years covered by the study a number of things happened which might have conceivably influenced corporate financial disclosure practices and the standards against which practices were publicly evaluated. For instance, as noted above, between 1900-1933, corporations first sought widespread public ownership; the investor base was both broadened and enlarged; and the differentiation between ownership and management became more distinct and more prevalent. Corporations became vested with a "public interest." In addition, the New York Stock Exchange, the Investment Bankers Association of America, the American Institute of Accountants and several other groups all began to develop and adopt recommendations, rules and regulations which were designed to influence management's practices related to corporate financial disclosure to investors. The needs of the users of financial data, in particular investors, also underwent a change during 1900-1933 as new techniques of analysis and new criteria for evaluation of corporate securities were developed. And, finally, the government intervened. Thus, during this thirty-three year period a number of persons and institutions outside the firm sought to, or in fact did, influence the creation of new standards and practices related to financial disclosure. A bibliography showing the various materials--primary and secondary--used in the study of this period is presented at the end of the thesis.

<u>Prospectuses</u>

The analysis of management financial disclosure practices was limited to those revealed in prospectuses rather than, say, annual reports for at least three reasons. First, the history of prospectus disclosure during the period 1900-1933 represented the "life cycle" of a management instrument--the prospectus--which, in the case of industrial firms, all too rapidly passed from a state of non-regulation to regulation. Second, the Securities Act of 1933, the so-called "truth in securities bill," was, and still is today, the most significant externally imposed restriction on management's financial reporting freedom. Third, between 1900 and 1933, the information disclosed in prospectuses was important to investors since in a number of instances no other source of information was available.

In all, over 500 prospectuses offering a variety of industrial securities, issued by almost every conceivable type of industrial corporation, and marketed by a number of different investment bankers, were closely examined. These prospectuses were randomly selected from the extensive collection of prospectuses on file at Baker Library, Harvard Graduate School of Business Administration. This collection, in the absence of evidence to the contrary, the author considers representative of the range of prospectuses issued between 1900 and 1933.

<u>The Thesis Outline</u>

Since management lost through the passage of the Securities Act a considerable amount of its freedom to decide what financial data was to be disclosed or not disclosed in prospectuses, the organization of a significant proportion of the thesis material about the history of securities regulation seemed appropriate. Accordingly, the material was so organized.

The thesis is divided into nine chapters. The first chapter traces the legislation of prospectus and financial disclosure standards in England up to the enactment of the English Companies Act of 1900. The principle of securities regulation established by this 1900 Act was to influence greatly later American securities regulation, particularly on the federal level. Chapters two through eight, inclusive, present the American history during the period 1900 to 1933 of the following: securities legislation on the state and federal level; the demands for more honest and complete prospectus and corporate financial disclosure; and prospectus financial disclosure practices.

Chapters two through nine of the thesis are divided under the following headings: chapter two: the critics of big business, 1900-1917; Chapter three: the demand for disclosure of corporate affairs, 1900-1917; chapter four: state security regulations, 1850-1933; chapter five: major federal securities legislation proposals, 1918-1929; chapter six: proposed financial disclosure standards, 1918-1929; chapter seven: prospectus disclosure practices, 1900-1930; and chapter eight: the Securities Act of 1933. Chapter nine presents the conclusions to the historical portion of the study as well as the implications for today's administrator which can be derived from these conclusions.

*****

The thesis is a study within the framework of a dynamic society of management's responsibility and practices related to financial disclosure. It is not an analysis of accounting theory <u>per se</u>.

CHAPTER ONE

THE LEGISLATION OF PROSPECTUS AND FINANCIAL DISCLOSURE STANDARDS IN ENGLAND BEFORE 1900

The origins of the regulatory philosophy underlying the Securities Act of 1933 can be found in the British legislation related to securities enacted prior to 1900. In fact, the British experiences in the area of corporate financial disclosure to investors, and the related topic of securities regulation, greatly influenced, as will be seen later, a number of those who spoke on these topics in the United States during the period 1900-1933.

English statutory regulation pertaining to securities, securities dealers and the protection of the investor can be traced back to the reign of Edward I. Much later, however, in 1720, the first British statute, the so-called Bubble Act, to establish state control over the activities of the promoters of joint stock companies was passed. This Act,which was enacted after a period of uncontrolled security speculation, sought to protect the investor by limiting the availability of the instrument of his speculation -- securities. The Act in essence prohibited, except by special permission of parliament, the issuance of securities in joint stock companies. Subsequently, in 1825, under the pressure of increasing industrializa-

DOI: 10.4324/9781003169420-1

tion, the Bubble Act was repealed.

Beginning in 1844, Parliament passed a series of comprehensive statutes, called Companies Acts, which were designed to regulate the formation, management and winding up of public companies. Each one of these nineteenth century acts, and the events surrounding them were relevant in some way to the establishment of the concept of "disclosure," rather than direct regulation, as the philosophy underlying modern British and American (federal) securities regulation. Of those English acts passed after 1844, the following are mentioned below: The Directors Liability Act of 1890; and the Companies Acts of 1844, 1847, 1855, 1862, 1867, and 1900.

The Bubble Act

The Bubble Act was passed in 1720. This Act was not the first British statute relating to securities for, as early as the thirteenth century, a statute of Edward I had authorized the London Court of Aldermen to license securities brokers in that city.[1] The 1720 Act, however, was the first attempt by Parliament to establish effective administrative control over the securities offered by corporate promoters to the public.

[1] Louis Loss, Security Regulation (Boston: Little, Brown and Company, 1951), p. 1.

Later, in 1825, the Bubble Act was revoked and within twenty years the first of the modern English Companies Acts emerged.

Beginning in 1690 the English entered a period of financial speculation which lasted until 1720. During these 30 years, a number of people from every class of society engaged in extravagant speculation in the freely transferable shares of the numerous joint stock companies then organized to undertake enterprises of varying degrees of plausibility.[1] These enterprises were no ordinary corporations, for the operations of several of the larger joint stock corporations, the stocks of which were among the most popular traded, were also linked up with the public budget.[2] The most notorious of these quasi-public companies was the South Sea Company whose "stock was the most fashionable speculation ever to grip Great Britain."[3] One writer, Virginia Cowles, in speaking of the speculation in the South Sea Company stock said:

---

[1]For examples of some of the "lunatic" enterprises to which the public were invited to subscribe during 1720, see Virginia Cowles, The Great Swindle (New York: Harper and Brothers, 1960), p. 120 ff.

[2]Armand Budington DuBois, The English Business Company after the Bubble Act 1720-1800 (New York: The Commonwealth Fund, 1938), pp. 1-2.

[3]Cowles, op. cit., p. 132.

> One must remember that the great majority of investors...knew nothing of finance. It did not occur to them...to study a balance sheet before risking their money. They bought on hunch and hearsay. The government was behind the South Sea scheme; the King was Governor of the Company: what could be more solid or respectable?[1]

By the mid-1690's Parliament had become so alarmed by the effects upon the trade of England of this widespread speculation that a commission was appointed to inquire into the matter.

In 1697, the report of the commission was published. This report and the motive for establishing the commission gave some indication of a dual goal which was to influence the type of British company law eventually adopted during the nineteenth century. Simply stated, the twin purpose of these acts was the protection of the investor from security frauds and the encouragement of the promotion of new legitimate businesses. The 1697 report stated:

> The pernicious Art of Stock-jobbing hath, of late, so perverted the End and Design of Companies and Corporations, erected for the introducing or carrying on, of Manufactures to be the Private Profit of the first Projectors, that the Privileges granted to them have, commonly, been made no other Use of, by the first Procurers and Subscribers, but to sell again, with Advantage, to ignorant Men, drawn in by Reputation, falsely raised, and artfully spread, concerning the thriving State of their Stock. Thus the first Under-

---

[1] Ibid.

> takers, getting quit of the Company, by selling their Shares for much more than they are really worth, to Men allured by the noise of great profit, the Management of that Trade and Stock comes to fall into unskilful Hands; whereby the Manufactures, intended to be provided by such Grants, and put into the Management of Companies, for their better Improvement, come, from very promising Beginnings, to dwindle away to nothing, and be in a worse Condition than if they were perfectly left free, and unassisted with such Laws, or Patents; and Instance whereof, we humbly conceive, is to be found in the Paper and Linen Manufactures, which, we fear, feel the Effects of this Stock-jobbing Management, and are not in so thriving a Condition as they might have been, had they not fallen under this kind of Misfortune.[1]

The mania of speculation persisted until 1720, By then, however, it had reached such frightening proportions that a desperate Parliament in May of that year passed the so-called Bubble Act: "An Act to Restrain the Extravagant and Unwarrantable Practice of Raising Money by Voluntary Subscriptions for carrying on Projects Dangerous to the trade and Subjects of this Kingdom."[2]

Briefly, the 1720 Act sought to limit stock speculation by prohibiting the creation of joint-stock companies except by special Act of Parliament

---

[1]Felix Frankfurter, "The Federal Securities Act," <u>Fortune</u>, Vol. 8, No. 2, August 1933, p. 53.

[2]6 George 1, c. 18 (1720).

or Charter from the Crown.[1] In addition, any broker trading in the shares of an unlawful company was liable to lose his license. Another provision of the Act allowed merchants and traders whose businesses were injured by the activities of an unlawful company to sue for treble damages.[2] Now, for the first time in England, stock companies were placed under government control and, "for good or for ill, Parliament had committed the business company to the ward of administrative officials, and to this accountability, company law of the succeeding century owes its amorphousness."[3]

In 1825 Parliament, so as to make available more sources of capital to promoters, repealed the Bubble Act.[4] Parliament now realized that the joint stock company, with its transferable shares, was the one form of commercial organization which legitimate promoters could effectively use to raise capital in such amounts as would ensure the development of a national economy based on manufacturing and trade.

---

[1]The "Bubble Act" did not put an end to speculation in England. Speculation in the stock of unlawful companies continued for some time after the passage of the Act. Again, after the Napoleonic wars, there was another paroxysm of speculation.

[2]Loss, op. cit., p. 5.

[3]DuBois, op. cit., p. 12.

[4]6 George 4. c91 (1825).

If business was to be regulated a new concept of regulation was necessary. The old was inappropriate: it neither protected the investor nor promoted trade.

The 1844 Companies Act

By 1840, freed from government control, the joint-stock form of commercial enterprise had substantially increased in number and importance. Unfortunately, the number of fraudulent joint stock companies promoted also increased and again there arose among members of Parliament a demand for the establishment of some more adequate form of government supervision over business activities. Accordingly, in 1841, a Select Committee on Joint Stock Companies was appointed by Parliament, "to inquire into the state of the Laws respecting Joint Stock Companies (excepting for Banking) with a view to the greater security of the Public."[1] The eventual report of this committee was to introduce a new form of regulation based on the full and fair disclosure of corporate financial and management affairs.

In 1842, Sir Robert Peel became Prime Minister and, one year later in 1843, he appointed William Gladstone, then the President of the Board of Trade, Chairman of the Select Committee on Joint Stock Com-

[1]First Report of the Select Committee on Joint Stock Companies, British Parliamentary Papers. Vol. VII, 1844, p. ii.

panies. Subsequently, in 1844, under Gladstone's direction the Select Committee submitted its report to Parliament. One important conclusion Gladstone's committee drew was that better protection of investors might be achieved if prospectuses were registered and their contents prescribed by law; the goal being to provide the investing public and their advisors with adequate and reliable knowledge pertaining to the companies whose stock they owned or were solicited to purchase.

The Select Committee divided "bubble companies"--joint stock companies--into three classes:

> 1st, those which, being faulty in their nature, inasmuch as they are founded on unsound calculations, cannot succeed by any possibility; -
>
> 2dly, those which, let their objects be good or bad, are so ill constituted as to render it probable that the miscarriage or failures incident to mismanagement will attend them; and -
>
> 3dly, those which are faulty, or fraudulent in their objective, being started for no other purposes that to create shares for the purpose of jobbing in them, or to create, under pretence of carrying on a legitimate business, the opportunity and means of raising funds to be shared by the adventurers who start the company.[1]

To protect the public from this third class of company, those fraudulent in their objective, the remedy the Committee said was "easy": publicity of directors names, the dead of settlement, and the

---

[1] *Ibid.*, p. iv.

amount and nature of the enterprises's capital. With such information available "the public would have the means of knowing with whom they deal; and agents and bankers would be enabled to avoid participating in the discredit of such concerns, by giving the sanction of their names to questionable undertakings."[1]

The formulation of a suitable remedy was more difficult for the second class: companies created for good objects but ill constituted. The remedies suggested earlier for the limiting of fraudulent companies would, the Committee said, be insufficient in this case. The solutions suggested by the Committee were: periodic stockholder meetings; periodic balancing, audit and publication of accounts; and the making of directors more responsible to shareholders. The report said: "periodic accounts, if honestly made and fairly audited, cannot fail to excite attention to the real state of a concern; and by means of improved remedies, parties to mismanagement may be made more amenable for acts of fraud and illegality."[2]

The only class which was beyond certain cure by legislation, the Committee believed, was the first class: companies faulty in their nature. "No antecedent check will avail; any authority appointed to

---

[1]*Ibid.*, p. v.

[2]*Ibid.*

act as censor would be liable to be deceived as the promoter of the schemes, and it might sometimes sanction bad, and at other times prevent good, schemes."[1] The best suggestion the committee could offer to reduce the risk of loss through an investment in the first class of company was the early publication, resulting from registration with the Board of Trade, of the prospectuses and circulars of such companies.

Thus, the general solutions recommended by the Committee were publicity of accounts and registration of prospectuses so that "the share-holder and other persons professionally employed in making investment... [may] learn more easily and more accurately the real nature of these Companies; so that, at least, the ignorant may not be so misled by the example of persons of weight and intelligence...."[2]

After reviewing the Committee's report, Parliament passed the Companies Act of 1844[3] which incorporated in a modified form a number of Gladstone's recommendations related to corporate and prospectus disclosure. The Act introduced the principle of compulsory disclosure through the device of requiring certain information

---

[1] Ibid.

[2] Ibid., p. vi.

[3] 7 and 8 Victoria, c. 110 (1844). The act also introduced the principal of general incorporation.

describing the promoters, and a copy of each prospectus issued, to be registered and filed with the Registry Office of the Board of Trade. These documents were available for public inspection.

The Act also sought to protect further the investor by requiring all registered companies to publish an annual report. It was thought the publication of financial statements, particularly those related to solvency, would cut back the number of acts of fraud and illegality by company promoters and directors since, hopefully, the various activities of a dishonest management would soon be discovered by those "knowledgeable men in business" who counseled the investing public. Henceforth, these companies registered under the Act were obliged to keep books on account and to present to their shareholders an annual report which was to consist of at least a "full and fair" balance sheet audited by one or more auditors, at least one of whom had to be appointed by the shareholders. Copies of its audited balance sheet were to be filed annually with the Registrar of Joint Stock Companies.

Finally, the 1844 Act also contained an anti-fraud provision. Acts of fraud of wilful omission by a director or officer with respect to the information contained in the prospectus, books of accounts, books of register or any document belonging to the company was deemed to be a misdemeanor.

The Act did not specify the duties of the auditor or the form of content of either the balance sheet or the prospectus. The most probable reasons for this omission are three in number. First, there was no established auditing code. Second, generally accepted accounting conventions as we know them today were non-existent. And third, there prevailed a general desire not to interfere unduly with legitimate business activities.

Disclosure: Decline and Revival 1845-1889

Subsequently, between 1845 and 1862, in order to assist new enterprises in their search for capital three more relevant companies acts were passed in 1847, 1855, and 1862. The content of these three acts was strongly influenced by Parliament's desire to create conditions favorable to the continued creation of new commercial enterprises upon which, it was then believed, the maintenance of England's leadership in the world industrial economy depended.[1] The success of this general policy of promoting industrialization may be judged from the rapid increase in the number of registered companies after 1862. In 1862, 165 new companies

[1]For example, the 1847 Act made it easier for companies to register as incorporated bodies and the act of 1855 and 1862 established limited liability for shareholders of joint stock companies.

had been registered; in 1863, 790; in 1864, 997; and in 1865, 1,034 new companies were registered.[1]

However, between 1845 and 1862, Parliament, in its enthusiasm to promote industrial expansion, relaxed or removed a number of the statutory requirements related to disclosure. For instance, the 1847 Act revoked the prospectus filing requirements of the 1844 Act as this particular provision was "found to be very bothersome to the promoter." The 1856 Act swept away all disclosure, accounting and auditing requirements.[2] Both the 1856 and 1862 Acts[3] contained clauses which made it possible for companies to avoid the statutory requirement that stockholders receive annual reports. The abandonment of these disclosure provisions can also be traced to the above-mentioned strong contemporary feeling against the intervention

---

[1]Nicholas A. H. Stacey, English Accountancy 1800-1954 (London: Gee and Company, 1954), p. 8.

[2]The widely published failure, in 1856, of the Royal British Bank due to the falsification of balance sheets and other financial reports did not convince those responsible for legislation that adequate disclosure based on compulsory accounting and auditing clauses was necessary. It was argued, compulsion in this area may lead to relaxed vigilance by investors. Anyway, it was said, the unscrupulous could easily avoid such clauses. A. C. Littleton and B. C. Yamey, Studies in The History of Accounting (Homewood: Richard D. Irwin, Inc., 1956), p. 367.

[3]The Act of 1862 (25 & 26 Victoria c. 89) was a so-called Consolidation Act., e.g., it consolidated into one act all the existing company law.

by Parliament in business matters.

The relaxation of the disclosure and registration statutory requirements did not, however, remove all of the restraints upon the claims promoters could make regarding their promotions. In 1861, the court in the case of Brunswick Company v. Muggeridge,[1] after admitting that the object of a promoter to make his company as attractive as possible was understandable, cautioned promoters thus:

> Those who issue a prospectus, holding out to the public the great advantages which will accrue to persons who will take shares in a proposed undertaking, and inviting them to take shares on the faith of the representations therein contained, are bound to state everything with strict and scrupulous accuracy, and not only to abstain from stating as a fact that which is not so, but to omit no one fact within their knowledge, the existence of which might in any degree affect the nature and extent or quality of the privileges and advantages which the prospectus holds out as an inducement to take shares.[2]

The above remarks were often referred to thereafter as "the golden rule as to framing prospectuses."[3]

In 1867, following the financial panic of 1866 and the "chronic distrust"[4] it generated, Parliament

---

[1]1, Dr. and Sm. 383.

[2]Ibid. See also A. C. Connell, Companies and Company Law (London: Pitman & Sons, 1924), p. 61.

[3]Connell, Companies and Company Law, p. 61.

[4]The Banker's Magazine, Vol. 27, September 1867, pp. 885 ff.

hastily enacted a series of amendments[1] to the 1862 Companies Act. These 1867 amendments, among other things, specified the minimum legal content of prospectuses. Section 38 of the Act provided:

> Every Prospectus of a Company, and every Notice inviting Persons to subscribe for Shares in a Joint Stock Company, shall specify the Dates and the Names of the Parties to any Contract entered into by the Company, or the Promoters, Directors, or Trustees thereof, before the Issue of such Prospectus or Notice, whether subject to Adoption by the Directors or the Company or otherwise; and any Prospectus or Notice not specifying the same shall be deemed fraudulent on the Part of the Promoters, Directors, and Officers of the Company knowingly issuing the same, as regards any Person taking Shares in the Company on the Faith of such Prospectus, unless he shall have had Notice of such Contract.

A copy of the prospectus, however, did not have to be filed with the Board of Trade.

In practice, the effectiveness of section 38 was greatly weakened. For instance, the courts in interpreting this particular section of the 1867 Act insisted that only material contracts need be revealed.[2] Also, the courts allowed promoters to issue prospectuses containing a clause stating the applicant for shares would waiver compliance by the promoter with

---

[1]29 & 30 Victoria, c. 131 (1867).

[2]Nash v. Calthorpe 2 ch., 237.

this statutory requirement.[1] The waiver clause was needed, it was argued, so as not to force promoters to reveal vital competitive data, particularly secret contracts.

During the 1870's Parliament passed a number of Acts which reversed the trend away from the compulsory disclosure of accounts: a trend which had begun with the 1847 Act. Initially, the new statutes related only to "special" types of companies such as financial institutions and public utilities. Beginning in 1868, the Regulation of Railways Act[2] required that railroad companies publish annual reports and file annual returns with the Board of Trade. Next, in 1870, the Life Assurance Companies Act,[3] provided for life assurance companies to make available audited annual reports to shareholders and to file annual returns with the Board of Trade. Later, public utilities were made subject to similar requirements by the 1871 Gas

---

[1] Macleay v. Tart A. C. 24. The waiver clause, however, was not to be "tricky and fraudulent." In Greenwood v. Leather Shod Wheel Co. 1 ch., 421, the court held: "the waiver clause is clearly tricky and fraudulent. It is printed in small type so as to escape attention. It is worded so as to conceal and not to afford notice of the contract...to which the promoter was a party. The clause was void."

[2] 31 & 32 Victoria c. 119.

[3] 33 & 34 Victoria c. 61.

Works Clause Act,[1] and the 1882 Electric Lighting Act.[2] This movement toward the reintroduction of statutory provisions requiring disclosure of financial accounts may well have resulted from the widespread public concern over the increasing number of business and banking failures, such as the notorious City of Glasgow bank failure,[3] which had involved gross mismanagement and constructive falsification of accounts by directors.

The Directors Liability Act, 1890

In 1890, The Directors Liability Act[4] was passed so as to define more clearly the responsibility of those issuing prospectuses. One year earlier, in 1889, the courts had held in Derry v. Peek[5] that a director was not responsible for statements in a prospectus which he honestly believed to be true even though there was no reasonable ground for his belief. To this decision, which the court believed was in accord with the existing common law related to deceit,

---

[1] 34 & 35 Victoria c. 41.

[2] 45 & 46 Victoria c. 56.

[3] In 1878 the City of Glasgow Bank failed. Its Directors had concealed the weak financial position of the bank by overvaluing assets, understating liabilities and incorrectly describing balance sheet items. In addition, dividends had been paid out of capital. Littleton and Yamey, op. cit., p. 370.

[4] 53 & 54 Victoria, c. 64 (1890).

[5] Derry v. Peek, 14 App. Cas. 337.

a number of people took exception and within Parliament there arose a demand for a more stringent statutory definition of the duties and responsibilities of directors. In response to these demands the Directors Liability Act was passed on August 18, 1890.

The Directors Liability Act, which was construed as one with the existing Companies Acts, made directors and promoters liable for statements in prospectus and other documents which solicited applications for securities. Now, a director was liable to compensate any person who was damaged by a false statement unless:

(i) The Director had reasonable grounds for believing it to be true; or

(ii) He made the statement upon the authority of an expert whom he had reasonable grounds for believing to be competent; or

(iii) The statement was a correct copy of an official document.[1]

The Directors Liability Act proved to be inadequate since it did not in practice significantly lessen the frequency with which false statements appeared in prospectuses. The principal limitations of the 1890 Act and existing common law were two in number. First, it did not make nondisclosure of material facts grounds for recovery of damages. Second, proceedings could only be undertaken on the

---

[1]Alfred F. Topham, Principles of Company Law, Second Edition (London: Butterworth & Co., 1908), p. 64.

basis of either "fraudulent conspiracy" or "fraudulent misrepresentation." On this second deficiency, the 1897 Report of the Inspector-General in Company Liquitation had this to say:

> It is frequently said that the law is strong enough to deal with cases of fraud, but this view is hardly supported by practical experience. There have been numerous cases in which criminal proceedings have been successfully undertaken in respect of "fraudulent misrepresentation"; but "fraudulent conspiracy" requires proof of dishonest intention on the part of two or more persons, whereas nothing is more common in connection with the formation of companies than dishonest intention on the part of one person only (the real promoter), although such intention is carried into practical effect through the instrumentality of ignorant or careless directors acting under the influence of the promoter, but who have themselves no dishonest intention. Such cases cannot, I understand, be made the subject of a prosecution for conspiracy.
>
> And, so far as I am aware, there are no cases in which proceedings against one person only have been successful upon a charge of fraud and deceit caused by "concealment." Yet it is evident that it is by means of concealment chiefly that these frauds occur. Nothing is more simple than to draw a prospectus which does not contain a single misrepresentation, but which by its concealment of some of the most important and material facts is equally calculated to deceive and defraud. The view that such action is not at present capable in all cases of being reached either by civil or criminal proceedings, except on the ground of conspiracy, is not merely based upon the experience of the Department, but appears to receive support from high judicial _dicta_, such as that of Lord Cairns, who, in the case of _Peek v. Gurney_ (6 H. L. 403) laid down that mere nondisclosure of material facts, however morally censurable would in [his] opinion form no ground for an action for misrepresentation.

> So long as this is the case, and misrepresentation as thus limited is deemed to be an essential element in a prosecution for fraud, it is to be feared that many practices which are truly fraudulent, inasmuch as they produce all the effects of fraud, and are animated by a fraudulent spirit and intention, may be practised under the Companies Act with impunity. It is perhaps a matter for consideration how far a reform of the company law will prove really effective unless it is accompanied by provisions rendering promoters criminally responsible who, by any means, with intent to deceive and defraud, either themselves make use, or induce others to make use, of the machinery of the Companies Acts to the loss and injury of the company or of any of its shareholders or creditors.[1]

Clearly, the Inspector-General, on the basis of his experience, believed the intent of the promoter was the primary determinant of what information was disclosed or concealed from the public. The problem was to render "promoters criminally responsible who, by any means, with intent to deceive and defraud," caused injury to investors and creditors.

The Demand for Reform 1890-1895

By the 1890's, it was generally believed in Britain that some remedy had to be found to the growing number of abuses to which the company law was open. Awakened by the widespread publicity given to the misfeasance of company directors, "all sorts and

---

[1] Seventh General Annual Report by the Board of Trade under Section 29 of the Companies (Winding Up) Act, 1890 (London: Her Majesty's Stationery Office, 1898), pp. 24-25.

conditions of men" felt that the company law called for great reform.[1]

In particular, the financial press reflected this discontent and, as a result, demanded compulsory publication of more adequate and reliable accounting information.[2] In 1895, for example, The Statist, a leading journal of finance and trade, stated:

> We believe, and have always believed, that it would pay to be honest in company promotion. The present seems, at any rate, a favourable time for making the experiment. Company promotion as now conducted is utterly discredited. The state of affairs could not be worse than it is. It is taken for granted that the statements in a company prospectus are misleading, and as nearly false as the compiler dares to make them. It is quite understood that the certificates of profits or values of even high-classed accountants and valuers must be carefully weighed, and that many firms merely certify what they are paid to certify, their fees being increased in proportion to the divergence of their certificates from facts. It is recognised that the publication of the names of bankers, brokers, solicitors, and directors on a prospectus, although all of them may be otherwise men of honourable reputation, is no guarantee whatever that its statements are in any way trustworthy. It is assumed as of course that the waiver clause conceals agreements of which the parties to them are so much ashamed that they dare not allow them to be disclosed. All these things, to which, for years past, The Statist has been persistently calling attention, are now generally acknowledged. So utterly rotten in the public estimation has the whole business of company promotion become, that it is now almost useless to offer for subscription an issue of Ordinary shares in an industrial enterprise. If a few more issues of Preference shares and debentures such as some of those that have

---

[1] Banker's Magazine, Vol. 60, September 1895, p. 363.

[2] Littleton and Yamey, op. cit., p. 369.

> lately been brought out are offered, the public will soon become disgusted with these also.[1]

Later, The Statist outlined the elements of a prospectus "as honourable company agents would like to issue."[2] Such a prospectus would present the names of the real vendor; all contracts including mortgages with which investors ought to be acquainted; the vendor's interests in the issue; the minimum capital needed; and trustworthy reports upon sales, profits and properties and their valuations. Comparative information related to sales, net profit and capital, The Statist believed, should be presented in all prospectuses. If such information was revealed, The Statist claimed, company promotion might be profitable — "which under the present system of extravagant charges it rarely is...."[3]

The principal causes of this outcry for reform were also revealed in the above-mentioned 1897 report submitted by the Inspector-General in Companies Liquidation to the Board of Trade. During the period 1890-1897, the Inspector-General reported an "alarming number" of liquidations and fraudulent promotions and

---

[1] The Statist, Vol. 35, No. 885, February 9, 1895, p. 185.

[2] The Statist, Vol. 35, No. 887, February 23, 1895, p. 246.

[3] The Statist, Vol. 35, No. 896, April 27, 1895, pp. 537-538.

"a growing want of confidence in the integrity of joint stock enterprise."[1] For instance, the 1897 Report, after indicating about 16,000 companies were registered with the Board of Trade, noted that in 1893, as against the addition of 2,332 companies added to the register, winding-up proceedings were commenced for 1,018 registered companies. Clearly these wholesale liquidations had far-reaching and possibly disastrous consequences for a nation such as Britain whose welfare depended upon the tapping of the savings of every class of society so as to insure the continuous development of a healthy economy. If the confidence of investors in commercial investments was destroyed surely the flow of capital into commerce would stop. Certainly, some remedy was necessary. It was imperative that investors be encouraged, not discouraged, to provide new capital for England's economic development.

The British, however, were not disillusioned with the principle of the Companies Acts. For instance, the 1897 Report of the Inspector-General also concluded that the Compampies Acts,despite their limitations, had in fact led to an abundant flow of new capital into all

---

[1]Board of Trade, op. cit., p. 5. Lord Russell, the Lord Chief Justice, reported that between 1891 and 1897, £ 27 million was lost through liquidations, £ 20 million by shareholders, and £ 7 million by creditors of registered companies. Times, November 10, 1898.

sorts of legitimate commercial enterprises. The Report also observed that those companies which had supplied investors with the most full and complete information had not found such disclosure contrary to their interests. Therefore, the Inspector-General said, the needed capital might be obtained if the disclosure practices voluntarily adopted by the "honest companies" be applied to all companies. Such a modification to the existing company law might, he said, be taken without fear of injuring legitimate companies.

> On the other hand, it must be admitted that the question of dealing in any practical and effective manner with the abuses which have arisen in the working of the Companies Acts is attended with considerable difficulties. It is clear that the legitimate use of these Acts had led to a great development of industrial enterprise by procuring a more abundant flow of capital into commercial, mining, and manufacturing channels; and any restrictions which would materially interfere with this tendency would be open to serious objection. <u>Per contra</u>, even the introduction of capital and the extension of industrial enterprise by <u>deceitful means</u> cannot be deemed legitimate or really beneficial to the community. The best companies, which are honestly promoted and managed, do not find that honesty and candour are contrary to their interests The prospectus which most fully and completely supplies the information which a subscriber for shares desires to have, and which would most thoroughly enable him to judge of the real merits of the enterprise, is not likely on that account to check the flow of capital into sound and legitimate enterprise, although it is more than probable that it will check the flow if illegitimate gain into the pockets of the intermediary promoters. On this point, therefore, the principles which honest companies

> naturally adopt of their own accord might probably be applied by law to all companies without any fear of injuriously affecting legitimate enterprise.[1]

The 1897 Report of the Inspector-General mentioned above also presented a summary of the leading abuses attending the working of the Companies Acts. As regards prospectuses, he noted, that rarely, if ever, were the names of the true promoters disclosed. Other prospectus abuses mentioned included the failure to disclose the terms of the Articles of Association; the want of independent property valuations; the combination of tangible assets and "goodwill"; and concealment of material facts.

One remedy to the above abuses was suggested in June 1894 by Judge Emden who, because of his experience in company liquidation, was well qualified to comment upon the companies acts and his opinion carried "great weight."[2] In an article he wrote for the Nineteenth Century, entitled "The Crying Need For Reforms In Our Company Law," Emden suggested an amendment to Section 38 of the 1867 Act. Section 38, it will be recalled, related to prospectuses. The Judge's amendment, as reported in the Banker's Magazine, would have required "all material facts which had a bearing on the position of the business" and were "within the knowledge of the

---

[1]Ibid.

[2]The Banker's Magazine, Vol. 58, July 1894, p. 18.

promoters, or those engaged in forming the company, should be communicated to persons invited to subscribe for shares in a manner sufficient to give them the same means of forming an opinion as the promoters and their friends."[1]

A reviewer for the Banker's Magazine, a publication not favorably disposed toward the "experiments in commercial legislation" as it called the Companies Acts, said of Emden's proposed amendment:

> ...No doubt Section 38 requires amendment, and fuller information should be given to intending subscribers; but after all they do not purchase the whole business, often only a very small share of it. Is it necessary, or in many cases practically possible, to give every shareholder the same means of forming an opinion as the promoters?
>
> ...It is too much to expect every shareholder to investigate all the affairs of the company for himself; life is not long enough. What the investing public look to is the trustworthiness of those who appear to them to be responsible for the formation and promotion of a company, and this responsibility should be something more than a name.[2]

Thus, even the conservative element of society saw the issue as one of how much disclosure: not of disclosure *per se*.

---

[1] *Ibid.*

[2] *Ibid.*, p. 19.

The Davey Report and the 1900 Companies Act

In 1895, the Board of Trade appointed a committee, whose members were called by one contemporary commentator, the "highest authority in the world of commerce and law,"[1] to investigate the workings of the various Companies Acts. The Davey Committee, as it became known, sought to devise ways of protecting the investing public without curtailing "the facilities for the formation of companies which bring so much business to England, or embarrassing the administration of companies, or deterring the best class of men from becoming

---

[1]"These gentlemen, needless to say, speak on the matters they were called together to discuss with an ex cathedra tone." The Banker's Magazine, Vol. 60, September 1895, p. 363. The Chairman of the committee was Lord Davey. Other members of the committee were Mr. Justice Chitty; Mr. Justice Vaughan Williams; Sir William Houldsworth, Bart, M.P.; Sir A. E. Rollet, M.P.; Mr. H. B. Buckley, Q.C.; Mr. F. B. Palmer; Mr. John Smith, the Inspector-General in Bankruptcy; Mr. Alexander Wallace; Mr. John Hollams; Mr. Frank Crisp; Mr. Edwin Waterhouse; and Mr. George A. Jamieson. One year earlier Lord Davey had been appointed Lord of Appeal in Ordinary. The Accountant said at the time of Sir Horace Davey's elevation to the nation's principal bench: "The appointment...is satisfactory in more respects than one. The qualifications of Lord Justice Davey to occupy a seat in the highest tribunal in the land are beyond question. His wide legal attainments, his great career at the Bar, and the reputation he had Acquired as a judge during the nine months he has sat on the Bench, entitle him to the honour that has now been conferred upon him. The appointment is particularly welcome...." The Accountant, Vol. 20, New Series. No. 1028. August 18, 1894, p. 705.

directors."[1]

Later, in 1895, the Davey Committee issued its report. Among the Committee's recommendations were a number related to prospectuses which had been drawn up on the basis of the following assumptions: the law cannot protect people from themselves; the majority of businesses were honestly formed; and the maxim of caveat emptor was of limited application in public security offerings. Two other assumptions were: the best protection the law could afford investors was to require full publicity of those corporate facts which could conceivably influence the investor of average prudence; and if the investor did not avail himself of such publicity, it was the investor, not the law, which was at fault. The report stated:

> ...legislation cannot protect people from the consequences of their own imprudence, recklessness, or want of experience. The legislature cannot supply people with prudence, judgement, or business habits. It must be remembered, the majority of companies are honestly formed for carrying on a legitimate though it may be a speculative enterprise or business, and the business is conducted with honesty and reasonable ability and judgement....

---

[1]Report of the Departmental Committee Appointed By The Board Of Trade To Inquire What Amendments Are Necessary In The Acts Relating To Joint Stock Companies Incorporated With Limited Liability Under The Companies Acts, 1862 to 1890, British Parliamentary Papers LXXXVIII (1895), p. vi.

> On the other hand, it must be generally acknowledged that a person who is invited to subscribe to a new undertaking has practically no opportunity of making any independent inquiry before coming to a decision. Indeed, the time usually allowed between the issue of a prospectus and the making of an application does not permit of any real investigation. The maxim of Caveat Emptor has in the opinion of your Committee but a limited application in such cases.
>
> It is therefore of the highest importance that the prospectus upon which the public are invited to subscribe shall not only not contain any misrepresentation but shall satisfy a high standard of good faith. It may be a counsel of perfection and impossible of attainment to say that a prospectus shall disclose everything which could reasonably influence the mind of an investor of average prudence. But this in the opinion of your Committee is the ideal to be aimed at, and for this purpose to secure the utmost publicity is the end to which new legislation on the formation of companies should be directed.
>
> The law may enforce the giving of information or supplying the means of information, but it must never be forgotten that if people will not avail themselves of the means of information, or even use the information when given, it is not the law which is in fault. It must be borne in mind that in a large number of cases applicants for shares are indifferent to the terms of the prospectus, as they apply, not for investment, but for speculation with the view to sale at a premium.[1]

Based on these assumptions, the Committee offered a number of recommendations related to the content of prospectuses. These recommendations sought "to enable the public who are asked to subscribe to a Company to get at the real and ultimate vendor...and to ascertain

---

[1] *Ibid.*

to whom the price to be paid by the Company is to go, and how it is to be applied, what the real purchase money is, what expenses are to be paid, and what will be left to the Company for working capital."[1] In particular, the Committee listed thirteen specific items related to the promoters, the issuing company and the securities on which, in the Committee's opinion, information should be included in every prospectus issued. The Committee believed it was necessary to list those specific items to be covered in prospectuses since a general requirement that all "material" facts be revealed was "unfair to promoters, vendors and directors." The list was limited to thirteen items, the Committee said, so as not to overload the prospectus.[2]

In addition, the Committee recommended stockholders receive at least every 15 months an audited balance sheet. Certain particulars of this balance sheet, the Committee believed, should also be made compulsory. The compulsory items included a full description of the company's capital structure; a clear distinction between current and long term debts ; a statement of accounts receivable showing the provision, if any, made for bad or doubtful accounts; a statement describing the pro-

---

[1]<u>Ibid</u>., p. xi.

[2]For a list of these minimum requirements as they were later enacted into law see p.32 , footnote 1.

visions made for depreciation reserves; and a description of the method used to value the reporting company's assets. However, on the subject of the computation and reporting of income, the Committee "regreted" it was unable to make any recommendations. This matter the Committee suggested should be taken up later by a smaller group of experts.

With respect to the recommendations related to financial accounting the Committee's report noted they "have been carefully considered and approved by the experienced accountants who sat on this Committee."[1] One year later, in 1896, a bill embodying the Committee's recommendations was placed before Parliament.

Subsequently, the Companies Act of 1900[2] put into effect a number of the Committee's recommendations including the thirteen specific items to be covered in prospectuses. Commenting on the delay between the introduction of the original bill and the passage of the Act, The Accountant, the official organ of Chartered Accountants throughout the world, said: "Incidentally, the fact that more than three years has passed since the first introduction of the measure is a point worth noting, as showing that - even where all parties are agreed upon the necessity of reform - the precise manner in which to set about it is a matter

---

[1] Ibid., p. xvi.

[2] 63 & 64 Victoria c. 48 (1900).

which cannot be readily settled off hand."[1]

The 1900 Act set the pattern for subsequent British legislation in the area of security regulation. Henceforth the British company law was wedded to the philosophy of disclosure. The Act, in addition to both strengthening the Directors Liability Act and providing for audited annual reports to stockholders, also provided that every prospectus issued by or on behalf of any company would be dated, signed and filed with the Registry Office of the Board of Trade : a "prospectus" being defined as almost any written offer of stocks or bonds to the public. In addition, the Act, as noted above, outlined the minimum legal content of prospectuses issued after January 1, 1901.[2]

---

[1] The Accountant, Vol. 23, New Series, No. 1280. June 17, 1889, p. 654.

[2] The minimum content of prospectus was described in the 1900 Act thus:

(a) The contents of the memorandum of association, with the names, descriptions, and addresses of the signatories, and the number of shares subscribed for by them respectively; and the number of founders or management shares, if any, and the nature and extent of the interest of the holders in the property and profits of the company; and -

(b) the number of shares, if any, fixed by the articles of association as the qualification of a director, and any provision in the articles of association as to the remuneration of the directors; and -

(c) The names, descriptions and addresses of the directors or proposed directors; and -

Later, the minimum legal prospectus disclosure

(d) The minimum subscription on which the directors may proceed to allotment, and the amount payable on application and allotment on each share; and in the case of a second or subsequent offer of shares, the amount offered for subscription on each previous allotment, and the amount actually allotted; and the amount, if any, paid on such shares; and -

(e) The number and amount of shares and debentures issued, or agreed to be issued, as fully or partly paid up otherwise than in cash, and in the latter case the extent to which they are so paid up, and in either case the consideration for which such shares or debentures have been issued or are proposed or intended to be issued; and -

(f) The names and addresses of the vendors of any property purchased or acquired by the company, or proposed so to be purchased or acquired, which is to be paid for wholly or partly out of the proceeds of the issue offered for subscription by the prospectus, or the purchase or acquisition of which has not been completed at the date of publication of the prospectus, and the amount payable in cash, shares, or debentures, to the vendors, and where there is more than one separate vendor, or the company is a sub-purchaser, the amount so payable to each vendor; and -

(g) The amount (if any) paid or payable as purchase money in cash, shares, or debentures, of any such property as aforesaid, specifying the amount payable for goodwill; and -

(h) The amount (if any) paid or payable as commission for subscribing or agreeing to subscribe, or procuring or agreeing to procure subscriptions, for any shares in the company, or the rate of any such commission; and -

(i) The amount estimated of preliminary expenses; and -

(j) The amount paid or intended to be paid to any promoter and the consideration for any such payment; and -

requirements were strengthened by the passage of the Companies Acts of 1907 and 1928.[1] However, these subsequent amendments did not depart from the philosophy of disclosure upon which the 1900 Act was established. These later acts simply made more explicit what constituted, in Parliament's opinion, the minimum statutory requirements of adequate disclosure.[2]

* * * *

The solution the British evolved to their problem of how to protect investors without discouraging the

---

(k) The dates of any parties to every material contract, and a reasonable time and place at which any material contract or a copy thereof may be inspected; Provided that this requirement shall not apply to a contract entered into in the ordinary course of the business carried on or intended to be carried on by the company, or to any contract entered into more than three years before the date of publication of the prospectus; and -

(l) The names and addresses of the auditors (if any) of the company; and -

(m) Full particulars of the nature and extent of the interest (if any) of every director in the promotion of or in the property proposed to be acquired by the company, with a statement of all sums paid or agreed to be paid to him in cash or shares by any person either to qualify him as a director or otherwise for service rendered by him in connection with the formation of the company.

[1]7 Edward 7 c. 50; and 18 & 19 George 5, c. 44. Each one of these Amending Acts was followed in the next year by a Consolidating Act.

[2]Pages 37 - 46 show an English prospectus issued in 1912.

necessary promotion of legitimate business was expressed in the Companies Act of 1900. This Act, which was based upon a philosophy of disclosure, applied to all companies the current practices of the "best" companies. Adequate disclosure of corporate affairs, it was argued, would discourage a number of those fraudulent promotions which could not stand the light of publicity. In addition, the investor would be better protected, it was claimed, since he and those who advised him would now receive the minimum information needed to formulate informed investment judgments. The legislation setting forth civil penalties for misstatement also provided, it was said, better protection of the investor by strengthening the common law related to fraud. Given this kind of protection, it was hoped, the potential investor would feel more confident about investing his savings in new corporate securities. Thus, the needed flow of capital to maintain England's industrial and commercial expansion could be encouraged without discouraging legitimate promotions.

Henceforth, an individual would be free to speculate in any type of new security he wished. Parliament would attempt, however, to prevent others from selling to him securities which were either fraudulent or inadequately described by requiring the minimum disclosure of certain material facts related to the issue.

Eventually, the United States Congress would pass legislation based on the British disclosure philosophy but, not until after the States had attempted to directly regulate security issues -- a method previously rejected by the Gladstone and Davey Committees. The history in the United States of securities legislation, including the influence of the British experience upon such legislation, and the development of prospectus and corporate financial disclosure standards begins in chapter two and continues through chapter eight.

ENGLISH PROSPECTUS ISSUED 1912

A Copy of this Prospectus has been filed with the Registrar of Joint Stock Companies in Scotland

The Subscription List will open on Monday, the First day of July, 1912, and will close on or before Wednesday, the Third day of July, 1912

THE SCOTTISH IRON AND STEEL COMPANY LIMITED

[Incorporated under the Companies (Consolidated) Act, 1908]

SHARE CAPITAL £750,000

DIVIDED INTO

300,000 Six per cent Cumulative and Participating Preference Shares of £1 each

(Ranking also as regards Capital in priority to the Ordinary Shares), and

450,000 Ordinary Shares of £1 each

£300,000 Five per cent Redeemable First Mortgage Debenture Stock

DEBENTURE STOCK

The mortgage debenture stock will be secured by conveyances of the company's heritable property to the trustees for the debenture stock holders and by a deed of trust relative thereto. It will be repaid at 100 per cent not later than 31st December, 1934 by a cumulative sinking fund of 2½ per cent, to be applied annually to the redemption of the stock by purchases when obtainable under 100 or by drawings at that price. The amount payable to meet interest and sinking fund in respect of the year 1912 will be £15,000 (representing one-half year's interest and a whole year's sinking fund) and in each subsequent year £22,500. In addition to this, the trust deed provides that after paying the 6 per cent cumulative dividend on the preference shares and before paying any dividend on the ordinary shares, the sinking fund will be increased by a further 1¼ per cent per annum (£3,750) of the amount of the debenture stock (£300,000), out of the surplus profits of the company. The company further reserves the right to increase the payments to the sinking fund in any year. In the event of a voluntary winding-up for the amalgamation or reconstruction of the company, the stock will be repaid at par.

PREFERENCE SHARES

The preference shares will carry a fixed cumulative preferential dividend of 6 per cent per annum, with the right to one-fourth of the profits in every year remaining after provision of a non-cumulative dividend at the rate of 6 per cent on the ordinary share capital.

The preference shares will also rank as to capital in priority to the ordinary shares, and in the event of liquidation, after the ordinary shareholders have been paid the par value of their shares, the two classes of shares shall rank equally until the holders of the preference shares have received an additional 5 per cent on the par value of their shares. Thereafter all remaining assets shall belong to the ordinary shareholders.

ORDINARY SHARES

The whole of the present issue of ordinary shares will be taken by the vendors in part payment of the purchase price of their businesses.

The dividend on the ordinary shares is, by the articles of association, restricted to 10 per cent per annum, payable out of the profits of any one year, until a special reserve fund amounting to £50,000 shall have been accumulated to secure the dividend on the preference shares, which, as provided by the articles, must be invested outside the business of the company.

Subscriptions will be received by the company's bankers:

THE LONDON CITY AND MIDLAND BANK LIMITED, Threadneedle Street, London, and Branches;
THE BRITISH LINEN BANK, Glasgow, Edinburgh, and Branches;
THE CLYDESDALE BANK, LIMITED, Glasgow, Edinburgh, and Branches;

For the Issue of £300,000 Five per cent Redeemable First Mortgage Debenture Stock at 95 per cent, and

150,000 Six per cent Cumulative Participating Preference Shares of £1 each at par

Payable as follows:	Debenture Stock	Preference Shares
On application	£5 0 0	£0 1 0
On allotment	45 0 0	0 9 0
On 12th September, 1912	45 0 0	0 10 0
Total	£95 0 0	£1 0 0

The whole of the instalments may be paid on allotment only, and interest at four per cent per annum will be paid on such prepayments.

Bearer scrip will be issued after allotment, to be exchanged for registered debenture stock certificates after 1st October, 1912, the stock being transferable in amounts not involving a fraction of £1. Certificates for the preference shares will be issued in due course in exchange for bankers' receipts and fully-paid allotment letters.

The interest on the debenture stock will be payable half-yearly on 30th June and 31st December in each year, the first payment being on 31st December, 1912, calculated on the instalments from the respective dates of payment.

It is proposed to make the dividends on the preference shares payable in April and October in respect of the periods ending 31st December and 30th June in each year. The first payment will be calculated on the instalments from the respective dates of payment.

The preference and ordinary shareholders shall be entitled to one vote for every share held.

TRUSTEES FOR THE DEBENTURE STOCK HOLDERS

ARCHIBALD COLVILLE, Chairman of David Colville and Sons, Limited, Dalzell Steel and Iron Works, Motherwell.
JOHN HENDERSON, General Manager, Clydesdale Bank, Limited, Glasgow.

SOLICITORS TO THE TRUSTEES

MACKENZIE ROBERTON & CO., 176 St. Vincent Street, Glasgow.

DIRECTORS

C. F. MACLAREN, Stenton Iron Works, Wishaw (Chairman),	Iron Manufacturers.
WM. DOWNS, Coats Iron Works, Coatbridge (Vice-Chairman),	
DAVID JOHN GARRETT, Waverley Iron Works Coatbridge,	
GEORGE B. BENNETT, Woodside Iron Works Coatbridge,	
ROBERT CRICHTON, Victoria Iron Works Coatbridge	
THOMAS R. MILLER, Globe Iron Works, Motherwell,	
J. W. ARTHUR SPENCER, Phœnix Iron Works, Coatbridge,	
ROBERT WATERSTON, North British Iron Works, Coatbridge,	
WM. WYLIE, Clifton Iron Works, Coatbridge,	

BROKERS

BUCHANAN, GAIRDNER, and TENNANT, 19 St. Vincent Place, Glasgow.
EGERTON JONES and SIMPSON, 2 Copthall Buildings, London, E. C.

SOLICITORS

MOTHERWELL, M'MURDO, and MITCHELL, 10 Bank Street, Airdrie.

AUDITORS

MOORES, CARSON, and WATSON, 209 West George Street, Glasgow, Chartered Accountants.
GRAHAMS and Co., 212 West George Street, Glasgow, Chartered Accountants.

SECRETARY—JAMES HAMILTON.

REGISTERED OFFICES (pro tem)—209 WEST GEORGE STREET, GLASGOW.

PROSPECTUS

The company has been formed for the purpose of acquiring, amalgamating and working as one concern the following businesses of malleable iron and steel manufacturers in Scotland with a view to securing economy of manufacture and administration:

Name of Company or Firm — Name and Place of Works

ARCHIBALD BAIRD & SON, Ltd., Cairnhill Iron Works, Coatbridge.
DOWNS & JARDINE, Coats Iron Works, Coatbridge.
THOMAS ELLIS, Ltd., North British Iron Works, Coatbridge.
GLENCAIRN IRON AND STEEL COMPANY, Ltd., Glencairn Iron Works, Motherwell.
C. F. MACLAREN & COMPANY, Stenton Iron Works, Wishaw.
HUGH MARTIN & SONS, Coatbridge Iron Works, Coatbridge.
A. & T. MILLER, Globe Iron Works, Motherwell.
JOHN SPENCER (Coatbridge), Ltd., Phœnix Iron Works and Drumpellier Iron Works, Coatbridge.
WILLIAM TUDHOPE & SON, Ltd., Crown Iron Works, Coatbridge.
THE VICTORIA IRON AND STEEL COMPANY, Ltd., Victoria Iron Works, Coatbridge.
WAVERLEY IRON AND STEEL COMPANY, Ltd., Waverley Iron Works and Rochsolloch Iron Works, Coatbridge.
WYLIE & COMPANY, Clifton Iron Works, Coatbridge.
THE WOODSIDE STEEL AND IRON COMPANY, Ltd., Woodside Iron Works, Coatbridge.

DESCRIPTION OF BUSINESS—These firms and companies last year produced in malleable iron and steel about 225,000 tons.

Capital has been freely expended recently in the erection of the latest type of furnaces and machinery and in consequence the company will have a reserve capacity sufficient to meet the probable requirements of many years to come.

With two exceptions all the firms in Scotland which are strictly malleable iron manufacturers are included in this company, and with these two firms and a few others which make a small quantity of malleable iron as an adjunct of their larger business, arrangements are being made for a working agreement.

Malleable iron manufacture is one of the oldest metal industries in Scotland. Scotch iron has a first-class reputation both at home and abroad and the output is probably now equal to that of any district in the Kingdom.

The works proposed to be taken over have an excellent trade with the makers of boiler, gas, water, and steam tubes, rivets, bolts and nuts, the fencing and constructional trades, the Clyde and Belfast shipbuilders and engineers, locomotive builders, railway companies, and wagon builders.

EXPORT TRADE—The companies and firms have a considerable business with London, the various districts of England, Ireland, and the Continent of Europe. In the export trade the various brands and trade-marks are well-known in Canada, Australia, New Zealand, South Africa, Straits Settlements, India, and the East generally.

In regard to specialties of the malleable iron trade, such as for government work at home and abroad, this locality has come into prominence during the last few years. Many of the firms about to be amalgamated by this company are on the British admiralty, war office, India office, and other official lists.

In consequence of the situation of these works in the heart of the coal and pig-iron district of the West of Scotland, with abundant supplies of fuel and raw materials, the company will be in a specially favourable position to compete on the best terms in home and foreign markets. The works being conveniently situated for the ports of Glasgow, Greenock, Adrossan, Leith, Grangemouth, and Bo'ness, enjoy exceptional shipping facilities to all parts of the world.

The present managers of the various companies and firms are being retained by the new company, so that continuity in business and efficiency in manufacture are assured.

Valuation of Properties Acquired by the Company—The works, including ground, buildings, and fixed machinery and plant of the various firms and companies, have been valued by Messrs. Fuller, Horsey, Sons, and Cassell, Valuers, London, who have had a long and intimate connection with works of this description, and have practical knowledge of the trade, at the sum of £518,962.

The loose plant and tools have also been valued by the same valuers at £57,314.

The following is a copy of their certificate:

FULLER, HORSEY, SONS, and CASSELL. 11, Billiter-square
CERTIFICATE London, E. C., 21st June, 1912

To the Directors of The Scottish Iron and Steel Company, Limited:

Gentlemen—In accordance with your instructions, we have attended at the undermentioned iron and steel works, rolling mills, and other properties, and have made a survey and valuation of same, together with the fixed and movable plant and machinery therein:

(1) Waverley Iron and Steel Works at Coatbridge, and a neighboring disused quarry used as a tip; (2) The Rochsolloch Iron and Steel Works; (3) The North British Iron Works at Coatbridge, together with an adjoining block of dwelling houses and tenements; (4) The Phœnix and Drumpellier Iron Works at Coatbridge, and a block of tenements in Phœnix Square, Coatbank Street; (5) The Globe Iron and Steel Works at Motherwell, together with certain tenements, a shop, and a fully licensed store; (6) The Coats Iron and Steel Works, situate in Coatbank Street, Coatbridge; (7) The Woodside Steel and Iron Works, situate at Langloan, near Coatbridge; (8) The Stenton Iron and Steel Works, situate at Wishaw, together with a row of 28 cottages in Alexander Street; (9) The Victoria Iron and Steel Works at Coatbridge; (10) The Clifton Iron and Steel Works at Coatbridge; (11) The Crown Iron Works, situate in Main Street, Coatbridge; (12) The Cairnhill Iron and Steel Works, situate at Calder, near Coatbridge; (13) The Glencairn Iron and Steel Works, situate at Flemington, near Motherwell; (14) The Coatbridge Iron Works at Coatbridge.

Each of the foregoing properties is held in perpetual feu, and is subject to a feu duty or duties amounting in the aggregate to £1, 621 8s 3½d per annum, in some cases with duplications and nominal casualities.

We are of opinion that the fair value as a going concern, as on 1st January, 1912, of the above-mentioned iron and steel works, rolling Mills, and other properties, together with the whole of the fixed plant, machinery, and fixtures, loose plant, tools, utensils, patterns, and other movables, is the sum of Five Hundred and Seventy-six Thousand Two Hundred and Seventy-six Pounds (£576,276), divided as under:

Land, buildings, and fixed plant and machinery ...	£518,962
Loose plant, furniture, patterns, and other movables	57,314
	£576,276

These figures are exclusive of any value for stock, stores, material, work-in-progress, registered brands, trade-marks, or good will.

We are, Gentlemen, yours faithfully,

(Signed) FULLER, HORSEY, SONS, and CASSELL.

The stock-in-trade of each firm at 31st December, 1911, has been carefully taken and verified both as to quantity and quality by a representative from another firm. The pricing of the stock has been carefully supervised by a committee of the vendors. This stock will be taken over by the company.

Working Capital—It is calculated that the sum of at least £180,000 will be available as working capital out of the present issue after payment of the preliminary expenses. This sum the directors consider sufficient for the purpose of the business.

Past Profits—The books of the firms and companies now proposed to be acquired have been examined by Messrs. Moores, Carson and Watson, Chartered Accountants, Glasgow, and Messrs. Grahams and Company, Chartered Accountants, Glasgow, and the following is a copy of their certificate thereon:

To the Directors of The Scottish Iron and Steel Company, Limited:

Gentlemen—We have examined the books of the following companies and firms: (1) Downs and Jardine, Coatbridge; (2) Thos. Ellis, Ltd., Coatbridge; (3) C. F. MacLaren and Co., of Wishaw; (4) Hugh Martin and Sons. Coatbridge; (5) A. and T. Miller, of Motherwell; (6) John Spencer (Coatbridge), Ltd., Coatbridge; (7) William Tudhope and Son, Ltd., Coatbridge; (8) Victoria Iron and Steel Company, Ltd., Coatbridge; (9) Waverley Iron and Steel Company, Ltd., Coatbridge; (10) Wylie and Co., Coatbridge; (11) The Woodside Steel and Iron Company, Ltd., Coatbridge, for the eleven years ending December 31st, 1911; and of Messrs. Archibald Baird and Son, Ltd., in so far as these relate to their business at Cairnhill, Coatbridge, for the four years ending December 31st, 1911.

The aggregate profits calculated to December 31st in each case, before providing for interest, depreciation, management salaries, and income tax were as follows:

1901, eleven businesses	£80,308	10	3
1902, " "	64,623	18	9
1903, " "	72,891	15	7
1904, " "	80,439	12	1
1905, " "	84,631	7	7
1906, " "	106,387	13	10
1907, eleven businesses	£87,031	13	0
1908, twelve "	53,402	19	10
1909, " "	36,652	18	0
1910, " "	32,279	11	7
1911, " "	75,412	17	2

The annual average of the profits of the vendor firms on the basis of eleven years' working of eleven businesses, four years' working of one business, and apart from the results of the Glencairn Iron and Steel Company, Ltd., a company which has only been working for one year, and whose books have not been examined by us, has been £72,-181 12s 9d.

The amount charged for maintenance and renewals before arriving at the above profits is equal to an average of not less than £28,000 per annum. In addition to this, the wages expended on maintenance and renewals have been charged to revenue, but it has not been possible to ascertain the amount thereof.

We are, yours faithfully,

GLASGOW, June 21st, 1912.

(Signed) MOORES, CARSON and WATSON, C.A.
(") GRAHAMS and Co., C.A.

During the years 1909 and 1910 exceptionally keen competition prevailed amongst local makers, and prices were for a time reduced to an unremunerative level. In addition to this, several of the works were for varying periods closed for alterations and reconstruction. The profits for 1911 have shown a satisfactory recovery, and it is anticipated that irrespective of any benefits from amalgamation, 1912 will show much better results.

The amount required to pay the interest on debenture stock and the fixed dividend on the preference shares is:

£300,000 first mortgage debenture stock at 5 per cent	£15,000
2½ per cent for redemption of debentures	7,500
£300,000 in preference shares at 6 per cent	18,000
	£40,500

By reason of the economies hereafter referred to, coupled with the general improvement in the trade, it is considered that increased profits can be earned, which would mean additional dividends on the preference shares.

The works proposed to be taken over are at present fully employed, and the contracts already booked will keep them so for many months.

ECONOMIES TO BE DERIVED BY AMALGAMATION—The economies which can be effected by the consolidation of this trade are very marked. The profits obtainable can be largely augmented owing to the fact that the malleable iron industry is peculiarly fitted to benefit from improvements in methods of working, which are only rendered possible by amalgamation. The rolling of the many and varied sections and the range and dimensions in these sections involves frequent roll-changing in the mills, but under amalgamation this will be reduced to an absolute minimum, giving thereby:

(1) Greatly increased output from present plant in a given time, and consequent reduction in overhead charges.

(2) Saving in consumption of fuel.

(3) Less waste of metal due to much greater uniformity and regularity of work at furnaces and mills.

(4) The utilization of plant on lines to give outputs greater than are possible when working as individual firms.

The economies in expenditure on rolls and other plant will also be considerable.

The advantages of buying in larger quantities and the lessened competition in selling should tend to increase the margin of profit obtainable.

The businesses will be taken over as from the 1st January, 1912, the debts and liabilities to that rate being discharged by the respective vendors, the benefit of the trading after that date accruing to the company, which will therefore benefit by the large rise which has taken place in the selling prices of its products since that date. The profits to the date at which the company is entitled to commence business will afford a fund available towards the payment of the preliminary expenses.

SECURITY FOR DEBENTURE STOCK AND PREFERENCE SHARES—As will be seen from the valuers' certificate.

Lands, buildings, fixed plant and machinery represent a value of	£518,962
Loose plant represents a value of	57,314
To which has to be added the value of	576,276
Goodwill, including value of brands and trade-marks	249,384
Working capital, including stocks, provided by the present issue	180,000
Making a total of	£1,005,660

or, excluding goodwill, etc., of £756,276. On the latter reduced figure it will be seen that the debenture stock is covered over two-and-a-half times, and the preference shares one-and-a-half times as to capital.

The following particulars are furnished in accordance with the requirements of the companies (consolidation) act, 1908:

A copy of the memorandum of association of the company, with the names, descriptions, and addresses of the signatories thereto, and the number of shares subscribed for by them respectively, is annexed to this prospectus, and forms part thereof.

The articles of association provide that the qualification of a director shall be the holding of shares of the company, whether preference or ordinary, of the aggregate nominal value of £1,000.

The provisions of the articles of association as to the remuneration of directors are:

ARTICLE 96. The remuneration of the directors, and their remuneration for services performed previous to the first general meeting, shall be determined by the company in general meeting.

ARTICLE 97. If any director shall be called upon to perform extra services and to make any special exertions for any of the purposes of the company or the business thereof, the company may remunerate the director or directors so doing, either by a fixed sum or otherwise as may be determined, and such remuneration may be either in addition to or in substitution of his or their remuneration as provided for above.

ARTICLE 117. The board may appoint any one or more of their number to be managing director, or general manager, or manager, or managing directors, or general managers, or managers, of the company, and may allow to him or them such remuneration in respect thereof, in addition to his or their remuneration as director or directors fixed in accordance with the preceding clause, as they think fit.

ARTICLE 118. The board may delegate to such managing director, or general manager, or manager, or managing directors, or general managers, or managers (provided that, in the case of a general manager, or manager, or general managers, or managers, he, or they, be a director or directors), all or any of the powers hereby made exercisable by the board except those relating to shares and borrowing, and any others as to which special provisions inconsistent with such delegation are herein contained.

The price payable by the company to the vendors, including price of stocks, is £956,508 9s 3d, of which £249,384 represents goodwill, payable to the respective vendors, as to £150,000 in fully-paid preference shares, as to £450,000 in fully-paid ordinary shares, and as to £356,508 9s 3d in cash out of the proceeds of the present issue. The purchase price payable to the vendors in preference and ordinary shares and in cash will be divided among them as follows, *viz.*:

Archibald Baird & Son, Limited, 8,435 preference shares, 26,513 ordinary shares, and £13,095 18s 6d in cash; Downs & Jardine 14,155 preference shares, 44,489 ordinary shares, and £21,319 17s 5d in cash; Thomas Ellis, Limited, 13,761 preference shares, 43,253 ordinary shares and £15,433 12s 6d in cash; Glencairn Iron and Steel company, Limited, 7,050 preference shares, 22,396 ordinary shares, and £11,378 1s 1d in cash; C. F. McLaren & Company, 13,081 preference shares, 41,115 ordinary shares, and £21,134 1s 6d in cash; Hugh Martin & Sons 6,289 preference shares, 19,768 ordinary shares, £8,646 14s 7d in cash; A. & T. Miller 13, 758 preference shares, 43,243 ordinary shares, and £19,331 7s 1d in cash; ohn Spencer (Coatbridge), Limited, 15,499 preference shares, 48,714 ordinary shares, and £25,769 19s 10d in cash; William Tudhope & Son, Limited, 6,843 preference shares, 21,508 ordinary shares, and £11,325 4s 4d in cash; The Victoria Iron and Steel Company, Limited, 11,182 preference shares, 35,147 ordinary shares, and £15,849 18s 6d in cash; Waverley Iron and Steel Company, Limited, 30,071 preference shares, 34,698 ordinary shares, and £144,000 14s 8d in cash; Wylie & Company, 9,876 preference shares, 31,042 ordinary shares, and £12,999 16s 2d in cash; The Woodside Steel and Iron Company, Limited, 38,114 ordinary shares, and £36,223 3s 1d in cash.

Such fully-paid preference and ordinary shares are the whole of the shares issued or agreed to be issued as fully or partly paid up otherwise than in cash.

The minimum subscription upon which the directors may proceed to allotment is 150,000 preference shares.

The whole of the present issue has been guaranteed for a commission (which includes underwriting and over-riding commissions) payable by the company at the rate of 4 per cent in the case of the mortgage debenture stock, and of 6½ per cent in the case of the preference shares.

The preliminary expenses other than the above, including the expenses and stamp duties of the conveyances to the company, are estimated to amount to £25,000. These are payable by the company.

The following contracts have been entered into:

Here follow details of twenty-six contracts.

The following directors are respectively interested in the promotion of the company, and in the business and others to be acquired by the company, as follows, *viz.:* Colin Faulds MacLaren, as a partner of C. F. MacLaren and Company; William Downs, as a partner of Downs and Jardine; David John Garrett, as a shareholder of Waverley Iron and Steel Company, Limited; George Bowen Bennett, as a shareholder of the Woodside Steel and Iron Company, Limited; Robert Crichton, as a shareholder of the Victoria Iron and Steel Company, Limited; Thomas Ronald Miller as one of the trustees of the late Alexander Ronald Miller, iron manufacturer, Motherwell, who carry on business under the name of A. and P. Miller; John William Arthur Spencer, as a shareholder of John Spencer (Coatbridge), Limited; Robert Waterson, as a shareholder of Thomas Ellis, Limited; and William Wylie, as a partner of Wylie and Company.

The following directors are interested in the underwriting, having subunderwritten (at a commission at the rate of 2½ per cent in the case of the debenture stock and at a commission at the rate of 4 per cent in the case of the preference shares), debenture stock to the amount and preference shares to the number following their respective names, *videlicet:* C. F. MacLaren, 4,000 preference shares; William Downs, £1,300 debenture stock and 5,120 preference shares; David John Garrett, 2,500 preference shares; Thomas R. Miller, £4,700 debenture stock and 6,000 preference shares; J. W. Arthur Spencer, £3,000 debenture stock and 4,200 preference shares; Robert Waterson, 3,000 preference shares; and William Wylie, £600 debenture stock and 1,400 preference shares.

By the contracts above mentioned it is also provided that several of the directors should, along with other officials of the vendor companies and firms, receive engagements with the company on the terms therein specified.

Application will be made for a settlement and quotation for the debenture stock and the preference and ordinary shares of the company on the London, Glasgow, and Edinburgh Stock Exchanges.

Applications for debenture stock and preference shares must be made on one of the accompanying forms, and must be sent to the bankers of the company with a remittance for the amount payable on application.

If the amount of debenture stock or number of preference shares allotted to any applicant is less than the amount or number applied for by such applicant, the surplus will be credited in reduction of the amount payable on allotment, and the balance (if any) will be returned.

Failure to pay any instalment when due will render the allotment liable to cancellation and previous payments to forfeiture.

A brokerage of one-half per cent will be paid by the company to brokers and other approved agents upon all debenture stock and preference shares allotted on forms of application, other than underwriting applications, bearing their stamps.

Prospectuses and application forms may be obtained at the offices of the company, and from the British, Foreign, and Colonial Corporation, Limited, 57 Bishopsgate, London, E. C., and from the bankers, the brokers, and solicitors. Dated the 27th day of June, 1912.

THIS FORM MAY BE USED

This form should be sent with a deposit of 5 per cent to The London City and Midland Bank, Limited, Threadneedle Street, London, E. C., or branches; or to The British Linen Bank, Glasgow, Edinburgh, or branches; or to The Clydesdale Bank, Limited, Glasgow, Edinburgh, or branches.

No. A

FORM OF APPLICATION FOR DEBENTURE STOCK

THE SCOTTISH IRON & STEEL COMPANY, LIMITED

[Incorporated under the Companies (Consolidation) Act, 1908]

Issue of £300,000 Five Per Cent Redeemable First Mortgage Debenture Stock at 95 Per Cent

To the Directors of The Scottish Iron and Steel Company, Limited:

Gentlemen—Having paid to the company's bankers the sum of £...... being a deposit of 5 per cent on application for £......... of the above mentioned five per cent redeemable first mortgage debenture stock, I (we) hereby request you to allot to me (us) that amount of debenture stock, and I (we) agree to accept the same or any less amount that may be allotted to me (us) upon the terms of the prospectus, dated the 27th day of June, 1912, and to pay the balance due as provided by the said prospectus.

Ordinary Signature ....
Name (in full) ....
Address ....
*Occupation or Description ....
Date ...., 1912

*If a lady, state whether "Mrs." or "Miss."

Please write distinctly

Cheques should be made payable to The London City and Midland Bank, Limited, The British Linen Bank, or The Clydesdale Bank, Limited.

THIS FORM MAY BE USED

This form is to be filled up and forwarded with a deposit of 1s per share to the London City and Midland Bank (Limited), Threadneedle Street, London, E. C.; or branches; or to the British Linen Bank, Glasgow, Edinburgh, or any of its branches; or to the Clydesdale Bank (Limited), Glasgow, Edinburgh, or any of its branches.

No. A

FORM OF APPLICATION FOR PREFERENCE SHARES

THE SCOTTISH IRON & STEEL COMPANY, LIMITED

[Incorporated under the Companies (Consolidation) Act, 1908]

Issue of 150,000 Six Per Cent £1 Cumulative Participating Preference Shares at Par

To the Directors of The Scottish Iron and Steel Company, Limited:

GENTLEMEN:

Having paid to your bankers the sum of £.........., being a deposit of 1s per share on.......... six per cent £1 cumulative participating preference shares of the Scottish Iron and Steel Company (Limited), I request that these shares may be allotted to me upon the terms of the prospectus, dated the 27th June, 1912, and memorandum and articles of association, and I agree to accept the same, or any less number that may be allotted me, and to pay the further instalments as provided in the said prospectus.

Ordinary Signature ....
Name (in full) ....
Address ....
Occupation ....
Date ...., 1912
If a lady, state whether "Mrs. or "Miss."

CHAPTER TWO

THE CRITICS OF BIG BUSINESS: 1900-1917

Between 1900 and 1917, the larger corporations in the United States were under verbal attack from a variety of critics. In fact, during these seventeen years the issue of "big business"[1] was probably the most important continuing moral, economic, political and social problem in the United States. The topic of the study -- financial disclosure standards of management -- and the closely related issue -- securities legislation -- were an integral part of this assault on the giant corporation and hence, can only be understood within the context of that larger controversy. Therefore, chapter two presents a brief introductory survey of some of the major events comprising the attack on big business as well as the attitudes, expectations and arguments of both the critics and defenders of the so-called trusts and combinations. Later, chapter three will focus upon

---

[1]A number of other terms such as "trusts," "industrial combinations," "monopolies," "corporations," "giant corporations," and "pools" were also used at various times as synonyms for big business. Sometimes the term "big business" seemed to include all corporations -- large and small. Also, on occasion, the word "trust" was used to cover both industrial and financial concentrations irrespective of whether or not they were organized under the trust form.

DOI: 10.4324/9781003169420-2

the related and concurrent controversy which raged over the desirability of greater publicity of corporate affairs.

During the period 1900-1917, the attack on big business involved a number of diverse groups and individuals and was highlighted by several commissions, investigations and hearings sponsored by either the legislative or executive branches of the federal government. These investigations, plus the writings of a number of those interested in the issue of big business, are the basis for the following discussion of the attack on, and the defense of, big business.

The Environment, 1900-1917

The years from 1900 to 1917 roughly bound a period known in American history as the "Progressive Era", a period during which the American people were on a "quest for social justice."

> Less than three score years after the common man won enlarged rights in government and society in the tumultuous days of Andrew Jackson, the democratic principle in America faced another grave crisis. The profound social changes resulting from the growth of giant industry, the dislocations wrought by rapid urbanization, the decline of rural opportunity as the free lands were exhausted, the increasing rapacity of "malefactors of great wealth" and their subservient allies, the political bosses of city, state and nation, the menacing growth of class feeling--all these helped to create a condition of affairs in which the vaunted "unalienable rights" of "life, liberty and the pursuit

of happiness" had become the despair of an ever larger proportion of average humanity ...."To many thoughtful men in the opening years of the twentieth century it seemed that America in making her fortune was in peril of losing her soul."

...The old doctrine of extreme individualism and a purely competitive industrial system, relics of a rural civilization, were breaking down before the new complexities of American life; a Hamiltonian exertion of governmental power had become necessary in order to restore Jeffersonian conditions of equal opportunity. The battle was waged on many fronts. To the traditional Western advocacy of popular rights was now added the aggressive championship of the reform parties in the great urban centers....

Although American politics had never before been so preoccupied with the vital concerns of the plain people, the social note was as strongly sounded in nearly every other phase of human activity. Under the hammering blows of the Muckrakers captains of business discovered the wisdom of conciliating the consuming public upon whose goodwill their prosperity rested. Organized labor consolidated its position and, sobered by power, advanced more swiftly the cause of better conditions for the wage earners. Resolute drives were launched against the squandering of the nation's natural wealth, against the waste of life in industry, against food adulteration and the liquor evil. While women continued their march toward economics and political equality, the generation made perhaps its greatest humanitarian contribution in an energetic concern for the long-neglected rights of childhood.

Organized religion caught the new spirit and, heedless of denominational barriers, gave earnest attention to the exigent problems created by man's inhumanity to man. Novelists and playwrights, after a brief dalliance with the romantic past, turned almost fiercely to the stern realities of the present. Scientists and scholars likewise made their contributions to human welfare....

> ...Many of the achievements reflected similar measures in other lands; America was not living aloof from the world. Yet in the energy, the optimism and sometimes the precipitancy with which the new ideas were put into effect they evidence their authentic American character. The great task of the generation was to put the national house in order....[1]

This Progressive Era was a period of great change. It was also a period during which "big business" was under a most constant attack[2] from a number of economic, social, moral and political critics: the so-called "progressives."[3]

Initially, the progressives' attack upon big business focused on the giant corporations: the impact of the many newly formed industrial combinations being of course obvious to all. Later, sometime after 1910 and especially after the 1912-1913 Money Trust Investigation, the attackers shifted the object of their

---

[1]Arthur M. Schlesinger and Dixon Ryan Fox, Editors' Foreword to Harold Underwood Faulkner's The Question for Social Justice, 1898-1914 (New York: The Macmillan Company, 1931), pp. XV-XVII.

[2]Should the reader question the appropriateness of the word "attack" it might be well to recall that a number of the critics of big business often used such terms as "attack," "hostile forces," "pending struggle," and "battlefield" in their denunciation of the "evils" of big business. As far as this author is concerned, big business -- if not all business -- was unedr attack and the reaction of a number of businessmen to the critics' offensives was conditioned by their recognition that they were fighting for the survival of their businesses and the social order, some might say myths, which had made such giant businesses possible.

[3]A number of the progressives were, in fact, as reactionary as the businessmen they criticized.

wrath to the "Money Trust" -- J. P. Morgan, George F. Baker, James Stillman and their fellow investment bankers. This was the "money trust" which, through its control of big business allegedly ran the country.

The shift in the progressive thinking after 1910 as to the locus of the control over big business, however, did not cancel or divert the attack on big business. Now, the progressives saw the institution of big business as the key to the money trust's grip over the nation. For instance, in 1913, Louis D. Brandeis, starting with Woodrow Wilson's assertion that a great industrial nation is controlled by its system of credit, went on to argue the most dangerous monopoly in the United States was the "money monopoly."

The money monopoly, Brandeis said, was dominated by a few men--investment bankers--within whose hands the country's system of credit was concentrated. So long as this situation existed, irrespective of these men's motives, Brandeis argued, the continued existence of America's traditional freedom and individual energy was out of the question.

The investment banker, Brandeis claimed, by virtue of his dominant role in the "financial oligarchy's" creation of big business had become the "directing power" in a number of railroad, public service, and industrial corporations. Also, investment bankers had become the "directing power" in certain banks and trust companies, in order to acquire the control over and use of "other people's money" to promote new combinations. Thus, Brandeis stated, the key to the power of the investment banker was commercial and financial "combinations" of all kinds including big business. Therefore, to destroy the "financial monopoly" big business, the most evil of the combinations, must first be dissolved. Then, and only then, Brandeis insisted, could the promise of The New Freedom[1] so "joyously proclaimed" in 1913 by Woodrow Wilson be achieved.[2]

During the period 1900-1917, there were more than the liberals' verbal attacks on big business. These 17 years were also highlighted by a number of investigations by the federal government of the industrial trusts and their financial allies: The Industrial Commission, 1898-1902; the various investigations concluded by the Bureau of Corporations, 1903-1914; and the Money Trust Investigations, 1912-1913. In addition, the Justice Department prosecuted a number of major antitrust suits involving such giant corporations as Swift and Company, Standard Oil of New Jersey,

---

[1]Woodrow Wilson, The New Freedom: A call for the emancipation of the generous energies of people (New York: Doubleday, Page & Company, 1913).

[2]Louis D. Brandeis, Other People's Money (New York: Frederick A. Stokes Company, 1913), pp. 1-6.

International Harvester Company and American Tobacco Company. Major legislation in this area included the 1914 Federal Trade Commission Law and the 1914 Clayton Act. Clearly, Congress, the Administration, and the Courts, were not insensitive to the demand for corporate reform: occasionally hesitant, but definitely not insensitive.

Hopefully, the above brief survey of the political and social environment between 1900 and 1917 will be sufficient to (re)introduce the reader to the sometimes hostile and confusing, but always changing, world faced by many American businessmen during the early part of the twentieth century. The remainder of this chapter will be concerned with the attitudes of the critics and defenders of big business for it was these attitudes which determined the nature of the corporate publicity controversy and its related subissues discussed in chapters three through seven.

The Critics[1]

The critics of big business came from no one particular political or religious "school" and included

[1]Before proceeding, I wish to make it quite clear that I am not concerned with the validity of merit of the arguments present below. For my purposes these would not be useful questions. What is relevant, however, is that such a controversy, right or wrong, existed and influenced the behavior of a variety of people including management, stockholders, investors, creditors, legislators and voters.

people of dissimilar backgrounds such as "independent" businessmen -- usually displaced or potential competitors; eminent jurists; academics; religious leaders; poets; novelists; labor leaders; farmers, and political leaders including Presidents Roosevelt, Taft, and Wilson. That these people had, from time to time, widespread influence there can be little doubt: the critics struck a responsive chord among the American people. The best selling novels of such authors as Jack London and Upton Sinclair definitely had an anti-business bias, and, one political party -- the Progressives -- campaigning in 1912 on an anti-big business platform, attracted a large number of voters. However, not all those who wanted the government to regulate or dissolve the giant corporations did so for the same reasons. In general, the criticisms of big business can be placed in three categories: economic; social and political; and moral and ethical. Each is briefly discussed below.

The major economic criticisms can be reduced to two proportions: big business was inefficient; and big business was monopolistic. Both these assertions flowed from the obvious disparity between the actual world of big business and the traditional economic abstraction labeled "laissez faire capitalism." Clearly, big business was not carried on by a large number of independent small units and, therefore, according to the classical theory of economics it could not be efficient. In addition, the economic critics stated a number of more particular charges related to the indictment of inefficiency: big business couldn't be managed efficiently -- it was too large and too complex; the growth of big business had resulted from ruthless and unfair competition, not efficiency; big business was profitable because its managers arbitrarily set prices at artificially high levels -- their goal being to enrich the promoter at the expense of the consumer, laborer and investor; the profits of big business resulted from having a monopoly, not from cost savings; and, finally, big business held back technological progress. More explicit statements pertaining to the "monopoly charge" were: the consumer was "plundered"; and monopolistic competition led to a waste of the nation's resources. In short, big business was inimical to the economic welfare of society. How the defenders of big business answered these particular criticisms, and the additional ones presented below, will be discussed later.

About 1900, many persons believed that the American hope of a democratic life was falling short of its earlier promise. The cause? Big Business. Such political and social criticism of big business was based on three beliefs: big business ran the country;

it was incompatible with the economic basis of democracy; and it was incompatible with the social basis of democracy. The belief that big business controlled the nation's government, credit, schools and press, was a widespread and, in general, a deeper fear than the economic criticisms mentioned above. The two criteria--economic and political--were not unrelated since it was argued the ultimate basis of political power was economic power. Furthermore, the critics said, in a democracy, political power must, by definition, be distributed equally among the people who, as an expedient, may consent to confer certain powers upon the government. Therefore, since economic power was concentrated in hands other than the people or their government, political power must also be so concentrated. Thus, it was said, the economic basis needed for a true democracy was not present in the United States. Businessmen, the critics said, had too much power and exercised this power irresponsibly and for antisocial ends.

It was also argued big business subverted democracy by creating a large class of wage earners, the so-called "payroll dependents." Working in factories for wages, the critics said, dehumanized people and made them subservient and unable to cope with the complex problems of life in as democratic a fashion as, say, a nation of independent businessmen and farmers: the critics' preferred social base for a true democracy.

The target of the ethical and moral critics was the same as the previous two groups discussed: big business. However, a number of those constituting this third group were objecting, not only to big business, but also to much of that which distinguished the twentieth century from, say, the seventeenth century: widespread urban living; a high level of industrialization; and an expanded commercial class. As these critics looked about them they thought they saw in society much which displeased them: excessive materialism; irresponsible individualism; and a civilization which was pernicious and inhuman. The cause of this unpleasant situation? Again big business. In short, these critics said man was suffering from a spiritual poverty brought about by the type of unique civilization created by businessmen and business.

Thus, the critics, for a variety of reasons, said the institution of big business was "evil". Big business, or the power of those people who controlled it, had to be either curbed or destroyed.

The Defense

The prominent defenders of big business included corporate executives, corporation lawyers and certain eminent economists. These people took their stance for a variety of reasons: to protect the existing distribution of economic, political and social power; to defend the institution of private property; to preserve the freedoms of enterprise, contract and exchange; and to promote economic efficiency. A number of the executives associated with the trusts, however, did not actively participate in the controversy: as to the clamour for reform many businessmen were apparently insensible, indifferent or unconcerned.

In answer to the social and political, and moral and ethical critics, the defenders of big business produced no compelling rebuttals. Against the economic critics, however, the defenders of big business were able to muster some strong arguments. The monopoly charge, they said, was inaccurate. Despite their size the giant corporations were, in general, not monopolies. None of these corporations was the sole seller within any industry: each had actual and potential competitors. Since the prevailing economic theory recognized only two general models, the competitive and the monopolistic, if the trusts had competitors they could not be monopolies <u>ergo</u> they must be competitive.

As to the charge that big business was inefficient the defenders replied with facts: a number of the trusts were profitable; big business had adopted mass production techniques and passed the cost savings on to the consumer in the form of lower prices; and from the industrial giants an abundance of new products were indeed flowing into the marketplace.

A legalistic argument presented by the defenders of big business was that corporations such as the American Sugar Refining Company, which was "owned" by over 10,000 stockholders and controlled most of the nation's sugar output, were "private" corporations and hence, immune from any government regulation. Congress, the defenders said, could not legislate away the right of private individuals and corporations, even if engaged in interstate commerce, to enjoy the institution of private property and the freedoms of enterprise, contact and exchange. Anyway, the defenders claimed, the existing statutory and common law already gave the government adequate authority to prosecute all illegal combinations in restraint of trade. To legislate further against these alleged private corporations would, the defenders said, violate the fundamental principles of federal jurisprudence and the recognized and accepted federal-state relationship. The law, in the opinion of these defenders, was static: not evolutionary. Here the case for big business rested.

The defense of big business was no more elaborate,

extensive or convincing than outlined above for a variety of reasons. Unfortunately, a number of businessmen--not all--acted, or at least said they did, in just the predatory fashion described by their critics. In one government investigation after another it was revealed how executives, promoters, and financiers[1] had used inside information to "fleece" investors; actively sought to establish monopolistic control over an industry so as to limit output and raise prices; or, collected fat promoters' fees. The critics, of course, used such testimony to good advantage. It was difficult to refute.

However, what is perhaps more striking to the modern reader studying the testimony of businessmen before the various pre World War I Congressional groups which looked into commercial matters is the complete lack of responsibility toward the public displayed by some top managements of publicly owned corporations. Such irresponsibility reflected much of the philosophy of the managements which were synonomous with ownership and not responsible to "outside" investors. Glover has said:

---

[1]During this period the public drew no clear-cut distinction between those who financed, promoted, directed, or managed big business: all were businessmen. Perhaps such distinctions would not have been meaningful in practice since in fact the various functions were often either mixed, combined, or joined.

> The total irresponsibility and disregard for public sensibilities shown in those days /circa 1900/ by the officers of some of the combinations and trusts is something which today /1954/ must amaze even the most case-hardened "rugged individualist." This avowal of irresponsibility, not only toward the community at large, but toward employees, and even toward stockholders has to be examined at first hand to be believed.[1]

Possibly, the following extensive excerpts from the frank testimony of Mr. Henry O. Havemeyer, president, American Sugar Refining Company before the Industrial Commission, may illustrate the attitude of at least one prominent businessman towards the public as well as suggest why the critics took their various positions.[2]

Mr. Havemeyer, testifying on June 14, 1899,[3] read

---

[1]John D. Glover, The Attack on Big Business (Boston: Division of Research Graduate School of Business Administration Harvard University, 1954), p. 33.

[2]Quotations of Henry O. Havemeyer have been used extensively in the thesis for two reasons. First, he was often quoted by the critics of big business. Second, Havemeyer's statements reflected almost all of the arguments presented at various times by the defenders of big business.

[3]By 1899, America was pre-eminently a manufacturing nation; the McKinley administration seemed somewhat complacent toward the problem of big business; prosperity had returned after the depression of 1893; and the major concern of the people was the war with Spain. The 1898 Congress, somewhat reluctantly made one concession to those persistent people who demanded action to correct the faults of the industrial system. It passed Public Law No. 146 which established the Industrial Commission. The task of this Commission, which consisted of five Senators, five Representatives, and nine other members, was to "collate information and to consider and recommend legislation to meet the problems presented by labor, agriculture and capital." The Commission's reports were published between 1900 and 1902.

the following from a prepared statement:

> There appeared to be in the public mind a distinction between robbery by an individual and that by a corporation. What is commendable in an individual appears to be dishonest in a corporation.
>
> I maintain it is immaterial to the public in what form business is done - whether by an individual, firm, corporation or even trust. There are merely forms of conducting business, or, in other words, machinery for the operations of business....
>
> *****
>
> The Sugar company undoubtedly tries to do its utmost to enlarge its business, but does it in a way, which they consider the only proper one, i.e., by making the price so low as to defy competition.
>
> *****
>
> It is my opinion that corporations are under no obligation whatever to any of the states for their existence. Quite the reverse; the states are under obligation to them....
>
> *****
>
> Business is not philanthropy. Capital and labor will adjust their own relations. Interference always operates against one or the other; that means to the disadvantage of both....
>
> *****
>
> There is a prevailing hostility to wealth. This is perfectly illogical. Everyone wants money. It is the abuse of money, not its possession, which is opposed to the public interest.
>
> This hostility finds its outlet in hostile legislation, in unequal and unjust taxation. All this is probably unconstitutional. It is directly against the interests of the very class, I mean the poorer class, whom it is supposed to benefit.
>
> *****

> Corporations, whether directly such or in the form of trusts, are an expedient for uniting the interests of a large number of persons of smaller means into large aggregations of capital.
>
> Attack upon them is, therefore, an attack upon their stockholders....In the absence of all disturbing causes, the direct tendency of a combination of capital is to promote economy, reduce expenses, and diminish price....
>
> *****
>
> Trade will always take care of itself. If it is left to pursue ordinary channels, A will see to it that B does not have any extraordinary advantages. It is only when the state interferes that a situation is created of which advantage can be taken against the interest of the community.
>
> *****
>
> In these days there are only two forms, and only two forms of monopoly. One, that which results from a patent and copyright. It is universally recognized that this is in the interest, not against, the public.
>
> The other, that which comes from unfair tariff discrimination.[1]

---

[1]Earlier, Mr. Havemeyer had said: "The mother of all trusts is the customs tariff bill." Mr. Havemeyer claimed all the existing trusts, with the exception of the sugar trust, were created and nurtured by exorbitantly high tariffs — they were creatures of the government. Unlike some trusts which were protected by tariffs as high as 100% ad valorum, the sugar trust operated under a protective tariff of 3½% ad valorum. No tariff, Havemeyer claimed, should be higher than 10%. However, in the interest of equity he suggested the sugar tariff be increased to 8%. During much of his testimony Havemeyer was, in fact, arguing for a high tariff and therefore his attitudes may well have been greatly influenced by this consideration. See, for example, Industrial Commission, *Preliminary Report on Trusts and Industrial Combinations*, Vol. 1 (Washington: Government Printing Office, 1900), p. 101.

*****

> Citizens are divided into two classes - the industrious and those who wish to live on the industry of others. It is they who are without capital who are hostile to it. This is only another mode of stating the obvious proposition that it is those who are without means who wish to have wealth without work.

*****

In concluding his prepared statement Havemeyer said:

> It must be kept in mind that this is a rich country, not a poor country....
>
> The hostile action to which I have re-referred, legislation against corporations, if followed to its legitimate results, would make the country less powerful, its people less prosperous, and would destroy the influence which comes from the richness of the land and its people.[1]

In short, Havemeyer said: the public had two standards when dealing with corporations and individuals; the legal form in which business was carried on was immaterial; the public was misinformed as to the nature of trusts; price cutting was a legitimate means to achieve the desirable goal of "bigness"; and corporations were under no obligations to the states. Business was not philanthrophy. Government intervention led to imperfect solutions; hostility toward wealth was illogical and only hurt the poorer class; and big business was an aggregation of the capital of a

---

[1]*Ibid*., pp. 101-106.

number of people of small means. The attack on big business was, in reality, an attack on its stockholders; businessmen through competition, not government intervention, would eliminate the abuses of trade; in 1899, there existed only two forms of monopoly, i.e., patents and copyright, and unfair tariff discrimination; big business had made the nation prosperous; and, finally, those who attacked big business were parasites.[1]

*****

Businessmen were a heterogeneous lot: not all joined the battle and few spoke publicly in defense of big business. As one contemporary commentator observed: "[businessmen did] not seem to have the faculty for expressing publicly their defense to the frequent unjust attacks upon them by the many would-be reformers whose only qualifications appear to be glib tongues or facile pens."[2] Others, like Havemeyer, when forced to face the issue in public, adopted a position which in the

---

[1]Subsequently, under cross-examination by the members of the Industrial Commission, Havemeyer modified some of the above statements and related others directly to the question of "publicity of corporate affairs": the topic of the next chapter.

[2]Elijah W. Sells, "The Accounting Profession: Its Demands and Its Future," The Journal of Accountancy. Vol. 20, No. 5. November 1915, p. 325.

long run was to prove untenable. Irrespective, however, of their role in the controversy businessmen, in general, were on the defensive. The attitude of corporate executives toward the publicity of corporate affairs question was, as we shall now see in chapter three, greatly influenced by their position with respect to the issue of big business. The issues of big business and corporate publicity were closely related.

CHAPTER THREE

THE DEMAND FOR DISCLOSURE OF CORPORATE AFFAIRS, 1900-1917

During the period 1900 to 1917, one of the several proposals designed either to curb or destroy the power of the so-called trusts was a demand for greater publicity of corporate affairs. This publicity demand reflected an American political tradition which held that if the people are given the true facts and allowed to discuss them freely the right solution to any political problem will be found. In general, those who advocated more adequate and truthful corporate activities sought thereby to protect the public -- consumers, employees and independent businessmen -- from the evils of trustification. Others wanted a greater disclosure of corporate affairs so as to reveal to all the alleged abuses of corporate power. Full publicity for this second group was only a prerequisite for further more stringent corporate regulation.

During much of this period, the protection of investors through adequate prospectus financial disclosure standards, while often discussed, was in general, of minor concern: it being only a subissue

DOI: 10.4324/9781003169420-3

of the larger question of corporate publicity. Later, some time after 1917, the issue of prospectus financial disclosure standards became, in its own right, an important question: the origins of which, however, stemmed from the various attacks on big business and the related corporate publicity controversy which raged during the period 1900-1917.

So as to best illustrate the range, intensity and scope of the corporate publicity controversy, the remainder of the chapter will be devoted to a discussion of those portions of the reports of the following which pertained to corporate publicity: the Industrial Commission; the Bureau of Corporations; and the Money Trust Investigations. Other investigations such as the Armstrong Insurance Investigation which dealt primarily with financial institutions are not discussed. In addition, the final section of chapter three will present the views with respect to the publicity controversy of some of those who did not participate directly in these three government investigations.

The Industrial Commission reports, especially the one issued in 1900 and devoted to trusts and industrial combinations, presented numerous examples of the thinking of businessmen--corporate executives--on the topic now under review: publicity of corporate affairs. The work of the Bureau of Corporations between 1903 and 1914, particularly during the presidency of Theodore Roosevelt, was an example of how one government agency did use publicity of corporate transactions as a powerful weapon in its attack on the so-called "bad" trusts; the Bureau did not regulate in any way prospectuses or security issues. In addition, portions of the 1913 report of the Money Trust Investigation are presented since it proposed a new technique whereby the government might indirectly force a greater publicity of corporate affairs. Finally, the published statements relating to corporate publicity of Louis Brandeis and certain investment bankers and public accountants are presented since such people either influenced or at least sought to influence financial reporting practices. The Bureau of Corporations and the Money Trust Investigation are treated only briefly: the bulk of the text being devoted to the Industrial Commission and the views of those individuals who did not participate in the government sponsored investigations.

The Industrial Commission, 1898-1902

In 1898, Congress established the Industrial Commission "to consider and recommend legislation to meet the problems presented by labor, agriculture, and capital." One of the many concerns of the Commission was the desirability of achieving greater disclosure of corporate activities since, as noted above, it was generally believed by some that greater corporate publicity might lead to the end of the supposed social, political and economic evils brought about by the various trusts and combinations.

In 1900, after hearing from a number of witnesses on the general topic of trusts and industrial combinations, the Industrial Commission submitted to Congress two sets of recommendations related to the disclosure of corporate affairs. The first set, which pertained to disclosure standards for newly formed corporations, were the first recommendations of any federal body to propose federal legislation governing industrial prospectus disclosure standards. The report said:

> To prevent the organizers of corporations or industrial combinations from deceiving investors and the public, either through suppression of material facts or by making misleading statements, your Commission recommend:
>
> (a) That the promoters and organizers of corporations or industrial combinations which look to the public to purchase or deal in their stocks or securities should be required to furnish full details regarding the organization, the property or services for which stocks or securities are to be issued, amount and kind of same, and all other material information necessary for safe and intelligent investment;

(b) That any prospectus or announcement of any kind soliciting subscriptions, which fails to make full disclosures as aforesaid, or which is false, should be deemed fraudulent, and the promoters, with their associates, held legally responsible.

(c) That the nature of the business of the corporation or industrial combination, all powers granted to directors and officers thereof, and all limitations upon them or upon the rights or powers of the members, should be required to be expressed in the certificate of incorporation, which instrument should be open to inspection by any investor.[1]

The Commission members, like a number of others who advocated greater publicity, were fuzzy as to what specific details ought to be disclosed so as to ensure "safe and intelligent investment." The proposed requirement "to furnish full details regarding organization, the property... and all other material information" was, to say the least, vague, uncertain and indefinite. Possibly, since various Commission members had, during the hearings, asked a number of questions related to the desirability of revealing the "real" value of patents and plant the Commission members regarded such information as being relevant to the investment decision. Certainly, the question of "stock watering" or overcapitalization,[2] to which plant and

---

[1]Industrial Commission, op. cit., pp. 5-6.

[2]Overcapitalization, at this time, meant the par value of the stock issued was in excess of its tangible book value. Tangible book value was calculated thus: appraised asset value less intangible assets, current liabilities and fixed debt.

patent value were closely related, was a topical concern.

The second set of publicity recommendations, which were in the critic's mind apparently the more important of the two, related to established corporations, and, as the quote below indicates, were proposed so as to curb the power of big business and to protect the interest of existing stockholders, consumers and employees. Later, in 1903, these recommendations, in part, led to the establishment of the Bureau of Corporations:

> The affairs of a corporation or industrial combination should be carried on, without detriment to the public, in the interest of its members, and under their lawful control. To this end the directors or trustees should be required:
>
> (a) To report to the members thereof its financial condition in reasonable detail, verified by a competent auditor, at least once each year;
>
> (b) To inform members regarding the method and conduct of business by granting them, under proper restrictions, access to records of directors' meetings, or otherwise;
>
> (c) That the nature of the business of the corporation or industrial combination, all powers granted to directors and officers thereof, and all limitations upon them or upon the rights or powers of the members, should be required to be expressed in the certificate of incorporation, which instrument should be open to inspection by and investor;
>
> (d) To provide for the use of members, before the annual meetings, lists of members, with their addresses and their several holdings; and

(e) To provide, in whatever other ways may be named in the certificate of incorporation, means whereby the members may prevent the misuse of their property by directors or trustees.

The larger corporations--the so-called trusts--should be required to publish annually a properly audited report, showing in reasonable detail their assets and liabilities, with profit or loss; such report and audit under oath to be subject to Government inspection. The purpose of such publicity is to encourage competition when profits become excessive, thus protecting consumers against too high prices and to guard the interests of employees by a knowledge of the financial condition of the business in which they are employed.[1]

That the Commission was well aware of the British experience in this field can be of little doubt. The thinking underlying the above recommendations clearly reflected the current British "disclosure philosophy".[2]

---

[1]*Ibid*. The Final Report of the Industrial Commission--Volume XIX of the Commission's Reports--issued in 1902 repeats the above recommendations. In addition, it also contains a "supplementary statement" by Thomas W. Phillips, a commission member. Mr. Phillips had wanted the Commission to amplify its recommendations in the area of corporate publicity to provide for a government official to whom all corporations would submit audited annual reports containing a specified list of points on which data were to be provided. In addition, Phillips proposed, he be given a staff of examiners who would at irregular periods and without notice appear at the offices of each corporation to examine, verify and report upon its books. The reports of the examiners were to be made public.--*Final Report of the Industrial Commission*. Vol. XIX (Washington: Government Printing Office, 1902), pp. 669-673.

[2]The American advocates of publicity saw it as a means of *reforming* corporate abuses, whereas the English saw disclosure as the way whereby new investors could be *encouraged* to invest in new enterprises.

as expressed in the 1895 Davey Report and the Companies Act of 1900. Also, several Commission members asked specific questions of witnesses involving the English Companies Acts.[1]

The Industrial Commission's recommendations to Congress were based on evidence which suggested to the Commission that a greater publicity of corporate affairs was needed to overcome, in addition to a number of the other "evils" of trustification and combination, the particular "evils" of speculation and overcapitalization. Associated with these two particular practices were the misrepresentation or concealment by management of material facts from investors; and the use of "inside" information by management at the expense of its stockholders. The Commission's Report summed up the evidence of these points thus:

> ...Another evil[2] often charged against these newer combinations is that the promoter, by virtue of misrepresentations or by the concealment of material facts, is frequently able to secure very large profits for himself at the expense of the people at large who buy the stocks, and that in this way undue speculation is encouraged.

---

[1]Industrial Commission, Preliminary Report. See, for example, the testimony of James B. Bell, attorney at law, pp. 1082-83.

[2]The other "evils" mentioned were: unemployment due to the closing of surplus or redundant industrial plants; unfair competition, particularly price cutting; monopolistic price setting; freight rate discrimination; destruction of independent action by firms and persons; and the sapping of courage and initiative of potentially influential persons. <u>Ibid.</u>, pp. 33-34.

> Connected with this evil which comes with the modern method of promotion is that of overcapitalization. Stock is frequently issued to four or five, or even more, times the amount of the cash value of the plants that are brought into the combinations. These stocks then placed upon the market go into the hands of persons ignorant of the real value of the property, who afterwards are likely to lose heavily. Pools are sometimes made to control the stock market, or other of the common ways of disposing of the stock by unfair methods are employed.
>
> At times also the officers and directors of the large combinations seem to have taken advantage of their inside knowledge of the business to speculate on the stock exchange in their own securities to the great detriment of the other shareholders.[1]

The proposed cures for the above abuses, suggested by the various witnesses, reflected, as might be expected, their proposers' positions with respect to the combinations under investigation. Those opposed to the trusts, for either social or business reasons, advocated through direct government action, either the direct suppression of monopolistic combinations[2]

---

[1] *Ibid.*, p. 34. This summary reflects the testimonies of James B. Dill, attorney at law (p. 1080); F. P. Thurber, president, United States Export Association (p. 20); Samuel Dodd, president, International Silver Company (pp. 1058, 1060-1061); N. Burton Rogers, vice president, C. Rogers & Bros. (p. 1067); James L. Meyers, member of the legislature of Massachusetts and chairman of the Judiciary Committee of the House of Representatives (p. 1133); John R. Dos Passos, attorney at law (p. 1166); and Francis L. Stetson, counselor at law (p. 976).

[2] *Ibid*. See, for example, testimony of P. E. Dowe, president, Commercial Travelers National League, pp. 28, 36; John McNulta, receiver, Distilling and Cattle Feeding Company, p. 237; and, Charles C. Allen, attorney at law, pp. 1193-1197.

or the outright prohibition of destructive competition.[1] It is interesting to note those businessmen who opposed the trusts for business reasons did not advocate publicity. Presumably, they did not want to reveal their "private" affairs any more than, as we shall see, did the trusts; the independents' goal being primarily to destroy a larger and more powerful competitor. One witness, J. W. Lee, a president of three independent pipe line and oil companies, dismissed the greater publicity argument as being an ineffective reform measure since the trusts "do not seem to care about [public opinion]; they are largely defying public opinion."[2]

Greater publicity, a number of the witnesses and the Commission's report said, was a feasible remedy for at least three reasons. First, by revealing to all the monopoly profits of the trusts new firms would seek to compete with the trusts and combinations for these profits[3] which, it was said, would lead to lower

---

[1]Ibid. See, for example, testimony of J. W. Lee, a former senator of the State of Pennsylvania and president of three independent pipe line and oil companies, p. 294; T. W. Westgate, independent refiner, p. 383; M. L. Lockwood, independent producer of oil, p. 394.

[2]Ibid., p. 296.

[3]Ibid. See, for example, Professor Jenk's questions to King, p. 1109. Professor J. W. Jenk's of Cornell was reputed to be an expert on trusts and industrial combinations. He had been hired by the Commission to assist in its study.

prices to the consumer. Second, employees through a greater knowledge of their employers financial condition would be better able to protect their interests.[1] Finally, by forcing firms to reveal the "real" value of plant and patents the practice of overcapitalizing firms would end. Hopefully, investors would refuse to invest in "overcapitalized" firms if presented with a statement of these companies' real "worth". Hence, the incentive to overcapitalize would be removed.[2]

In general, those connected with the trusts advocated a "let-alone policy" for at least three reasons: it was beyond the constitutional powers of the federal and state governments to regulate corporate activites; the mechanism of competition would automatically prevent monopoly and exhorbitant prices; and the rights of the stockholder and the investor were amply protected under existing statute and common law.

On the topic of publicity, several witnesses associated with the trusts conceded the demands for legislation requiring compulsory disclosure of the results of operations of public service corporations--railroads and power companies--was reasonable. Any attempt to

---

[1]*Ibid*. See, for example, Dos Passon, pp. 1158, 1166. It is of interest to note, Dos Passos, in his testimony, sought to defend the right of property rather than trusts *per se*. He saw in the current attacks on trusts an attack on the institution of private property.

[2]*Ibid*., p. 1158.

extend such legislation, however, to include "private" corporations, these witnesses added, would be illegal, dangerous and intolerable.[1] Furthermore, the investor had little right to expect information related to the issuer of any stock he is offered: caveat emptor was the traditional rule which covered such transactions.

On the topic of disclosure, in response to questions posed by Industrial Commission members Thomas Phillips, S. N. Dexter North and Representative L. F. Livingston, one witness mentioned earlier--Henry O. Havemeyer--had this to say:

Phillips: You have spoken in regard to the benefits of trusts, both in your paper and in your testimony, and you say they should not be regulated by law. As I understand, you would take the same position in regard to a combination of railroads. If railroads can in any sense be governed by law or taxes, has not the Government the same right to tax the great trusts or combinations in industry extending over the whole country and regulate them?

Havemeyer: I doubt if they have the constitutional power.

---

[1] Ibid. See, for example, Stetson, p. 981 and Havemeyer, pp. 122-123 and 135-136.

Phillips: The States have the power, each individual State?

Havemeyer: I doubt if a State has any power over the sugar company in the regulation of its prices; I do not think so.

Phillips: Do you believe that these trusts should be put more specifically under governmental control than they are, that they should have examination or inspection similar to the national banks?

Havemeyer: Not at all. I think the Government should have nothing to do with them in any way, shape, or manner.

Phillips: You think, then, that when a corporation is chartered by the State, offers stock to the public, and is one in which the public is interested, that the public has no right to know what its earning power is or to subject them to any inspection whatever, that the people may not buy this stock blindly?

Havemeyer: Yes; that is my theory. Let the buyer beware; that covers the whole business. You cannot wet-nurse people from the time they are born until the time they die. They have got to wade in and get stuck, and that is the way men are educated and cultivated.

Phillips: Then, you think that they have a right to charter corporations and allow them to offer stock to the people - to the whole community - and that the community then has no right to a knowledge of what the earning power of that stock is?

Havemeyer: Precisely. Take the other side. A lot of men get together in New York City and organize a company, and a capital of $10 million is to be put up. I go into New York City and say, "Gentlemen, put your money up whether you want to or not." They do not do it. They are not compelled to buy the stock. The State does protect these people as against any false statements, as against any fraud; but where a man goes into the stock exchange today and buys 100 shares of sugar and pays $160 and it is $110 tomorrow, and he goes to the State and gets down on his knees: "Mother dear, pay me the difference, and let us put the sugar trust out of existence." I say, hands off; there is nothing in it; hands off; let them settle it among themselves.[1]

---

[1] *Ibid.*, pp. 122-123.

Mr. Havemeyer might well have had other reasons for not wishing to publicize his trust's operating results:

North: Are you now carrying on business at a loss?

Havemeyer: I have answered that before; I have no answer to give it.

North: You refused to answer it before.

Havemeyer: Well, I refuse to answer it now.

North: How do you carry on business at a loss and still declare dividends?

Havemeyer: One is an executive act and the other is a business matter.

Phillips: Where do you get the money, though?

Havemeyer: We may borrow it; the sugar company has got pretty good credit.

North: How many years can the American Sugar Company keep up that practice?

Havemeyer: That is a problem to everyone. We[1] would either buy or sell the stock if we knew that.[2]

*****

---

[1]About 1900, American Sugar Refining Company had over 10,000 shareholders. William Z. Ripley, Main Street and Wall Street (Boston: Little, Brown & Co., 1927), p. 157.

[2]Industrial Commission, Preliminary Report, p. 132.

Livingston: Did you answer or not the question: What were the dividends paid by your company; what per cent? Do you mind answering that?

Havemeyer: The question as to what we have paid has not been asked. I think it had averaged about 10% on the entire capital; 7% on the preferred and 12% on the common; that makes an average of 10% on the whole.

Livingston: How will you mind going a step further and say what your profits for 12 months were?

Havemeyer: I wish I knew.

Phillips: Have you stated the amount of capital stock in the American Sugar Refining Company?

Havemeyer: $75 million.

Livingston: One thing further. Did you pay the last dividend out of the earnings or out of the surplus?

Havemeyer: I did not mention that.

Livingston: Do you mean to say you would not like to answer that?

Havemeyer: I mean to say that I did not mention it.

Phillips: Do you refuse to answer that question?

Havemeyer: I think it had better remain as it is, Mr. Chairman.[1,2]

---

[1]*Ibid*., pp. 135-136.

[2]"Until 1910, when it was abolished, the New York Stock Exchange maintained a so-called 'unlisted' department, where dealings were permitted in securities of corporations refusing to furnish any substantial information as to their business and which therefore could not be admitted to the regular list. Such securities appeared in the same table with those regularly listed and were differentiated from them only by a star in front....In this manner such active stocks as those of Amalgamated Copper and the American Sugar Refining Companies were dealt in on the exchange for many years without the public having any information regarding their affairs....They were in effect conducted and maintained as 'blind pools." Those in control were then enabled more freely to use their information for speculative purposes."--Report of the Committee appointed Pursuant to House Resolutions 429 and 504 to Investigate the concentration of control of Money and Credit. H. R. Report No. 1593. 62nd Congress, 3rd Session, p. 37.

Strictly speaking the above quote is incorrect. Each year, for instance, the American Sugar Refining Company, which was chartered in Massachusetts, was required by Massachusetts Law to file a balance sheet with the Secretary of the Commonwealth of Massachusetts: no income statement was required. In 1901, for example, American Sugar Refining filed the following meager balance sheet:

Assets		Liabilities	
Real estate and machinery	$34,328,664	Capital	$ 88,280,370
Cash and debts receivable	36,862,702	Debts	24,364,027
Sugar, raw refined, etc.	12,248,640	Reserves, balance	9,907,491
Investment in other companies	39,111,883		
	$122,551,888		$122,551,888

Ripley, *op. cit*., p. 158.

No doubt investors, irrespective of their position with respect to the attack on big business, would have liked to have known what was the financial condition of American Sugar Refineries. Mr. Havemeyer knew---but he was not telling.

In spite of a number of statements similar to Havemeyer's, several of the witnesses, including Havemeyer, who were sympathetic to the nonintervention argument, when questioned by the Commission admitted: "Certain measures tending toward giving the public, and particularly the stockholders, more information regarding the nature of the business might be advisable."[1] For instance, Henry O. Havemeyer after firmly stating in his prepared statement that the public had no right to information on corporate affairs, subsequently admitted under direct examination that companies like American Sugar Refineries, whose business involved food, might because of the nature of their products be considered by some to possess a "quasi-public character." If there were so, the public, from the public's viewpoint, could demand, irrespective of what he, Havemeyer, thought, more information on Sugar Refineries' operation. Possibly, Havemeyer said, the direct results of greater publicity might result in there being less pressure on Congress to revoke the present sugar tariff.

[1]Industrial Commission, Preliminary Report, p. 35.

With greater publicity, he said, the "senseless clamor against trusts" would end and "the industry would be fairly treated," which to Havemeyer meant the passage of a higher sugar tariff.[1] Later, another executive, John D. Archbold, vice president, Standard Oil Company of New York, said compulsory publicity would be acceptable especially if it was introduced as part of a national incorporation law.[2] If the trusts were to be compelled to publicize their activities they wanted a direct _quid pro quo_.

Among those few witnesses representing the trusts and combinations who under cross examination admitted the need for greater disclosure of corporate affairs there was a little agreement as to the scope and character of any reform in this direction. In fact, when questioned as to what details ought to be disclosed, the only specific suggestion forwarded was that stock books should be available for inspection by stockholders and judgment creditors.[3]

Several of these witnesses associated with the trusts who were willing to recognize the need for

---

[1]_Ibid._, pp. 136-137.

[2]_Ibid._, p. 578.

[3]_Ibid._ See, for example, testimony of Charles C. Clark, an independent distiller, who in the past, had been a willing member of several whiskey pools. P. 187.

greater publicity wished to distinguish between the standards governing financial disclosure by proposed ventures and established companies. New ventures, it was said, should provide investors with more information than they had in the past, whereas going concerns need not provide any additional information. All of the trust witnesses, it should be noted, represented established companies.

Still another point of view, which while recognizing that stockholders and persons with contractural relations with corporations probably deserved more information than they then received, held the public should be given little more information than they currently received.[1]

The basic argument supporting these two positions was that firms and individuals engaged in the same business may profit from any information revealed by a going concern to the public. One of the persons who presented the "competition argument" before the Commission was Charles W. King, the Secretary and General Manager of the New Jersey Corporations Agency.[1]

---

[1]How stockholders were to get more information without revealing such data to the public was never explained or asked.

[2]The New Jersey Corporations Agency was formed in 1895 for the purposes of furnishing corporations chartered in New Jersey, but operating out of state, with the necessary facilities for complying with the laws of the State of New Jersey. Mr. King's office represented several hundred such corporations including the Amalgamated Copper Company; the American Car and Foundry Company; the American Thread Company; the Pressed Steel Car Company; and the American Soda Fountain Company.

Mr. King was replying to questions posed by Professor Jenks and Representative Livingston.

Jenks: [Earlier, Mr. King had mentioned a statutory report all corporations chartered in New Jersey had been required to file annually with the secretary of state.] You spoke of the annual report that had to be made by these corporations. Can you state what is contained in that annual report?

King: A list of the officers and directors, and when they were elected, and how long they are elected for.

Jenks: With the addresses, I suppose, of the officers?

King: Well, yes; they have to give their business address.

Jenks: They may give as their business address your office?

King: If the corporation is located with us they can give their business address with us, and all communications that come to our office for any stockholder or director or officer of the company are forwarded to him.

Jenks: Do you yourself think that it would be a greater protection to the public - that is, to the purchasers of the goods of these companies - if they were required to give, in addition to these facts, in their annual report also a balance sheet showing the condition of the business, so that would-be competitors would be able to judge somewhat better whether it would be worth their while to engage in competition with them?

King: No; I do not. I think that would be giving away the business of the concern to the competitor.

Jenks: The assumption is, of course, that if a report of that kind were required a similar report would be required from all of the competitors, so that no special advantage would be given to one over the other in that particular. Do you think that this would be giving more than the public interest would require?

King: I do; yes.

Livingston: You have got a public franchise granted by the sovereign State of New Jersey. Why not give the citizens of New Jersey all and any information that will better their condition? Why do you want a public franchise and then want a private corporation? What is there right about that?

King: The citizens of New Jersey may not be dealing with that corporation at all, and why should they want any information regarding it?

Livingston: Why do you want any franchise at the hands of the people if you are not willing to give the people all the information they ask? Practically you get this franchise from the people through their representatives?

King: That is right.

Livingston: Now, then, when the people ask for information, why not just give it? You say because it would be giving away your private business. Well, you did not think of that when you went to the public for your franchise, did you?

King: The public may not be your competitors; but you may have competitors, and in giving it to the public you would have to give it to your competitors.[1]

The record speaks for itself. Before 1917, a number of corporate executives (and their critics) were reactionary, irresponsible and, in general, out of step with the changing moral, social, political and economic environment. These corporate officers saw the demand for greater publicity as part of the attack on big business: to be repelled in the same fashion and for much the same reasons

---

[1]*Ibid.*, pp. 1109-1110.

The Bureau of Corporations: Publicity as a Regulatory Tool

In 1903, Congress at the behest of President Theodore Roosevelt established the Bureau of Corporations. This federal agency, which was authorized by Congress to conduct investigations of the business affairs of corporations, other than transportation companies, doing interstate or foreign commerce, during its lifetime[1] published a number of public reports covering the activities of various business combinations. The manner in which these reports were used, especially by Roosevelt, to punish the so-called "bad" trusts is briefly outlined below. Publicity in this case became an auxiliary tool of the Justice Department in its antitrust work.

The report of the Industrial Commission mentioned above, which recommended greater publicity of corporate affairs, greatly strengthened the cause of those seeking federal regulation of industrial combinations through publicity. One of those who advocated such a policy was Theodore Roosevelt who, in January 1900, while Governor of New York, proposed to the New York Legislature as a remedy for the abuses of power by corporate managers and promoters compulsory publicity of corporate

---

[1] In 1914, the Bureau of Corporations was absorbed by the newly created Federal Trade Commission.

affairs. Roosevelt, after urging caution in dealing with trusts which, in his opinion, were the inevitable outgrowth of modern industrial life and in themselves not injurious to the public, said:

> The first essential is knowledge of facts, publicity. Much can be done at once by amendment of the corporation laws so as to provide for such publicity as will not work injustices between business rivals.[1]

In September 1901, after President McKinley's death, Roosevelt became President of the United States, and, in his first annual message to Congress, observed that there were "real and grave evils" in the business world: "one of the chief being over capitalization." However, again he urged caution in dealing with corporate abuses:

> ...the mechanism of the modern business world is so delicate that extreme care must be taken not to interfere with it in a spirit of rashness or ignorance.[2]

Next, Roosevelt presented his solution to the trust problem:

> The first essential in determining how to deal with the great industrial combinations is knowledge of the facts--publicity. In the interest of the public the Government should have the right to inspect and examine the workings of the great corporations engaged in interstate business. Publicity is the only sure remedy which we can now invoke....[3]

---

[1]William Griffith (ed.), The Roosevelt Policy. 2 vols. (New York: 1919), Vol. 1, pp. 19-20.

[2]*Ibid.*

[3]*Ibid.*

Roosevelt, who saw publicity only as the first step toward achieving a more effective and broader form of government regulations over business activities, went on to say:[1]

> Artificial bodies, such as corporations and joint stock or other associations, depending upon any statutory law for the existence or privileges should be subject to proper governmental supervision, and full and accurate information as to their operations should be made public regularly at reasonable intervals.[2]

Later, in 1903, Congress enacted the Department of Commerce and Labor Bill which, among other things, provided for a Bureau of Corporations.

> The purpose of the Bureau was...stated to be the procurement of information and data to enable the President "to make recommendations to Congress for legislation" for regulation of interstate commerce. Publication of the results of the Bureau's work was to be at [the President's] discretion.[3] Common carriers subject to the Interstate Commerce Commission were specifically exempted from the jurisdiction of the new agency, but the Commissioner of Corporations was given the power already conferred on the [Interstate Commerce Commission] to compel testimony and the production of the documents.[4]

---

[1]During the summer of 1902, Roosevelt speaking in Providence, Rhode Island stated: "...publicity would by itself tend to cure the evils of which there is just complaint; it would show us if evils existed and where the evils are imaginary, and it would show us what next ought to be done." Ibid., pp. 180-181.

[2]Ibid.

[3]In this way competitive information was to be withheld from industrial rivals.

[4]Arthur M. Johnson, "Theodore Roosevelt and the Bureau of Corporations," The Mississippi Valley Historical Review. Vol. XLV, No. 4, March 1959, p. 575.

The so-called "private" corporations were not subject to a new form of federal government intervention: the Bureau of Corporations. The power of this agency being derived from its ability to influence public opinion through publicity.

Following the presidential election of 1904, Roosevelt, who now had been elected President in his own right by an overwhelming majority, embarked upon an aggressive antitrust drive.[1] Subsequently, as Roosevelt's enthusiasm for publicity alone as a remedy for corporate abuses waned, he increasingly used the Bureau of Corporation's investigatory powers as a means of supplementing the Justice Department's antitrust prosecutions. The first notable instance of this switch in policy was the publication of the Bureau's Beef Trust Report in March 1905 - just prior to the calling of a federal grand jury to consider possible violations by the meat packers of the Sherman Act. Clearly, Roosevelt sought to use the report to whip up

---

[1]Roosevelt never had control of the Republican Party's conservative wing, which under the leadership of Senator W. Aldrich, held firm control of Congress. Roosevelt was too wise a politician not to recognize the strength of such formidable opponents. Instead of pressing on the legislative front, he acted in areas such as antitrust in which he did not need congressional collaboration. Also, he relied on a widespread popular following to aid in whipping Congress into line with his legislative recommendations. The use of the Bureau of Corporations reports was an outstanding example of this latter practice.

public support for the Administration's antitrust charges.

The Bureau's publication dealing with the Beef Trust, which was an arid, tedious and voluminous analysis of the meat packing industry, was not favorably received by the public. The public had expected the report to substantiate in a dramatic and decisive fashion the charges made against the Beef Trust by the so-called muckrakers. The public was disappointed--a reaction Roosevelt neither expected nor wanted.

> In the fiasco of the beef report, Roosevelt was brought face to face with two of the conflicting demands of his program for dealing with big business. The use of the Bureau for the investigation of economic conditions and business behavior as a basis for legislation demanded objectivity and restraint. Effective publicity to create widespread popular support for such legislation demanded sensationalism. In his initial foray, Roosevelt had chosen the first course, stressing that the beef report was to be unassailably correct in its facts and figures. Certain information, moreover, was withheld from publication to avoid interference with the pending antitrust prosecution of the packers.[1]

Following this failure, Roosevelt later used the Bureau's reports more effectively in the administration's attacks upon the "bad" trusts. For instance, the Bureau's revelations pertaining to Standard Oil's rail-

---

[1]<u>Ibid</u>., p. 581. Later, all of the data gathered by the Bureau in its investigation of the Beef Trust was turned over to the Justice Department.

road rate practices played a timely role in gaining passage of the Hepburn Amendment to the Interstate Commerce Act, and the Bureau's 1906 report on Standard Oil was an important factor in the successful federal prosecution of that company. According to Johnson "the importance of the Bureau's role in these prosecutions cannot be overstressed."

In short, in the absence of voluntary full corporate disclosure, the various Bureau reports, by publicizing corporate abuses, helped to produce a favorable climate for federal action in the area of corporate reform. Also, the Bureau demonstrated that the federal government could and would intervene in the affairs of so-called "private" corporations. The expectations and actions of one man--Roosevelt--opened the way for others, if they should choose to do so, to impose more stringent federal regulations upon business disclosures--financial and non-financial. The Bureau of Corporations was an important precedent. Later, another Roosevelt--Franklin D. Roosevelt--was to build upon this precedent and introduce federal securities legislation designed to force through the Bureau's successor, The Federal Trade Commission, full disclosure of corporate affairs to investors.

The Money Trust Investigation

A brief discussion of the report of the Money Trust Investigation of 1912-1913, the so-called Pujo Hearings, is included for only one reason: it suggested to Congress an indirect means whereby Congress could improve corporate publicity. The suggested approach was tothreaten to limit the use of the mails by stock exchanges unless the various exchanges insist upon full and fair financial disclosure by listed companies. Such a proposal, the report claimed, would be effective since Congress did in fact possess the power to regulate the mails; the stock exchanges could control listing requirements; and corporations valued their listings on recognized exchanges. The mails were important to the stock exchanges and the stock exchanges were important to corporations. By pressure on the stock exchange corporate reform might be achieved without direct government regulation.

During part of 1912 and 1913, the House Committee on Banking and Currency, under the chairmanship of Representative Arsène Pujo of Louisiana, conducted an investigation to discover if a "Money Trust"[1] existed

[1]The Committee defined a "money trust" thus: An established and well-defined identity and community of interest between a few leaders of finance which has been created and is held together through stock holdings interlocking directorates, and other forms of domination

and if this "trust" had the nation under its control. Subsequently, after hearing a total of only 24 hours of testimony from a number of witnesses drawn from the financial community, the Committee submitted a report to Congress listing the Committee's conclusions and recommendations in three areas: clearing-house associations; "money trusts"; and stock exchanges. The portion dealing with stock exchanges---particularly the New York Stock Exchange---is of direct interest to this study and is discussed below.

The Pujo Committee[1] saw the various stock exchanges as a key to achieving corporate reform including more uniform and complete corporate publicity. The Committee developed its proposal thus:

First, the Committee briefly described the role and operations of stock exchanges. In the Committee's view, the stock exchanges in the principal cities--

---

> over banks, trust companies, railroads, public service and industrial corporations, and which has resulted in a vast and growing concentration of control of money and credit in the hands of a comparatively few men -

Report of the Committee Appointed Pursuant to House Resolutions 429 and 504 to Investigate the Concentration of Control of Money and Credit. Op. cit., p. 130.

[1]The Pujo Committee consisted of seven lawyers, one banker, one publisher, one farmer and one manufacturer from towns the total population of which was less than 200,000, one being as small as 700. H. S. Martin, The New York Stock Exchange and the "Money Trust." Copyright 1913 by H. S. Martin, p. 12.

New York, Chicago, Philadelphia and Boston--were "essential instrumentalities in the conduct of modern business and finance." Two aspects of the Exchange's practices were noted by the Committee: the Exchange's power to regulate listing agreements; and the significance of the mails for the successful and profitable operation of the Exchange. On the subject of the New York Stock Exchange the Committee had this to say:

> The New York Stock Exchange undertakes to prescribe the form and conditions of every corporate security in which it authorizes dealings and its determination is final through its control over the listings of such securities. It reserves the right to exact minutest details of the business and affairs of issuing corporations...all this on the ground that it is performing a national public function.
>
> It jealously controls the reports as to every transaction on its floor....Courts of justice, trustees, financial institutions, and the public the world over act on this information. It...sells its quotations to interstate and international telegraph companies for large sums of money and scatters them broadcast over the country through the newspapers, over the telephone and telegraph, but always under its control.[1]

Next, the Committee noted the power and importance of the New York Stock Exchange were essentially derived from the value of listing securities to corporations: "listing on the New York Stock Exchange gives a security a wider market and a more definite current value, making

---

[1]The Report of the Committee Appointed Pursuant To House Resolutions 429 and 504, op. cit., p. 36.

it easier to sell and easier to borrow upon."[1]

The report then listed a number of the features of the operations of certain stock exchange members the Committee found objectionable: unwholesome speculation; irresponsible rehypothecation of customers' securities; price manipulation; and the lending by brokers of their customers' stocks to persons who had sold short and needed stock with which to make deliveries.

The Committee doubted if Congress had the power to regulate stock exchanges directly so as to end the above "abuses." Congress, however, could regulate the mails and thereby force the exchanges to reform themselves by denying the use of the mails and other essential facilities to those stock exchanges which continued to allow their members to practice the above abuses.

> It is doubtful, however, whether the Federal Government has power generally to regulate stock exchanges....But whether stock exchanges in their wholly local and internal relations may be regulated by Congress or not, where they lend their facilities for transactions injurious to the public interests at large, Congress may prevent any instrumentality under its control from being used to multiply and spread such transactions; and it is its obvious duty to do so.

In other words, the facilities of the

---

[1] *Ibid*.

> New York Stock Exchange are employed largely for transactions producting moral and economic waste and corruption; and it is fair to assume that in lesser and varying degree this is true or may come to be true of other institutions throughout the country similarly organized and conducted. Your committee believes, therefore, that Congress has power unconditionally to prohibit the mails, the interstate telegraph and telephone, the national banks, and all other instrumentalities under its control, from being used in executing, negotiating, promoting, increasing or otherwise aiding transactions on such stock exchanges.[1]

However, this proposed bill was not designed solely to protect the investor by reforming the nation's twenty or so stock exchanges: the bill had broader implications related to corporate reform and corporate publicity.

> Great and much-needed reforms in the organization and methods of our corporations may be legitimately worked out through the power wielded by the stock exchange over the listing of securities. Much of the confusion and many of the defects in corporate regulation due to the diversity of State laws and to the bidding of the states against one another in laxity of administration in order to attract corporations within their borders may be corrected and uniformity of methods introduced through the listing department of the exchange.
>
> Thus complete publicity as to all the affairs of a corporation may be uniformly enforced. The scandalous practices of officers and directors in speculating upon inside and advance information as to the action of their corporations may be curtailed if not stopped. In short, its opportunities as an agency of corporate reform are endless,

---

[1] *Ibid.*, pp. 115-116.

> provided its own practices can be reformed so as to entitle it to exercise these broad powers.[1]

With respect to publicity the Pujo Committee's bill provided for a formal listing statement to be completed by all companies which desired to list their securities on any exchange. This statement, which was to be sworn to, was to show: assets and liabilities, "in every form"; net earnings; for what purpose stock was issued; who received stock; what consideration in cash or services was received for the stock; and the net return to the company from the issue. Listed companies also were to file with the exchange on which they were listed annual reports covering all these items. Later, the Securities Act of 1933 and the Securities Exchange Act of 1934 were to embody similar provisions.

The various stock exchanges, and especially the New York Stock Exchange, as might be expected, took exception to the Pujo Committee Report and the proposed legislation. For instance, the assistant secretary of the New York Stock Exchange, H. S. Martin, labeled the measure as "morally, economically and legally...unsound."[2] Furthermore, Martin said, the New York Stock Exchange had a far better record than

---

[1] _Ibid._, pp. 114-115.

[2] Martin, _op. cit._, p. 55.

the government in requiring publication of the business and earnings of corporations. In fact, he claimed, since 1868, the exchange had constantly demanded publication of statements by corporations. Currently, it required listed companies to both publish annual reports to stockholders and file annual statements in the "utmost detail" with the Exchange. In addition, the application statements of those companies seeking to list securities were made public.[1] What Mr. Martin neglected to say, however, was that the amount of information contained in application statements varied with each company---there were few formal and uniform requirements---and a number of listed companies either neglected or refused to meet the prescribed conditions relating to the annual reports. In fact, until 1910 the New York Stock Exchange permitted its members to conduct "blind pools" involving listed stocks.[2]

While the Pujo Committee failed to prove the stock exchanges were as corrupt as it claimed neither did the actions of the exchanges substantiate their pretense of virtue. Perhaps, as Mr. Martin said, the New York Stock Exchange was in fact a proponent of greater publicity

---

[1]*Ibid.*, pp. 53-54.

[2]The New York Stock Exchange listing agreements are discussed in greater detail later. See page

of corporate affairs but, in 1913, the Exchange was apparently more concerned with more immediate problems: establishing effective control over its members; increasing the number of listed companies; and gaining the goodwill of the dealers in securities. In 1913, when the Pujo report was issued, the exchanges, including the New York Stock Exchange, neither had the power nor the inclination "to go out into the highways and byways and compel" companies to list securities under the conditions laid out by the Pujo Committee. The companies who issued securities and the people who dealt in these securities could successfully operate outside the exchanges with complete impunity.[1]

Other Critics

Between 1900 and 1917, not all who advocated greater publicity of corporate affairs participated in the federal activities described above. This concluding portion of chapter three will briefly present samples of the views of some of these non-participants including Louis D. Brandeis and several investment bankers and public accountants.

---

[1]The exchanges played no role at all in the issuance of securities and dealers in securities could operate in the many security markets which existed outside the framework of the exchanges. Not being listed carried few disadvantages.

Louis Brandeis

Among those who advocated greater publicity of corporate affairs few were as widely read and respected as the future Supreme Court Justice Louis D. Brandeis. In 1913, Louis Brandeis, whom Loss has described "as the man who left the greatest mark on the philosophy of federal securities regulation in this country,"[1] said:

> Publicity is justly commended as a remedy for social and industrial diseases. Sunlight is said to be the best of disinfectants; electric light the most efficient policeman.[2]

Brandeis, like Roosevelt, saw publicity as the means whereby the "hostile forces" could be located, counted, and appraised; the first step--and a long one--toward relief.

He insisted disclosure must be real and it must be directed to the investor. The filing of a statement of facts with some government or stock exchange official was insufficient; the investor must receive the facts directly.

> To be effective, knowledge of the facts must be actually bought home to the investor, and this can best be done by requiring the facts to be stated in good, large type in every notice, circular, letter and advertisement inviting the investor to purchase. Com-

---

[1]Loss, _op. cit._, p. 123.

[2]Louis D. Brandeis, _op. cit._, p. 93.

> pliance with this requirement should also be obligatory, and not something which the investor could waive. For the whole public is interested in putting an end to the bankers' exactions. England undertook, years ago, to protect its investors against the wiles of promoters, by requiring a somewhat similar disclosure; but the British act failed, in large measure of its purpose, partly because under it the statement of facts was filed only with a public official and partly because the investor could waive the provision.[1] And the British statute has now been changed in the latter respect.

Furthermore, Brandeis, partly in an endeavor to break the power of the "money trust" advocated disclosure in prospectuses of all the participants in an underwriting. With this information, Brandeis believed, investors could determine whether the banker advising them to buy securities was in fact disinterested. In addition, Brandeis recommended for two reasons investment bankers when issuing securities be compelled to make public the commissions or profits they received. First, the inestor has a right to know the middle-man's profit. If the banker's profits were too high the investor, Brandeis argued, would not buy and thereby force bankers to quit taking "excessive commissions"; the supposed basis for the financial oligarchy's "unjustly acquired wealth." Second, the investor by

---

[1] *Ibid.*, p. 104. The British Companies Act Brandeis was referring to here was the defunct British Companies Act of 1867. See pp. 15-16.

knowing the size of the banker's "spread" would be better able to judge the safety of the investment since bankers, according to Brandeis, received larger commissions for underwriting weak securities than for "safe" issues. The law, however, should

> ...not undertake (except incidentally in connection with railroads and public-service corporations) to fix bankers' profits. And it should not seek to prevent investors from making bad bargains. But it is now recognized in the simplest merchandizing, that there should be full disclosure. The archaic doctrine of <u>caveat emptor</u> is vanishing. The law has begun to require publicity in aid of fair dealing. The Federal Pure Food Law does not guarantee quality or prices; but it helps the buyer to judge of quality by requiring disclosure of ingredients.[1]

Brandeis' advocacy of greater publicity--particularly prospectus disclosure--was based on a curious mixture of motives: he wished to dissolve big business and break the power of the money trust; he saw a need to improve the protection afforded investors; and he desired to eradicate the corporate and financial abuses by implementing remedial action which would be in accord with his absolutist interpretation of the civil liberties clauses of the Constitution. Later, in 1933, "it was Mr. Frankfurter--surrogate for Justice Brandeis--in his visits to Albany and Hyde Park who argued, day in and day out, for this approach to business regula-

---

[1]<u>Ibid</u>., p. 103.

tion."[1]

Investment Bankers

As early as 1912, the investment banking community in general, supported, or at least said they did, the demand for greater publicity of corporate affairs.[2] For instance, on August 8, 1912, George B. Caldwell,[3] speaking as chairman of the organization meeting of the Investment Bankers' Association of America said:

> ...There is also the question of a Federal Corporation Law; at present, business initiative is greatly hampered by the multiplicity of laws governing interstate corporations. Federal law, providing for national incorporation, making interstate corporations subject to uniform requirements with annual reports to be accompanied by a sworn statement, subject to investigation by a Federal Bureau, it is suggested, would greatly improve the quality of our industrial securities and avoid much expense and confusion....[4]

If Mr. Caldwell's remarks can be interpreted as representing the investment bankers' point of view, it

---

[1]Rexford G. Tugwell, "The Progressive Orthodoxy of Franklin D. Roosevelt," Ethics, Vol. 64, No. 1, p. 16.

[2]On the state level, as we shall see, the Investment Banking Association of America did not advocate publicity as the means whereby security issues could be effectively regulated. In this case, the Association fought, first, for dealer licensing laws and later, for antifraud statutes. See, for example, pp. 164 ff.

[3]Vice President Continental and Commercial Trust and Savings Bank, Chicago, Illinois.

[4]George B. Caldwell, Chairman's Address, Proceedings of the Organization Meeting of the Investment Bankers' Association of America. August 8, 1912, pp. 18-19.

would appear that investment bankers saw improved corporate publicity as a crutch for the securities market: a narrow and selfish view. However, little was done by the Association at this time to promote greater publicity of corporate affairs. The fledgling organization was concerned with more immediate problems such as increasing its membership and the challenge of the blue sky movement.[1]

Not all those dealing in securities, however, saw publicity solely as a support for the securities market. At least one person associated with investment banking, Alexander Smith, had another view of the role, problems and limitations of publicity. He approached the controversy from the point of view of the user of financial data and as such was highly critical of the accounting profession's practices and ethics.

In October, 1912, Smith, who was associated with Peabody, Houghteling & Co., a Chicago firm dealing in securities, addressed a meeting of the American Association of Public Accountants on the subject of "The Abuse of the Audit in Selling Securities."[2] He said:

---

[1]See chapter four.

[2]The Journal of Accountancy, Vol. 14, No. 4, October 1912, p. 243.

> The abuse of the Audit, especially in relation to the sale of securities, constitutes a serious menace to the community, and the correction of this abuse is a matter worthy of most serious consideration. It is impossible to contemplate complete and universal honesty in business transactions and, to that extent, it is impossible to devise practical means of entirely eliminating this abuse, but I hope to convince you that it is within the province and ability of the American Association of Public Accountants to remedy existing conditions, and to eliminate entirely some of the main procuring causes that lead to the abuse of the audit.[1]

Mr. Smith claimed the three leading causes of the audit abuses were:

First - The lack of scientific method of accounting, and the lack of uniform principles and expressions of accounting.

Second - Dishonesty or incompetency of the accountant, and especially his indifference towards the abuse of his certificate by other parties.

Third - The inefficiency of the banker and his dishonesty in wilfully misinterpreting the audit.

Alexander Smith, speaking as a layman who regularly used accounting data, suggested several remedies to the above abuses which would also help solve his problems in working with accountant's reports. Smith believed "accounting is, or should be, a science--not a system of ethics but an exact science, amenable to definite laws, constructed on definite laws, constructed

---

[1] *Ibid.*

on definite axioms, and capable, in proper practice, of producing definite and exact results."[1] The responsibility and the power to make accounting such an "exact science" as, say chemistry, Smith maintained, rested with the American Association of Public Accountants. In fact, he said, the Association must give definite rulings on the correct accounting treatment of such items as depreciation, bond discount and organization expenses since the variety of accounting treatments of these items often confused the nonaccountant. The Association, Smith claimed, would by promulgating "proper scientific laws" for the guidance of its members and adopting uniform methods of expressing the results of these laws remove "the most potent and common cause of the abuse of the audit." Such action would take away from the dishonest banker and the dishonest promoter the "principal cloak under which they are now able to cover their frauds."[2]

Smith suggested some specific courses of action to the Association:

> First - Let this Association appoint a committee to investigate and report to it as to the feasibility of adopting exact and uniform principles and expressions of accounting.... When you have agreed among yourselves on these fundamental rules, publish your findings

---

[1] *Ibid.*, p. 252.

[2] *Ibid.*

> and send them to the members of the American Bankers Association and similar bodies, and for their concurrence or criticism.
>
> Second - When your certificate is misquoted or misinterpreted in public announcements to the investing public, you must, at all costs and by all means at your command, correct this abuse....
>
> Third - You must be careful to give your certificate in such form that it will be the least capable of misinterpretation....
>
> Fourth - See to it that membership in your association is *prima facie* evidence of efficiency and integrity.[1]

In summary, Smith as a user of accounting data appealed for a uniformity of accounting principles, a stronger accounting association, and a well-defined code of ethics for accountants. His plea was to be repeatedly echoed by many more users of financial statements.

Public Accountants

During the period 1900-1917, a number of public accountants published articles advocating greater publicity of corporate financial affairs. These accountants urged the adoption on the federal level of corporation laws similar to the English Companies Acts. The principal accounting society--The American Association of Public Accountants--unofficially supported the efforts of these men, but took--except for one limited

---

[1] *Ibid.*, pp. 252-253.

case--no official action to actively promote, as a society, better standards of financial disclosure. At this time, the main efforts of this stripling accounting society were absorbed by other more pressing tasks: the improvement of the education and training of accountants; the passage of Certified Public Accounting legislation;[1] the establishment of professional standards; and the formulation of a definition describing the duties and responsibilities of public accountants.

The public accountant, perhaps more so than any other group external to the firm, faced in his daily practice the problem of financial disclosure. Increasingly the public accountant was being called upon to certify the earnings and financial position of corporations for a variety of purposes including the issuance of securities, application for bank credit, acquisition of corporations, and preparation of annual reports to the stockholders. Therefore, it is not surprising a number of accountants, acting in their individual capacity, did write on the topic of disclosure. In

---

[1]Prior to the passage of effective certified public accounting legislation there were a number of "bogus" accountants willing to lend their names to the unsavory schemes of the fraudulent promoter. The competition from this source was a constant irritation to the legitimate public accountant.

fact, the first issue of The Journal of Accountancy[1] carried an article entitled "Duties and Responsibilities of the Public Accountant with regard to New Issues of Stocks and Bonds"[2] by A. Lowes Dickinson, a transplanted British Chartered Accountant. Mr. Dickinson's article and several of the other articles which related to the general subject of financial disclosure that appeared in The Journal of Accountancy during the 17 years now under review are discussed below.

A. Lowes Dickinson, directing his remarks to accountants, discussed in both general and specific terms the attitude a public accountant should adopt when hired to certify financial statements for publication in a prospectus. In general, Dickinson was hopeful that prospectus financial disclosure in the United States would soon be governed by some form of federal legislation similar to the 1900 English Companies Act. Also, he noted, in addition to the many technical

---

[1]The Journal of Accountancy at this time was published under the auspices of the American Association of Public Accountants. I believe it would be fair to say that, in general, its editorials supported the institution of big business; federal incorporation; and more adequate publicity of corporate affairs. The editors were highly critical of the Supreme Court's antitrust decisions and the treatment received by big business at the hands of the popular press. The Journal of Accountancy was, and still is today, the principal professional journal of public accountants.

[2]The Journal of Accountancy, Vol. 1, No. 1, November 1905, pp. 16-27.

accounting problems related to income determination there was one other of equal, if not greater importance, to which the accountant must pay attention when certifying prospectus financial statements. Namely, the accountant must decide, before signing his certificate, if the prospectus' financial statement fully disclosed to the investor all the material facts necessary to enable the investor to form a judgment upon the value and safety of the securities offered to him. Clearly, such a point of view reflected, in part, Dickinson's early training and work as a Chartered Accountant in England.

Before stating what he conceived the responsibility of the auditor to be, Dickinson described the current practice, both in the United States and Great Britain, with respect to certification of prospectus financial statements. His description is of interest because it offered some insights into the contemporary American practice in the area of prospectus disclosure and the attitudes of those associated with prospectus preparation and use--corporate executives, investment bankers and investors. Dickinson said: corporate executives were technically incompetent in the area of accounting and left the responsibility for statement preparation to subordinates; management desired to put the best possible complexion on the state of affairs; and in cases of doubt as to which of several accounting treatments to adopt management decided, not necessarily improperly, in favor of their own interests. The Investment Bankers' main desire, Dickinson said, was to sell the issue and make a quick profit. And the public was satisfied with receiving the facts surrounding the issue and issues in the form of unverified statements supplied by the vendor. In 1905, the user accepted the current practice and demanded no more. Finally, Dickinson, after reviewing the current prospectus disclosure practices concluded the neglect of the honest promoter to present an independent verification of the data contained in his prospectus made the task of the dishonest promoter easier.[1]

---

[1]...In Great Britain, where the value of the services of public accountants is more generally recognized, it is almost the universal custom that the prospectus should contain a certificate by a chartered accountant as to the earnings of a period of years; and frequently also as to the financial position.

In this country this certificate is, in far too many cases, replaced by a mere letter from the vendors or from the president or directors of the corporation, or from the bankers who recommend the investment, stating the results of operations and the present condition. While the standing of the officers of the company, or of the bankers, is generally such as to merit confidence in the bona fides of any statements which they make, a consideration of the difficulties involved in determining profits will show that too much reliance should not be placed thereon, unless they are supported by a certificate of a reputable public accountant...the questions involved in the determination of profits are often highly technical...

Dickinson believed the responsibilities of the accountant when certifying financial statements for inclusion in prospectuses were very onerous. The accountant had a responsibility to two parties: the investor and the vendor. The accountant must, Dickin-

---

and a departure from correct principles may easily make what is really a losing business appear as a comparatively profitable one. The proprietors or chief officers of the vendor concerned must rely upon their subordinates to a large extent for the facts which they furnish to the bankers or to the public. They have not, as a rule, the necessary skill in accountancy to detect errors, whether of principle or of detail, in the statements submitted to them; they do not properly appreciate the distinction between facts and estimates, which might perhaps be more properly described as "expert guesses"; and finally they are interested in putting the best possible complexion upon the general state of affairs and will naturally, and not necessarily improperly, be biased in cases of doubt in favor of the view which is most to their own interests. The main desire of the bankers is to sell the stocks or bonds which they are offering to the public and make a quick profit on the turnover. Their reputation and standing requires them to take very reasonable precaution to satisfy themselves that the investment they are offering is a thoroughly sound and reliable one; and while it is doubtful if letters from or facts supplied by the vendors are sufficient precautions, yet as long as the public demands no more there is no reason why bankers should offer more. In the meantime, the natural bias of the promoter helps the banker with a favorable statement and the verification by a public accountant might show a less favorable condition and diminish the banker's profit. It may be added that the neglect of such obvious precautions by the honest promoter makes the task of the dishonest one comparatively easy, and in the interests of commercial morality and for the protection of the public it is hoped that a change may soon be made in this respect and that the certificate of a reputable public accountant in a prospectus will become as common in this country as in Great Britain.--*Ibid*., pp. 16-17.

son said, insist that the "real facts" be disclosed to the investor but, at the same time, he must not select data to be revealed which would reflect as permanent those conditions which were in fact only temporary. So as to guide the accountant in making right decisions in this area Dickinson offered a number of specific suggestions as to what ought to be included or not included in prospectuses: audited financial statements covering three to five years; a segregation of reoccuring operating income from income derived from nonoperating and nonreceiving sources; the results of each year's operations clearly stated--not averaged; exclusion of interest paid on loans to partners from profits;[1] notes appended to the financial statements indicating what provisions had been made for such items as management salaries, depreciation and renewals; and, finally, a description of all current enforceable "special" contracts entered into by the firm. Dickinson also stated that it was inadvisable and dangerous for accountants to lend their names to any estimates of future earnings which the vendor wished to include in

[1]At this time, investors in increasing numbers were being invited to purchase securities in public corporations which a short time before had been private companies. Dickinson was principally concerned with the problem of recasting the past financial statements of such former partnerships and proprietary companies in a form that would reflect the company's new corporate status.

his prospectus. The accountant dealt only with verifiable facts.

In summary, Dickinson believed "the question of the responsibility of the accountant for a certificate which he gives to vendors or purchasers and which is published in a prospectus issued to the public, [was] a matter of considerable importance."[1] Clearly, Dickinson saw financial disclosure standards as being more than the sum of a number of accounting techniques. To him, the attitudes toward disclosure of the vendor, the public accountant involved in the certification of the vendor's financial statements and the user of such data were, in any situation, the real determinants of the degree of disclosure actually achieved.

Later, in February 1910, J. E. Strerrett, then the President of the American Association of Public Accountants, published an article[2] in The Journal of Accountancy in which he also suggested effective federal control over the activities of corporations might be obtained through the passage of a federal incorporation statute based on the English Companies Acts. He, like a number of other public accountants, held the English acts in

---

[1]Ibid., p. 26.

[2]"Legislation for the Control of Corporations," The Journal of Accountancy, Vol. 9, No. 4, February 1910, pp. 241-247.

high regard:

> ...Under [the Companies Acts] English companies have multiplied and prospered. The securities of established businesses have a stable market and investors are protected from false rumors and insinuated half truths that so often work injury to the investor in American securities. At the same time new and speculative ventures, which while involving a higher risk of loss have often proved the means of progress, are not necessarily restricted. In brief while speculation is not prohibited, the dice must not be loaded.... It is significant also that probably without exception the corporations whose courses of conduct have been made the subject of severe criticism within the past few years have failed to follow a policy in accord with the principles just outlined.
>
> It may fairly be added that such abuses as have been proved against these corporations would, in a large measure at least, have been prevented had the offenders been subject to the control laid down by the English laws or those recommended for this country by the Industrial Commission....[1]

In Strerrett's opinion the American law of corporations should be in accord with the practices outlined in the English Companies Acts. Enact similar legislation in the United States, he said, and the investor will be better protected; criticism of big business will be less severe; and those who would abuse corporate power deterred.

The prominent accountants of the day clearly saw adequate, truthful and verified publicity of corporate affairs as an essential ingredient of any government

---

[1] Ibid., pp. 246-247.

plan to control big business. Hopefully, such regulation would be based on laws similar to the English Companies Acts. Just as clearly, these leading accountants saw a role for the public accountant in any such a government regulation. For instance, in October 1912, Robert H. Montgomery, a well-known and respected public accountant, said:

> ...The people are not afraid of big business. They want it, but they know that it must be controlled. Control is of great interest to professional accountants, because if any one of the suggestions for new legislation[1] be enacted into law, vital questions relating to accountants immediately arise. If combinations are to be permitted, as I think they must be, there will be some plan of publicity which will require that the results of operations be published. Unless these results are dependable gross abuses will arise.
>
> Without a knowledge of profits there can be no regulation, no control. Furthermore, the amounts of profits must not be a secret between the corporations and the government if there is to be effective control, but no plan is feasible which does not require publicity of a sort which can be depended upon. Profits must be reported to every stockholder and under modern conditions this

---

[1]In 1912 Democratic Party Platform called for the establishment of a commission to report both to the President and to either branch of Congress as to the costs of production, effieiency of labor, capitalization, industrial organization and the general competitive position in this country and abroad of industries seeking protection from Congress. This commission, if established, was to have plenary power to elicit information, and for this purpose, prescribe a uniform system of accounting for the industries protected by tariff. Already, the Interstate Commerce Commission had established a uniform system of accounts to which all interstate common carriers were required to conform in their financial reports.

> means to the public generally. The temptation to understate profits will be as strong in the future as was the temptation to overstate profits in the past. Therefore, every plan of federal control must provide for the certification of profits and balance sheets by independent accountants, recognized by law and who will be supported by public opinion when fearless in the performance of their duty, and made amenable to constitutional laws if recreant to their trust.
>
> As stated above, accountants benefit financially more by the adoption of laws which are unscientific than by those which are intelligently drawn. We may be misunderstood by the government and the corporations when we state that the failure to consult and recognize us officially in relation to all legislation concerning federal control of corporations will result in economic waste;[1] but the fact is true nevertheless....
>
> In all plans of control it is to be assumed that suitable provision will be made for the certification by professional accountants of the accounts of all corporations subject to federal control, and that accounts so certified shall be presumed to be correct unless reasonable cause for suspicion to the contrary exists.[2]

Montgomery, and a number of other public accountants, realized that if federal legislation based on the English experience was enacted the accounting profession might well receive, not only more work, but

---

[1]Here Montgomery is obviously referring to the 1909 Income Tax Regulation. This Act, which was drawn up by government lawyers used a cash basis rather than an accrual basis for determining taxable income. A number of leading accountants had pointed out this error to the drafters of the bill but the accountants' protests produced no change.

[2]Robert H. Montgomery, "Federal Control of Corporations," The Journal of Accountancy, Vol. 14, No. 4, October 1912, pp. 282-283.

also the prestige and legal recognition it so eagerly sought. Such legislation, they claimed, might also benefit the investor, government and business.

In January 1916, the first official statement of the American Association of Public Accountants related to publicity was issued by the Association's Committee on General Relations under the title of "Protection of Investments."[1] This official pamphlet, which purported to be a "plea for adoption of the principle of election of auditors by stockholders," approved the objectives of the recently passed blue sky laws;[2] recommended passage of a federal law similar to the English Companies Act; and claimed that the investor would receive greater protection if he had direct access to the unabridged corporate reports of the auditor. The short pamphlet made no specific suggestion as to what ought to be covered by the auditor's certificate.

*****

During the years 1915 and 1916 the intensity of the attack on big business lessened. In fact, as early as 1914, George B. Caldwell by now the President of the Investment Bankers Association of America observed:

---

[1] The Journal of Accountancy, Vol. 21, No. 1, January 1916, pp. 52-53.

[2] See chapter four.

> After 10 years of agitation we are apparently approaching the time when public sentiment is changing and when people will not continue to listen to attacks upon big business, and constructive wealth. They begin to realize that their welfare depends upon the welfare of those companies in which their savings are invested for the protection of old age, disablement, and their widows and orphans.[1]

The presidential campaign of 1916 was fought on the issue of America's entry into World War I: not big business. And for the next two years the nation was to be concerned with the war in Europe: big business was reprieved.

Chapters two and three are the key to a proper understanding of the historical aspects of this thesis. The problems, attitudes and practices of corporate executives and their critics discussed herein, not only determined, in part, the character of the period 1900-1917, but continued, to some degree, to influence the response of businessmen to the rapidly changing environment during the next 17 years.[2] Since these two chapters are so important, before moving on to chapter four--the regulation of securities on the state level--

---

[1]President's Address. Proceedings of the Annual Convention of the Investment Bankers Association of America. November 12 and 13, 1914, p. 22.

[2]In fact, many of the criticisms of big business expressed during the progressive era still persist today: a topic refered to in chapter nine.

it may be wise to pause to summarize and comment upon the material already presented to date in chapters two and three.

During the period 1900-1917, for a variety of reasons, big business in the United States was under almost constant attack from reform-minded Administrations, frightened intellectuals, disgruntled farmers, oppressed workers, outraged consumers and frustrated competitors. One of the several demands of these many critics of big business was for more publicity of corporate affairs; a demand which reflected a long-standing American belief in the ultimate power of public opinion to remedy social abuses. Businessmen saw this publicity issue for what it was--part of the general attack on big business--and answered it in a similar fashion, and for much the same reasons, as they met the more general assault. Their response to this challenge was primarily conditioned by two outmoded beliefs: caveat emptor ruled all commercial transactions; and industrial corporations were essentially private companies and as such their business was no business of the public which, on occasion, included stockholders. Corporate executives did not believe the public--stockholders, investors, consumers--had the right to expect "full and fair" disclosure of corporate affairs.

The critics' demand for a greater publicity of corporate affairs was broader than just an appeal for more financial data. The critics wanted the publication of information on such diverse corporate matters as pricing, labor policy, corporate salaries, promoter's profits, director's lists, distribution of share ownership, and trust agreements. In general, the critics agreed that once data of this type was made public political protection for those individuals and institutions threatened by the power of big business would follow automatically. The desired protection would come from either governmental control or the dissolution of big business.

Some of these associated with commercial life---investment bankers and public accountants---suggested a greater publicity of corporate affairs might be more desirable. In fact, the Investment Bankers Association of America, the American Association of Public Accountants and the New York Stock Exchange all recommended, for different reasons, greater corporate publicity, however, each of these organizations was faced with more immediate organizational problems and the publicity issue was either neglected, postponed or avoided. And, one <u>user</u> of accounting data was so bold as to suggest to the American Association of Public Accountants that it undertake a program to remove the "abuse of the audit" by formulating and enforcing uniform accounting practices, principles and ethics.

In addition, a number of accountants and investment bankers, acting in their individual capacity, did propose greater publicity of corporate affairs. Their reasons were many: to protect investors; to increase their profession's prestige; to create a more stable securities market; and to end the "unjust" attacks on business. Several of these individuals, particularly accountants, believed publicity alone was not enough. Truthful, reliable and accurate disclosure was needed and the only way to achieve such disclosure was for corporations to issue financial statements audited by certified public accountants as required under the existing English company law.

CHAPTER FOUR

STATE SECURITY REGULATIONS, 1850-1933

In the United States, state regulation of securities was achieved long before the passage of the first federal securities act in 1933. In contrast to the English Companies Acts, which were based on a philosophy of disclosure, the securities statutes enacted by the various states, particularly after 1911, sought to directly regulate either the issue, issuer or seller of securities. Discussed below is the evolution of the regulation on the state level of securities, the various types of state acts, and the reaction of the business sector to these acts.

The earliest security regulations in the United States were those state statutes passed during the last half of the nineteenth century to control the issuance and sale of new securities by public service corporations. These acts were designed primarily to regulate the costs and the character of the service performed by public service corporations, rather than to protect potential investors from fraud. It was from these early statutes, however, that the form of the later state securities regulation related to corporate issues was derived.

DOI: 10.4324/9781003169420-4

In 1911, the state of Kansas passed the first comprehensive licensing statute related to corporate securities in the United States. This act, which sought to protect the citizens of Kansas from fraudulent and unsound investments, authorized the Kansas Bank Commissioner to prohibit the sale of any security in Kansas unless, in his opinion, the enterprise issuing the security gave promise of a fair return and being managed by honest, fair and just men. Subsequently, other states enacted laws similar in purpose to the Kansas statute and, by 1933, Hawaii and every state, with the exception of Nevada, had passed a general statute regulating in some fashion the issue and sale of securities to the public. The majority of these state statutes, which were called blue sky laws, were based on a paternalistic regulation philosophy rather than the previously discussed disclosure philosophy embodied in the 1900 British Companies Act.

Chapter four is divided into three parts. First, there is a brief description of the securities regulation enacted on the state level before 1911. Next, a section is devoted to an analysis of the so-called blue sky movement and in particular the passage and administration of the 1911 Kansas Blue Sky Law. Finally, there is a sample of the reaction of the business and financial sector to the blue sky movement.

Part I: Before 1911

Prior to 1911, except for a few isolated cases, which will be described later, nearly all of the state statutes regulating securities sought to regulate the issuance and sale of new securities by public service corporations. These statutes regulated the capitalization of the issuer, not the practices of the dealer in these securities or the content of prospectuses. In fact, during much of this period, the investor received little protection as it was "tacitly agreed that a man runs his own risk in choosing securities in which to invest, goes into such projects with his eyes open, and deserves no governmental protection from swindlers and companies of unsound organization."[1]

Public Service Corporations

The early regulation of public service securities sought, with limited success, to achieve honest capitalization through law. As might be expected, the public service corporations first subjected to

---

[1]Arthur V. Ayres, "Governmental Regulation of Securities Issues," Political Science Quarterly, Vol. XXVIII, No. 4, December 1913, p. 586.

financial regulation by the state were the railroads.[1] The earliest of these state statutes[2] controlling security issues of railroads was a Massachusetts law of 1852 which prohibited a railroad, if chartered in Massachusetts, from constructing its road until it had filed a certificate with the Secretary of the Commonwealth stating that 20 per cent of the par value of all the company's authorized stock had actually been paid into the company's treasury. The statute further required that the stock be subscribed to by "responsible parties." Prior to 1852, Massachusetts had permitted railroads to be started on the basis of a prospectus and a down-payment on a portion of the stock--a practice which had led to a number of speculative and unsound enterprises.

Subsequently, in 1868, Massachusetts tightened its 1852 law by forbidding the issuance of stock by railroad corporations unless the par value of the shares so issued were first fully paid in cash.[3]

---

[1]The right of the state to regulate industries "affected with public interest," when the public good required it, had long been established in common law. See, for example, _Munn v. Illinois_, 94 U.S. 113 (1877).

[2]Prior to this time, and for a number of years afterwards, the principal railroad regulatory tool of the states was the charter. However, in practice, the charter was used more effectively as a means to encourage railroad construction rather than to regulate the roads.

[3]Edward C. Kirkland, _Men, Cities and Transportation_, 2 vols. (Cambridge: Harvard University Press, 1948), vol. 1, pp. 323-324.

One year later, in 1869, Massachusetts established a railroad commission whose activities were confined to the investigation and the preparation of reports based thereon for submission to the attorney general or the legislature, according to the nature of the evils revealed. The commission did not set rates: "The Commission was simply a medium, a species of lens by means of which the otherwise scattered and powerless rays of public opinion could be concentrated to a focus, and brought to bear upon our corporation."[1] Publicity was the essential regulatory tool of this commission. Its power was to be derived solely from the influence of public opinion upon those who charged inequitable rates.

Subsequently, especially between 1893 and 1894, a number of the businessmen of Massachusetts[2] became

---

[1]William A. Crafts, State Railroad Commissions (New York: The Railroad Gazette, 1883), p. 11.

[2]See, for example, Albert E. Pillsbury, Arguments of Ex-Att'y-Gen'l, In Behalf of the Boston Associated Board Of Trade, Massachusetts State Board of Trade, And Boston Merchants' Association In Support Of The Bill To Prevent Stock And Debt Watering, And To Provide For Supervision Of The Issue Of Securities by Railroad, Street Railway, Gas, Electric Light, Telegraph, Telephone, Aqueduct, And Water Companies, And To Provide Further Supervision of Railroads And Street Railway Leases And Consolidations Before The Joint Special Committee On Revision Of Corporation Laws, April 9, 1894 (Boston: Geo. O. Ellis, 1894), p. 1.

disillusioned with the concept of publicity as a rate controlling device and there arose among those dealing with the railroads and other public service corporations a strong agitation for more stringent and direct government control over the capitalization of such companies.[1] In response to this demand the Massachusetts legislature passed the 1894 "anti-stock watering act."[2] This act prohibited the issue of share capital other than at a market value which was to be determined by the railroad commissioners.

The 1894 Massachusetts statute, plus later public service laws, followed a Massachusetts policy under which no railroad, and later no utility, security could be issued except for cash and at a price which was not less than par value. The clear intent of this regulatory policy was to limit the amount of dividend-bearing stock so as to reduce the rate base. That the stock of public service corporations might become more valuable owing to the reduction in the amount of watered stock issued was an incidental

---

[1]At this time, it was believed that public service rates depended upon the amount of stock outstanding. The more stock outstanding the greater the dividend requirements and, consequently, the higher the rates.--Irston R. Barnes, Public Utility Control in Massachusetts (New Haven: Yale University Press, 1930), p. 34.

[2]The 1894 Act was prompted, in part, by the adverse public reaction to the issuing of bonds by the Connecticut River Road to pay a dividend to the stockholders. See William Z. Ripley, Railroad Finance and Organization (New York: Longman's, Green and Co., 1920).

benefit derived from such legislation by the investor.

During the late nineteenth century, a number of states including Texas, New York, Maine and New Hampshire passed legislation prohibiting the issuance of new securities by common carriers without the specific approval of some public authority. Again, as in the case of Massachusetts, the primary goal of such regulation was the regulation of the cost and character of the service. For instance, in 1893, Texas passed a Stock and Bond Law requiring that all new railroad issues be authorized, approved and registered by the state's railroad commission. This Texas Act, according to William Z. Ripley, was prompted purely by the state's interest in the regulation of rates.[1]

Later, beginning with New York's Gas and Electric Commission Act of 1905, a number of states passed public service laws which typically contained clauses providing for commission regulation of the securities issues of public utilities. These later statutes, which have been described as the "middle period" in public service company regulation, sought to extend the protection of the commission to the investor.[2]

---

[1] *Ibid.*, p. 301.

[2] Arthur V. Ayres, *op. cit.*, p. 586.

However, this protection proved to be much less than the average investor supposed,[1] as in every state, except New York, the commission could not refuse to grant a certificate for a new issue if the minimum technical provisions of the law had been met. Generally, the commission's powers were limited to passing judgment on the size of the issue relative to the proposed uses of the funds so raised: a task not too different from the earlier concern of limiting the capitalization of public service corporations.

It is generally acknowledged that these early attempts on the state level to control security issues were a form of public utility and common carrier regulation rather than security regulation *per se*[2] and, as such, a fuller discussion of them is beyond the scope of this study. However, a brief exploration of early public service corporation financial regulation was necessary since, in a number of cases, later state securities legislation sought to apply to the security

---

[1]Commissioner Halford Erickson of the Wisconsin Commission, one of those public service commissions created after 1905, said: "We know that from experience that investors often attach a great deal of importance to government regulation of securities.... In fact, investors often buy securities on the strength of the existence of such regulation alone, without inquiring into its character and scope."

[2]Louis Loss, *Security Regulation* (Boston: Little, Brown and Company, 1951); Louis Loss and Edward M. Cowett, *Blue Sky Law* (Boston: Little, Brown and Company, 1958), p. 5.

issues of all companies a number of the regulatory practices which had evolved during the period before 1911.

Private Corporations

Before 1911, the regulation of new security issues of corporations other than public service corporations, except for three isolated and limited cases, was nonexistent. The three exceptions were a Connecticut statute of 1903; a Nevada statute of 1909; and a Rhode Island amendment to its corporation law of 1910. None of the statutes passed prior to 1911 sought to regulate, in any way, the content of the prospectus or circulars issued by promoters.[1]

---

[1]Of course, the criminal statutes and common law related to fraud could have been used to punish those who sold securities on the basis of fraudulent statements. However, as Loss pointed out: "common law afforded the public insufficient protection against plain fraud both in the issuance of securities and in postissuance trading."--Loss, op. cit., p. 15.

In 1921, the Massachusetts Special Commission to Investigate the Sale of Corporate Securities and Related Matters said: "...it has been demonstrated that criminal legislation is not sufficient to effectively check the sale of fraudulent securities.... Criminal legislation only locks the door after the horse is stolen. The fraudulent promoter has not committed a crime until people have been robbed,--the attempt alone is hard to prove,--and before he is arrested he has usually squandered or concealed the stolen money, or has fled from the jurisdiction."--Report of the Massachusetts General Court, House no. 1175. Special Commission to Investigate the Sale of Corporate Securities and Related Matters. January, 1921, p. 26.

In 1903, Connecticut enacted a statute which regulated, for the first time, the securities of a corporation other than a public service corporation. The Connecticut statute made it illegal for a mining company to offer securities to the public without first filing certain information in the office of the Secretary of State. Included in the information to be filed was a certificate showing the financial position of the company. Exempted from the jurisdiction of this statute were those mining companies whose mines were all located in Connecticut.

Next, in 1909, Nevada passed an act which sought to achieve disclosure in the sale of mining stock. Under this statute, every mining company engaged in mining in Nevada which sold and offered any of its stock in Nevada had to file semiannually in the office of the Attorney General, and the office of every county recorder of each county where the company had mining operations, a sworn statement containing information related to the company's capital structure, compensation of officers, and certain types of expenditures.[1] Members of the public could avail themselves of this information if they so desired.

---

[1]This act "was watered" down in 1911 and repealed in 1915. Since 1915, Nevada has had no Blue Sky Law of any kind. Loss and Cowett, op. cit., p. 6.

In 1910, Rhode Island amended its corporation law to include a general securities regulation provision. Specifically, the new provision regulated the issuance of "stocks, shares, or installment shares, in any investment company or in any real estate, mining, or cooperative corporation, society, association or organization, other than building and loan associations or notes or bonds or other securities thereof." The act provided that no companies, of the type named in the act, could issue or sell securities in Rhode Island unless the company had first "filed in the office of the Secretary of State a statement certificate showing its financial condition, the location of the property or properties, with plans of the same, the amount of work done thereon, the amount of cash expended for improvements thereon, and the condition of the plant and machinery if any connected therewith."[1] A similar statement was to be filed annually thereafter. This provision, like the earlier Connecticut and Nevada statutes, was "in essence nothing more than a simple notification statute."[2]

---

[1]Rhode Island Acts and Resolves 1910, c. 557, p. 39.

[2]Loss and Cowett, op. cit., p. 7.

In addition to these few statutes related to security issues, some states had regulations which were related to the more general topic of corporate publicity.

In 1903, Frank Edward Horack undertook a study of the state legal requirements regulating the reporting practices of corporations. He reported his findings under two main headings: reports submitted to some public authorities and reports submitted to stockholders. The reports required by state authorities, he said, were, in general, considered as confidential statements between the State and the corporation and as such not available for public inspection. These reports or statements which corporations were required to make to State officers were of three kinds: detailed reports, those requiring financial statements, in some detail, as to assets and liabilities; general statements as to the condition of the company; and simple reports, those requiring the names and residences of directors, the agent or person upon whom processes may be served etc. Detailed reports were required in sixteen states, general statements in five states and simple reports in six states.

The second class of reports--reports to stockholders--was broken down by Horack into three sub categories: periodic reports to the stockholders;

reports at the demand of the minority stockholders; and reports which combined the two prior categories. Nine states fell within the first division, seven under the second and three under the third.[1]

Part II: 1911 Onwards

After 1911, beginning with Kansas, a number of states enacted comprehensive licensing statutes or antifraud acts applicable to securities, investment bankers and securities salesmen. These state laws, which became known as blue sky laws, varied greatly in scope and method. All, however, sought to accomplish, at least as a minimum goal, the same general purpose--the protection of the purchaser of the securities from fraudulent promoters. Several of the states went further than this minimum objective and enacted statutes which were designed to protect investors from not only fraud but also "unwise" investments, even though the transaction was an honest one. Generally, as will be shown later, the philosophy underlying these statutes was one of direct regulation rather than one of disclosure.

No two blue sky statutes were identical. However,

---

[1]Frank Edward Horack, The Organization and Control of Industrial Corporations (Philadelphia: C. F. Taylor, 1903), pp. 79-122.

two acknowledged authorities on the subject, Louis Loss and Edward Cowett, have concluded that the "typical" blue sky law did three things:

1. Contained fairly broad antifraud provisions,

2. Imposed registration requirements upon broker dealers and agents, and

3. Provided that securities must be registered either by notification (carrying with it an automatic effectiveness) or by qualification.[1]

By 1933, when the Federal Securities Act was passed, every state--except Nevada--had some type of blue sky statute regulating security sales. At least 38 of these 47 statutes had been passed by 1921.[2]

The Kansas Act

Within two years after Kansas passed its 1911 act requiring registration of securities and security salesmen, 23 other states passed similar acts.[3] Of

---

[1]Loss and Cowett, op. cit., p. 39.

[2]Report of the Massachusetts General Court, op. cit., p. 25.

[3]Between 1911 and 1920, the following states passed securities statutes:

1911: Kansas
1912: Arizona, Louisiana, South Carolina, Vermont.
1913: Arkansas, California, Florida, Georgia, Idaho, Iowa, Maine, Michigan, Missouri, Montana, Nebraska, North Carolina, North Dakota, Ohio, Oregon, South Dakota, Tennessee, Texas, West Virginia, Wisconsin.
1915: Alabama.
1916: Mississippi, Virginia.
1917: Illinois, Minnesota, New Hampshire.
1919: Indiana, Oklahoma, Utah, Wyoming.
1920: Kentucky.

In addition, Manitoba, Canada, and New South Wales, Australia, promptly passed almost identical legislation to the Kansas Act of 1911, Jacob Murray Edelman, Security Regulation In The 48 States (Chicago: The Journal of State Governments, 1942).

these acts, all but six were either identical to the Kansas Act or modeled upon it.[1] Therefore, in view of the influence of the Kansas Act upon succeeding legislation in other states, a brief discussion of the Kansas Act and its architect, J. N. Dolley,[2] is presented below.

During the first decade of the twentieth century Kansas, along with the other agrarian states, experienced unprecedented prosperity.[3] This prosperity attracted to the area unscrupulous promoters who, in a number of cases, were able to convince the citizens of Kansas to exchange their savings for stock in

---

[1]Loss, op. cit., p. 10.

[2]"There is no doubt that the zealous bank commissioner [Dolley] fathered the paternalistic approach to state securities regulation."--Loss and Cowett, op. cit., p. 9.

[3]Between 1900 and 1910 the value of the nation's farm products rose from 106.4 to 189.2 (1899=100)--Theodore Saloutos and John D. Hicks, Agricultural Discontent in the Midwest, 1900-1939 (Madison: University of Wisconsin Press, 1951), p. 21. In Kansas, between 1896 and 1910, Kansas bank deposits increased from less than $9 million to over $73 million.--Biennial Reports of the Kansas State Bank Commission, 1896 and 1910, pp. 2-9 and p. 447, respectively.

enterprises such as mining, oil,[1] and land and loan companies which all too often proved to be financially unsound or fraudulent.[2] Often these investors knew little of either the business instruments such as bonds and stocks or the enterprises in which they were asked to invest. According to one Kansas, J. N. Dolley, who was the president of a local savings bank, a prominent merchant and the one-time chairman of the State Republican Party, Kansas was "literally infested" with swindlers, fakers, and "blue sky merchants." In 1910 Dolley, in a circular letter to the state's newpapers said:

---

[1]While describing the impact upon Standard Oil Company (New Jersey) of the speculation in crude oil production in Kansas and the subsequent price declines during the period 1894-1904, Ralph W. Hidy and Muriel E. Hidy in their book Pioneering in Big Business 1882-1911, said:

> "The pattern of financing crude production in the state accentuated the agitation. I Kansas many of the approximately 500 producing companies, some not too soundly financed, were unable to pay dividends to their large number of local stockholders as prices declined; in fact, some of the companies needed a spectacular high price per barrel to operate successfully...."

Ralph W. Hidy and Muriel E. Hidy, Pioneering in Big Business 1882-1911 (New York: Harper & Brothers, 1955), p. 672.

[2]According to Loss, "Some of these frauds became so barefaced that it was stated that they would sell building lots in the blue sky in fee simple." Loss, op. cit., p. 7.

> I find that Kansas has been tolled millions and millions of dollars during the past few years by these confidence men, and 98% of the money so paid has been entirely lost by the investor.[1]

Following the 1910 Kansas elections in which Walter R. S. Stubbs, the Republican candidate for governor, was reelected and his Republican party swept into power,[2] Stubbs appointed his political ally, J. N. Dolley, Bank Commissioner. Stubbs, Dolley, and their political associates, who represented the progressive and reform-minded element in the Kansas Republican Party, have been described as: "men of substantial means who had seen the need for reform and were determined to bring it to pass."[3]

Soon after his appointment, Dolley established within the office of the bank commissioner a department to investigate securities publicly offered in Kansas; instigated a vigorous publicity campaign to warn the public against known fraudulent stock; and,

---

[1]A circular letter dated December 16, 1910, to the editors of Kansas papers sent by J. N. Dolley, Bank Commissioner of the State of Kansas, 1910-1913.--Thomas Mulvey, Report Upon Existing Registration in Canada and Elsewhere Prepared By The Under Secretary Of State (Ottawa: Government Printing Bureau, 1913), p. lxix.

[2]See William E. Connelley, A Standard History of Kansas and Kansans (Chicago: Lewis Publishing Company, 1918), p. 1137 ff.

[3]William Frank Zornow, Kansas. A History of the Jayhawk State (Norman: University of Oklahoma Press, 1967), p. 215.

through his office, offered investment advice to prospective investors.[1] Subsequently, largely as a result of the bank commissioner's persistent efforts to obtain a statutory basis for his department's activities, the Kansas Blue Sky Act of 1911[2] was passed.

The Kansas Act sought not only to protect its citizens from fraudulent promotions but also from unwise investments in poorly conceived ventures which were otherwise honest. The Act's provisions, which were at least in theory particularly stringent, applied to all issuers of securities and security salesmen located nn the state.

The law required each issuer to file with the bank commissioner:

> ...a statement showing in full detail the plan upon which it proposed to transact business...a copy of all contracts, bonds, or other instruments which it proposes to make or sell its contributors, its name and location, an account of its financial condition, and its articles of incorporation, association, copartnership, or charter.[3]

---

[1]"It has been said that the people do not need a guardian to supervise their investments. Why not? Bankers are subject to the very strictest of supervision. Almost every state in the union has a banking department to regulate and supervise the banks. Why should the bank be regulated any more so than the stock selling company? History and statistics show that losses through banks are but a drop in the bucket compared with the money which is lost through investment in worthless stocks and bonds." A quote of J. N. Dolley, reproduced by Loss and Cowett, op. cit., p. 9.

[2]Kansas, Sessions Law 1911, c. 133.

[3]Edelman, op. cit., p. 2.

False statements as to the financial position of the company were punishable by fine or imprisonment.

Added to these simple disclosure requirements was a departure from previous American (and British) statutes related to corporate securities: the so-called "paternalistic" provision. Under this innovation in security regulation no security could be issued or sold unless a "permit" covering such securities had been issued by the bank commissioner. A permit could be denied if:

> ...said bank commissioner finds that such articles of incorporation or association, charter, constitution and by-laws, plan of business or proposed contract, contain any provision that is unfair, unjust, inequitable or oppressive to any class of contributors, or if he decides from his examination of its affairs that said investment company is not solvent and does not intend to do a fair and honest business, and in his judgment does not promise a fair return on the stocks, bonds or other securities by it offered for sale, then he shall notify such investment company in writing of his findings, and it shall be unlawful for such company to do any further business in this state....[1]

In addition, companies registered in the bank commissioner's office were required to file semiannual reports and keep certain books and accounts, which

---

[1]Kansas, Sessions Law 1911, c. 133. See also Loss and Cowett, op. cit., p. 8.

were subject to examination by the bank commissioner.[1]

Why did the state of Kansas pass such a stringent and paternalistic statute? The answer is probably to be found in the mood of the people of the time; the lingering populist influence upon Kansas politics; and the composition of the 1910-1912 legislature. That the agricultural citizens of Kansas were outraged by the frauds--both real and imaginary--which they believed to have been recently perpetrated in their midst there is little doubt--Dolley's publicity campaign had helped to create that mood. The people demanded prompt and effective state action to protect them from such exploitation--half measures would not do.[2]

It was only to be expected that the citizens of Kansas, whose political thinking had been, and still was, greatly influenced by the populist movement, should turn to the state for protection from "fraud-artists." While the Populist Party was dead, the

---

[1]In 1915 Kansas amended its 1911 Act. The new act sought to regulate the sale of "speculative" securities rather than the company selling them. At the same time the administration of the act was transferred to the state charter board. In addition, the number of exemptions to the act was increased.

[2]"In 1911...fraudulent promotions became so gross among the agricultural population of Kansas that the farmers literally revolted." Report of the Massachusetts General Court, op. cit., p. 24.

populist philosophy still lingered on among a number of those in and out of politics. This philosophy "boiled down.../to/ two fundamental proportions; one, that the government must restrain the selfish tendencies of those who profit at the expense of the poor and the needy; and another, that the people, not the plutocrats, must control the government."[1]

A number of those elected to the 1910-1912 Kansas Legislature, both Democrats and Republicans, had been, in earlier days, either associated with or sympathetic toward the populist movement. Added to their populist heritage and the current popular sentiment for action was Dolley's pressure for a securities act; the leadership of a reform minded governor; and a legislature controlled by progressive Republicans. Given these conditions, it is little wonder that the Kansas legislature drafted and passed the type of

---

[1]John D. Hicks, The Populist Revolt (Minneapolis: The University of Minnesota Press, 1931), p. 406. Later on pages 412-413, Hicks wrote:

"The control of the government by the people was to the thoughtful Populist merely a means to an end. The next step was to use the power of the government to check the iniquities of the plutocrats....Once permit the people really to rule, once insure that the men in office would not or could not betray the popular will, and such regulative measures as would right the wrongs from which the people suffered would quickly follow."

securities act it did.[1]

Encouraged and authorized by the new statute, Dolley stepped up his activities in the securities area and accomplished, according to Dolley, "some wonderful results":

> ...I estimate that it has saved the people of this state at least $6 million since its enactment. Between 1,400 and 1,500 companies have been investigated by this department since the enactment of this law, and of this number less than 100 have been granted permits to sell their securities in Kansas.[2] The law is rapidly gaining fame all over the world and I believe that a large number of the states will accept a similar law at the coming session of their legislatures. I believe that a movement has been started that will eventually result in the regula-

---

[1]The reform-minded 1911 legislature also passed a workman's compensation law; appropriated money to construct a new insane asylum; disbanded the ineffective elective Board of Railroad Commissioners; and created a new Public Utilities Commission. Ibid., p. 218.

[2]In 1913 the Hon. Thomas Mulvey, the Under Secretary of State for Canada, conducted a personal survey of the Kansas Blue Sky Law and its administration. He reported on this particular claim of Dolley's thus:

"A personal investigation of the files of the bank commissioner's office casts serious doubts upon the accuracy of this statement. It appears that down to April 1, 1913 permits were granted to 49 companies and refused to 62. The balance was held for consideration, and in some cases temporary permits were granted on the personal authority of the commissioner, such authority not being granted by the law. It is well known that serious frauds were committed through these temporary permits....However, it should be pointed out that while the statute was irregularly administered and while frauds were being perpetrated under it, businessmen of the state were convinced of its good effect...." Mulvey, op. cit., p. lxxii.

> tion and supervision of all kinds of companies in the same manner as banks are now regulated and supervised....[1]

Dolley, in addition to publicizing the benefits of the act in Kansas, sent numerous reports, releases and statements to the press and officials in other states. So successful was Dolley's campaign "that there have been few if any statutes which have been so thoroughly advertised through the press and magazines of the United States."[2]

Thus was born the blue sky movement and the first blue sky law.

<u>Widespread Fraud</u>

During the early decades of the twentieth century, it was a widely held belief that unscrupulous investment companies and individual promoters were perpetrating gross frauds upon the public. The blue sky movement sought to eliminate, at least as some people saw it, "the evils resulting from the unbridled sale of alleged securities [which] had become so inimical to the welfare of the citizens of various states."[3] No doubt, such reports as the 1913 report

---

[1]*Ibid.*, p. lxxi.

[2]*Ibid.*

[3]Brief for Appellants. *Hall v. Geiger-Jones Co.*, 242 U.S. 539 (1917), p. 10. A "test" case, involving the 1913 Ohio blue sky law, argued before the Supreme Court during 1916-1917.

of the United States Postmaster General helped to foster the impression that widespread fraud existed:

> The stock selling proposition appears to appeal to the public more than any other one fraud scheme conducted and the amount of money taken in by promoters operating this class of scheme is enormous.[1]

In 1916, a spokesman of the National Association of Attorneys General of the United States said:

> Generally speaking, the evil in connection with the sale of stocks and bonds has gradually been increasing for the past 20 years.... The evil spread until corporations were being formed in almost every state in the Union for the express purpose of issuing worthless stock to be sold to a large class of people throughout the United States who by thrift or inheritance had a small sum of cash, but whose knowledge of business, made them an easy victim for men who were skilled in the art of deception."[2]

This same statement went on to note that "capable businessmen" had been deceived by reason of the fact that a number of "prominent men" in the community had allowed their names for one consideration or another to be connected with the "innumerable domestic corporations which had been organized for the express purpose of defrauding the public."[3]

---

[1]*Ibid*., pp. 10-11.

[2]Brief for National Association of Attorneys General as *amicus curiae*, *Merrick v. N. W. Halsey & Co*., 242 U.S. 568 (1917), p. 5.

[3]*Ibid*., pp. 5-6.

At least one group, the Investment Bankers Association of America, of whom more will be said later, believed the practice of selling fraudulent securities was not as prevalent as commonly believed:

> Despite the repeated generalizations as to the extent of loss through fraud in "get-rich quick" securities, it is impossible to get from official or any other source a reliable estimate, even an approximate estimate, of actual losses. The statements published cannot be verified by those who make them. Much less is it possible to ascertain to what extent such losses are due to fraud in the actual sale of securities. Many of these statements are attributed to the Post Office Department. But an inquiry at the department for specific information has made it clear that it has issued none, and that there is none."[1]

The above quote goes on to state that there was considerable confusion as to the extent of genuine securities frauds in the total losses from "fake" schemes. In fact, in the investment banker's opinion, the losses from security flotation frauds were magnified and confused with fraud in the operation of the business. For instance, during 1914, of the 200 fraud cases prosecuted by the Post Office Department only 15 cases were related to securities fraud, a less alarming situation than the 1913 Post Office Report mentioned above would indicate. In addition,

---

[1]Brief for Investment Bankers Association of America, as _amicus curiae_. _Hall v. Geiger-Jones Co._, _op. cit._, p. 33.

a number of the estimates of the losses due to fraud included situations where the losses were due to causes other than fraud, such as lack of adequate finance for honest ventures, incompetent management and reckless optimism.

Later, the investment bankers' statement noted:

> As against these estimates of losses in various "fake" schemes, a part of which are stock flotations, may be cited in the fact that close to $2 billion in new securities are issued and that several more billions change hands every year. There is not and has not been any charge that fraud is prevalent in this normal business."[1]

The Investment Banking Association only questioned the common belief as to the extent of the fraudulent dealings in securities--it did not deny fraud existed. In 1917, the Association's committee on fraudulent advertising stated:

> Millions of dollars of the savings of our people have each year been filched from them by the promoters of fraudulent operations in camouflaged swindles.[2]

The Association was particularly anxious that the public distinguish between the Association's members, whom it referred to as "legitimate dealers in securities," and those "fly-by-night" operators who were outside the

---

[1] *Ibid.*

[2] Report of Committee on Fraudulent Advertising. Proceedings of the Sixth Annual Convention of the Investment Bankers Association of America. Nov. 12, 13, 14, 1917, p. 190.

Association. It was the latter, not the former, who should, in the legitimate investment bankers view, be regulated. However, since a number of the blue sky laws did interfere with the business of the "legitimate dealers in securities" the Association found itself, at least in its early days, in opposition to the blue sky movement.[1]

Another estimation as to extent of fraud in the securities business during the late 1910's was given in 1925 by E. H. H. Simmons, President, New York Stock Exchange.

> Many estimates have been made of this gross income of the security swindling industry in America. The U.S. Treasury has stated that in 1918-1919 approximately $400 million of Liberty Bonds were taken from investors through various swindling methods. Some years ago both ex-Secretary of the Treasury W. G. McAdoo and the Fraudulent Securities Committee of the Investment Bankers' Association agreed in estimating the annual public loss at $500 million. But the U. S. Post Office Department, I believe, as well as several prominent private businessmen, have since been inclined to double this figure.[2]

Thus, while a number of people had confliciing opinions as to the extent and nature of the fraud

---

[1]More will be said on the relationship of the Investment Bankers Association and the blue sky movement later. See p.164.

[2]E. H. H. Simmons, <u>Cooperation Against Security Frauds</u> (New York: Committee on Publicity New York Stock Exchange, 1925), p. 30.

practised upon investors during the first two decades of the twentieth century, there did exist a widespread concern over this matter on the state level. It was in response to this concern that the blue sky movement spread so rapidly.

Categories

The blue sky movement, when translated into legislation, assumed a number of different forms. As noted above, no two blue sky laws were identical. However, one authority on blue sky laws, Forrest Bee Ashby, divided, according to their principal regulatory device, the state securities statutes into two major categories: regulatory acts and fraud acts. Regulatory acts he further divided into two subcategories: dealer-licensing acts and specific-approval acts.[1] Each of these basic types of statute represented different means of achieving the same end--protection of the investor from fraud.

---

[1]Forrest Bee Ashby. The Economic Effect of Blue Sky Laws (Philadelphia, 1926).

"Although several authors have attempted to classify the legislation of the various states in different ways, the analysis adopted by Forrest B. Ashby in his pamphlet entitled Economic Effects of Blue Sky Laws appears to be the least confusing." A Study of the Economic and Legal Aspects of the Proposed Federal Securities Act. Department of Commerce Report. Hearings before the Committee on Banking and Currency. United States Senate on S.875, 73rd Congress 1st Session (1933), p. 319.

The first class--regulatory laws--were those statutes which sought to prevent fraud before its occurrence by supervising either the sellers of securities or the securities themselves. This major group, which later encompassed the vast majority of state securities statutes, can be subdivided, depending upon the emphasis of the act, into two sub-classes: dealer-licensing acts and specific-approval acts. The statutes comprising the dealer-licensing sub-class were those statutes which sought to protect the investor by "primarily supervising dealers through licenses."[1] By 1933, this type of statute had been employed by Maryland, Connecticut, Maine and Pennsylvania. The remaining regulatory statutes can be included in the second sub-class labeled specific-approval acts. This category included those statutes which regulated "each individual issue of securities through specific approval by the state commission."[2] The specific-approval act has been enacted in its most complete form in the Middle West--the Kansas Act of 1911 having set the pattern.

In 1933, only two states, Delaware and New Jersey, had state securities statutes which were principally

---

[1] Ashby, op. cit., p. 7.

[2] Ibid.

of the antifraud type.[1] According to Ashby:

> These acts apply to the issuance and sale of securities the principles of the criminal law which apply to fraud in general. There is no attempt at supervision before issuances or sale of securities, but injunctions are sought (or orders issued) to check suspicious transactions, while criminal prosecutions are waged against the swindler.[2]

In those 47 states with securities statutes in 1933, the above clasees of securities statutes existed in a variety of permutations and combinations. For instance, a number of the blue sky laws included comprehensive fraud provisions comparable to those in New Jersey; nearly all states required in some fashion the registration of brokers and dealers; and practically every state required, subject to a variety of exceptions, the filing of some documents related to security registration.

At least 50 per cent of those states with registration provisions provided, either by statute or administrative decision, for a prospectus to be used. However, in practice, these states used the material so disclosed primarily to assist the securities

---

[1]The best known of the fraud acts was the 1923 Martin Act of New York State. Later, in 1932, this Act was supplemented by a simple form of broker-dealer registration and, hence by 1933, New York was placed in the dealer-licensing class.

[2]Ashby, op. cit., p. 8.

commission to approve or disapprove of the issue according to the statutory standards of the particular state. Without exception, the standards as to what constituted an acceptable investment kept an issue from being offered in security registration states regardless of the degree of disclosure that the prospectus made.[1]

In 1933, there was only one state act which was basically of the disclosure type: the Colorado statute. Under the Colorado Act, any security could be sold as long as the issuer had filed a prospectus and was willing to deliver a copy of the prospectus within forty-eight hours to any investor making a written request for it. In the case of subsequent litigation involving the securities, the purchaser of securities was deemed to have relied on the prospectus when purchasing the securities. In addition, the Colorado law provided for civil liabilities for false statement. This act had been based upon a federal securities bill unsuccessfully introduced into the United States Congress between 1921 and 1923 by Representative Taylor of Colorado. Taylor's original bill had been modeled upon the British Companies Acts.

Except for the few states that registered

---

[1] *Ibid.*, p. 38.

securities purely on fraud or disclosure standards, the philosophy underlying most of the state securities laws, particularly those which required the registration of securities, was one of regulation rather than one of disclosure. As Loss stated:

> ...the law does not assure merely that accurate and adequate information is made available to the public, through a specified prospectus or otherwise, and leave each investor to decide for himself whether a particular security is for him. The approach is a more paternalistic one: a state agency decides whether each security satisfies specified statutory standards--the standards are typically very broad and give the authorities a good deal of discretion--and, if not, the security is not considered sound enough to be offered in the state.[1]

---

[1]Loss, op. cit., p. 37. This method of regulation had been condemned and rejected in England by the Davey committee as early as 1894. In that year, as noted above, the Davey committee reported:

> Your committee may observe that they have dismissed from their consideration every suggestion for a public inquiry by the registrar or other official authority, into the soundness, good faith, and prospects of the undertaking at this or any other stage of the company's formation. To make any such investigation into the position of every new company complete or effectual would demand a very numerous staff of trained officers, and lead to great delay and expense, while an incomplete or perfunctory investigation would be worse than none. It would be an attempt to throw what ought to be the responsibility of the individual on the shoulders of the state, and would give a fictitious and unreal sense of security to the investor, and might also lead to grave abuses.

Report Of The Departmental Committee Appointed By The Board Of Trade To Inquire What Amendments Are Necessary In The Acts Relating To Joint Stock Companies Incorporated With Limited Liability Under The Companies Acts, 1862 to 1890. Op. cit., p. xiv.

Part III: The Business Sector

The principal agitation for the blue sky legislation came from local businessmen, commercial bankers and, in the agrarian states, the farmer. In general, the executives of large corporations which issued securities from time to time were opposed to the blue sky laws since such laws imposed an added cost to security offerings. In addition, the registration process involved much executive time in preparing the documents necessary to comply with the machinery of these laws.

While the officers of the nation-wide corporations were unfavorably disposed toward blue sky laws, they did not actively seek to remove this burden.[1] One group associated with big business--the Investment Bankers Association of America--did, however, take a strong stand on this question and actively sought to influence the type of state securities regulation passed.

---

[1]During the period 1900-1933 businessmen seldom made public statements or wrote articles for the various professional journals. The principal source of information pertaining to the attitudes of businessmen was the various congressional investigations. This source, however, was not always reliable, representative or accurate as businessmen were, in general, answering unfriendly questions posed by men who were unfamiliar with business practices and unfavorably disposed toward big business. Regrettably, businessmen sought to answer their critics under the most unfavorable of conditions.

The Businessman, Commercial Banker and Farmer

The local small businessman, banker and, in the agrarian states the farmer, were the principal advocates of blue sky legislation. Apparently, executives of the giant corporations, while they were opposed to such legislation, played a minor part in the blue sky movement.

There is much evidence suggesting that local businessmen and bankers supported the blue sky type of law. For instance, in 1912, Warren S. Hayden, of Hayden, Miller and Company, Cleveland, told the Investment Bankers Association of America:

> First, in my own state of Ohio I happen to know that one of the most influential chambers of commerce in the state has had a definite intention for several months to see to it that a blue sky bill is introduced at Columbus this winter. I also know that last summer at the convention of the Ohio Bankers' Association a resolution was adopted unanimously, looking toward giving the endorsement of the association to blue sky legislation of some sort...[1]

Also, it is not without significance that Mr. Dolley was a banker and his political associates businessmen.

Farmers, local businessmen and small town bankers were the most active promoters of blue sky legislation for a variety of reasons. The bankers lost loaning

---

[1]Warren S. Hayden, "Blue Sky Laws and Their Relations to the Investment Banker," Proceedings of the First Annual Convention of the Investment Bankers Association of America. November 21 and 22, 1912, p. 140.

capacity when their depositors withdrew money to invest in out-of-town investments; the local businessman often suffered a decline in trade and bad debt losses when his customers' savings were wiped out by the failure of unsound investments; and the farmer was the class of person most often preyed upon by "blue sky merchants." Direct regulation of security issues to eliminate the promotion of fraudulent and unsound investments appealed to these groups for this was the type of regulation the local farming and business interests had traditionally supported and understood. Earlier, it will be recalled, it was these groups who had fought the hardest for regulation of railroad rates and capitalization.

As noted above, the officers of large nationwide corporations were opposed to the various blue sky laws. Rather than fight these laws they preferred to avoid them by failing to seek qualification in those states where the qualification procedure was particularly burdensome. A 1925 report of the Industrial Securities Committee of the Investment Bankers Association of America on the topic of corporate management and "blue sky laws" said:

> One of the most serious problems which managements of industrial concerns have to face in putting out and making a market for their securities is the question of the

increasing burden of the Blue Sky Laws. The complexity of these laws is now so great that only experts can supply the experience which is necessary to meet the conditions of these laws...corporations of highest class which put out securities find that they are being put on the defensive, and that in some cases the judgment of Commissioners is being substituted for the judgment of their own experienced executives. This means that the companies in putting out securities must either try to adapt their security issues to the conditions imposed by numerous and not always consistent laws--and try to estimate the probable rulings and local opinions of each Commission--or must take their chances of a refusal to allow their securities to be sold.

.. in some cases issues of the best corporations have been denied entrance to some of the Blue Sky states, but it is almost universally true that such corporations are being caused large expense and much vexation in satisfying various state commissioners, not only of the details of their accounts, but of the soundness of their business judgment....Managements and bankers alike have both money and reputation at stake in offering securities to the investing public. This being the case, the officials of such corporations have a right to ask, as they do ask, why they should spend valuable time and incur substantial expense in getting out special reports for the authorities of various states. It is very difficult to answer the president of a corporation who wishes to know why, because some state is trying to catch fraudulent promoters, he should have to spend perhaps hundreds of dollars in order to satisfy investigators so that his own high-grade securities may be allowed to find their proper market. The answer at present is that if companies wish a national market for their securities, as many of them do, they must comply with the requirements which various states set up. In many cases, protesting strongly against the principle of the thing, they decide that it is not worth the

> expense of qualifying in order to be able to sell their securities in some particular state.[1]

The executives of large corporations--the ones most likely to seek capital through security issues--did not participate in the blue sky movement. This is not surprising. At first glance it would seem that businessmen would have been extremely interested in any legislation which had the tendency to limit the sale of corporate securities. However, it must be remembered that before 1917 few large industrial corporations had made more than one or two public offerings of securiiies. Therefore, most businessmen would come in contact with the blue sky laws only occasionally: investment bankers labored under such laws every day. Also, to date, the sale of these securities had been predominantly in the East where the blue sky movement had had few successes, thanks to the investment banking lobby which was fairly influential in most of the eastern states. In addition, since typically security issues were underwritten by investment bankers, selling of the securities issued was predominantly the bankers' problem, not the businessman's. The businessman got his capital irrespective

---

[1]Report of Industrial Securities Committee. Proceedings of the Fourteenth Annual Convention of the Investment Bankers Association of America. December 7, 8, 9, 10 and 11, 1925, pp. 265-266.

of whether the banker sold or did not sell his securities. Anyway, businessmen had more important political battles related to the attack on big business to fight on the federal level. It was the investment bankers who fought on the state level--not their corporate clients.

The Investment Banker

Prior to the enactment of the blue sky laws the investment banker in the conduct of his business was relatively free from state interference. The Kansas Act of 1911, and the subsequent blue sky laws ended this state of affairs. The investment bankers, while in sympathy with movements to eliminate the sale of fraudulent securities, considered the blue sky law's typical licensing provisions to be burdensome upon those who dealt in and issued "legitimate" securities. Accordingly, a number of investment bankers, backed by their newly formed association--the Investment Bankers Association of America,[1] flooded the courts with litigation contesting the licensing provisions of those state securities statutes on the basis of their con-

[1]Founded in 1912 and constituted purely of investment bankers. It was "organized primarily to improve the standard of those engaged in investment banking and the general protection of the investing public." Proceedings of the First Annual Convention of the Investment Bankers Association of America. November 21 and 22, 1912, p. 1.

stitutionality. In addition, the Investment Bankers Association, often in collaboration with other groups, tried to influence the type of securities legislation enacted.

The Investment Banker's Attitude

The Committee on Legislation of the Investment Bankers Association stated its official position thus:

> The committee is in sympathy with any fair and practical statute which will prevent the distribution of wild-cat securities and which will protect investors against fraud but it is opposed to the crude paternalistic measures adopted in many states. It was against the enactment of such laws, the enforcement of which would practically destroy the legitimate business of responsible investment bankers, that the association, where possible, protested....We cannot believe that a business as sound, legitimate and economically necessary as is ours, shall, or can be, ruthlessly destroyed by the ill-considered bills of unthinking legislators.[1]

Later, in 1916, a spokesman for the investment bankers spoke out more strongly against blue sky legislation:

> It should be added that, despite the fact that these laws have not been enforced according to their terms, they have in a substantial degree hindered and destroyed the normal business, particularly between the states. They have tended also to throw the business into

---

[1]Report of the Committee on Legislation. Proceedings of the Second Annual Convention of the Investment Bankers Association of America, October 28, 29, 30, 1919, p. 54.

> the hands of local houses, licensed in the particular state. If they are upheld and enforced, these effects will undoubtedly be far-reaching and disastrous, both upon the interstate business as such and upon the present wide distribution of securities which is vital to our industrial and financial welfare.[1]

The investment bankers adopted this attitude toward the blue sky movement primarily because such laws placed a number of limitations upon the investment bankers' accustomed way of conducting business. The various state laws interfered with the market for securities, which, at this time, was slowly growing from an intrastate market to an interstate one served by several large New York banking houses and their friends located in the 10 to 20 major cities of the nation. In those states with the Kansas-type blue sky law each issue a banker wished to sell had to be approved individually by each one of such states---a rather difficult and expensive undertaking for the investment banker (and the state department responsible for the administration of the statute). The expenses associated with obtaining the approval of state officials would, of course, be deducted from the bankers' profit---an unnecessary expense in the view of the established dealers in securities who considered

---

[1]Brief for Investment Bankers Association of America. Hall v. Geiger-Jones Co., op. cit., pp. 39-40.

their securities to be neither fraudulent nor speculative. Consequently, the blue sky laws, in the opinion of the Investment Bankers Association, placed an unfair and unnecessary burden upon their industry. In fact, as noted above, if strictly administered, the laws, in the opinion of some bankers, would inevitably destroy the business of dealing in securities.

The Investment Banker's Reaction

Among investment bankers it was considered that there were at least three ways they could react to the challenge of the blue sky movement: attack the existing statutes in the courts; work with other groups interested in drafting and promoting "workable and effective" blue sky laws; or ignore the existence of the movement. As to what the Investment Bankers Association might do to defend its members from the "oppressive" blue sky laws, a speaker at the Association's 1912 convention said:

> ...as to what this association may do: I received a letter the other day from a member of this association, in which a good deal of doubt was expressed as to the advisability of stirring this thing up at this time. He said, 'perhaps it is wise to let sleeping dogs lie.' I have already shown, I think, that the dogs are not sleeping, and we therefore cannot let them lie. If that is true, it certainly seems wise that we bestir ourselves in time to have something to do with the moulding of this legislation which is impending. We are much more likely to be effective by affirmative action than we are by negative action. It is always

> an awkward thing to be on the defensive, trying to tear down what someone has painfully built up, particularly if those building it up are working with good intentions, even though their information is rather scant. We ought, it seems to me, to formulate our own ideas so that we can offer an affirmative program to those who are seeking to accomplish what, really, is an entirely praiseworthy object....[1]

Subsequently, the Association decided to both challenge the constitutionality of selected existing blue sky laws in the courts and to work with other groups for the purpose of drafting a model blue sky law. Each of these programs will be discussed in turn below.

In 1912, the year the Investment Bankers Association of America was founded, Kansas was the only state with a blue sky law. However, by the end of 1913, as noted earlier, a total of 24 states had enacted state securities statutes--all of which affected in some way the interests of investment bankers and their clients. A number of these statutes--particularly the Kansas type--were considered by the Investment Bankers Association to be unconsitutional, since these acts not only placed an undue burden upon interstate commerce but also violated the due process and equal protection of law clauses of the Constitution.

---

[1]Hayden, op. cit., p. 147.

By 1914, several investment banking firms, with the encouragement of their Association, had entered into litigation contesting the 1913 Iowa, Ohio, West Virginia and Michigan Acts[1]--all of which were based upon the Kansas plan. In these suits the Association's general counsel cooperated with the local counsel in preparing the briefs or in the arguments before the courts or both. Subsequently, lower federal courts held the Iowa, West Virginia and Michigan statutes to be unconstitutional and hence invalid.[2] Later, in 1916, the Ohio act was also held unconstitutional on the authority of the earlier cases.

These four acts were voided since the court objected, among other things, to their paternalistic features. For the state to undertake to protect a man from making an investment, even though free from fraud, unless the administrator of the act thought it would result in a wise investment was, in the opinion of the

---

[1]Wm. R. Compton Co. v. Allen, 216 Fed. 537 (S. D. Iowa 1914); Geiger-Jones Co. v. Turner, 230 Fed. 233 (S.D. Ohio 1916); Bracey v. Darst, 218 Fed. 482 (N. D. W. Va. 1914); Alabama & New Orleans Transportation Co. v. Doyle, 210 Fed. 173 (E.D. Mich. 1914); N. W. Halsey & Co. v. Merrick, 228 Fed. 805 (E.D. Mich. 1915).

[2]In other decisions the blue sky laws of Arkansas, Florida, and North Carolina were upheld. In addition, the courts refused to consider the constitutional question in cases related to the Montana and Oregon Acts. The Investment Bankers Association of America did not participate in these suits.

court, beyond the police powers of the state. In the decision involving the Michigan Act the court, after first noting the act's stated purpose was "to stop the sale of stock in fly-by-night concerns, visionary oil wells, distant gold mines and other like fraudulent exploitations," went on to state "if just this intent had been covered into effect by the act as passed, these cases would not be here." Clearly, the intent of the statutes went far beyond preventing simple fraud.

In 1915, following the invalidation of its 1913 act, Michigan passed a revised statute designed to overcome the court's objections to its original act. This act, plus the Arkansas and South Dakota statutes also enacted in 1915, was based upon a bill drafted by a 1914 committee appointed by the National Association of Attorneys General.[1] The committee's bill, it was hoped, would be in harmony with the nation's fundamental law and the recent decisions of the lower federal courts. The new act aimed to eliminate all paternalistic or guardianship features and require only the minimum of inspection and supervision of securities and security dealers as was necessary, in the committee's opinion, to prevent fraud. The

---

[1]The committee consisted of the Attorneys General of Michigan, Arkansas and Iowa.

Investment Bankers Association had offered to cooperate in drafting this proposed legislation but the Attorneys General committee had declined to accept their offer.

Subsequently, in 1915, the new Michigan[1] and South Dakota[2] acts were challenged and held invalid in two lower federal court decisions. The court, in considering the Michigan Act, could find no substantial changes from the original act:

> ...some minor details have been corrected, but the new law, like the old, impresses upon interstate commerce a burden which is direct and which is beyond the limits of the police power.[3]

The two cases involving 1915 South Dakota and Michigan statutes, plus the case involving the voided 1913 Ohio Act, were then appealed to the Supreme Court where they were argued and decided together.[4]

At the time the so-called blue sky cases were argued before the Supreme Court twenty-seven states

---

[1]N. W. Halsey & Co. v. Merrick, 228 Fed. 805.

[2]Sioux Falls Stock Yards v. Caldwell D.S.D., Nov. 18, 1915 (decree set out in Geiger-Jones Company v. Turner, 230 Fed. 233 at 236).

[3]N. W. Halsey & Co. v. Merrick, 228 Fed. 805 at 806.

[4]Caldwell v. Sioux Falls Stock Yards Co., 242 U.S. 559 (1917); Merrick v. N. W. Halsey & Co., 242 U.S. 568 (1917); Hall v. Geiger-Jones Co., 242 U.S. 539 (1917).

had enacted general securities statutes and all of these laws---except for the 1910 Rhode Island Act---contained some form of licensing provision. In addition, a number of other states had similar legislation under consideration and were obviously awaiting the decision of the court before enacting such legislation. If the blue sky movement was to be halted, its opponents would have to win a decisive victory in the Supreme Court at this time.

On January 22, 1917, the Supreme Court ruled that it was within the police power of the states to enact laws embodying comprehensive licensing systems to regulate securities if the state legislature believed by doing so it would protect its citizens against fraud and "the imposition of unsubstantial schemes and the securities based upon them."[1]

The 1917 Supreme Court decision removed any possible constitutional barrier to blue sky legislation.[2] The way was now open for those states contemplating securities statutes embodying comprehensive licensing provisions to enact such laws. Consequently, between 1917 and 1921, eleven additional states enacted blue sky laws--making a total of 38 states with statutes

---

[1]Hall v. Geiger-Jones Company, 242 U.S. 539.

[2]Loss and Cowett, op. cit., p. 13.

regulating the sale of securities. Henceforth, the Investment Bankers Association preferred to accomplish its goals with respect to modifying blue sky laws through cooperation with legislative committees and other interest bodies--the challenging of entire statutes in the courts by the Association had ended.

From its very beginning the Investment Bankers Association actively urged the various state legislatives to adopt blue sky laws which would control fraud and misrepresentation in the offering of securities without interference with legitimate business interests. To this end the Association drafted a model bill. By 1920, two states, Maine and New Hampshire, had adopted measures embodying the suggestions put forward by the Association. In addition, in 1915, the Association cooperated with the National Association of Supervisors of State Banks in drafting another model bill. Portions of this bill were adopted by several states, including Virginia, West Virginia and Minnesota. Subsequently, the Association worked with other groups, including the Conference of Commissioners on Uniform State Laws and the American Bar Association, on matters related to blue sky laws.

The suggestion that the Investment Bankers Association enact a model bill was made at the First Annual

Convention of the Investment Bankers Association by the previously mentioned Warren S. Hayden. Hayden urged the Association through its legislative committee, to study the subject of blue sky legislation and draft a "typical blue sky statute." The legislative committee, he proposed, would distribute papers on its finding to the membership of the Association. Then, when the state legislature was considering the enactment of blue sky legislation, the Association's members who were residents of the state concerned could put forward the Association's model law as a basis for the proposed legislation. The convention unanimously adopted a resolution based on Hayden's proposal.

Hayden, during his address before the convention, also spoke on a bill he and some of his associates in Ohio had drafted for submission to the Ohio legislature which, in 1912-1913, was considering the enactment of a blue sky law. Some of the features of his proposed Ohio statute, he thought, might well be considered by the Association for incorporation in its model statute. Subsequently, a measure, embodying many of Hayden's suggestions, was formulated.

Hayden's suggested provisions for incorporation in the Association's model bill fell under three headings: licenses, publicity and penalties. First

[1]Hayden, op. cit., p. 140.

the model bill would require that everyone who offered securities in a state obtain a license from the banking authorities of the state concerned. The license would be granted on the basis of the applicant's character and standing and revoked if its holder should engage in improper practices. Second, as to publicity, the state would furnish the investor the means of obtaining adequate data concerning any offering. So that the filing requirement would not be burdensome upon investment bankers dealing in "legitimate" securities, however, a number of transactions were to be exempted. These exemptions included those securities involved in normal brokerage transactions. In addition, those transactions between dealers, banks and corporations were also to be exempted. Hayden estimated that 90 per cent of the business of members of the association would be exempt from this publicity requirement. Finally, the proposed statute was to provide penalties for fraud and improper conduct. Later, in 1913, a state securities statute based on Hayden's dealer licensing suggestions was passed by Maine and, in 1917, New Hampshire passed a similar statute. The Maine statute was the first dealer licensing statute enacted in the United States.

The first outside group the Investment Bankers Association worked with for the purpose of preparing a model blue sky law was the National Association of Supervisors of State Banks. During 1914, Mr. Robert R. Reed, the general counsel of the Investment Bankers Association, spoke on the subject of blue sky legislation before the Atlantic City Convention of the National Association of Supervisors of State Banks, and, as a result of Mr. Reed's talk, as well as their general dissatisfaction with operation of the blue sky laws, the State Bank Supervisors appointed a committee to investigate the matter of blue sky legislation. The Committee on Blue Sky Legislation, as it was to be called, was fully authorized to cooperate with Mr. Reed and the Investment Bankers Association for the purpose of securing "uniform laws which will be practical in effect."

In 1915 the committee on blue sky legislation completed its task and presented a "proposed blue sky act" which was endorsed by both the Investment Bankers Association and the National Association of Supervisors of State Banks. The important features of the proposed statute were:

1. A fraud provision adopted from the existing federal postal law making fraud or intended fraud involving securities punishable by a fine of not more than $5,000, or imprisonment for not more than five years, or both such punishments at the discretion of the court.

2. A notification provision requiring that the appropriate state official be notified of all offerings of securities made within the state prior to the making of such promotions. Furthermore, any and all prospectus and circulars used in such promotion were to be filed. The state official could investigate and require such proof or information that he deemed necessary to determine the character of the securities or promotion. However, it was not necessary to gain the states approval of the securities before they could be offered. Any person filing materially false information, or failing to comply with the notification provision was liable to a fine of not more than $1,000 or imprisonment for not more than one year or both such punishments.

3. An exemption provision exempting from the notification provision all offerings or sale of any securities on any recognized exchange in the state and all securities advertised in magazines or newspapers published outside of the state.

4. A dealer registration provision requiring dealers in securities to register with the appropriate state official annually.

The two most important provisions, in the opinion of the committee were the fraud[1] and notification[2]

---

[1]"Such a provision should, in our opinion, be the basis of any legislation on this subject. Without it, a blue sky law may serve to ward off obvious frauds; it cannot be a deterrent, and is in fact an aid to insure skillful frauds which are not detected in the first instance:--Statement of the blue sky committee. Report of General Counsel. Investment Bankers Association of America. Fourth Annual Convention, September 20-22, 1915."

[2]"This publicity feature has, we believe, been the cause of the great success of the Kansas type of law, and for it credit is due to the originators of that law. It compels every promoter to make his presence and purpose known. This requirement standing alone is practically protective of two-thirds of the frauds." Ibid.

provisions.[1]

In addition to working with other groups interested in blue sky legislation, the members of the Investment Bankers Association also sought to influence directly those legislative bodies considering securities statutes. However, because of the frequent unsatisfactory nature of committee hearings, its early appearances before legislative committees were seldom successful. The 1913 Report of the Investment Bankers Association's commiteee on legislation had this to say:

> Our experience in connection with the blue sky bills in the various state legislatures emphasizes the fact that much of our unsound legislation is due not so much to the unreasoning demand of the popular electorate as to the system under which our laws are made. In practically none of our legislative bodies are bills given a judicial consideration. Proposed laws are presented in a most haphazard manner. We found that the blue sky bills were often introduced by legislators who had not the faintest conception of the nature and character of the business which the bills proposed to regulate. In some cases hearings were held by committees and when these committees impartially considered our arguments the bill usually reached a final form in which many of its objectional features had been eliminated.

---

[1]Subsequently, the fraud provision of the blue sky committees proposed law was incorporated in the 1915 West Virginia and 1917 Minnesota Securities Acts. The 1916 Virginia Securities Act consisted of both the fraud and investigation sections--the notification provision was omitted. In 1918, the Virginia legislative supplemented the earlier fraud act with a 1915 Kansas type act.

> Committee hearings, however, are often unsatisfactory. Frequently, the time allotted is insufficient to go thoroughly into the matter under consideration. Many of the committee members are called out of the conference and few of them hear the entire argument. It is also often true that if the bill is made a party measure the hearings is largely a matter of form and the bill is passed without giving any particular regard to the protests against it.
>
> Few legislatures have a Bill Drafting Bureau or drafting department thus we find many of the blue sky laws, particularly those which were passed without a hearing, are crude and ambiguous in the extreme. Certain paragraphs are inconsistent with others and some of the statutes as a whole are entirely unworkable.[1]

Later, beginning about 1920, the committee on legislation was able to report that its efforts to influence the passage of legislation on the state level, based on the Association's concept of adequate blue sky legislation, had met with encouraging success:

> It is felt that real progress has been made in this matter both in the way of new legislation on the subject and in the bringing about of cooperation with the various state officials in the practical applications of laws in effect.[2]

In 1920, the Association's committee on legislation could report to the annual convention that securities legislation of the type desired by the Association--elimination of the paternalistic concept--had

---

[1]Report of Committee on Legislation. Proceedings of the Second Annual Convention of the Investment Bankers Association of America, October 28, 29 and 30, 1913, p. 54.

[2]Report of Committee on Legislation. Proceedings of the Nineth Annual Convention of the Investment Bankers Association of America, October 4, 5, 6, 1920, p. 63.

been enacted in Maryland, New Jersey, New York, Louisiana, Kentucky and Indiana.

During the 1920's, the Investment Bankers Association took the initiative in a drive for uniformity of state securities statutes. In 1921, the President of the Investment Bankers Association stated the position of the Investment Bankers Association with respect to blue sky legislation:

> 1. As to the 38 states having blue sky laws it is not the intention of the association to attempt to remove those laws, but simply to amend them from time to time so as to make them more workable, and to accomplish the elimination of fraudulent securities.
>
> 2. As to the three states having fraud laws, we intend to oppose the introduction of typical blue sky legislation and to try and maintain and improve the fraud laws.
>
> 3. As to the remaining states having at the present time no blue sky laws or fraud laws we intend to use our best efforts to oppose the introduction of blue sky laws and to favor the introduction of fraud laws.[1]
>
> 4. As to the national situation we are as much opposed as the blue sky commissioners to a federal blue sky law which would supersede the state laws.[2]

The following year, 1922, the Association prepared a tentative outline of a uniform state securities law.

---

[1]Earlier, it will be recalled, the Investment Bankers Association favored dealer registration type statutes.

[2]Proceedings of the Tenth Annual Convention of the Investment Bankers Association of America, October 31, November 1 and 2, 1921, p. 283.

However, before the Association could take positive action in this matter, the Conference of Commissioners on uniform Laws took up the subject of a uniform state securities statute. Subsequently, in 1925, the Commission, after accepting the cooperation of the Investment Bankers Association and the American Bar Association, put forward a draft bill entitled the Uniform Sale of Securities Act. In 1929, this draft bill was approved by the American Bar Association. Later, the 1933 Federal Securities Act rendered this pre-1933 Uniform act obsolete since:

> The Securities Act of 1933 was on an entirely different theory to that of the several state laws. For the first time the principle of "full disclosure" became the basic theory of securities registration. This law made necessary a form for registering securities under it of an entirely different type to that of the state laws and was far more comprehensive and exacting in the information required. The registration statement required contained all and even more information than that required by the provisions of any state law.[1]

The 1933 federal securities act, however, did not supersede the various state security acts. In fact, it specifically preserved them.

Limitations of Blue Sky Laws

Today, it is generally acknowledged that the blue sky laws failed to provide adequate protection for

---

[1]Report of State Legislation Committee. Proceedings of the Thirty-Second Annual Convention of the Investment Bankers Association of America. November 2-5, 1943, p. 196.

the investor. The principal reason for their failure, according to Loss, was the inherent inadequacy of state legislation in an interstate economy.[1] Two other reasons mentioned by Loss were perfunctory administration of the statutes and legal "loop holes" in the statutes arising from the numerous exemption provisions.[2] In addition, the 1933 Department of Commerce report referred to earlier cited several other reasons; lack of uniformity of state statutes; willingness of victims to "compound" the offense or accept a compromise; and the absence of protective securities legislation in Nevada and in the territories.[3]

The most effective and widely used method of evading the blue sky laws consisted in operating across state lines.[4] Both honest and fraudulent promoters adopted this practice so as to avoid the registration

---

[1]Loss, op. cit., pp. 56-58.

[2]For instance, the 1916 Michigan Act exempted securities "which are listed in any standard manual of information approved by the commission." Subsequently, the Michigan Commission approved Moody's and Standard and Poors, despite an admitted policy on the part of these manuals to list any company in which the publishers considered there was a public interest regardless of the quality of the securities listed.

[3]Department of Commerce, op. cit., p. 323.

[4]Ibid.

burdens of the blue sky laws.[1] This subterfuge was based on the clauses of the Constitution of the United States which read "A person charged in any state with Treason, Felony, or other Crime, who shall flee from Justice, and be found in another state shall on demand of the executive authority of the state from which he fled, be delivered up, to be removed to the state having jurisdiction of the Crime."[2] As the court interpreted this clause, at least before the recent Uniform Extradition Act, a person could not be extradited unless he had "fled" from the state where he had, in the case of a violation of the blue sky law, sold fraudulent securities. Therefore, a salesman operating in New York and selling fraudulent securities over the phone

---

[1]Reed, Dougherty & Hoyt, the counsel for the Investment Bankers Association, offered the following advice to the members of the association:

A dealer naturally desires to regulate his business by the law of his own state. With this purpose and not any idea of evading blue sky laws as such, a formula in somewhat the following language may be used to advantage in any advertisement or circular offering securities:

"No sale is contemplated or effective upon an offer made by us except upon receipt of acceptance at our office. A sale upon an offer made to us is effective upon our acceptance by mail or telegram sent from our office. We neither offer nor sell securities in any state where such offering or sale by us is prohibited by law."

Reed, Dougherty & Hoyt, Blue Sky Laws prepared for the Investment Bankers Association of America, November 1, 1920, p. xxii.

[2]The Constitution of the United States of America, Article IV, Section 2.

to persons in, say, Kansas was safe from prosecution under the Kansas law as the salesman had not been in Kansas and, hence, could not have fled from Kansas justice. The blue sky statutes merely shifted the practice of fraud from an intra to an interstate operation.

*****

Between 1911 and 1933, forty-seven states enacted blue sky laws. These laws regulated, for the first time in the United States, securities issued by non-public service corporations. In general, the philosophy underlying these blue sky laws was one of regulation, not disclosure.

Those states which passed blue sky laws sought to achieve one goal: the protection of local citizens from fraudulent or unsound securities. Many persons, approving of the state's goal but despairing of the state's ability to achieve this goal, believed a federal blue sky law was both necessary and desirable. There was little agreement, however, as to whether such a federal law should be based on the English or Kansas solution. Chapters five and eight will discuss the so-called battle of the philosophies--regulation versus disclosure--on the federal level between 1918 and 1933.

CHAPTER FIVE

MAJOR FEDERAL SECURITIES LEGISLATION PROPOSALS, 1918-1929

Between 1918 and 1929, a number of securities bills were placed before Congress and several groups and individuals proposed improved financial and corporate disclosure standards. None of these bills were enacted and few corporations adopted the disclosure recommendations. Business and finance were in control of the government and the public was not in a reforming mood--they sought only "normalcy." This period, which has been called "the indian summer of the old order,"[1] began with the Armistice of 1918 and closed with the stock market crash of 1929.

The genesis of the federal 1933 Securities Act, as noted earlier, can be found in such previously mentioned topics as the British Companies Acts and the reports of the Industrial Commission. Discussed below are further important political incidents in the long series of events which culminated in the 1933 Securities Act: the 1918 Report of the Capital Issues Committee; the 1918 Taylor Bill; the 1919 Volstead

---

[1]Frederick Lewis Allen, The Big Change: America Transforms Itself 1900-1950 (New York: Harper and Brothers Publishers, 1952), p. 131.

DOI: 10.4324/9781003169420-5

Bill; and the 1921 Denison Bill.

Two other subjects, both of which greatly influenced the securities bills mentioned above, are also discussed in this chapter: the nature of the political and social environment between 1918 and 1929; and the rise of a new investor class. The discussion and formulation of financial disclosure standards by groups and individuals external to the firm during this period will be discussed in chapter six.

Briefly, the years 1918 through 1929, at least up to the stock market crash of October 1929, were highlighted by general economic growth, widespread business prosperity, and a swing in the political pendulum to the right. A war weary nation was in reaction against the preceding progressive era. The incidence of share ownership by the public increased; the gap between the control and ownership of a number of the nation's larger corporations widened; and the businessman experienced a new public veneration.

During World War I, Congress established the Capital Issues Committee[1] to oversee the allocation

---

[1]The Capital Issues Committee was officially created in 1918 under Title Two of the War Finance Corporation Act. The Committee's task was to conserve capital for war purposes by encouraging citizens, through appeals to their patriotism, to avoid investing in the new securities of industries not considered essential to the war effort. The Committee could not prohibit the issuance of any securities. It could only state whether a security issue was, or was not, in the Committee's opinion, compatible with the national interest. Hopefully, patriotic citizens would refrain from purchasing securities of issues deemed not to be in the national interest.

of capital into those enterprises which were most essential to the furtherance of the nations's war effort. In 1918, just prior to when it was dissolved, the Capital Issues Committee filed a report[1] with Congress which suggested, in order to end the prevailing widespread trade in fraudulent securities, some form of federal supervision over corporate security issues should be enacted. During the next few years several bills designed to remedy the sale of fraudulent securities were introduced in Congress. For instance, in 1918, Congressman Edward T. Taylor of Colorado submitted a proposed securities bill based on the disclosure philosophy of the English statutes; in 1919, Congressman Andrew J. Volstead of Minnesota introduced an antifraud type bill; and, between 1921 and 1925, Congressman Edward E. Denison of Illinois presented on several occasions a bill designed to strengthen the various state blue sky laws. As noted above, none of these bills were ever enacted into law.

At the same time, in the area of financial disclosure--the topic discussed in the next chapter--the Federal Reserve Board, the New York Stock Exchange and several associations of commercial and professional

---

[1]Report of Capital Issues Committee, H. R. Doc. No. 1485, 65th Congress, 3rd Session (1918).

men attempted to influence the financial disclosure standards of management. And a few social reformers, still fighting the progressive's battle, demanded a greater publicity of corporate affairs. In response to these activities and proposals corporate executives, in general, said or did little: corporate executives, investors and the public were apparently unconcerned with both the attempts to formulate financial and corporate disclosure standards and the spasmodic attacks on big business.

Chapter 5 is divided into two major portions: Part I briefly describes the environment during the 12-year period now under review; and Part II lists several of the securities bills placed before Congress between 1918 and 1929.

Part I: The Environment 1918-1929

Following World War I there was a reversal of the American political, social, economic and ethical climate. The nation was weary and disillusioned with the crusades of the progressive era--new things and new ideas gripped the public's imagination. A number of these changes, including the emergence of a new investor class, are briefly discussed below.

During the years 1918-1929 there occurred the second great period of rapid business consolidation and merger within the history of the United States. Big business got bigger. Yet no sustained, widespread, and savage outcry against big business arose. There were several reasons for this state of affairs: the political triumph of the businessman; economic prosperity;[1] the advent of the public-relations specialist; and the decline in the popular appeal of the critics of big business.

Beginning in the congressional elections of 1918 and continued in the presidential elections of 1920 the political pendulum swung to the right. During the Administrations of Warren G. Harding and Calvin Coolidge business and finance were again dominant. None of the measures to control business put on the statute books by Wilson were repealed but in their administration they were tempered.[2] Now, the federal agencies created to regulate business were in the hands of people sympathetic to business.

The nation was prosperous and business profitable. Both were expanding. Improving productivity and marketing were the twin concerns of management: not the attack on big business. Consumers were

---

[1]Only three of the 12 years covered by this chapter were "recession years": 1919-1921.

[2]V. O. Key Jr., Politics, Parties and Pressure Groups (New York: Thomas Y. Crowell Company, 1952), pp. 196-197.

interested in consumption, not agitation. And investors and speculators both looked for capital gains, not protection. However, within this period, which in many respects resembled the South Sea Bubble era, the seeds of disaster--economic and social--were being sown in the form of speculation, unsound business consolidation and the breakdown of the fiduciary tradition.

> What was destined to halt the forward progress of business was the fact that the businessmen of America had become bemused with paper values - with the piling up of speculative or artificially generated wealth which had little relation to the production of goods. At a time when the greatest economic need of the nation was for devices which would distribute as widely and fairly as possible the fruits of industrial progress, without destroying the incentives (to capital, to management, and also to workers) which sparked that progress, there developed a speculative mania which benefited immediately only those who could lay their hands on capital; and in addition, there were invented or improved a series of devices for distributing the fruits of prosperity - or what looked like them - into the pockets of the few.
>
> These devices included company mergers at inflated prices which gave insiders a chance to line their own pockets; the piling of holding companies one upon another until - as in the Insull and Van Sweringen empires - they were sometimes five or six or seven deep, with the result that the heaviest cream of the profits of the concerns at the base of such a pyramid could be drawn off by the owners of the concern at the top; the formation by banks of "security affiliates" which in effect used the depositors' funds to make investments, in securities and in real estate, such as were denied to the banks themselves by

> the law; the frequent practice of inflating corporate profits by selling properties back and forth among a group of companies at rising prices; and the formation of stock-market pools in which the officers of a company would join with brokers and well-heeled speculators to push up the price of the company's stock - and then unload the stock on a new lot of buyers, thus making money at the expense of those officers' own stockholders.
>
> These were only a few of the widely employed devices of that day. Not only did they represent, collectively, an appalling breakdown of the fiduciary tradition; but - this is the primary fact to bear in mind - they tended, collectively, to knit speculative or even phony values into the economic fabric of the country at so many points that if value fell, bank after bank and company after company - and their depositors and employees - would be hard hit. The irresponsible actions of men who did not stop to think that they were constructing a caricature of the capitalist system were paving the way for disaster....[1]

Business and businessmen were regarded with a new veneration and, in general, the public either knew nothing of or were unconcerned with the abuses described above: the public apparently neither understood nor cared about these events. A number of those Americans who a few years earlier would have been ardent progressives were now too busy enjoying prosperity with its attendant material and psychic benefits--cars, radios, sports heroes, and Lindberg. "Normalcy" was the mood of the nation.

---

[1]Allen, op. cit., pp. 140-141.

The public was receptive to the wooing of the newly launched corporate advertising and public relations programs. Business, the public was informed, was "The American Way," business leaders recognized they had a public trust and the fruits of prosperity would soon be shared by all. The crusaders of the prewar years, however, were not dead--just outnumbered. Below the surface the beliefs of the progressives lingered on among their modern counterparts--to be revived again after the "fat years" so dramatically ended in the chaos and disaster of 1930.

The "New" Investor Class

Between 1900 and 1929 the character of the market for securities changed in a number of ways--the most important aspects of these changes nearly all occurred sometime between 1910 and 1920. These changes, the most important of which was the growth of a large class of small investors, added a new dimension to the publicity controversy and were to have important consequences for those involved with investor-management-government relations.

Between 1900 and 1920, the principal classes of securities offered and the character of the purchasers of such securities changed. In 1900, for example, the major outlets for new securities, which up to that time had been mostly bond and preferred stock issues of railroad companies, were savings banks and other institutional investors, trust funds and the more wealthy segments of the nation's eastern population. However, within 20 years the majority of new security issues were either utilities or industrials;[1] the importance as a purchaser of securities of the nation's middle class, including many of those from the immigrant group, had increased; and the influence of institutional investors, who in many cases were limited by law to the holding of high grade bonds, was considerably less important as a direct purchaser of securities than 20 years earlier.

In addition, between 1900 and 1929, the total number of persons owning securities increased and the ownership of the larger corporations became more dispersed. Also during this period there was a general tendency for that percentage of the total number of industrial securities outstanding which were held primarily for investment purposes to increase. Con-

---

[1]In 1900 a breakdown of the total stock issues listed on the New York Stock Exchange into their principal classes showed Banks and Trust companies 19%; Railroads 49%; Industrials 13%; and, Miscellaneous 19%. By 1920, the distribution between these four classes was: Banks and Trust companies 6%; Railroads 25%; Industrials 44%; and Miscellaneous 25%--James Edward Meeker, The Work of the Stock Exchange (New York: The Ronald Press Company, 1922), p. 524.

versely, the percentage held principally for speculation steadily decreased. This shift of investor motive from speculative to investment was particularly true with respect to the securities of the larger industrial corporations which, before 1910, had been regarded as being so highly speculative by the New York Stock Exchange that the conduct of "blind pools" in such securities had been tolerated. These two factors--more widespread ownership of securities and relatively more ownership for investment rather than for speculation--contributed to yet another important trend: the divorcing of corporate ownership from effective control over corporate management.

During World War I and the immediate post armistice period these trends of the preceding 17 years gained added momentum: the number of people owning securities rapidly increased; the shift in security ownership from speculators to investors accelerated; and the character of the investing public, including its relationship to management, changed significantly.

From 1900 to 1930, the number of people in the United States who held stocks increased from about 500,000 to approximately 10,000,000.[1] Another

---

[1]Federal Reserve Board of Boston, "A History of Investment Banking in New England," Annual Report for 1960, pp. 32 and 38.

estimate placed the number of investors in 1928 at between 4 and 7 million.[1] While no reliable statistics do exist which show the change in the exact number of individual holders of securities, Gardiner C. Means has drawn up a fairly reliable estimate of the number of book stockholders in the United States in both 1900 and 1928. This study showed the number of book stockholders increased from 4,400,000 to 18,000,000 during this period.

The following two tables related to the changes in the total number of book stockholders between 1900-1928 were adapted from similar tabulations prepared by Means:

Diffusion of Stock Ownership[2]

Table I

Index of Number of Book Stockholders 1900-1928

Year	Est. No. of stockholders in the United States	Annual rate of increase during preceding interval (% compounded annually)	Average No. of $100 par value shares per stockholder
1900	4,400,000		140.1
1910	7,400,000	$5\frac{1}{4}$	86.3
1913	7,500,000	$\frac{1}{4}$	87.0
1917	8,600,000	$3\frac{1}{2}$	77.3
1920	12,000,000	12	57.3
1923	14,400,000	$6\frac{1}{4}$	49.7
1928	18,000,000	$4\frac{1}{2}$	51.0

[1]Adolf A. Berle Jr., and Gardiner C. Means, The Modern Corporation and Private Property (New York: The Macmillan Company, 1933).

[2]Gardiner C. Means, "The Diffusion of Stock Ownership in the United States," The Quarterly Journal of Economics, Vol. XLIV, No. 4, August 1930, p. 595.

TABLE II

Rate of Annual Increase in Number of Book Stockholders of Selected Corporations

	1900-1917 Per Cent	1917-1923 Per Cent	1923-1928 Per Cent	Entire Period 1900-1928 Per Cent
10 Railroads	5	7	0	4½
17 Industrials	5½	10	2¼	6
4 Public Utilities	11	20	9	12½
31 Companies	6	11¼	3 3/4	6 3/4

Clearly, Means said, the above figures inducated a tendency for individual corporations to be owned by an ever-increasing number of investors.

In addition to the dispersion of ownership and the increase in the number of stockholders, the total number of securities owned by people of moderate means--the professional man, middle management, small business owner--increased rapidly between 1916 and 1921. For instance, from 1916 to 1921 the share of corporate stocks owned by the rich and very rich, i.e., individuals with incomes of at least $35,000, declined from 58 to 36 per cent between 1917 and 1921 and remained constant thereafter, while the shares owned by individuals with small to moderate incomes, i.e., under $12,000 increased from 21 to 44 per cent."[1] In 1929, the distribution

[1]Means, op. cit., p. 62.

of dividends, which Berle and Means regarded as an indication of the distribution of security owners, among the various income groups was as follows:

Distribution of Dividends Among Various Income Groups in 1929[1]

Size of Taxable Income	No. of Individual Stockholders included in Income Group	Per cent of all Dividends Received by Group	Per cent Cumulated from Above
Over $1,000,000	513	5.74%	5.74%
$100,000 to $1,000,000	14,303	19.02%	24.76%
25,000 to $ 100,000	87,762	23.97%	48.73%
5,000 to $ 25,000	494,425	24.88%	73.61%
Under 5,000	3,5-6,500,000	26.28%	100.00%

Means concluded his 1930 study by saying:

> ...This study indicates that a great distribution of stock ownership took place during the war and immediate postwar periods, increasing both the number of stockholders and the proportion of corporate industry owned by persons of moderate means...This widespread ownership was a legacy of the war period...and that thereafter, while the number of stockholders continued to increase, this involved no appreciable shift in the proportion of corporate industry owned by the different income groups.[2]

The principal causes of this trend toward a larger investor class were several: the increasing number of securities available for trading on the organized exchanges; the widespread distribution of Liberty Bonds

[1]Berle and Means, op. cit., p. 60.

[2]Means, op. cit., p. 591.

during World War I; and the increase in the number of utility customer and corporate employee stock ownership plans. Underlying and contributing to these factors was a rising level of economic prosperity. For instance, from 1900 to 1930, the gross national income of the United States rose from about $15 billion to approximately $87 billion.[1] Also accompanying this rising level of national prosperity was a trend towards a higher per capita income--both real and statistical. For example, between 1900 and 1930, the per capita income, expressed in 1929 prices, rose from about $501 to $717.[2]

The increasing number of securities--particularly industrial and utility securities--potentially available for trading on the nation's 20-odd organized stock exchanges resulted from the wholesale conversion of private companies to public companies during the early 1900's; the creation of securities through new promotions sponsored by investment banking firms; and the need of industry to acquire outside capital for expansion purposes. A number of the securities so created were eventually listed on an exchange as,

---

[1] W. S. Woytinsky and E. S. Woytinsky, <u>World Population and Production</u> (New York: The Twentieth Century Fund, 1953), p. 383.

[2] <u>Ibid</u>., p. 408.

supposedly, such action improved the securities' marketability. Although not all securities were listed, the listed securities represented nearly all of the important issuers and were the securities most often traded in by the new class of small investors. The following table which shows the number of shares and issues listed on the New York Stock Exchange indicates, in part, the trend toward a great number of listed securities:

Number of Bond and Stock Issues and Shares Listed -- New York Stock Exchange, 1900-1930[1]

	January 1, 1900	January 1, 1917	January 1, 1930
Total Bond Issues Listed	830	1,175	1,543
Total Stock Issues Listed	377	613	1,293
Total Issues Listed	1,207	1,788	2,836
Number of Shares Listed	56 million	167 million	1,128 million

Thus, the total number of issues listed on the New York Stock Exchange rose by about 48% from 1900 to 1917 and approximately 59% between 1917 and 1930. An even more dramatic, and perhaps more relevant, comparison

[1]Adapted from a similar table presented by James Edward Meeker, op. cit., pp. 593-594.

was the contrast between the percentage change in the total number of shares listed during the same two periods. Between 1900 and 1917, and 1917 and 1930, these increases were nearly 200% and 600%, respectively!

During World War I, in order to finance the war effort, the United States Government sold Liberty Bonds to a number of people drawn from all of the major social, economic and geographical subdivisions of the nation. The impact of this widespread sale of Liberty Bonds upon the American public was that for the first time a number of people of moderate means were introduced to the practice of investing in securities. During the short period 1917-1918 the United States Government floated four "Liberty Loan" issues. In June 1917, four million persons subscribed to the First Liberty Loan. Later, in November 1917, 9,400,000 persons purchased Liberty Bonds in the Second Liberty Loan. These two issues were followed in 1918 by two larger issues, the Third and Fourth Liberty Loans, to which there were over eighteen and twenty one million subscribers, respectively. Subsequently, a number of these holders of Liberty Bonds purchased industrial and utility securities through the same legitimate investment banking house which had originally sold to them their Liberty

Bonds.[1] Investment bankers having been one of the principal sales outlets for the government's Liberty Bonds.[2]

Between 1919 and 1923 there was a rapid increase in both the number of utility companies which adopted customer ownership plans and the number of corporations which introduced employee stock purchase plans. Both these phenomena increased the newly created propensity of people of moderate means to acquire securities. For instance, between 1914 and 1918, inclusive, 29 public utility companies introduced customer ownership plans whereas during the next five years 156 such plans were adopted:

---

[1]In order to sell securities to a number of these persons investment bankers showed during the post-armistic period an increasing tendency to reduce the denominations of new bond issues from the traditional $1,000 to $500, and, in some cases, to as low as $100.--<u>Ibid</u>., p. 473.

[2]Unfortunately, a number of these holders of government bonds were also induced by unscrupulous security salesmen to exchange the low interest "governments" for fraudulent or unsound "industrials" carrying the promise of higher yields. It was this work of these swindlers which prompted the Capital Issues Committee to recommend to Congress the passage of a federal securities act.

Stock Sales Made by Public Utilities
to Customers[1]*
1914-1929

Year	Number of additional companies adopting customer ownership plan[1]	Sales made	Shares of Stock sold	Value of sales
1914	7	4,044	92,310	
1915	3	4,357	57,130	
1916	4	3,681	38,183	
1917	8	8,242	82,007	
1918	7	5,186	42,388	
1919	12	19,872	194,021	
1920	34	53,063	454,139	$ 43,000,000
1921	37	118,544	830,222	80,000,000
1922	49	156,725	1,450,707	130,000,000
1923	24	279,186	1,806,300	175,000,000
1924	23	294,467	2,478,165	254,000,000
1925	18	236,043	2,926,271	297,000,000
1926	2	248,867	2,686,187	236,000,000
1927	18	249,491	3,581,206	263,000,000
1928	5	227,961	2,081,071	181,000,000
1929		280,600	2,432,550	153,436,000
1930		217,000	2,030,000	135,000,000

*In the compilation of these statistics, each separate purchase of stocks has been recorded by many of the reporting companies as being the acquisition of an additional "stockholder". There are possibilities of duplications, arising from:

(a) Repeat purchases of stock of the same company by the same individual.
(b) The purchase of stock in two or more companies by the same individual.
(c) In addition, the situation is further complicated by the purchase of stocks by customers from other sources than through the company's office.

[1]Berle and Means, *op. cit.*, p. 370.

Before 1916, only 70 companies in the United States had adopted employee stock purchase plans but by 1923 this total had increased to 262.

The Increase of Employee Stock Purchase Plans in the United States[1]

Year	No. of Companies instituting stock purchase plans
1900 or earlier	5
1901-1905	13
1906-1910	14
1911	1
1912	7
1913	7
1914	6
1915	7
1916	10
1917	11
1918	8
1919	24
1920	46
1921	35
1922	17
1923	51
1924	29
1925	29
1926	13
1927	4
No information	49

In addition to an increase in the number of security holders, there was, in general, an apparent change in the distribution of people's motivations for acquiring securities in the larger industrial companies: more people held more industrial securities primarily for investment rather than for

[1]*Ibid.*, p. 371.

speculative purposes.[1] To "prove" this trend existed is difficult; however, one man J. Edward Meeker, a former economist to the New York Stock Exchange, on this subject said:

> In connection with this general tendency of securities to shift from speculators to investors it must of course be recognized that many years often elapse before the process approaches relative completion and the floating supply is reduced to small proportions. In the meantime the general trend may be halted from time to time by various adverse incidents. Sometimes, indeed, the trend may temporarily turn in just the opposite direction. Nevertheless, over a considerable period and in the instances of successful and well-managed companies, the general drift of shares from speculators to investors, together with a gradual decrease in the floating supply, is the normal tendency. Thus the average 100-share lot, after an adventurous and speculative youth in brokers's boxes and call loan envelopes, slowly settles down into a calm and dignified old age in the deposit box of some private or institutional investor.

In order to demonstrate the above proposition Meeker presented some data related to the proportion of United Steel Corporation stock registered to either brokers' or individual's names. The amount of stock

---

[1]People who buy securities primarily to purchase an income-yield property in order to get an annual income were for Meeker's purposes "investors." "Speculators", he defined as those people who buy securities with the idea of making profits out of fluctuating capital value. Of course, in practice, the distinction between investors who purchase for investment or speculation is seldom clear-cut. These two classes are in reality fictitious since most investors were most probably either more or less of each type.

held in a broker's name, Meeker said, might be regarded as an index of speculation. Conversely, the amount of stock registered in an individual's name was an indication of the investment motive.

> In order to illustrate this general trend in the large-scale distribution of securities, the case of the common and preferred stocks of the United States Steel Corporation is cited. Both issues, and particularly the common (5,083,025 shares), are large enough to preclude any abnormal conditions in their distribution arising from any unusual speculative purpose or condition. The United States Steel Corporation has endeavored to distribute its stock to investors for the past 20 years - a period in which the company has proved a conspicuous financial success. The quarterly reports published by the corporation give the proportion of both its stock issues which stand respectively in brokers' and individuals' names. While a little of the former may really represent investment, and a very little of the latter be held for speculative purposes, nevertheless in a general way it is fair to consider stock staniing in a broker's name as part of the speculatively held floating supply, and that standing in the name of an individual as investment stock.
>
> On the basis of this assumption, a comparative examination of these quarterly reports of the United States Steel Corporation from 1909 to 1920 shows that on December 31, 1909, 66.41% (or about two-thirds) of the common stock was in the floating supply, and only 33.59% (or about one-third) held by investors. Six years later, on December 31, 1915, 49.80% (or about one-half) of the same issue was speculatively held, and 50.20% (or about one-half) held by investors. On December 31, 1920, 25.1% (or only about one-quarter) remained in the floating supply, and

74.83% (or almost three-quarters) had been absorbed by investors. This is a striking illustration of the tendency of a stock to shift from speculative to investors' hands as it becomes seasoned.[1]

The significance of this rise in the "investment motive" was that more people, say between 1916 and 1925, tended, to an increasing degree, to have a continuing interest in the affairs of the enterprises, rather than the enterprise's stock, represented in their investment portfolio. The relevant data for more investors thus became the so-called investment fundamentals--earnings, assets, industry trends, etc.: not the price gyrations of the stock market which were of primary interest to the speculator.

Later, particularly after 1925 and throughout the subsequent bull market "the thinking of common investors had become indistinguishable from that of speculators; the only practical difference between

---

[1]Meeker, *op. cit.*, pp. 462-464.

Distribution of United States
Steel Common Stock, 1910-1920

Date 12/31	Held in Brokers' Names	Held by Individuals
1910	63.94%	36.06%
1912	57.36	42.64
1914	49.86	50.14
1916	58.04	41.96
1918	40.71	58.29
1920	25.17	74.83

Ibid., pp. 593-594.

them was that the former may have paid cash for the same stocks that the latter carried on a thin margin."[1] Both became wedded to the "growth stock principle" of investment which was based principally upon a firm's projected rate of change of earnings per share.

The changes in the character and scope of the investor class described above were to influence greatly the nature of, and justification for, the recommendations related to securities legislation and financial disclosure discussed below. The reaction of businessmen to these recommendations, as shown later, was conditioned by two factors: the 1918-1929 social, political and ethical environment discussed above; and continuance of those 1900-1917 attitudes of corporate executives toward corporate publicity previously examined in chapter three.

Part II: Legislative Proposals, 1918-1929

Between 1918 and 1929, so as to protect the small investor from fraudulent promotions, there were at least three serious attempts to pass securities legislation on the federal level. These efforts began in 1918 with the report of the Capital Issues Committee

---

[1]Benjamin Graham and David L. Dodd, Security Analysis: Principles and Techniques (New York: The McGraw-Hill Book Company, Inc., 1951), p. 389.

which recommended to Congress the enactment of a federal securities law to curb the prevailing widespread sale of securities in fraudulent and unsound ventures. During the years following the filing of the Committee's report, several bills designed to regulate security issues were introduced into Congress.

The Report of the Capital Issues Committee

On April 5, 1918, the Capital Issues Committee, the first formal federal body to exert control over the issuance of corporate securities,[1] was established by the War Finance Corporation Act to assist the government in the "conservation of financial resources, labor and material, so that they may be available for uses essential to the prosecution of the war."[2] In particular, the Act authorized the Capital Issues Committee to investigate any securities issued after April 5, 1918, and to determine whether the issue was compatible with the "immediate military or economic necessity."

The Committee's sole function was to ration capital. Unlike the various state "blue-sky" commissions, it did not seek to protect the investor by

---

[1]Homer V. Cherington, The Investor and the Securities Act (Washington: American Council on Public Affairs, 1942), p. 41.

[2]Capital Issues Committee, Rules and Regulations (Washington: Government Printing Office, 1918), p. 1.

passing upon the intrinsic investment merits of the securities to be offered for sale. In order to make clear to the public the true nature of the Committee's function, issuers of prospectuses advertising securities examined and approved by the Committee were requested to place the following statement upon the prospectuses:

> Passed by the Capital Issues Committee as not incompatible with the national interest, but without approval of legality, validity, worth or security.[1]

On December 2, 1918, shortly before it was dissolved, the Capital Issues Committee filed a report[2] with Congress recommending the continuation of federal supervision of security issues by some public agency with the view to checking the flow of unsound securities. The report stated:

> At no time has the obligation been so definitely placed upon the government to protect its public from financial exploitations by reckless or unscrupulous promoters. The field has been greatly enlarged by the wide distribution of Liberty bonds, and the purveyor of stocks and bonds is no longer put to the necessity of seeking out a select list of prospective purchasers with money to invest. He now has the entire American public, and the transaction becomes one of persuasion to trade a government bond bearing a low rate of interest for stocks or bonds baited with promise of high rate of return and prospect of sudden riches.[3]

---

[1] *Ibid.*, p. 7.

[2] Report of Capital Issues Committee, H. R. Doc. No. 1485, 65th Congress 3rd session (1918).

[3] *Ibid.*, p. 3.

In addition, the fear that investors' funds would be attracted away by fraudulent promotions from the "Victory Liberty Loan"--the bonds of which were to be offered between April 21 and May 10, 1919--prompted the Secretary of the Treasury, the Chairmen of the Federal Reserve Board and the Capital Issues Committee to ask the Federal Trade Commission to take such action as it believed necessary to prevent the sale of fraudulent securities.

Accordingly, "on the theory that the bad securities were in unfair competition with the good"[1] and hence subject to Federal Trade Commission regulation, the Commission adopted a form of inquiry blank consisting of 32 questions which the officers of those companies making public offerings were required to fill out and submit to the Stocks and Securities Division of the Commission before issuing securities. The questionnaire, a copy of which is reproduced in Appendix A, related to the security vendor's company's organization, business, plans, properties and financial condition. In addition, it was a penal offense, punishable by fine, to make a false statement in answering these questions. This measure, designed to

---

[1]Loss, op. cit., p. 155. According to Loss, "A member of the Commission expressed his thankfulness, when he testified in 1933 on the bill which became the Securities Act, that the Commission had never had to defend this theory in court."

prevent security fraud, was a post-wartime expedient and little ever came of it. Discussed below are some attempts to introduce a more permanent type of regulation through legislation.

Subsequent Proposals

Soon after the Capital Issues Commiteee filed its report, Congressman Edward T. Taylor of Colorado introduced a bill[1] embodying the Committee's suggestions. Taylor's bill, which had been drawn, in part, by Bradley W. Palmer, counsel of the Capital Issues Committee, had the approval of President Woodrow Wilson, Secretary of the Treasury Carter Glass and the Federal Trade Commission.[2] On August 8, 1919, President Wilson, concerned with the increase in fraudulent promotions, urged Congress to pass a Federal Securities Act. He said:

> May I not add that there is a bill /H. R. 188/ now pending before Congress which, if passed, would do much to stop speculation and to prevent the fraudulent methods of promotion by which our people are annually fleeced of many millions of hard earned money.[3]

Representative Taylor's bill, which was modeled on the British Companies Act, required the promoters, corporate officers and directors of each company

---

[1]H. R. 188, 66th Congress. 1st Session.

[2]Department of Commerce, op. cit., p. 327.

[3]Presidential Message to Congress, August 8, 1919.

offering securities to the public to file with the Secretary of the Treasury a statement setting forth certain detailed information related to the issuer, its corporate structure and the offered security. All prospectuses related to the registered securities were to state "further information could be obtained by consulting the registration statement on file with the Treasury and with the post office in the principal city of each state in which the security was offered."[1] In addition, the issuer, the registration statement signatory and any others authorizing any misstatement in the registration statement were all liable to civil suit. The courts were instructed under Taylor's proposal to presume the buyer of any registered securities had relied upon the information contained in the filed statement. Hence, in effect, the *onus probandi* was upon the issuer. In addition, the act would have excluded from the above provisions securities sold at a public auction or on stock exchanges approved by the Secretary of the Treasury. Moreover, the Secretary of the Treasury could at his discretion issue licenses to brokers, bankers and dealers authorizing them to sell new securities without otherwise

---

[1] Louis Loss, *op. cit.*, p. 117.

complying with the Act.[1]

There were a number of people and groups, including the Investment Bankers Association of America, who were opposed to the Taylor Bill, and it was never reported out of the House Committee on the Judiciary.[2] The principal objections to this bill presented by representatives of the investment banking community were: the registration requirement put an excessive burden on honest corporations and investment bankers; it was beyond the constitutional power of Congress to regulate the interstate sale of securities; and the right of the purchaser of securities to sue the vendor for damages would discourage honest investment bankers from promoting new issues and thus the function of investment banking would fall into irresponsible and perhaps dishonest hands. It was also argued that public access to the proposed registration statements would give the registrant's competitors an unfair competitive advantage.

In return, the investment bankers proposed a law which would have required that "all literature,

---

[1]Cherrington, op. cit., pp. 43-44.

[2]Subsequently, in 1923, Taylor's home State of Colorado passed a similar law. This Colorado law, as previously noted, was the only "blue-sky" law to be based on the publicity philosophy (Session Laws of Colorado, 1923, Ch. 168).

advertising and circulars regarding the offerings of shares' should be filed in Washington. Furthermore, the bankers proposed, some agency of the government should be given authority to call for additional information regarding any offering of securities. Such a request for more information would be made whenever it became necessary to do so in order to determine whether the 'offering was made in good faith, or whether it was simply a fraudulent scheme. If, after further investigation, it should be developed... it was a fraudulent scheme, the Federal Trade Commission, or some other suitable agency' might and to protect investors by ordering the sellers to cease and desist from fraudulent activity."[1] Such a bill, the investment bankers said, would prevent the sale of fraudulent securities.

Taylor's original goal had been to ensure by force of law that the intelligent investor in securities would be given enough information to be able to make a critical evaluation of any investment opportunity, including the honesty of the promoter. The bankers' goal--simply prevention of fraud--was a more limited objective.

The next year, 1919, Congressman Andrew Volstead of Minnesota introduced an "antifraud type" bill[2]

---

[1]Cherrington, op. cit., pp. 46-47.

[2]H. R. 12603, 66th Congress, 2nd Session.

similar to the blue sky legislation previously passed by New Jersey and Maryland. The Volstead bill, which was supported by the Investment Bankers Association, would have given the Attorney General of the United States power, upon investigation by the Justice Department, to prohibit the sale of fraudulent securities through the mails. The Volstead bill was never reported out of committee.

Between 1921 and 1925, Congressman Edward E. Denison of Illinois on several occasions presented before Congress bills[1] which sought to strengthen the various state blue sky laws by denying the use of the mails to those seeking to evade the state securities laws. The use of the U. S. mails to avoid compliance with state securities laws was, as we have seen, a common practice of both the honest and dishonest promoters and bankers. Under the original Denison bill, securities declared unlawful by the various states were to be unlawful in the mails or in interstate commerce. In 1921, the Denison bill, which had the support of a number of the "blue sky" commissioners, the American Bankers Association and

---

[1]See Hearings on H. R. 7215, 67th Congress, 1st Session; House Report 760 on H. R. 10598, 67th Congress, 2nd Session: House Report 132 on H. R. 4, 68th Congress, 1st Session; House Report 34 on H. R. 52, 69th Congress, 1st Session.

the Mortgage Bankers' Association but was opposed by the Investment Bankers of America, was passed by the House but never reported out of the Senate Committee on the Judiciary.[1]

The major objection to the Denison Bill was that its goal of providing federal aid in the enforcement of state statutes was unconstitutional since Congress was prohibited by the Constitution to delegate, directly or indirectly, its power to regulate interstate commerce to the states. The Investment Bankers Association, the principal spokesman of these matters for the business community, objected to the bill for much the same reasons it had objected to the state blue sky laws. If the federal government wished to deal with security frauds, the investment bankers said, then pass a federal anti-fraud "blue sky" statute similar to the recently enacted Martin Law of New York.

During subsequent sessions of Congress Denison unsuccessfully tried to introduce a modified version of his original bill.[2] Thereafter, until 1930 there

---

[1]Denison had invited the president of the National Chamber of Commerce of the United States of America to present his views on H. R. 7215 before the House Committee on Interstate and Foreign Commerce. The president of the Chamber, however, did not choose to appear before the Committee.

[2]On these occasions, because of certain exemptions included in the modified bill, the Investment Bankers supported Denison's bill but reserved the right to promote the passage of an anti-fraud type statute.

were no other major attempts in Congress to introduce securities legislation on the federal level.

*****

The introduction of these three securities bills and the Report of the Capital Issues Committee were indicative of the emergence of a new concern on the federal level of government. To the government wards of the past--consumers, employees and independent businessmen--a number of persons now wished to add the investor. The times, however, were not conducive to the passage of a federal securities statute; the question as to Congress' right to regulate the interstate sale of securities was not settled; and there were divergent views as to the most appropriate form of any such legislation. Despite the growth of a nation-wide investor class and the inability of the blue-sky laws to halt the sale of fraudulent securities, there was no popular support for reform in this area on the federal level--security fraud still was regarded in Congress as a local rather than a national issue.

CHAPTER SIX

PROPOSED FINANCIAL DISCLOSURE STANDARDS, 1918-1929

Between 1918 and 1929 a number of governmental and private groups, including the Federal Reserve Board, the Federal Trade Commission, the American Institute of Accountants, the New York Stock Exchange, the National Association of Credit Men and the Investment Bankers Association of America, all in some way sought to influence the formulation and adoption of improved accounting disclosure standards. In addition, such individuals as Clinton Collver, a prominent security analyst, and William Z. Ripley of Harvard University also spoke out on the subject of financial disclosure. What these groups and individuals had to say was important for, as will be seen in chapter eight, it was to be the proposals of these groups and individuals--not the practices of businessmen--which, in general, were the basis for the minimum prospectus financial disclosure standards established by the Securities Act of 1933.

"The Accountant's Bible"

In April 1917 the Federal Reserve Board in conjunction with the Federal Trade Commission and the

DOI: 10.4324/9781003169420-6

Committee on Federal Legislation[1] of the American Institute of Accountants published in the Federal Reserve Bulletin, under the title of "Uniform Accounting,"[2] a tentative proposal for a uniform system of accounting practices to be adopted for credit purposes by manufacturing and merchandising concerns. To date, this was the most comprehensive and authoritative document related to financial disclosure published in

---

[1]The Committee consisted of W. Sanders Davies, the president of the Institute, Harvey S. Chase, George O. May and Robert H. Montgomery.

[2]"Uniform Accounting," Federal Reserve Bulletin. Vol. III, April 1917, pp. 270-284.
This history of the document's origins was described in its "Introduction" thus:

> The Federal Trade Commission in the course of its investigation of business conditions has been strongly impressed with the lack of uniformity and has enlisted the aid of the American Institute of Accountants, with a view to remedying the condition....
>
> As a first step toward the standardization of balance-sheet audits and to insure greater care in compiling and verifying statements the Federal Trade Commission requested the American Institute of Accountants, to prepare a memorandum on balance sheet audits. This memorandum was duly prepared and approved by the council of the institute representing accountants in all sections of the country.
>
> After approval by the Federal Trade Commission the memorandum was placed before the Federal Reserve Board for consideration. The Federal Reserve Board, after conferences with representatives of the Federal Trade Commission and the American Institute of Accountants, and a careful consideration of the memorandum in question, has accepted the memorandum, given it a provisional or tentative indorsement, and submitted it to the banks, bankers, and banking associations throughout the country for their consideration and criticism,

the United States. Later, in 1917[1] and again in 1918, under the title Approved Methods for the Preparation of Balance Sheet Statements,[2] over 65,000 copies of this proposal were distributed in reprint form "for the consideration of banks, bankers, and banking associations; merchants, manufacturers, and associations of manufacturers; auditors, accountants, and associations of accountants." The Board of Governors of the Federal Reserve System believed the document would be of interest to the parties to whom it was addressed because:

> It is recognized that banks and bankers have a very real interest in the subject, because they are constantly passing upon credits based upon statements made by manufacturers or merchants.
>
> It is quite as much of vital interest to merchants and manufacturers, because they realize that their credit sometimes suffers by reason of losses incurred by bankers through credits given to merchants and manufacturers whose statements do not correctly reflect true conditions.
>
> Lastly, it is of immense importance to auditors and accountants because they have a professional as well as a practical interest in having the character of their professional work thoroughly formulated and standardized. Losses incurred by bankers by reason of credits given to merchants or manufacturers, if such credits were given because the state-

---

[1]Federal Reserve Board, Uniform Accounting (Washington: Government Printing Office, 1917).

[2]Federal Reserve Board, Approved Methods for the Preparation of Balance Sheet Statements (Washington: Government Printing Office, 1918).

> ments were either actually false or misleading in their nature, tend to discredit accountancy as a profession and to shake the confidence of bankers in the real value of any statements.[1]

Clearly, the proposal had been prepared from the point of view of the grantor of credit, not the general investor.

The pamphlet sought to do two things---improve and standardize the form of financial statements, and encourage the adoption of independent audit methods which would insure greater care in the compiling and verification of financial statements.

> In recent years bankers, through their associations and otherwise, have made rapid progress in the direction of more uniform and complete forms of statements. Much has also been accomplished in the improvement of the quality of the statements rendered and in securing statements which do not depend for their accuracy on the borrower's statement alone but are verified to a greater or less extent by independent scrutiny and audit. The advantage of a statement certified by trustworthy public accountants over an unverified statement is evident. At the present time, however, there is no uniformity as to the extent of verification in the case of statements put forward as having been verified.[2]

The bulk of the article's recommendations related to the scope, method and form of the balance-sheet audit. The last three pages, however, presented suggested forms for an auditor's certificate and

---

[1]Federal Reserve Board, 1917, *op. cit.*, p. 3.

[2]*Ibid.*, p. 5.

financial statements which would meet as nearly as possible the requirements and practice of Federal Reserve Banks. The recommended form for the auditor's certificate was:

> I have audited the accounts of Blank & Co. for the period from.......to......and I certify that the above balance sheet and statement of profit and loss have been made in accordance with the plan suggested and advised by the Federal Reserve Board and in my opinion set forth the financial condition of the firm....., and the results of its operations for the period.
>
> Signed A. B. C.[1]

The proposed form of the profit and loss statement and the balance sheet are reproduced below.

---

[1] *Ibid*., p. 24.

[FORM FOR PROFIT AND LOSS ACCOUNT.]

Comparative statement of profit and loss for three years ending......19

	Year ending—		
	19—	19—	19—
Gross sales	$.......	$.......	$.......
Less outward freight, allowances, and returns	....	....	....
Net sales	....	....	....
Inventory beginning of year	....	....	....
Purchases, net	....	....	....
	....	....	....
Less inventory end of year	....	....	....
Cost of sales	....	....	....
Gross profit on sales	....	....	....
Selling expenses (itemized to correspond with ledger accounts kept)	....	....	....
Total selling expense	....	....	....
General expenses (itemized to correspond with ledger accounts kept)	....	....	....
Total general expense	....	....	....
Administrative expenses (itemized to correspond with ledger accounts kept)	....	....	....
Total administrative expense	....	....	....
Total expenses	....	....	....
Net profit on sales	....	....	....
Other income:			
Income from investments	....	....	....
Interest on notes receivable, etc	....	....	....
Gross income	....	....	....
Deductions from income:			
Interest on bonded debt	....	....	....
Interest on notes payable	....	....	....
Total deductions	....	....	....
Net income—profit and loss	....	....	....
Add special credits to profit and loss	....	....	....
Deduct special charges to profit and loss	....	....	....
Profit and loss for period	....	....	....
Surplus beginning of period	....	....	....
	....	....	....
Dividends paid	....	....	....
	....	....	....
Surplus ending of period	....	....	....
	....	....	....

[FORM OF BALANCE SHEET.]

ASSETS.

Cash:			
1a. Cash on hand—currency and coin		....	
1b. Cash in bank		....	....
Notes and accounts receivable:			
3. Notes receivable of customers on hand (not past due)		....	
5. Notes receivable discounted or sold with indorsement or guaranty		....	
7. Accounts receivable, customers (not past due)		....	
9. Notes receivable, customers, past due (cash value, $..)		....	
11. Accounts receivable, customers, past due (cash value, $....)		....	
Less:			
13. Provisions for bad debts	......		
15. Provisions for discounts, freights, allowances, etc	......	....	....
Inventories:			
17. Raw material on hand		....	
19. Goods in process		....	
21. Uncompleted contracts	......		
Less payments on account thereof	......	....	
23. Finished goods on hand		....	....
Other quick assets (describe fully):			
....		....	
....		....	....
Total quick assets (excluding all investments)		....	....
Securities:			
25. Securities readily marketable and salable without impairing the business		....	
27. Notes given by officers, stockholders, or employees		....	
29. Accounts due from officers, stockholders, or employees		....	....
Total current assets		....	....
Fixed assets:			
31. Land used for plant		....	
33. Buildings used for plant		....	
35. Machinery		....	
37. Tools and plant equipment		....	
39. Patterns and drawings		....	
41. Office furniture and fixtures		....	
43. Other fixed assets, if any (describe fully)		....	
....		....	
		....	
Less:			
45. Reserves for depreciation		....	....
Total fixed assets		....	
Deferred charges:			
47. Prepaid expenses, interest, insurance, taxes, etc		....	....
Other assets (49)		....	....
Total assets		....	....

[FORM OF BALANCE SHEET.]

LIABILITIES.

Bills, notes and accounts payable:		
Unsecured bills and notes—		
2. Acceptances made for merchandise or raw material purchased	....	
4. Notes given for merchandise or raw material purchased	....	
6. Notes given to banks for money borrowed	....	
8. Notes sold through brokers	....	
10. Notes given for machinery, additions to plant, etc.	....	
12. Notes due to stockholders, officers, or employees	....	
		....
Unsecured accounts—		
14. Accounts payable for purchase (not yet due)	....	
16. Accounts payable for purchases (past due)	....	
18. Accounts payable to stockholders, officers, or employees	....	
		....
Secured liabilities—		
20a. Notes receivable discounted or sold with indorsement or guaranty (contra)	....	
20b. Customers' accounts discounted or assigned (contra).	....	
20c. Obligations secured by liens on inventories	....	
20d. Obligations secured by securities deposited as collateral	....	
		....
22. Accrued liabilities (interest, taxes, wages, etc.)	....	....
Other current liabilities (describe fully):		
....	....	
....	....	
		....
Total current liabilities	....	....
Fixed liabilities:		
24. Mortgage on plant (due date......)	....	
26. Mortgage on other real estate (due date......)	....	
28. Chattel mortgage on machinery or equipment (due date......)	....	
30. Bonded debt (due date......)	....	
		....
32. Other fixed liabilities (describe fully):		
....	....	
....	....	
		....
Total liabilities	....	....
Net worth:		
34. If a corporation—		
(a) Preferred stock (less stock in treasury)	....	
(b) Common stock (less stock in treasury)	....	
(c) Surplus and undivided profits	....	
Less—		
(d) Book value of goodwill		
(e) Deficit		
	....	
		....
36. If an individual or partnership—		
(a) Capital	....	
(b) Undistributed profits or deficit	....	
Total	....	....

This 1917 document, which was called by some "the accountants' bible", served as the most authoritative statement on the subject of balance sheet audits until the original bulletin was revised and distributed under the title, Verification of Financial Statements in 1929.[1] The authority of this revision, like that of the original, rested solely on the prestige of those who compiled it and the sponsorship of the Federal Reserve Board: compliance with it was voluntary.

---

[1]Federal Reserve Board, Verification of Financial Statements (Revised) (Washington: Government Printing Office, 1929).

The revision was prepared by a special committee of the American Institute of Accountants. The desire to revise the original statement arose from a survey of the field of accountancy by the Institute's Committee on Education during 1925 and 1926. The special committee selected to prepare the revision consisted of Arthur W. Teele, William B. Campbell, W. Sanders Davies, F. H. Hurdman, William H. West and John R. Wildman. In general, the revised version made few changes to the original preferred form of financial statement. The principal changes included the following: the wording of the auditor's certificate was changed; a provision for the disclosure of taxes, depreciation and "items in the surplus account attributed to prior years" were added to the proposed income statement; and, on the balance sheet, the surplus and contingent liabilities provisions were expanded. As in the earlier publications, the new release did not suggest the method used to value fixed assets be revealed or, a clear distinction between tangible and intangible assets be made. These had been two of the most prevalent requests of the users of accounting statement.

The American Institute of Accountants[1]

In 1917, The Journal of Accountancy, the official organ of the American Institute of Accountants, announced it was "heartily in favor of the policy of full disclosure,"[2] and during most of the next 13 years the Institute and a number of its members discussed this subject. The main efforts of the profession in this area, however, were limited in practice to promoting the adoption of balance sheet audits for credit purposes. Later, in 1926, one of the Institute's more prominent members, George O. May, was to suggest to the accounting profession that it accept larger responsibilities in the general area of corporate financial disclosure.

Encouraged by the publication, under the auspices of the Federal Reserve Board, of the Approved Methods for the Preparation of Balance Sheet Statements, mentioned above, the Institute's main efforts in the area of corporate financial disclosure were devoted to

---

[1] In 1916 the American Association of Public Accountants was disbanded and reincorporated under a new name--the Institute of Accountants in the United States of America. In 1917, the name was again changed by vote of its members to The American Institute of Accountants. During the period 1917-1930, the Institute, like its predecessor, was chiefly concerned with organizational problems, certified public accountant legislation and competition from other accountants' societies.

[2] "Promotion on Right Foundation," The Journal of Accountancy. Vol. 23, No. 1, January 1917, p. 45.

the promotion among granters of credit of the recommendations related to balance sheet audits outlined in that document. In addition, the Institute worked with several outside groups in an endeavor to promote the widespread adoption, primarily for credit purposes, of the balance sheet audit.

A number of individual accountants in their writings followed the Institute's line. Some of these accountants also recommended the Federal Reserve Boards's suggestions be extended to cover financial statements prepared for such prrposes as prospectuses and annual reports to stock exchanges and stockholders.

The interest of the Institute in the question of balance sheet audits for credit purposes can be traced back at least to 1913 when the Institute's predecessor, the American Association of Public Accountants, published, with the hope of promoting more widespread adoption of an accountant's certificate as a prerequisite for credit applications, a pamphlet entitled The Influence of Accountants Certificates on Commercial Credit.[1] This pamphlet reported favorably upon a survey conducted by the Association of the attitude of bankers toward independent audits of

---

[1]American Association of Public Accountants, The Influence of Accountants Certificates on Commercial Credit. Copyright, 1913.

borrower's statements. Later, the accountants' efforts in this area, as noted above, were given a boost by the Federal Reserve Board's tentative affirmation of the Institute's 1917 memoranda related to balance sheet audits.

The road ahead, however, was still difficult and two years later, in 1919, the editor of The Journal expressed a fear that accountants had been preaching "the doctrine of the value of audited statements for so many years that they sometimes become discouraged at the apparently slow progress with which the campaign of education makes."[1] The slow progress, the editor believed, was caused by bankers "refraining from insisting upon audited statements chiefly because of the fear of driving away customers."[2]

All was not without hope, however, for in November 1919 the New York Credit Men's Association observed: "It has become the custom among many progressive manufacturers and merchants to have attached to their financial statements the certificate of a competent public auditor, and several prominent New York banks and commercial note brokers are endeavoring

---

[1]Editorial, "Value of Audited Statements," The Journal of Accountancy. Vol. XXVIII, No. 6, December 1919, p. 454.

[2]Ibid.

to make the custom universal."[1] Later, other associated with the granting of credit also spoke highly of the value of audited financial statements but at the same time voiced a concern over the lack of uniformity of audit reports and financial statements. For instance, in 1920, Julien H. Hill, a prominent Virginia commercial banker, after noting the increasing use of audited financial statements by bankers, expressed the hope that accountants would find a way to standardize as nearly as practical their reports.[2]

In 1922, the Robert Morris Associates appointed a committee on cooperation with the American Institute of Accountants and at a series of conferences with the corresponding committee of the Institute "one of the main points raised by the credit men was that there did not seem to be any standard of verification followed by the accountants in their audits and that the certificate of one accountant might mean something very different from a precisely similar certificate given by another."[3] From the point of view of the

---

[1] Ibid.

[2] Julien H. Hill, "Information Desired by the Banker," The Journal of Accountancy. Vol. 30, No. 5, November 1920, p. 338.

[3] William B. Campbell, "Cooperation Between Accountants and Bankers," The Journal of Accountancy. Vol. 45, No. 1, January 1928, p. 1.

professional user of audit reports, the problem was lack of uniformity,[1] not the fear of losing customers. Recognizing this fact, the Institute and the Robert Morris Associates continued, for a number of years to work together to encourage their respective members to adopt the suggested practices and forms authorized in the pamphlet Approved Methods for the Preparation of Balance Sheet Items.

In 1928, A. P. Richardson, the editor of The Journal, could report with pride on the results of the Institute's associations with these credit organizations:

> Bankers have been induced to adopt more rigorous and therefore beneficient rules for the extension of credit, and accountants have been able to understand better than before the desires of the credit grantor and so make many improvements in the manner and method of preparing statements to be used as the basis of application for credit.[2]

As late as 1928, despite the successful efforts to improve the minimum standards of financial disclosure for credit purposes, there was little carry-over of those influences on corporate financial

---

[1]Several of similar user groups including the National Association of Credit Men developed and adopted standard forms for financial statements for use by their members. For examples of these forms, which dealt mainly with balance sheet items, see Arthur E. Fixell, False Financial Statements (New York: Mathew Bender & Company, 1924), pp. 7-44.

[2]"Cooperation with Bankers," The Journal of Accountancy. Vol. XLVI, No. 4, October 1928, p. 286.

reports to the public. According to William B. Campbell, an accountant who served on the Institute's committee which cooperated with the Robert Morris Associates, one reason for the widespread lack of adoption of the standards set forth in the Federal Reserve Board's publication for public reports was:

> In accounts which are prepared primarily for presentation to the stockholders and are available to the public at large, it frequently happens that clients take the position that too much information is presented in this form of statement and that this information may be used to their detriment by competitors. It is therefore customary in statements prepared for wide disculation, to give only a very condensed statement of profit and loss.[1]

The "competitive argument," it will be recalled, had been used as early as the Industrial Commission hearings; apparently the attitude of some businessmen toward financial disclosure had not undergone any significant change since 1900.

In general, during the period 1917-1930, the Institute supported, with one major exception discussed below, the work of the New York Stock Exchange in the area of corporate financial disclosure. The exception was the Exchange's unwillingness to stipulate all financial statements submitted to it be independently audited: under the Exchange's rules employees of the listed company could prepare required public reports.

---

[1] *Ibid*., p. 12.

In 1926, the editor of The Journal said "conservatism" and "tradition" were the reasons for the Exchange's failure to require an independent audit:

> The stock exchange is bent upon bringing about reform. The officers and committees are evidently imbued with a desire to do all that is possible to protect the investing public, but it is extraordinary that one of the most evident means of assuring impartiality should be overlooked. One wonders why there is so marked a disregard of what most accountants consider an obvious safeguard. It is not conceivable that the authorities of the New York Stock Exchange are ignorant of the value of accounting services properly rendered. No one supposes that the men of Wall Street would prefer ex-parte statements of condition to absolutely unprejudiced reports. There must be some reason that does not appear on the surface. The first thought will be that accountants have not become sufficiently established in their reputation as impartial observers....This, of course, is pure foolishness....It is clear, therefore, that there must be some other reason for the unwillingness of the stock exchange to take the plain open path toward full publicity by way of independent investigation. We are inclined to think that the reason is one that would be denied by almost any many associated with financial interests in this day and generation. Probably if one were to say to an investment banker that his conservatism was due to nothing more substantial than a tradition he would repudiate the allegation; and yet it seems that the only reasonable explanation of the attitude of the financial world in America is fealty to a tradition and nothing more.[1]

Later Richardson said the reluctance of the Exchange to stipulate independent audits arose, not because of any failure on the part of the accountant,

---

[1]"Financial Statements for Stock Exchange," The Journal of Accountancy, Vol. 42, No. 1, July 1926, pp. 37-38.

but rather because of the financial community's "marked swing toward ultra-conservatism, or, perhaps one should say to mid-Victorianism."[1]

Richardson's bitter attack on the Exchange for its omission of the audit requirement, when compared with the facts, appears to stem from doctrine rather than reality, for in 1926, over 90 per cent of the financial statements of the industrial companies listed on the Exchange were subjected to some form of independent annual audits.[2]

Apparently, the Institute, or at least the editor of its official organ, was more concerned with the failure of the Exchange to recognize the importance of the accounting profession than with the Exchange's failure to protect investors through audits. Of course, Mr. Richardson may have not been aware of the statistic just quoted since, in 1926, even such a perceptive man as George O. May was "surprised" to learn that in the case of listed industrial companies the presentation of audited financial statements "had become almost universal."[3]

---

[1]Ibid., p. 39.

[2]George O. May, "Corporate Publicity and the Auditor," The Journal of Accountancy, Vol. 42, No. 5, November 1926, p. 322.

[3]Ibid.

The quality of the form, contents and compilation of the listed company's audited statements, however, varied greatly: an audit certificate was no guarantee of adequate disclosure or comparability between the financial statements of different companies. The principal reason for this diversity was that public accountants, in general, were still hired by management and acted as the agents of management, and each management controlled the form of its particular financial statements.

In 1926, George O. May, having now come to the realization that, as noted above, the practice of having audits had become so general, declared it was no longer necessary for the Institute to demonstrate the value of the audit, a task which had consumed much of its energy since 1917. The time, May said, was ripe for auditors to assume a larger responsibility.

The new goal May proposed for the profession was the universal adoption of the financial disclosure standards as set forth in the English Companies Acts. The Institute, by taking the lead in this matter, would "help its members to render a higher service to the community." It was impractical, he said, to consider bringing about such a condition in the United States through legislation; rather, the Institute, should seek this end through cooperation with "such bodies as the leading stock exchanges, the investment bankers and the commercial banks which grant credit."[1] May, however, did not mention cooperation with businessmen as a means whereby his proposed goals could be achieved: an omission inevitably made by others who sought also to improve disclosure standards through the cooperation of private groups.

Later, in 1928, the type of cooperation with investment bankers envisioned by May promised to become a reality when the Investment Bankers Association of America and the Institute agreed to conduct a series of meetings "to bring about clear understanding of the financial statements of companies whose securities are offered for sale."[2] Of this agreement Richardson said:

> For many years it has been generally admitted that the statements or pseudo-statements issued in conjunction with the flotation of stocks and bonds have not been invariably explicit. Recently the need for reform has been accentuated by the large increase in the number and variety of securities displayed for sale. The investors of this country are steadily growing in geographical distribution, quantity and perhaps in quality -- although one is not positive about the last. Consequently it is imperative that the information supplied to prospective purchasers be full and

---

[1] Ibid., p. 323.

[2] "Cooperation with Bankers," The Journal of Accountancy, Vol. XLVI, No. 4, October 1928, p. 285.

> frank. The fact that the investor has often had to grope in the darkness heretofore is lamentable, but the lack of comprehensive information is not entirely the fault of any one group of men. In part the blame attaches to the investor himself who has not been properly inquisitive. In part the investment banker is responsible because he has been content often to give no more specific detail than sale of the securities demanded. In part the accountant is at fault because he has not always insisted as he should have insisted that the truth be told so plainly that the simplest buyer could have no valid excuse for saying that he had bought in ignorance. It would be invidious and it would not contribute anything to the cause of harmony and reform to attempt to designate the most blameworthy of these three. It is enough to say that all are responsible and that the movement toward reform is begun.[1]

The president of the Investment Bankers Association of America, Pliny Jewell,[2] however, expressed a slightly different reason for his Association's cooperation with the Institute in this matter. Of this agreement with the accountants Jewell said:

> As a result of [a] study of circulars, it became clear to the chairman of the Committee on Industrial Securities that in matters of accounting there appeared to be rather wide differences....The Institute of Accountants is prepared to meet official representatives of the Investment Bankers Association at any time on any matters affecting general policies of accounting. If we avail ourselves actively of this opportunity, it should lead to standard-

[1]*Ibid.*, p. 285.

[2]In 1927, Mr. Jewell was associated with Coffin & Burr, Inc., Boston.

> ization, with resulting benefit to the investor and to our member houses.[1]

The accountants, as noted above, hoped the proposed meetings would lead to more "full and frank" information being supplied to investors, whereas the Investment Bankers saw "standardization" of accounting practices and principles as the desired outcome of the cooperation between the two groups. These were, of course, not mutually exclusive goals, but it is necessary to note the particular interest of each group was related to that group's needs: Accountants were interested in increasing the adoption of audits---their "bread and butter"; the bankers, as users of such reports, wanted uniformity of accounting principles so as to be able to more easily compare the financial statements of different companies---a daily investment problem.

Before leaving the description of the accounting profession's activities in the area of financial disclosure during the years 1917 through 1929, one criticism of the relationship of accountants, accounting and corporate directors should be noted. Adolf A. Berle, Jr. and Gardiner C. Means, two critics of big

---

[1]Address of the President, Proceedings of the Sixteenth Annual Convention of the Investment Bankers Association of America. September 26, 27, 28, 29, and 30, 1927, p. 51.

business, speaking in 1933 of the historic control over the computation of a company's income by directors during the 1920's, said:

> Directors have a large measure of control over the company's income account. So long as accounting standards are not hardened, and the law does not impose any specific canons, directors and their accountants may frame their figures, within limits, much as they choose.... The methods of accounting by which this result can be achieved are various. Among the simplest are the charging or failing to deduct depreciation; charging to capital expenses which properly should be charged against income account; including nonrecurrent profits as income though their real place is in surplus; and creation of "hidden reserves."
>
> One of the reasons why the power of the directors in this regard is so wide lies in the fact that accountants themselves have as yet failed to work out a series of standard rules....[1]

Thus, while the Institute could congratulate itself on its success in the area of audit certificates particularly for credit purposes and its preliminary efforts to implement May's challenge, others were already beginning to look behind the audit certificate at the underlying accounting--not audit--principles and practices. And what they saw there--lack of rigorous and uniform accounting standards--displeased them greatly. Such an absence of standards, the critics said, had allowed management to manipulate, misrepresent and conceal information related to corporate activities.

---

[1]Berle and Means, *op. cit.*, pp. 202-203.

The New York Stock Exchange

During the period 1917-1929, the influence of the New York Stock Exchange upon financial disclosure standards fell most directly on the reporting practices of those corporations listed with the Exchange.[1]

---

[1]The New York Stock Exchange had, of course, no direct control over prospectus financial disclosure. In 1922, the Exchange's position on the subject of prospectus disclosure was summed up by Seymour L. Cromwell, President of the New York Stock Exchange, thus:

> A simple way of getting right down to the bottom of our problem would be the passage of a law requiring full publicity in connection with the issuance of securities and the status of the issuing companies. That is in line with the English practice.
>
> Require that sworn statements be filed prior to the issuance of securities and semiannually thereafter, and that the statements give adequate information concerning the flotation and the financial position of the issuing companies or parties, and also concerning their operations and earnings. That would strike a vital blow at the fake promotion because you would get the jump on it from the start.
>
> Officials of companies whose securities are offered for sale would immediately lay themselves open to punishment and could be easily reached by the present laws if they furnished doctored information to bolster up a swindling promotion. Let us pin the responsibility where it belongs, on the people who furnish the background for the dealer in fake securities, and we will soon make it impossible for such dealers to operate.
>
> That kind of legislation the stock exchange will support--something that is simple, direct, easily enforceable and that will really give protection to the public.

"Regulation of Security Issues," The Journal of Accountancy, Vol. 34, No. 5, November 1922, pp. 351-352.

The New York Stock Exchange, as previously noted, had attempted for a number of years through its listing requirements to exert some influence over the financial reporting practices of those companies listed on the Exchange. These efforts, however, had not always met with success either because of the Exchange's lack of enthusiasm for the task or the obstinancy of corporate executives. During the period now under review, the Exchange renewed its efforts to improve the quality and frequency of the financial statements issued by listed corporations and, in 1927, William Z. Ripley, of whom much more will be said later, stated:

> Beyond peradventive of doubt the New York Stock Exchange is today the leading influence in the promotion of adequate corporate disclosure the world over.[1]

Briefly, whenever a corporation desired to have its stocks or bonds listed it made a formal application to the Exchange's Committee on Stock List.[2] The formal application consisted mainly of a printed questionnaire requiring answers to a number of questions related to

---

[1]Ripley, Main Street and Wall Street, p. 210.

[2]"A committee on Stock List to consist of five members. It shall receive and consider all applications for placing securities upon the list of the exchange, and make report and recommendation thereon to the Governing Committee, giving full statement concerning organization, capitalization, resources and indebtedness....New York Stock Exchange Constitution, Article XI, Section II (a).

the nature of the securities and their issuer. For instance, in 1922, the application procedure required the submission of detailed statements describing the issuer's assets and liabilities, the character of its capital structure, its mortgages and leases, its past earnings and similar matters. All of the material so filed by the corporation seeking listing was available for public inspection.

In addition to these requirements for the original listing of a stock, the issuer was requested to make public at suitable intervals information related to its earnings and other current financial statistics. From at least 1912 onwards, each new corporation seeking listing was requested to agree:

> To publish at least once in each year and submit to the stockholders, at least 15 days in advance of the annual meeting of the corporation, a statement of its physical and financial condition, an income account covering the previous fiscal year, and a balance sheet showing assets and liabilities at the end of the year; also annually an income account and balance sheet of all constituent, subsidiary, owned or controlled companies; or a consolidated income account and a consolidated balance sheet.[1]

Once a company agreed to meet the above agreement--and not all listed companies did agree--failure to publish interim or annual financial reporting could have resulted in the securities of the negligent companies being suspended from the exchange's trading list.

---

[1]Meeker, op. cit., p. 585.

These listing requirements had evolved over the years and were to continue to change during the period 1917-1929. It may be of interest to the reader to trace the history of these listing agreements related to publicity from their origins in 1869 through to 1929. The Exchange's problems in this matter were: to get listing applicants to agree to the stock list recommendations; to make the stock list requirements more stringent; and to persuade listed companies to adopt the more stringent stock list requirements which had been formulated subsequent to their original agreement with the Exchange. During most of this period, it was to what the applicant for listing was willing to agree, rather than the Exchange's formal requirements, which governed the final agreement related to financial disclosure between the Exchange and the issuer. Each advance in this area was a concession by businessmen for which the Exchange had to fight.

In 1869 the Exchange established the Committee on Stock List to consider all applications for listings of securities. This committee set forth six requirements which it recommended each corporation seeking listing "must state." One of these requirements was that the company seeking listing, once listed, would publish some form of an annual financial statement--a stipulation to which not all companies would agree to observe.

On the subject of publicity the Exchange moved cautiously and, in fact, it was not until September 24, 1897, that the first substantial promise by a corporation to publish financial data was made. In its listing application the Kansas City (Mo.) Gas Company promised: "The company will, from time to time, make publication of its net profits not less than twice in each year." One year later, on November 20, 1898, the Glucose Sugar Refining Co. agreed that at its annual meeting "a detailed statement will be made public," and on October 16, 1899, the Gramercy Sugar Company stated "the company will publish an annual statement of its operations."[1]

Next, on February 27, 1900, the National Tube Company and the New York Stock Exchange made the following agreement:

> The company agrees that it will publish at least once in each year proper detailed statements of its income and expenditures, also a balance sheet giving a detailed and accurate statement of the condition of the company at the close of its last fiscal year.[2]

Subsequently, the following companies agreed to publish annual reports: The Lehigh and Wilkes-Barre Coal Co., June 25, 1900; The International Steam Pump Co., November 20, 1900; and The American Hide and

---

[1]Birl E. Shultz, Stock Exchange Procedure (New York: New York Stock Exchange Institute, 1936), p. 17.

[2]Ibid.

Leather Co., January 3, 1901.[1]

In general, between 1900 and 1910 the promises relating to publicity included in listing agreements were similar to the above National Tube agreement. Notable exceptions were the 1909 agreement of the American Sugar Refining Co. which agreed to "publish an annual report to its stockholders," and the 1909 agreements of the American Woolen Company and the E. I. du Pont de Nemours Powder Co. These two companies agreed to:

> ...publish at least once in each year, and submit to the Stockholders at the annual meeting of the Company, a detailed statement of its physical and financial condition and income account covering the previous fiscal year, and a balance sheet showing the assets and liabilities at the end of each year; also income account and balance sheet of any subsidiary Company.[2]

The above was by far the most extensive financial disclosure agreement to date.

In 1910 the New York Stock Exchange abolished its Unlisted Department which had been created in 1885 when th new industrial companies could not, or would not, meet the existing requirements of the Committee on Stock List.[3]

---

[1] *Ibid.*

[2] *Ibid.*, p. 18.

[3] "The purpose in admitting unlisted stocks to trading was to grasp much of the business which was going to outside street markets. Unfortunately for the speculating public, it proved a handy tool for bankers and promoters who were thus able to place behind unsound stocks of untried companies the prestige of the New York Stock

Following the abolition of the Unlisted Department most of the previously unlisted stocks and bonds were listed under agreements similar to the above National Tube agreement. One company, however, the Niagara Falls Power Company, included two new features in its agreement: "to publish an annual report prior to March 15"; and to "also publish quarterly income statements." To date, not one other company had agreed to these particular stipulations.

Subsequently, also in 1910, the Pacific Gas & Electric Company made the first agreement to publish comparative statements. Later, on January 14, 1914 the Peabody Company agreed to publish a semiannual income statement and in November 1916 the General Motors Corporation agreed to modify its original agreement and "to publish semiannually beginning June 30, 1917, a consolidated income account and balance sheet." Other companies which, soon after the General Motors Agreement, also agreed to publish semi-annual statements included the American Smelting and Refining Company in July 1917; the Certain-Teed Products Corporation in April 1918; and, the Endicott Johnson Corporation in June 1918.

Exchange. This was taken advantage of to an outrageous extent....The advantage was this: The Stock Exchange did not compel "unlisted" corporations to furnish detailed information (required or properly listed stocks and bonds) concerning their securities. Ignorance and blindness are two powerful weapons of manipulation."
--Humphrey B. Neill, <u>The Inside Story of The Stock Exchange</u> (New York: B. C. Forbes & Sons Publishing Co., Inc., 1950), p. 122.

The above agreements to publish semiannual statements were the exception rather than the rule. In general, as late as 1923 the typical listing agreement called only for an annual report, the contents of which were not specified. Later, in July 1923, the Inland Steel Company signed a modification to its original agreement. This modification called for the company "to publish statements of earnings quarterly." Henceforth the Inland Steel type of agreement became quite common. In fact, in 1924 one company, the Metropolitan Edison Company went so far as to agree to publish monthly statements of earnings. Later, in 1926 the Exchange officially recommended the publication of quarterly reports by all listed companies.[1] Not all listed companies, however, followed this suggestion of the Exchange.

The above short history is an indication of the rate and type of success achieved by the Committee on Stock List in its continued efforts to improve corporate disclosure standards. The principal concern of

---

[1]At the time this announcement was made a census showed that of the 957 companies listed on the exchange 242 were already making quarterly reports, 79 were reporting semi-annually, 339 issued annual statements and 297 companies had no agreements with the Exchange respecting the issuance of such statements. Many of this last group were transportation companies which were subject to the reporting requirements of the Interstate Commerce Commission, and utility companies which were under the authority as to publicity of the various state public service commissions.--Ripley, Main Street and Wall Street, p. 187.

the Exchange, with one exception,[1] was more disclosure--not the content of such disclosure.

The progress was slow for a variety of reasons: corporate executives were not receptive to the Exchange's suggestions, since many an executive held the publicity requirements to be "arbitrary and unreasonable;"[2] and the listing committee could only apply its current disclosure standards to new listings. In addition, the Exchange, in order to add new companies to its lists, often had to make concessions, since corporations had alternative markets to list securities--ignoring the publicity requirement being an easy concession to make. Finally, the Exchange had little direct power over corporate execu-

---

[1]In 1929, the governing committee of the New York Stock Exchange issued a statement for the benefit of the Exchange's members setting forth a recommended accounting treatment of stock dividends. At the time an increasing number of companies were issuing stock dividends and there was a question as to whether such dividends constituted income for their recipient.

[2]Richard Whitney, "Business Honesty." An address before the Philadelphia Chamber of Commerce, April 24, 1931.

tives; its only weapon was moral persuasion.[1]

By 1930, the Exchange was not yet able to demand that its financial disclosure rules and regulations be lived up to, to the letter. In 1931, Richard Whitney, then President of the New York Stock Exchange, said of the Exchange's past reluctance to enforce its publicity agreements:

> You may well ask me why we have not taken a more decided stand and removed from the exchange the securities of a company which has indulged in unethical methods. Such a power undoubtedly exists in the governing Committee of the Exchange, but in every instance the Exchange has had to consider what effect its

---

[1]Another measure of the success achieved by the Committee on Stock List in this area might be gauged from the change in the length and content of the listing agreements. For instance, before 1900, the listing application seldom was longer than one and a half pages and was often only half a page in length. In general, the information contained therein was limited to a description of the type and amount of the issue to be listed and a few facts pertaining to the company's operations. Occasionally, a meager current balance sheet or income statement was presented. By 1920, the "typical" listing application was somewhere between three and five pages long; contained a current balance sheet and income statement; and listed the agreements with the Exchange entered into by the applicant. Around 1927, listing applications, in general, ran to seven or eight pages and showed the following information pertaining to the issuer and issue: capitalization; history; organization; business; stock provisions or bond covenants; subsidiaries; plant and property; funded debt; employees; production; depreciation policy; dividends; agreements with Committee on Stock List; and general data such as the name of the transfer agents. The financial statements included were often in comparative form and, from time to time, quite detailed.

> actions would have upon the innocent stockholders of the offending company, since, when a stock is stricken from the list, it automatically ceases to have the same value for borrowing purposes. It often also suffers a radical decline in price because it no longer enjoys the advantages of a free and open market. Striking a stock from the list, therefore, imposes a tremendous penalty upon the stockholders who are innocent of wrong doing but does not necessarily punish the officers and directors who are really at fault.[1]

The Exchange had introduced the listing requirements pertaining to financial reporting to protect the stockholders and now such agreements could not be enforced because the stockholder would suffer a loss. Thanks to this unfortunate paradox, the balance of power still lay with the corporate executive, not the Exchange.

The success of the spasmodic efforts of the New York Stock Exchange in the area of corporate disclosure can better be appreciated when one considers how far the degree of disclosure recommended by the Exchange was in advance of the existing legal requirements of the day. For instance, in 1930, no state required disclosure directly to the public of even the minimum financial data usually considered essential in making open market security investment decisions. There was no legal requirement necessitating disclosure of financial information to bondholders. In several states, including Massachusetts, corporations chartered in these

---

[1]Whitney, op. cit., pp. 10-11.

states were required to file an annual balance sheet with some state official. These meagre reports were usually available for public inspection. In addition, practically every state contemplated some form of an annual meeting of stockholders at which it was customary to submit an annual report. These meetings were inevitably poorly attended and few states required the mailing of the reports of these meetings to stockholders.

In general, these statutory corporate disclosure requirements were based on the underlying assumption that "such information must be considered as a private matter, of interest only to its stockholders; and even in that regard limits in the extreme the information which the corporate management must make available, even to its own shareholders."[1] Clearly, the law embodied much of the thinking of corporate executives on this subject previously discussed in chapter three. Also, in 1929, the state law related to corporate publicity was similar to that which had existed about 1900.

---

[1]Berle and Means, op. cit., p. 318. In general the laws of the various states with respect to corporate publicity do not appear to have changed substantially since 1900. See, for example, chapter four page 138. During much of the period 1900-1933 the states were in vigorous competition with each other in the area of granting corporate charters. To have insisted upon full and fair financial disclosure of corporate affairs as a condition of incorporation, given the attitude of businessmen toward corporate publicity, would not have increased a state's chance of success in this competition between states.

Given the inadequacy of statutory requirements, the cautious work of the Exchange to improve the reporting of corporate affairs to the investors was noteworthy. In fact, no other group, including the accounting profession, was to achieve the same degree of success prior to 1930.

The Investment Bankers Association of America

Between 1917 and 1929, the Investment Bankers Association of America on several occasions attempted to define for the benefit of its members standards governing financial disclosure in prospectuses. These efforts are discussed below.

During World War I and the immediate postarmistice period there was, as noted earlier, a rapid expansion in the number of small investors. At the same time, the total of industrial securities offered increased,[1] and the frequency of fraudulent security promotions rose. The investment bankers were acutely aware of the opportunities and dangers inherent in these trends and they responded in a number of different ways. Initially

---

[1]According to the annual summary published in the Wall Street Journal, industrial companies furnished less than 20% of the amount of new bond and note issues sold during 1915. The percentage in succeeding years was roughly 30%, 39%, 37%, 40%, and 55% in 1920. Report of Industrial Securities Committee. Proceedings of the Tenth Annual Convention of the Investment Bankers Association of America. October 31, November 1 and 2, 1921, p. 302.

they sought to defend themselves from the competition of fraudulent promoters by supporting the antifraud work of the federal government---particularly the Post Master General's Department---and encouraging state agencies to enforce against promoters of nebulous investment schemes the existing laws related to fraud. The Association's work to curb the activities of promoters of fraudulent securities through blue-sky legislation has already been discussed. It was through such measures that the investment bankers hoped to guard themselves from undesirable competition and retain the goodwill of the small investor.

In 1920 the Investment Bankers Association adopted a new approach designed to shield legitimate investment bankers and unsophisticated investors from the activities of the sellers of fraudulent issues. In that year the Association's Industrial Securities Committee suggested "the bankers' responsibility to the investing public renders it essential that sufficient information be given in connection with the offering of an issue of securities to allow it to be judged by the same general considerations that governed the banker in assuring himself of the integrity of the company and that dictated the structure of the issue." The type of information which the committee recommended be included in all circulars offering industrial securities "was an adequate balance sheet", so that the investor might be able to gauge whether the issuer would need to seek additional capital, and correct and ample information on the management---"the first consideration of the banker in passing on a loan." Given such information in the past, the Committee believed, many investors would not have purchased so many of the recently issued securities which were either "out-and-out speculations" or "deliberate frauds."[1]

After presenting the 1920 annual Report of the Industrial Securities Committee, Harold Stanley,[2] Chairman of the Committee, placed before the convention an interim report, which dealt with the need to establish standards of prospectus disclosure, prepared for the Association's Board of Governors the previous spring. The interim report, Stanley said, would be of "supreme interest" to all investment bankers since previously there had "been no real effort to standardize information regarding industrial securities."[3]

Stanley told the convention there was both a lack of information in the prospectuses offering industrial

---

[1]Report of Industrial Securities Committee, Proceedings of the Ninth Annual Convention of the Investment Bankers Association of America, October 4, 5, and 6, 1920, p. 153.

[2]Mr. Stanley was associated with the Guaranty Company of New York, New York.

[3]*Ibid.*, pp. 160-161.

securities as well as no recognized standards in this area that investors could expect to rely on. At the least, according to Stanley, the same information the banker acted upon in buying the issue should be disclosed in sufficient detail to allow the individual investor to form his own opinion. If such information was disclosed in prospectus, he said, it would be the best method of putting promoters of fraudulent securities out of business, since no such promoter could, without fear of prosecution, supply this information to the public. Finally, Stanley warned the convention that "if reputable houses handling high-grade securities did not disclose this information they could hardly be expected to compete with fly-by-night schemes and promotions"[1] for the savings of the investor.

Aside from the protection of investors, adequate prospectus financial disclosure standards were also needed, the interim report said, to safeguard the investment banker. Often, the report claimed, bankers were asked to participate in syndicates on the basis of the information outlined in the prospectuses. Such information, the report said, was insufficient to form a sound judgement as to the worth of the security and to present the securities so offered in an effective manner to the banker's salesmen and customers.

---

[1] Ibid.

In addition, the report said, by giving the investor a full statement of the facts as presented by the issuer, the banker might avoid customer criticism should some of these corporations whose securities he recommended later prove unsuccessful.

Finally, the report predicted, unless the investment banker saw to it that the intelligent investor received full financial information from those corporations reluctant to publish financial data there might arise a demand for federal intervention. Failure to provide investors with the information needed to make informed investment decisions would inevitably lead to some form of federal registration legislation which might well require publication by the corporation issuing securities of information "in greater detail than bankers or investors would ordinarily require." Thus, as early as 1920, some investment bankers recognized that a failure to achieve reform in the area of financial disclosure to investors might, from the bankers' point of view, well lead to undesirable and unnecessary federal legislation.[1]

---

[1]...the attention of the committee has been called to the lack of uniformity of information contained in circulars and public offerings of corporate securities, which is noticeable in industrial issues and may be worth considering in the case of railroad and utility offerings as well. Without any formal action on the part of the committee, it was thought proper to suggest some reasons why the Investment

The convention unanimously adopted the Committee's

Bankers Association of America should be especially interested in recommending to its members greater uniformity in this respect.

Members of the committee have made some study of recent offerings and it seems apparent that there is no recognized standard of information which is expected to be given to investors. It appears as if the material contained in the offerings has probably been determined in each case either by what the companies gave out or by the facts that would especially appeal to investors, rather than being furnished in accordance with a schedule of required information....

Aside from the desirability of a full presentation of facts to investors, another and very practical consideration is the matter of the presentation of facts to bankers who participate in syndicates. Formerly, with small syndicates, or with reasonable time to examine material, it was not difficult for bankers who associated themselves in the distribution of an issue to get the needed information and form their own judgment, presenting the securities in an effective manner to their salesmen and their customers. At the present time, however, when large syndicates are the rule and offerings are made at once on receipt of a syndicate letter or a telegram, it is little exaggeration to say that in some cases the distributing banker knows no more about the issue than does his customer. He sometimes is obliged to both buy and sell without any circular at all and, usually, without any further information than is contained in the circular itself. As this method seems to be accepted at the moment, for various reasons, as giving the best results in syndicate operations, it is especially important that the information which forms the basis of the judgment both of the distributing banker and his customer should be exactly the information which they require....

It is frequently said that the investor does not require full information about the issues which he buys, that what he wants is the assurance of the issuing house that the security is good, and that figures and facts only bewilder him. This is not the whole story, however. Aside from the undesirability of encouraging unintelligent investment in the face of a general demand for the education of investors, it is for the banker's own protection to have sold his securities accompanied by a full statement of the facts on which he based his con-

Committee's interim report without discussion.[1]

---

clusions. Especially is this the case when a company later proves unsuccessful and the banker can show that he or an official of the company presented all the essential facts at the time of purchase and that these facts showed a justifiable basis for investment.

Another point which is sometimes brought forward is that some of the best companies object to furnishing full information to go beyond the eyes of their bankers and that in such cases it would be impossible to live up to any prescribed standard. Nevertheless, it seems as if the bankers should deal with these cases as exceptional, raalizing that if securities of such companies are to be sold they must be sold practically upon the strength of the banker's assertions rather than upon a presentation of facts. A further thought along this line is that it is quite probable, unless the bankers who sell the highest grade of securities give at least such information as an intelligent investor requires in forming his judgment, that the demand for this information may lead to a national registration plan of some kind which will oblige companies, issuing securities, to put on public record information probably in greater detail than bankers or investors would ordinarily require.

Methods are being sought to prevent the exploitation of investors by unscrupulous promoters. Among others who are seeking remedies, the Treasury Department of the United States calls our attention to the offerings put out by such promoters, chiefly in regard to the lack of vital facts concerning the issues which they advertise. One way in which the Investment Bankers Association of America can help to put these promoters at a disadvantage is by accustoming investors to such a frank presentation of the important facts in regard to the securities offered by its members that the omission of such facts from a prospectus will put the investor instinctively upon his guard. For this reason, as well as for better service to investors, and better use of the resources of the distributing bankers, it seems wise to set up some standard of information to be included in public offerings.--*Ibid.*, pp. 162-166.

[1]Later, in 1923, the Business Practice Committee of the Investment Bankers Association recommended as "better practice" that members of the Association in their offering circulars concerning securities of holding companies set forth: a consolidated statement of capitalization *or* a balance sheet; a consolidated statement of

Five years later, in 1925, the annual convention of the Investment Bankers Association of America again returned to the question of the preparation and use of circulars. One year earlier, the Association's Board of Governors had appointed a Special Committee on Circulars and, subsequently, in 1925, the Special Committee made its report to the Convention. The report, quoting from an earlier 1923 report of the Real Estate Securities Committee, stated the assumption underlying the Special Committee's recommendation was:

---

earnings; and an income of profit and loss acouunt of the holding company. In addition, there should be readily available through annual reports, statistical manuals and other media the following information: the securities of the subsidiary companies owned by the holding company and those owned by the public; and statements for each subsidiary company giving earnings, expenses, maintenance expenditures and reserves, fixed charges, dividends, assets, capitalization and other liabilities--Proceedings of the Twelfth Annual Convention of the Investment Bankers Association of America. October 29, 30, 31, 1923, p. 294.

One year later, the Committee on Ethics and Business Practice in reference to the 1923 disclosure recommendations related to holding companies noted a number of striking instances of failure by investment banking houses to observe these standards. The Committee was "inclined to think there may be some cases of indifference on the part of offering houses to the recommendations" adopted at the 1923 Convention. Proceedings of the Thirteenth Annual Convention of the Investment Bankers Association of America. September 22, 23, 24, 1924, pp. 210-211.

> The importance and great value of good faith and good judgment on the part of the issuing house are fully recognized, but it is believed that, as a matter of principle, investments should be sold on their own merits, and that a circular put out by any investment dealer who is a member of the Investment Bankers Association of America should not only be in such form as would satisfy its trusting customer, but would also satisfy the scrutiny of fellow members in other investment houses who may be called on to give their advice regarding the security in question, or to pass upon the collateral value of the bonds for bank loan purposes.[1]

This reaffirmation by the Special Committee of an earlier suggestion by a lesser committee that a security should be sold on its own merits was indeed

---

[1]Report of the Committee on Real Estate Securities. Proceedings of the Twelfth Annual Convention of the Investment Bankers Association of America. October 29, 30, 31, 1923, p. 254.

The report also stated: "Your Committee is most emphatic in urging that all essential facts be clearly stated in circulars; that there be no evasion or silence on points which might lead the investor to the wrong conclusion." Subsequently, the report stated better practice demanded the inclusion in circulars offering real estate securities material related to the following points: details of the land and building appraisal; name of appraiser; name and address of the borrowing corporation; the issuing houses' personal interest, if any, in the property; a full description of the property; terms of any leases in considerable detail; avoidance of misleading references to the value of the mortgage; earnings over a period of time; property analyzed and set forth in detail; if the building is to be constructed or is constructed; proposed construction insurance; names of trustees, approving attorneys, guarantor of title and any other experts; and illustrative cuts showing the building.--*Ibid*., pp. 253-254.

an important one. This proposal challenged one of the most entrenched beliefs of the older bankers. Earlier, before World War I, it was almost universally maintained by bankers that securities need only be sold on the basis of the investor's confidence in the banker. If the banker had recommended the security, ipso facto the security was, unless otherwise stated, of good investment quality.

Not all bankers were willing to adopt the Special Committee's suggestion since, as late as 1923, the report of the Publicity Committee stated: "confidence is the bulwark in the relationship between dealer and client."[1] The whole movement toward greater financial disclosure, of course, went against the grain of this tradition which had evolved when it was possible for the banker-client relation to be a personal one. The banker bought securities from the issuer if the "man was right"[2] and "the questions of brick and mortar and turnover and sale of profit and all the other fine points [were] secondary considerations,"[3] and the banker

---

[1] Report of the Publicity Committee. Proceedings of the Twelfth Annual Convention of the Investment Bankers Association of America. October 29, 30, 31, 1923, p. 302.

[2] Report of the Industrial Securities Committee. Proceedings of the Seventh Annual Convention of the Investment Bankers Association of America. December 9, 10, 11, 1918, p. 94.

[3] Ibid.

expected his customers to deal with him on the same basis. In the 1920's such relationships because of the growth of national syndicates and a larger investor class were not practical, but, as we know, tradition, like old soldiers, never dies---it just fades away.

The Special Committee on Circulars said with regard to the objective to be obtained in circulars

> ...it seems fair to demand that after an investor has read the contents of the circular he shall be in possession of all the essential facts concerning a security issue on which investors are accustomed to base their decisions, and he shall further have confidence that there have been no omissions of facts or circumstances which would cause him to change his decision if he knew that they existed. Unless he is possessed of special information, the investor can only base his decision on what is placed before him, and it seems only fair to require that this shall be sufficiently comprehensive, and with nothing concealed which might lead to his accusing the investment bankers of bad faith if he discovered it later.[1]

In addition to the above general statement, the Committee set forth eleven separate and different schedules listing the type of relevant information which should be contained in prospectuses offering the following classes of securities: Government Bonds; Municipals; Railroads; Public Utility; Holding Company; Industrials; Real Estate; Coal; Lumber; Irrigation; and Marine. For instance, the schedule for Industrials read as follows:

---

[1]Report of the Special Committee on Circulars. Proceedings of the Fourteenth Annual Convention of the Investment Bankers Association of America. December 7, 8, 9, 10, and 11, 1925, p. 272.

Industrials

Circulars should contain information on the following points.

1. Description of industry
2. Position of company in industry
3. Description of management
4. Description of property, including size, capacity or some measure of output.
5. Understandable balance sheet with comments on inventory, working capital, etc.
6. Earnings, by years, not averages, with statement as to depreciation, etc., and dividend record.
7. Security for issue -
   a. Character of security (mortgage note, etc.)
   b. Property covered.
   c. Prior liens.
   d. Value of equity if possible.
   e. Restrictions, escrow clauses, etc.
   f. Sinking fund, depreciation reserve, etc.
8. Purpose of issue.
9. In the case of stocks, voting rights should be stated clearly, as well as any provisions for the protection of the holders.[1]

Furthermore, each Committee responsible for fields of investment covered by the above eleven classes of securities was charged by the Association's Board of Governors with "the responsibility of reporting to it any alleged violation of an established principle of 'better practice' and the development of any practice which should be corrected or improved"[2] in the area of prospectus financial disclosure.

---

[1]*Ibid.*, pp. 281-282.

[2]Report of Public Service Securities Committee. Proceedings of the Fifteenth Annual Convention of the Investment Bankers Association of America. October 11, 12, 13, 14, and 15, 1926, p. 244.

During the next year, 1926, the Public Service Securities Committee and the Real Estate Securities Committee of the Association conducted surveys of the prospectuses offering securities in the areas of each one of these particular Committee's responsibility. These circulars were evaluated against the standards set for that class of securities by the 1925 Special Committee on Circulars. Both the Public Service and Real Estate Committee noted that a considerable number of circulars had not met the minimum standard. In fact, the Public Service Committee said "it had been necessary to report to the Board several [holding company offerings] which seemed most lacking in this respect."[1]

In general, it was assumed most of the omissions of essential information observed by the two Committees were "due either to carelessness or a lack of knowledge on the part of the members"[2] as to what were the 1925 standards. The Public Service Securities Committee, however, believed "much good will come of this plan for a supervision of circulars and we sincerely hope it will be adhered to and faithfully carried out."[3]

---

[1]*Ibid.*

[2]Report of Real Estate Securities Committee. Proceedings of the Fifteenth Annual Convention, p. 248.

[3]Report of Public Service Securities Committee, *op. cit.*, p. 244.

Next year, 1927, the Industrial Securities Committee, in addition to reporting on its meeting with The American Institute of Public Accountants noted above, issued a report on a survey of recent industrial prospectuses it had conducted. This survey sought to determine just how well prospectuses offering industrial securities were meeting the prospectus disclosure standards set by the 1925 Special Committee on Circulars. The survey covered 312 prospectuses which represented 96 per cent of the total industrial financing in the United States during the first seven months of 1927.

From its investigations the Industrial Securities Committee concluded: "these circulars have for the most part shown an evident endeavor on the part of the majority of the members to follow in general the suggestions of previous Industrial Securities Committees and the report of the Special Committee on Circulars."[1]

---

[1]Report of Industrial Securities Committee. Proceedings of the Sixteenth Annual Convention of the Investment Bankers Association of America. September 26, 27, 28, 29, and 30, 1927, p. 143.

The committee, however, felt obligated to call attention to one type of circular--the circulars offering the securities of manufactured ice companies! Apparently, these circulars erroneously had followed the schedule of the Utility rather than the Industrial class to which the Committee considered they belonged.

More substantial complaints by the Committee were the failure, in many cases, to present adequate data on the current position of the issuer and how the issuer's earnings were in fact generated.

It was directly from the result of this survey that the Chairman of the Industrial Securities Committee met, as noted above, with The American Institute of Accountants.

The intent of the members was in the right direction--improving prospectus disclosure standards.

Compliance with the various disclosure standards outlined above was voluntary. At the same meeting to which the 1927 report of the Industrial Securities Committee was submitted the President of the Association, Pliny Jewell of Coffin & Burr, Inc., Boston, said:

> You will recall that a year ago last spring the Association set in motion machinery for the scrutiny of circulars. This was the logical consequence of the Association's constant aim at the presentation of adequate information to the investor. Circulars are scrutinized after the offerings are made, for the policy of the Association is to follow tendencies rather than to exercise any arbitrary power. It is hardly necessary to point out that no one--the Association least of all--desires to assume exacting labors of this kind. This function is undertaken, with others, on the theory that, if we conduct our business with due regard for the rights of the public, we shall obviate the necessity for official supervision by people who, as President Morris said last year, "know less about our business than we do."[1]

The Association, the President had said, would not regulate its members. Here lay the weakness of the Investment Bankers Association's efforts to improve prospectus disclosure practices. Given the philosophy of voluntary adoption and the 1927 visionary report of the Industrial Securities Committee, the "machinery for the scrutiny of circulars" soon began to rust: the whole program had apparently lost much of its authority and

---

[1]Address of the President. Proceedings of the Sixteenth Annual Convention of the Investment Bankers Association of America. September 26, 27, 28, 29, and 30, 1927, pp. 50-51.

urgency. And other questions and other events were soon to demand the attention of the Association. Nevertheless, the attempts of the Association to define in rather specific terms the content of prospectuses was by far the most ambitious program undertaken in this field to date.

Clinton Collver: A Pioneer Industrial Security Analyst[1]

It was not until after World War I that industrial securities were widely recognized to be of "investment class" rather than the wildest of gambles. In addition, the investing public--professional and amateur--realized that the techniques used previously to appraise railroad securities and government bonds were of little assistance when faced with the task of intelligently appraising an

---

[1] Who's Who in America, 1930-31, listed Collver thus: "Collver, Clinton, security analysis;...U. of Wis., 1904-07; B.C.S., New York Univ., 1908, M.C.S., 1911.... On editorial staff Wall Street Journal, 1907-08; pub. accountant with Haskins & Sells, Everett Audit Co. and Lybrand Ross Bros. & Montgomery, 1909-11; served as member editorial staff of Systems Magazine, 1912; N.Y. mgr. Brookmire Economic Service, 1912-13; editorial staff, Iron Age, 1913-14; dean Baltimore Sch. of Commerce Account. and Finance, 1915-16; security expert Moody's Investor's Service, 1916-18; mgr. investment dept. Lyman D. Smith & Co., 1918-29; dir. Gowin United Cos., American Securities Service, Am. Executives Inst., N.J. Bond & Shareholding Corporation, Internat. Shopping Service, Fellow Royal Econ Soc., mem. Am. Assn. Security Analysts (pres. since 1925), Am. Econ Ass., Acad. Polit. Science, Am. Acad. Polit and Social Science, American Statis. Association....Author: How to Analyze Industrial Securities 1917; Industrial Securities, 1922; The Choice of Stocks 1924. Co-author: Trading and Investing, 1925...."--Albert Nelson Marquis ed., Who's Who in America, Vol. 16, 1930-1931 (Chicago: The A.N. Marquis Co., 1930), p. 555.

industrial security as either a speculation or an investment. In response to this inadequacy theories related to the analysis and valuation of industrial securities slowly developed. The first comprehensive work on this subject was a 200-page book by Clinton Collver entitled <u>How to Analyze Industrial Securities</u> published by Moody's Investors Service in 1917. Discussed below are Collver's general recommendations in the area of financial and corporate disclosure. Later, in chapter seven, Collver's specific suggestions related to intelligent security analysis are outlined.

Collver, as a user of the financial data published by industrial concerns in prospectuses and annual reports was most dissatisfied with the current level of financial disclosure to investors. His chief complaints were two in number: an absence of "accepted standards of industrial accounting;"[1] and, all too often, financial statements were "noteworthy for what they omit or conceal rather than what they convey."[2] Hopefully, he said, the Federal Trade Commission's 32 question questionnaire discussed above would "be the prelude to a real Blue-Sky law such as the English Companies Acts."[3]

In addition, Collver believed, "it was reasonable to expect that uniform forms of accounting [would]

---

[1]Clinton Collver, <u>How To Analyze Industrial Securities</u>, 2nd edition (New York: Moody's Investors Service, 1919), pp. 206-208.

[2]<u>Ibid</u>., p. 70.

[3]<u>Ibid</u>., Preface.

eventually be provided for the different industrial lines as they have for railways."[1] Fortunately, he said, a few corporations seeking a more friendly public attitude toward them had voluntarily adopted new standards of publicity, but on the other hand, unfortunately, a policy of adequate publicity was far from universal. Regulations governing financial disclosure and the compulsory adoption of uniform forms of accounting, Collver said, would force the laggard corporations to publish more adequate financial data and make possible the "intelligent analysis of industrial corporation securities."[2]

In order to be able to analyze securities of any kind, Collver said, it was essential that complete, prompt and truthful reports of earnings and financial condition be available: "Without light we are in the dark and darkness in the financial world is the moral breach of trust of the use of 'inside information' possessed by the few---and the hopeless gambling of uninformed outsiders."[3] To obtain the necessary explicit and detailed information needed to analyze intelligently industrial securities Collver recommended

[1]*Ibid.*, p. 70.

[2]*Ibid.*, p. 2.

[3]*Ibid.*, p. 1.

the adoption by managements of the following balance sheet and supporting schedules:

<u>Assets</u>

Fixed or Capital Assets.
- Plant and Property, Schedule 1.
- Investments, Schedule 2.
- Treasury Stock at Par.
- Treasury Bonds at Par.
- Patents.
- Trademarks.
- Goodwill.

Working and Trading Assets.
- Inventories, Schedule 3.

Current Assets:
- Cash, Schedule 4.
- Securities, Schedule 5.
- Accounts Receivable.
- Accrued Interests on Bonds Owned.
- Dividends Declared on Stock Owned.
- Drafts and Notes Receivable.
- Interest Accrued on Drafts and Notes Receivable.
- Due from Subscribers to Capital Stock.
- Total Current Assets.

Sinking Fund for Bonds.
- Schedule 6.

Insurance Fund.
Pension Fund.
Deferred Assets, Schedule 7.

Total....................

<u>Capital, Liabilities and Surplus</u>

Capital Stock
- Preferred:
  - Authorized.
  - Less--Unissued.
  - Issued and Outstanding...
- Common:
  - Authorized...............
  - Less--Unissued.
  - Issued and Outstanding...
  - Capital Stock Subscribed.

First Mort. 5% bonds.
- Authorized.
  - Less--Unissued.
  - Issued and Outstanding...

Five year 6% Notes issued and outstanding...........
Current Liabilities........
- Taxes accrued.............
- Payroll Accrued...........
- Accounts Payable.
- Notes and Drafts Payable.
- Expenses Accrued.
- Interest Accrued on Notes and Drafts Payable.
- Dividends Payable.
- Interest Accrued on First Mort. Bonds.
- Interest Accrued on Five Year Notes................
- Total Current Liabilities.

Reserves. Schedule 7 [sic]
Profit and Loss Surplus.
Capital Surplus...........

Total.....................

Contingent Liabilities with particulars.

Schedules Supporting Balance Sheet

1. Plant and property;
   - Land and buildings.
   - Additions to buildings.
   - Plant equipment.
   - Horses, wagons and motors.
   - Furniture and fixtures.

2. Investments:
   - Securities owned: Names and amounts of stocks and bonds with dividend and interest yield, price paid and present market price.

3. Inventories:
   - Raw materials.
   - Manufacturing department.
   - Finished goods, manufacturing.
   - Finished goods, trading.
   - Shipping department.
   - Coal, oil and waste.
   - Stable and garage supplies.
   - Postage, stationary, etc.

4. Cash in hand and on deposit:
   - Cash in bank.
   - Impressed cash, and Expense fund.
   - Freight deposit.

5. Securities:
   - See Schedule No. 2.

6. Sinking Fund:
   - See Schedule No. 2.

7. Deferred charges to expense:
   - Discount on bonds.
   - Legal expense deferred.
   - Organization expense.
   - Insurance prepaid.
   - Rent paid in advance.
   - Taxes paid in advance.
   - Advertising.
   - Advances for subsidiaries:

8. Reserves for:
   - Depreciation, Buildings, Equipment, etc.
   - " Outside investments.
   - " Subsidiary securities.
   - " Treasury stock.
   - " Treasury bonds.
   - " Raw materials.

Depreciation, Current asset securities.
" Accounts and notes receivable.
" Sinking and other fund securities.
Extinguishment of assets.
Dividends.[1]

Income statements as currently presented to the public, Collver declared, were often of dubious value, open to misrepresentation, incomplete and lacked comparability between years and companies. In time, he said, the form of income statements in public reports would be regulated by some government agency. On the subject of income statements Collver made the following observations:

> In all commercial enterprises earnings are the final criterion of progress....Yet the skepticism of a 'Down East' horse trader must accompany the examination of even the most promising income account. No more than the balance sheet it is devoid of possibilities of misrepresentation and abuse.
>
> It is unfortunate that the lack of standardization prevents exact comparison of income accounts of different companies. In time, standards will be worked out, perhaps by the Federal Trade Commission, and enforced by special authority. Until some such action is taken accounts will only gradually approach any semblance of standardization....
>
> The best accountants...differ violently as to the form of the simplest Income Account and as to the very names of the items....
>
> Yet the Income Account is usually much easier of comprehension than the balance sheet, and assuming that the methods of accounting in individual corporations remain unchanged, the Income Accounts may be analyzed with some satisfaction....

---

[1]*Ibid.*, pp. 77-79.

> Income Accounts are usually lamentably incomplete and presented only in devitalized form. To the extent that they are lacking in definiteness and detail they are baffling to intelligent speculation and investment.

Obviously, Collver was not happy with the existing income reporting practices of management. The remedy he suggested was the adoption of the condensed comparative income statement tentatively proposed by Federal Reserve Board reproduced above.

The next person to be discussed, William Z. Ripley, was also concerned with management's practices related to accounting and financial reporting to investors. Like Collver, Ripley, in 1926, also saw the need for action related to corporate financial disclosure by the Federal Trade Commission and the passage of a federal law similar in intent to the British Companies Acts.

William Z. Ripley.

In 1926 there arose "quite a flutter in financial centers"[1] over an article, "Stop, Look, Listen!" published in the September issue of the *Atlantic Monthly*.[2]

---

[1]"Desirability of Publicity," *The Journal of Accountancy*, Vol. 44, No. 6, December 1927, p. 441.

[2]William Z. Ripley, "Stop, Look, Listen!" *The Atlantic Monthly*, Vol. 138, No. 3, September 1926, p. 380. Later, in 1927, this article was to form the basis of chapters six and seven of Ripley's book *Main Street and Wall Street*. These two chapters were titled--chapter six, "Light at the Crossways: Stop, Look, Listen;"and chapter seven, "Impublicity; What To Do About It." The reference to "light" and a later one in the book to "electric flood lights," are similar to the earlier analogy used by Brandeis.

In the article the author, Professor William Z. Ripley of Harvard University, after discussing a number of cases, some over 30 years old, where the right of the investor and shareholder to adequate information related to their corporations's financial condition had been abused, suggested as a remedy: "let the word go forth that the Federal Trade Commission is henceforward to address itself vigorously to the matter of adequate and intelligent corporate publicity, and taken in conjunction with the helpful agencies at work the thing is as good as done."[1] Hopefully, Ripley believed, the threat of government established and imposed uniform accounting method and disclosure standards for all public companies would frighten businessmen into giving to the state, general public and stockholders the adequate information on those corporate financial affairs to which Ripley believed such public groups were entitled. Ripley's article is further discussed for it was an important article for what it represented; what it said; and what was said about it.

---

[1] Ibid., p. 399. Ripley claimed the F.T.C. had the power to take such action under Section 6 of the original Federal Trade Commission law of 1914. The majority of the members of the commission said Ripley's suggestion was impractical and bordered on illegality. Two members of the commission, John F. Nugent and Huston Thompson, of whom more will be said later, did not share the majority's viewpoint--"Current Events and Discussions," The Commercial and Financial Chronicle, Vol. 123, No. 3192, August 28, 1926, p. 1051.

Before discussing why the shareholder and the public had a right to certain corporate data and the possible remedies for the abuses of this right, Ripley described the current reporting practice--both good and bad--of some major companies:

> On my table is a great pile of recent official corporated [sic] pamphlets. The premier concern on the list is the Royal Baking Powder Company, which fails to register in this collection at all, in as much as it has never issued a balance sheet or financial statement of any kind whatsoever for more than a quarter of a century.... despite a considerable distribution of the stock, which is fairly active both in the unlisted market and on the New York Curb.... Akin to it is the Singer Manufacturing Company, which handles 80% of the world's output of sewing machines. Neither hide nor hair of financial data is discoverable in the usual sources of information. The dance-card, balance-sheet, or picture-book variety of corporation report follows hard upon these. For concerns like the National Biscuit Company such newfangled gewgaws as income accounts or depreciation simply do not exist. American Can gives you depreciation, for 1925, but never a whiff concerning its accrual through past years. Diminutive, dainty, tied up with fancy strings, perhaps, these reports are tenderly reminiscent of the parties of our youth....Some, like the Gillette Safety Razor Company (counting almost 7,000 shareholders in 1925), are inviting pictorially, however, uninformative they may be.[1]

---

[1]In addition to the non reporting companies and the uninformative reports described above, a number of large companies such as American Woolen Company., California Packing Corporation and National Lead Company, rendered their reports to the public well after the close of the fiscal year.--N. Loyall McLaren, <u>Annual Reports to Stockholders</u> (New York: The Ronald Press, 1947), p. 6.

> This brings one to the truly informative type of official report, which fortunately, is coming more and more to be recognized as not only good form but the best of business as well. The United States Steel Corporation, now owned by 179,000 people, has from the outset achieved high merit in this regard. From the first annual statement, outspread over entire newspaper pages in 1903, down to the present time, its record has been consistently admirable. The General Motors Company, first in its industrial class the world over, is a worthy second. In has 56,000 shareholders.... These and other entirely adequate statements, full-figured, compact, and businesslike, used to be the exception, but it is greatly to be hoped that in the early future they may become the rule. How to bring this to pass is a matter of the utmost importance.[1]

Ripley believed it was necessary for the state, the public, employees and stockholders to receive adequate financial information on corporate affairs for a variety of reasons.

The first reason related to the previously discussed power of publicity as an "automatic" regulator of big business.

> ...of wider scope, is the bearing of complete corporate disclosure upon the so-called trust question. It is now a quarter century since the United States Industrial Commission put forward this remedy, first among a number of proposals for dealing with industrial combinations Little attention was paid at the time to the argument that such revelation of profits by concerns which threaten to oppress the public would operate almost automatically like a lowering of tariff barriers, to invite corrective competition....[2]

---

[1]Ripley, "Stop, Look, Listen!" pp. 382-385.

[2]Ripley, Main Street and Wall Street, p. 167.

The second reason pertained to the supposed need of employees to receive full corporate information. Such information, it was said, would improve the ability of employees to bargain with their employers.

> ...Publicity also is significant in connection with the legitimate activities and aspirations of those who work with their hands. Wage earners, whether interested as incipient capitalists or not, certainly feel as they become class-conscious that they have a right to know what is the relation of the return for the work of their hands to the rewards which accrue to the employer for employment of his brains....[1]

The third reason presented by Ripley was that those who advised stockholders needed more ample, honest and relevant information pertaining to corporate activity so as to better perform their important advisory function.

> ...such information, if rendered, will at all events serve as fair warning in case of impending danger. And this danger will be revealed, not because each shareholder, male or female, old or young, will bother to remove the wrapping from the annual report in the post, but because specialists, analysts, bankers, and others will promptly disseminate the information, translating it into terms intelligible to all.[2]

The fourth, and for Ripley perhaps the most important, reason for more adequate corporate disclosure was that the public security markets, which were auction

---

[1] *Ibid.*, p. 168.

[2] *Ibid.*, p. 169.

markets, could only operate effectively when all those who participated possessed identical and adequate information related to the securities being traded.

> ...Our great exchanges--and no little investor should ever own securities for which there is not a great open public market at all times--can perform their proper function of making true prices, consonant with valuation, only when there is such disclosure. This, then, is the ultimate defense of publicity. It is not as an adjunct to democratization through exercise of voting power, but as a contribution to the making of a true market price. This is a point but half appreciated at its real worth.[1]

Clearly, Ripley's main concern was the investor, of whom, he estimated there were "upward of 14,400,000" in 1923.[2]

Ripley went further than most popular writers on the subject of corporate financial disclosure: he pointed out some specific financial reporting abuses which arose because of the tolerance of "enigmatic" accounting practices by the public and the accounting profession. On the general state of reporting he observed:

> The two essentials of an adequate statement are the balance sheet and the income account....Of the two, the income account is perhaps the more significant, both immediately and prophetically. Yet of the two it is the income statement, as perhaps too informative, that is the more apt to be suppressed.[3]

---

[1]*Ibid.*, p. 170.

[2]*Ibid.*, p. 228.

[3]*Ibid.*, p. 171.

After making the above general observation, Ripley noted "at the threshold of intelligent corporate publicity stands a clear distinction between capital and income." From this assertion he went on to discuss some of the current accounting practices in such areas as depreciation and depletion, property valuation, consolidation, goodwill, surplus and no-par securities: all transactions where current abuses, he believed, could and did, confuse the distinction between capital and income. Other accounting practices Ripley objected to were sudden reversals in accounting policy to reveal past concealment of profits, deflation of liabilities as well as inflation of asset values to create "watered stock," and a failure to distinguish between fixed assets and "goods in trade." In reading this section of Ripley's work, no doubt, many a layman was introduced to the possibilities for "obfuscation" and "malfeasance" which existed thanks to the vagaries of accounting practice and theory.

Before presenting his remedy for the above abuses, Ripley discussed a number of the possible ways of achieving reform through a number of private and public agencies: the New York Stock Exchange; shareholder groups; and blue sky laws. The New York Stock Exchange through its stock list requirements was, Ripley said, "the leading influence in the promotion of adequate corporate disclosure the world over."[1] There were several limitations, however, to the New York Stock Exchange's influence. The first limitation Ripley saw was that the Exchange's control was restricted to only those corporations which sought to list securities with the Exchange. Another limitation was that the unlisted securities handled on the Curb and securities listed on the "provincial exchanges"--Chicago, Boston, Pittsburgh--were not only beyond New York's control but also subject to less rigorous requirements so as to attract "local lesser corporations, more closely controlled and less susceptible to educational appeal"[2]--the very corporations where the most need for improved financial reporting existed.[3]

---

[1]*Ibid.*, p. 210.

[2]*Ibid.*, p. 212.

[3]Earlier Ripley said:
"To a considerable degree within each industry it is a case of all or nothing. The laggard corporation, persistent in secretiveness, lays a heavy penalty upon its progressive rivals all down the line. This does not apply among public utilities, for they are industrial monopolies, more or less. But in the domain of private competitive enterprise it is only the all-powerful factor in the business, conscious of its own worth and importance,-like the Steel Corporation or the General Motors Company,-which can throw reserve to the winds, making a full disclosure of everything. In certain industries, also--the chain stores for instance--where profits are derived from a multitude of transactions in different commodities, the embarrassment of disclosure is less important. Profits of all kinds of things are averaged into a general figure, not disclosed for particular products. Competition, in other words, is much generalized. But let rivalry within an industry narrow down to two or three big competitors and it takes a hardy perennial to stand the wind and weather of publicity alone.--*Ibid.*, pp. 208-209.

Curiously, Ripley noted, a number of corporations gave the New York Stock Exchange more complete descriptions of their activities than they supply to their stockholders. Often, this practice, Ripley thought, was not done intentionally to deceive: "It springs from the impression among managements that public reports are not matters of prime importance."[1] Fortunately, this view, he said, was changing as the result of the education of public opinion as to the value of financial data.

Ripley posed the rhetorical questions: "Why should not the stockholders themselves, if necessary, bring about a reform in this business of publicity? Do they rest meek and mute because of their helplessness?"[2] Two possible courses of action, he suggested, which were open to stockholders were: investors either boycott the securities of the "sealed-up corporation"; or "force the issue in open annual stockholders meetings." However, both actions, he believed, were impractical since there were always people willing to speculate in the "mysterious corporations," and it was an expensive business for independent stockholders to effectively challenge management at annual meetings.

---

[1] *Ibid.*, p. 211.

[2] *Ibid.*, p. 396.

What stockholders ought to do, Ripley said, and do "right speedily too, either by private initiative or by induced legislation, is the introduction of shareholders' audit or of general checkup committees."[1] Such independent audit reports to shareholders, he observed, were already mandatory in Great Britain and Germany.

Another activity Ripley commended to shareholders, in the area of "checkup, revision, or supervision" of corporate management, had to do with the valuation of assets shown on the balance sheet. Too often, Ripley said, these valuations, either in prospectuses or annual reports, were made up by persons dependent on management for their income and advancement. In fact, in practice, Ripley observed, there were many cases of "downright deception in this regard."[2] Independent valuations, he said, were not only essential to avoid misrepresentation but were the right of shareholders.

The blue sky laws, which were directed at the prevention of fraud and possible mismanagement, Ripley claimed, failed entirely to deal with the most weighty aspect of the matter of shareholders' rights:

> Must one reiterate that the prevention of fraud, while important, is limited to a few companies, while the registration of a fair market price, consonant with the real earning power of the company, is a matter of daily and universal importance to every shareholder

---

[1]Ibid., p. 396.

[2]At this time a number of companies were revaluing, usually upwards, their assets.

> who may have occasion to buy or to sell securities? This instance is worth citing just to drive home the main defense of the proposed reform.[1]

State legislation designed solely to prevent fraud was inadequate, and the possibility of state action to stimulate or enforce publicity, he concluded, held little promise.

Thus, according to Ripley, the New York Stock Exchange's role was limited; the promise of effective stockholders' action difficult to achieve; and the possibility of adequate state regulation was doubtful. Ripley's remedy, as previously stated, was the threat of genuine Federal Trade Commission action in the area of corporate disclosure so as to force corporations into adopting the better financial disclosure standards for prospectuses and annual reports recommended by such private agencies as the Investment Bankers Association of America and the New York Stock Exchange. If, in the face of threatened Federal Trade Commission regulation, corporate managers failed to achieve self-regulation then government regulation of corporate disclosure practices would be necessary.

At the time Professor Ripley's article was published, it was widely discussed in a number of publications including the <u>Commercial and Financial Chronicle</u>, <u>Financial</u>

---

[1] <u>Ibid</u>., p. 219.

World, The Magazine of Wall Street, and the Journal of Accountancy by editors, corporate executives and others. In general, those associated with business and finance who commented upon Ripley's work, while agreeing with his belief that corporate financial reporting was inadequate, said his suggested remedy was too drastic. In fact, one financial editor predicted Ripley's remedy would lead to socialism.[1] Reproduced below are a sample of these comments on Ripley's article.

An editorial in The Magazine of Wall Street said of Ripley's proposals:

> In recent years we have repudiated the theory of more Government in Business....As to the protection of investors' rights, we believe our long fight in behalf of their interest entitles our views to some consideration. We believe in the efficacy of education, not only of the shareholder but the business executive...we believe that the general trend is already in the proper direction. The old business "principle" of misleading the investor through incomplete reports is gradually losing favor among the better class of corporation heads. In the final analysis, it is the business of the shareholders to demand whatever information they deem necessary as to the position of their companies.[2]

This editorial was representative of an emerging new point of view which was popular among the editors

---

[1]William Baker Flowers, Criteria for Disclosure of Post-Statement Events (Austin: Bureau of Business Research The University of Texas, 1960), p. 15.

[2]The Magazine of Wall Street, Vol. XXVIII, September 11, 1926, p. 923.

of financial journals: any necessary reform in the area of corporate publicity ought to come from stockholder action---a possibility Ripley had labelled as impractical.

The editors of The New Republic, a magazine which reflected the liberal sentiment, said of Ripley's article:

> Professor William Z. Ripley gallantly returns to the attack...demanding adequate accounting standards and full publicity enforced by the Federal Trade Commission... he had no difficulty in pointing out a variety of shortcomings in the practices of many large concerns whose stock is widely distributed.
>
> It is, however, a little difficult to get excited over so obvious a reform whose object seems to be the protection of the absentee owner...good information is the requisite before anything further, and we are strong for it.[1]

Subsequently, The New Republic's editorial said Ripley's demand for "uniform Federal standards of accounting" was a valid government function since "one of first duties of government" was the maintenance of standards and publicity. State legislation in this area, the editorial claimed, was "bound to be scattering, dilatory and diverse, and to advocate it is in effect to oppose any adequate legislation."[2]

---

[1] "The Week," The New Republic, Vol. XLVIII, No. 614, September 8, 1926, pp. 54-55.

[2] Ibid., p. 55.

The long-time editor of The Journal of Accountancy, A. P. Richardson, praised Ripley's article as being "a valuable contribution to a subject of great importance,"---information for shareholders. However, Richardson believed Ripley's suggested remedy---intervention by the Federal Trade Commission---was not a useful one: "We have enough bureaucracy now." The "true" remedy, Richardson said, was to be found in the extension of the audit by competent independent auditors through "private initiative and judicious pressure from such bodies as the New York Stock Exchange which only recently had set seriously about the task of protecting the investing public which deals in securities which it lists."[1] Richardson, like the Magazine of Wall Street's editorial quoted above, saw reform stemming from the efforts of private sources, which in Richardson's case meant private institutions and associations other than individual stockholders.

On August 28, 1926, the editorial of The Commercial and Financial Chronicle had this to say:

> Professor Ripley has contributed another important discussion on corporate practices. He complains of the inadequacy of many corporation reports, pointing out that the public...

---

[1]"Information for Shareholder," The Journal of Accountancy, Vol. 42, No. 4, October 1926, p. 281.

> has a right to know the facts as fully and as correctly as they can be presented. He is undoubtedly right in this respect...the heavy selling which news of this article[1] occasioned followed, no doubt, from the suggestion that the Federal Trade Commission be called upon to function in respect to industrial corporation accounting as the Interstate Commerce Commission has been functioning with reference to railroad accounting. The full and uniform statements now provided by the railroad companies are of inestimable value and appreciated by stockholders and bankers....
>
> It is a real question whether the stock exchanges cannot serve the public better in this way than can the Federal Government.... We are inclined to think the remedy lies with the shareholder who by collective action can bring pressure to bear upon directors unmindful of their duties in that respect.[2]

Later, the September 4, 1926 issue of The Commercial and Financial Chronicle reported: "President Coolidge Inclined to View That State Rather Than Federal Authority Should Govern Publicity of Financial Operation of Corporations." The President, it was said, was in full sympathy with Ripley's suggestions

---

[1]Earlier this particular editorial had noted: "On Tuesday morning [8/24/26] the market was bouyant....Before the day was over, however, there was a veritable deluge of selling and sentiment seemed completely turned....[as the result of the] news of an article on corporation practices by Professor Ripley of Harvard. Apparently, advance copies of the "Atlantic Monthly" for September were available on Tuesday, whereas delivery to the public was not made until Thursday."

[2]"The Financial Situation." The Commercial and Financial Chronicle, Vol. 123, No. 3192, August 28, 1926, pp. 1013-1014.

related to the need for corporations to supply more complete and accurate financial data. Since, however, corporations received their charters from the states, Coolidge held, "off hand," the remedy rested with the states. The President indicated he had been considering the reporting practices of corporations for "a long time" and that he desired to protect the interests of the "20 million or more stockholders in American business concerns in every way that was legally possible."[1]

Others who commented on Ripley's article included George O. May, partner, Price Waterhouse; E. T. Bedford, chairmain of the board, Corn Products Refining Co.; and Samuel Untermeyer, the former counsel for the Pujo Committee. May agreed with Ripley's objectives; quarreled with his evidence; and suggested true investor protection would be derived not from more disclosure _per se_, but disclosure based on an independent audit.[2] Bedford declared corporation executives and directors should "cordially endorse" Ripley"s suggestions related to the need for the publication, compulsory if necessary, of more comprehensive financial data. Earnings and financial statements, Bedford said, should be published

---

[1]"Current Events and Discussions," _The Commercial and Financial Chronicle_, Vol. 123, No. 3193, September 4, 1926, pp. 1200-1201.

[2]_Ibid._, p. 1201.

in comparative form at quarterly intervals.[1] According to Untermeyer, the Federal Trade Commission was "plainly the agency" through which compulsory "complete publicity of corporate affairs should be enforced for the protection of investors." The government, Untermeyer said, could exert the same control over the great industrial corporations as it did then over the railroads. The only obstacle to such control, he said, was "the overshadowing political power over legislation of these vast aggregations of capital."[2]

The public furor created by Ripley's article soon subsided. Richardson, one year after "Stop, Look, Listen" was published, observed:

> A little more than a year ago there was quite a flutter in the financial centers about some rather startling allegations to the effect that the public was being grossly deceived by the published accounts of corporations whose securities were the media of common investment. These stories were not all well-founded, but there was a sufficient amount of truth underlying the general criticism to arouse the people who have money to invest and also the exchanges, the bankers and brokers. As America is today the richest nation in the world and as its wealth is more widely distributed than the wealth of any other country, it naturally follows that the investing public is a very substantial percentage of the nation as a whole. What stirs the investor, therefore, stirs the whole

---

[1] *Ibid.*, p. 1202.

[2] *Ibid.*, pp. 1202-1203.

> people directly or indirectly. For a few months there was reason to believe that we were to have a great reform. Accountants seized the opportunity to write and speak for the cause of frank publicity. Exchanges professed a zeal for the work of improving conditions. Everyone who had anything to do with money or the sale of money was filled with enthusiasm---a kind of religious fervor swept over us. But a year has gone by. The conditions are not changed. There is little more frankness than there was. It begins to appear that the effect of the revival is, like the effect of many noble plans, almost exactly nil. Most of us have forgotten that the banner of the crusade was ever raised. We have stopped at Stamboul....
>
> What is before us is the sad and astonishing failure of the public to insist upon reform when the need for reform has not only been revealed but acclaimed. Truly, the American public is a marvellous entity. It is not physically inert or even lazy, but at times it does appear to be extraordinarily apathetic. The oldest observer of Wall Street would not have believed that within a year from the excitement which followed the call for facts the whole incident would have passed without action and have been forgotten. Perhaps the bull market which ran so long a course made people lose sight of everything else. If there had been a falling market, a shortage of money, a psychological or an actual depression in business, people would have had more time to devote to reform. No one longs for a dull market, but it may have its advantages.[1]

In 1927, to people such as Richardson, the effect of Ripley's article may well have appeared to be "almost exactly nil." As subsequent events were to show, however, Ripley's revelations and recommendations in the area of financial accounting and his call for

---

[1]"The Desirability of Publicity," The Journal of Accountancy, Vol. 44, No. 6, December 1927, pp. 441-443.

government action greatly influenced a number of those who were to support, advocate, and draw up the Securities Act of 1933.

Corporate Executives

During much of the period 1918-1929, in the absence of hostile government investigations and political attack, corporate executives were silent on the subject of financial disclosure. In fact, it was not till 1926 when, under pressure from the Ripley article, that a number of businessmen spoke on the subject of corporate publicity. These statements and a number of the previously mentioned observations on this matter by those external to the firm are briefly discussed below.

In general, corporate executives in reply to Ripley's attack, perhaps under the influence of their own public relations departments, publicly displayed a milder and more sympathetic attitude than had their predecessors during the 1900-1917 period toward the demands for improved financial disclosure. In fact, as already noted, those businessmen who commented on Ripley's article almost universally agreed there was a need for improved standards of financial reporting. Their only quarrel was with Ripley's proposed remedy.

Other indications of a change in the attitude of businessmen toward financial disclosure included May's statement which recognized the widespread adoption by industrial firms for public reporting purposes of independent balance sheet audits; and Ripley's praise for the several large corporations which issued satisfactory annual reports. In addition, the partial success of the New York Stock Exchange in increasing the frequency with which listed companies reported to their stockholders the firm's operating results and financial condition also indicated some improvement in corporate reporting practices.

In contrast to the above evidence, which would indicate a change in the attitude of corporate executives toward financial disclosure, the following observations of non-businessmen would indicate otherwise. For instance, William B. Campbell, a previously mentioned accountant, said business executives were reluctant to adopt for public reporting purposes the Federal Reserve Board's recommended financial statements for fear of providing competitors with vital information. A number of executives, according to Richard Whitney of the New York Stock Exchange, complained that the Exchange's publicity recommendations were "arbitrary and unreasonable." And the interim report of the Industrial Securities Committee noted "the best companies often objected to furnishing full information to go beyond the eyes of bankers."

In addition, the above mentioned William Z. Ripley, beside praising the financial publicity practices of several corporations, also listed a number of cases of non-reporting, non-disclosure and misrepresentation by corporate officers in the area of financial reporting. Often, he said, the failure to provide the investor with sufficient information to make intelligent investment decisions sprang "from the impression among managements that public reports are not matters of prime importance." In fact, Ripley observed, it would appear as if the laggard corporations in each industry, especially in oligopoly situations, dictated the level of financial disclosure achieved in that industry.

The reports of the above observers, who for the most part dealt with businessmen in their daily work, strongly suggest that a number of corporate executives were not yet ready to recognize the right of the public to receive truly informative and reliable financial reports. While the tone of the businessman's response to the demands for fuller publicity of corporate affairs had changed, their reluctance to accept these proposals still persisted.

*****

During the period 1918-1929, a number of things related to the corporate publicity issue occurred. In general, the American nation experienced prosperity and politically, morally and ethically, the vast majority of the public were in reaction against the crusades of the progressive era. However, some people such as Ripley, continued in the progressive mood, but their ideas were not widely accepted. The critics of big business, however, embraced the cause of the investor and recommended for his protection federal action to promote more reliable corporate accounting and reporting practices.

A number of professional and commercial groups closely associated with corporate activities, for a variety of reasons, formulated minimum standards of financial disclosure for prospectus, annual report and credit purposes. Few of these standards, it would seem, were adopted. Businessmen publicly proclaimed the need for improved financial disclosure standards but there was also much testimony which indicated the fundamental attitude of corporate executives toward financial disclosure remained unchanged.

On the federal level no legislation, designed either to protect investors from fraud or to make compulsory full and fair disclosure of corporate financial information, was enacted. However, by 1930 on the state level nearly all of the states had passed blue sky laws. But either through poor administration or the inherent inadequacy of state regulation in an interstate economy these laws had failed to protect the investor from fraudulent and unsound promotions. And overseas, in England, the British Parliament in their 1928 Companies Act once again reaffirmed their confidence in the philosophy of disclosure as expressed in the Companies Act of 1900.

The next chapter---chapter seven---will discuss the impact of the events, trends and attitudes outlined in the previous six chapters on the disclosure standards of management as revealed in prospectuses between 1900 and 1930.

CHAPTER SEVEN

PROSPECTUS DISCLOSURE PRACTICES 1900-1930

Between 1900 and 1930, despite the many demands discussed previously for more adequate corporate publicity--financial and general--the content and character of prospectuses offering industrial securities lagged, just as did annual report disclosure, far behind the demands for improved corporate disclosure practices. In fact, after 1918, the form of the prospectus in its most important respects remained unchanged.

In general, the prospectuses issued during much of this period consisted of four or fewer pages of written material and were either the representation of the investment banker marketing the issue or an officer of the corporation issuing the securities--the latter type being of particular interest to this study. After 1918, most prospectuses, irrespective of whether the issue was underwritten or not, were presented as being principally the representations of management. The first or title page of such prospectuses, which I have labelled "management prospectuses,"[1] customarily presented the following:

[1]In contrast to "banker's prospectuses" which were the representations of the investment banking firm marketing the securities.

DOI: 10.4324/9781003169420-7

a general description of the type of security offered; a summary prepared by an officer of the issuing corporation showing the important facts outlined in the subsequent pages; information related to the legality of the issue; subscription dates and terms; and the names of the principal underwriting firms.

Usually, the remainder of the management circular showed a copy of the letter signed by an officer of the corporation issuing the securities and addressed to the managers of the investment banking syndicate marketing the offering. This letter, the so-called president's letter, elaborated upon the summary shown on the title page and touched on such subjects as management, history of the firm, earnings, dividends, etc. Often, if testimony of an "expert," such as accountants or an engineer, was directly incorporated in the body of the prospectus his statements or certificate were placed at the end of the prospectus and below the president's letter.

In addition, from about 1914 onwards, nearly all prospectuses carried the so-called disclaimer clause which, in effect, said the investment bankers handling the offering could not guarantee the reliability of the information presented therein.

Discussed below are the following topics: the

form and content of prospectuses; the role of the prospectus and the information needs of investors; the utility to the investor and the reliability of the information, particularly financial data, contained in prospectuses; and, finally, the responsibility for the content of prospectuses.

The Content of Prospectuses[1]

Between 1900 and 1930, a number of different forms of written communication were used to offer industrial and other securities to investors. These many types can be placed, according to the degree of disclosure, into three general categories: full prospectuses, abridged prospectuses and circulars.[2] In general, the full prospectuses and, to some degree, the abridged prospectuses were intended to provide the investor with sufficient information to form an appraisal of the offered securities. The circular, in most cases, was issued by the investment banker solely to advertise the issue.

---

[1]Wherever possible I have attempted to substantiate my own observations by referring to contemporary descriptions of prospectus disclosure practices.

[2]See Introduction for discussion of these three classes. These class names are used throughout chapter seven in order to clearly show the different levels of disclosure and the uses of the different types of documents offering securities to the public. In other chapters, the term "prospectus" is used in its general sense.

The "full prospectus", the use of which for industrial securities, first became prevalent about 1914, customarily consisted of four pages (quarto or legal size) and provided, of the three classes, the fullest disclosure. Usually it presented most of the following information: the number, price and type of security offered, and any restrictions related to the issue; the names of the issuing corporation, transfer agents, registrars and principal underwriters; a brief history of the firm and a short description of its properties and management; a statement, often in a narrative form, covering the corporation's operative results, financial position and dividend record or policy; the purpose of the issue; and some general remarks by an officer of the issuing corporation as to its future prospects. Typically, this type of document was most often used to offer simple industrial and utility securities, particularly when a corporation was makings its initial public offering. As a company became more well known the investmeht banker and the issuer might use one of the more abbreviated forms discussed below to offer subsequent issues.

The "abridged prospectus,"[1] which was used

---

[1]Not to be confused with the "abridged prospectus" described in the British Companies Act.

throughout the 30-year period usually took one of two forms. One type, which was used more often after 1918, consisted of a single legal size sheet showing on one side material similar to that presented on the title page of the full prospectus[1] and, on the reverse side, perhaps a balance sheet. This form of offering document was designed to serve two functions: inform and advertise.

Another form the abridgedprospectus took was to present, in a format similar to the full prospectuses, only that information which was relevant to the position in the issuer's capital structure of the security offered. For instance, if first mortgage bonds were offered, detailed information pertaining to the terms, covenants and provisions of the mortgage instrument and the assets so encumbered would be presented. Little information, however, would be given on such topics as management, dividend policy, history, and capitalization junior to the offered securities. And, in general, financial data sufficient only to suggest the security was amply protected by assets and by earnings was presented. The theory behind such disclosure for debt issues was that "the junior issues are of little concern to the buyer--

---

[1]See p. 297.

an assumption which is more or less true, but probably less true than is generally believed."[1] The second class of abridged prospectuses was most frequently used "in connection with railway financing, notably prior mortgage bonds, equipment trust certificates, and the like."[2]

The third general category--"circulars"[3]--were of two kinds and were used most frequently before 1910. First, there was the type which presented on a single sheet only the names of the issuer and the underwriter; the number, type and price of the securities offered; plus a few of the issue's strongest selling points. Sometimes, comments by the banker as to the securities' safety or speculative value were also included. Frequently, these circulars were reproduced in newspapers as a form of advertising to alert the public to the availability of the issue.

A second type of circular occasionally used showed little more than a description of the security's rights and the names of the underwriter and

---

[1]Berle and Means, op. cit., p. 302. Berle and Means on the basis of their analysis of prospectuses and circulars, believed "three rough classifications" were discernible. Their three classes approximate my "full prospectus" category and the second forms discussed under the "abridged prospectus" and "circular" labels.

[2]Ibid.

[3]Not to be confused with the term "banker's circulars."

issuer. The use most often made of the particular short form method was in floating the complex securities of public utility companies. It was not a persuasive method and could only be employed by corporations well known to the market.[1]

Written communications related to security offering falling into the three general classes outlined above appeared throughout the period 1900-1930. During the early years of this 30-year span the circular form was perhaps used more frequently than the other two types for at least three reasons: the railroads which offered the bulk of the securities at this time were well known to investors; the managements of the few industrial corporations which did make public offerings were reluctant to reveal their firm's "private" affairs; and investors, in general, bought securities on the basis of the investment banker's recommendation. In addition, banker-client relations at this time were close and the number of investors small. Therefore, once the investor had been alerted to the existence of a particular issue should he have required more information the banker could easily supply, if it were available, the needed data.

Later, as more and more securities of industrial

---

[1] *Ibid.*

and utility companies became available for the first time, the abridged prospectus and the full prospectus became more prevalent for at least three reasons: the more detailed prospectus was needed to introduce the increasing number of unfamiliar industrial and utility corporations to investors; the collapse of some of the giant corporations created in the "halcyon days of careless finance," such as National Cordage Company, National Asphalt Company and the United States Shipbuilding Company, had shaken investor confidence in the ability of bankers to recommend safe investments; and as the number of investors increased the close banker-client relationship of earlier years became too difficult and costly to maintain.

By 1930, depending on the stage of the offering, the size of the issue, the attitude of the officers of the issuing corporation toward disclosure and the selling problems of the banker, any one or all of these three major types of written communication might be used to make a particular offering. Since, however, the full prospectus typically reproduced the complete text of the "president's letter"[1] and

---

[1]Often after (say) 1918 the material reproduced in abridged prospectuses and circulars was clearly labelled as having been taken from the original president's letter.

(by definition) present the fullest disclosure, the bulk of the remainder of chapter seven will be concerned with the disclosure standards of management as revealed in full prospectuses offering industrial securities.

The Development and Content of Industrial Prospectuses

The development of the form and content of the full prospectus fell roughly into two periods: 1900-1917; and 1918-1930. In 1900, most industrial securities were introduced to the market through investment bankers. Typically, the underwriter notified his customers of the availability of such issues by means of a sales letter which we would classify as a type of circular. Subsequently, between 1900 and about 1917, for a variety of reasons, the use of the form of prospectus which incorporated the president's letter gradually became more frequent;[1] the amount of information disclosed increased; and the prospectus became longer. Prior to 1917, however, a great variety and range of different types of circulars and prospectuses were used and the degree of management disclosure revealed therein varied greatly. But between 1914 and 1917 the format of the full prospectus was finally established. Later,

---

[1]Earlier, it had been used often in railroad promotions.

after 1918, of the three general classes, the full prospectus was the most frequently used and its format became more standardized.

About 1900, circulars were customarily used by investment bankers to offer industrial securities to the public. In line with the current accepted theories of investment, which will be discussed later, these circulars presented some brief information related to the issue's capitalization; dividends; price; and interest and dividend coverage. Reproduced below is a representative circular offering a new issue of industrial common stock to the public:

Washburn & Moen Manufacturing Company.

TWELVE PER CENT. STOCK.

Free of taxes in Massachusetts.

Dividends payable quarterly, January, April, July, and October.

This Company has lately increased its capital from $2,000,000 to $2,500,000.

For the last twenty years it has paid dividends averaging 12 per cent. on its capital stock.

WE OFFER, subject to sale or advance in price,—500 shares, at $200 per share, at which price it will net the investor 6 per cent.

KIDDER, PEABODY & CO.,

113 Devonshire Street,

Boston, Mass.

Boston, July 9, 1892.

The above circular speaks for itself--to say what it did not contain would take far too many pages. Seldom was more information provided the investor, and it was generally claimed by investment bankers and corporate executives that there was, as noted above, no need to present more. Bankers, it was said, always thoroughly examined before offering to the public the security and the issuing corporation. If the banker offering the security had a "good" reputation, ipso facto the investment was safe. Anyway, how was a banker to provide more information when corporate executives said the investor had no right to ask for more information: caveat emptor governed such transactions.

Initially, circulars such as the above were used at this time to offer industrial securities for at least three reasons. First, the belief that bankers fully investigated security offerings and then only offered the "safe" securities removed much of the need for full disclosure.[1] Second, the unwillingness

---

[1]Later, the banker's scrutiny of security offerings became less rigorous when, in order to create new securities, a number of investment bankers promoted mergers, combinations and new enterprises. And, just as the New York Stock Exchange lowered its standards to list industrials, so did a number of investment bankers lower their fiduciary standards so that they, rather than competitors, might underwrite the securities of these newly formed industrial concerns. A number of these enterprises subsequently, for a variety of reasons, underwent one or more reorganizations.

of corporate managers to disclose their corporation's affairs to bankers, stockholders and investors.[1] And, third, the absence of statutory regulations compelling full disclosure.

From 1900 to about 1917, the fundamentals of disclosure which were to distinguish the full prospectus from other types of written communication offering securities were slowly developed. By 1914, the use of the full prospectus to offer industrial

---

[1]In retrospect, the cynic might say it was not difficult to understand why a number of the newly formed industrial corporations wished to keep secret their financial condition and operating results. In general these concerns were the results of the merger of a number of smaller companies not all of which had been profitable before the merger. To combine these companies the promoters and the owners of the merging companies were issued stock, usually far in excess of the combined book value or the sum of the capitalization of the earnings of the constituent companies. The "water" created in the capitalization of the new corporation was justified, it was argued, through the capitalization of the increased earnings which the new company would make thanks to the cost savings resulting from the merger. Unfortunately, as Mr. Havemeyer's testimony indicated, those savings were not always realized. Under these conditions "blind pools" through which "insiders" could run the price of the securities up and down as desired would be preferable to having the public know the true state of affairs. After all, if the promoter and sellers of the merged companies were to realize a profit on the merger it was necessary that they liquidate their securities at as high a price as possible. Thus, the cynic might argue the "caveat emptor," "competitor" and the "private business" arguments were but camouflage to hide the "true" reason for "secrecy."

securities was far from universal.[1] However, from 1914 to 1917, the tendency of industrial offering to make use of the full prospectus form accelerated.

The evolution during the period 1900 to 1917 of the full prospectus, which presented a little more information than earlier prospectus forms, was caused by a number of the factors previous discussed. Namely, the demands for more information related to corporate activities from the government, critics of big business and the New York Stock Exchange; the increasing number of "unknown" industrial and utility companies offering securities to the public for the first time; and the increase in the number of stockholders not closely involved with the management of their corporations. Other previously mentioned factors included "blue sky commissioner's" requirements for the filing of particular information; the increasing pressure upon businessmen from bankers, accountants and federal authorities to adopt balance sheet audits for credit purposes; the use of nationwide underwriting syndicates for distribution of stock; and the growing need to present more information so that the investor

---

[1]If one was to graph the frequency of full prospectus versus forms showing less information used during this period the peak of the frequency distribution, assuming the origin represented no disclosure, would be well to the left of the full prospectus point on the x axis.

could better distinguish between fraudulent and legitimate investment proposals. The declining investor confidence in the ability of the investment banker to select only "safe" investments for public distribution; the passing away of the "rugged individualist" type of management such as Havemeyer represented; and the need of industrial enterprises for increasingly greater amounts of outside capital--all forced management to adopt, perhaps reluctantly, the practice of disclosing slightly more corporate financial information both for prospectus and annual report purposes.

In the area of prospectus disclosure a number of these above factors also led to a desire on the part of the investment banker to provide investors with a little more information so that the offering could be sold more quickly as well as to escape from the responsibility for such data disclosed. Discussed below is the type of prospectus--the full prospectus--which was developed by corporate executives and investment bankers in response to these many factors.

Before 1918

Full prospectuses issued before 1918 took one of either two basic forms which I have labelled "banker's prospectus" and "management prospectuses."[1]

---

[1]See Introduction for definitions of these terms.

It was the latter type, especially after 1914, which was eventually to prove to be the more popular form.

Prior to 1914, in addition to circulars, investment bankers from time to time issued more complete prospectuses which were the representations of the banker and those "experts" hired by him to examine the issue and issuer. Typically, the banker's prospectus offering industrial securities covered several pages and touched on such matters as the form of the security; its provisions and restrictions; the names of the transfer agents; the purpose of the issue; a description of the issuer's properties; a schedule setting forth the issuer's capitalization. Other items shown were: the payment schedule, allotment data, preference order and similar matters related to the handling of the offerings; the issuer's actual net profit figure for several years or an average profit figure for say, the last five years; a list of the issuer's officers and the location of the issuer's principal plants; and if available, statements related to the issue by the legal firm, auditors, and engineers hired by the banker to examine the issue. The intention behind such a prospectus was to assure the investor that the industrial security so offered was indeed "safe";

the testimony of the counsel, auditor and engineer added weight to the banker's recommendation. Reproduced below is a copy of a "typical" banker's prospectus issued before 1918.

KIDDER, PEABODY & CO.,

BOSTON, MASS.,

OFFER FOR SUBSCRIPTION:—

$1,000,000 First Mortgage 5 Per Cent. 20 Years Gold Bonds,
Subject to call at 110 and interest.

$1,000,000 7 Per Cent. Cumulative Stock, preferred as to principal and dividends,
Subject to call at 125%.

$1,000,000 Class "A" Common Stock, entitled for 5 Years to 8 Per Cent. dividends each year, cumulatively, before any dividend payments to Class "B."

OF

The Torrington Company

(Incorporated under the laws of the State of Maine),

on the following terms:—

The securities are offered severally for public subscription at par.

The payments for each class of security will be as follows:—

5 % on application.
45 % on allotment.
50 % on October 15.
100 %

Payment in full may be made under discount at the rate of 4 % per annum.

The subscription lists will be opened on Thursday, September 1, and will be closed on or before Saturday, September 3, 1898.

The right is reserved to reject or reduce the amount of any subscription.

Negotiable certificates will be issued upon allotment, and bonds and certificates of stock will be delivered as soon as received from the Company.

Total capitalization of the Company issued and outstanding:—

$1,000,000	First Mortgage 5 % Bonds.
1,000,000	7 % Preferred Stock.
1,000,000	Common Stock, Class "A."
1,000,000	" " " "B."

The First Mortgage Bonds dated September 1, 1898, and due September 1, 1918, interest payable March 1 and September 1, are issued in coupon form, in $1,000 pieces. Principal may be registered, if desired. Principal and interest payable in gold coin of the United States of the present standard of weight and fineness.

The par value of the shares, both common and preferred, is twenty-five dollars ($25), there being 40,000 shares each of preferred, Class "A," and Class "B" common.

Application will be made at once to have these securities listed on the Boston Stock Exchange.

Trustee of the Bonds and Registrar of the Stocks,

THE NEW ENGLAND TRUST COMPANY OF BOSTON.

Transfer Agents,

Messrs. KIDDER, PEABODY & CO., OF BOSTON.

Counsel in formation of the Company,

Messrs. GASTON & SNOW, OF BOSTON.

This Company has been formed for the purpose of acquiring and carrying on the business of the Excelsior Needle Company of Connecticut, which has been in business since 1866. It will own directly and through ownership of the shares of subordinate companies the factory and plant at Torrington, Connecticut, where are manufactured sewing-machine and knitting-machine needles, and also bicycle spokes and nipples and swaging machinery; also the factory at Springfield, Massachusetts, where are manufactured needles; and the needle factory in Redditch, England; also a considerable investment in store supplies in Boston, New York, Philadelphia, Chicago, and London, England, and in its bicycle spoke factory in Leicester, England. The officers of the old Company inform us that it produces a large majority of all the sewing-machine needles and bicycle spokes and nipples produced in this country. The new Company acquires all the old Company, free of all incumbrances, and will start with no outstanding liabilities except the above mentioned bonds and with about $175,000 cash on hand, beside cash assets.

The books of the old Company have been examined by Messrs. Deloitte, Devers, Griffiths & Co., chartered accountants of London and New York, who report as follows:

69 WALL STREET, NEW YORK, N.Y., August 26th, 1898.

Messrs. KIDDER, PEABODY & Co.,
Boston, Mass.

GENTLEMEN:

We have examined the accounts of the Excelsior Needle Company, Torrington, Conn., the National Needle Company, Springfield, Mass., and A. H. Smith & Co., New Haven, Conn., for the three years ended 30th June, 1898, and we find the total profits for the three Companies, before charging any depreciation and interest on capital, to be as follows:—

Year ended 30th June, 1896,	$480,074.31
Year ended 30th June, 1897,	398,640.60
Year ended 30th June, 1898,	465,725.87

These profits are arrived at after including the result of the transactions of the business in England and the various Agencies in the United States.

In the profits for the year ended 30th June, 1898, there is included an amount of $71,912.65, derived from the sale of patent rights in Germany.

We are assured that all depreciation is covered by the charges to Operating Expenses for renewals and repairs, and, from the character of the machinery and plant, we believe this to be the case.

Very truly yours,

DELOITTE, DEVER, GRIFFITHS & CO.

These profits, averaging over $400,000 per annum, will leave a handsome surplus after paying 5% on bonds, 7% on the preferred stock, and 8% on both classes of common stock.

The new Company has arranged to continue for a period of years the present management, and some of the former Directors will be Directors of the new Company.

BOSTON, August 27, 1898.

The financial data presented in banker's prospectuses, as in the case of the circular, was meager. In addition, the financial data shown in management prospectuses issued prior to 1918 was similar to that presented in bankers prospectuses. Discussed below are three important aspects of financial disclosure typically touched on in such prospectuses: capitalization; balance sheets; and income statements.

The issuer's capitalization presented was on many occasions described thus:[1]

Capitalization of the company outstanding -
$1,500,000 Bonds
$1,500,000 Preferred Stock
$15,000,000 Common Stock

Occasionally, a more elaborate statement of capitalization might read as follows:

Capitalization of company -
$1,000,000 First Mortgage 5% Bonds.
1,000,000 7%. Preferred Stock.
1,000,000 Common Stock, Class A
1,000,000 Common Stock, Class B

Data related to income was commonly presented in one of several ways. For example, a table of profits such as the one below may have been used:

---

[1]All examples shown were drawn from actual prospectuses issued by a number of different vendors.

1904	$170,961.69
1905	163,300.49
1906	160,383.92
1907	185,336.34
1908	244,261.76
1909	294,836.99
1910	205,255.93
1911	274,237.63
1912	210,100.94
1913	204,334.93

Another common method used to present earnings data was to include in the prospectus a statement, in narrative form, indicating what the issuing company's average earnings had been for the past, say, five years (without giving even an indication of the range about this average). Sometimes, the average earnings were presented by the investment banker, or issuer, in the form shown below:

> We have had made by Messrs. Niles & Niles, Chartered Public Accountants, New York City, a very complete audit of the company's books and accounts covering the operations of the five years ended April 30, 1912. The average net earnings...have amounted to, according to this audit, $306,735.88.

Rarely, if ever, in prospectuses related to industrial offering was an income statement showing sales and the major classes of expense presented. In fact, it was indeed unusual to find an annual sales figure in these prospectuses. When revealed, sales data was usually in the form of an average figure covering some period such as five years.

Occasionally, a balance sheet similar to the

following unaudited balance sheet dated November 29, 1911, might be presented:

Assets

Plant and good will	2,728,966.40	
Tenements and land	65,056.58	2,794,022.98
Merchandise	323,571.68	
Cash	161,960.53	
Accounts receivable	575,652.29	
Investments	34,465.61	1,095,650.11
Prepaid insurance		1,038.00
		3,890,711.09

Liabilities

Capital Stock, First Preferred	1,000,000.00	
Capital Stock, Second Preferred	1,000,000.00	
Capital Stock, Common	1,500,000.00	
Notes Payable	0.	
Accounts Payable	216,859.49	
Reserve for replacement	5,600.00	
Profit and Loss	168,251.60	3,890,711.09

If a balance sheet was not shown, which was often the case, information on the issuing company's assets was, in general, presented in either the form of a brief description of the issuer's principal properties or a statement, in narrative form, such as:

> The real estate, buildings, machinery and appliances have been carefully examined and valued by competent experts at $1,879,700, and the merchandise, open accounts, stores on hand and personal property to be transferred to the new company are guaranteed by the vendors to be in value not less than $950,000.

Between 1900 and 1917 the banker's prospectus slowly fell from favor and was modified: first, by the addition of a statement to the effect that the data contained therein was obtained from information supplied to the underwriter by the management of the corporation issuing the securities; and later, about 1914, by the addition of the so-called "disclaimer clause." This disclaimer clause was, in effect, a statement by the banker that he would not guarantee the reliability of the statements presented in the prospectus. Another change was the adoption of the "president's letter" form of prospectus which had been used previously to offer railroad securities. The type of prospectus which incorporated the president's letter I have labelled "management prospectus."

Initially, the management prospectus was similar in format and content to the banker's prospectus except that the information related to the issue and corporation issuing the securities was contained within a letter from an officer of the issuing company addressed to the underwriting firm. Now, the bulk of material shown in the prospectus was the representation of management. About the only change from the banker's prospectus format was that headings were often used to highlight the different topics covered in the prospectus. The degree of disclosure of financial data, however, was no different in substance and range from that disclosed in the banker's prospectus discussed above and, consequently, will not be repeated.

After 1918

By 1918 the basic form and content of the management prospectus was well established and underwent few changes during the next 12 years. In addition, variations from this standard form became less frequent. There were at least five reasons for absence of change. First, the absence of intolerable pressure for such change on executives from the investing public, government and the critics of big business. Second, the inertia of the corporate executive in this area. Third, the need for corporate "secrecy" as a prerequisite for speculation by "insiders". Fourth, the rise of national syndicates which led to a decrease in the number of local variations of the prospectus form. And, fifth, as will be indicated later, the standard form, as devised by lawyers, diminished, so far as possible, the legal responsibility of everyone concerned with a flotation for the information shown in the prospectus.

The standard form of the management prospectus, as noted earlier, generally covered four pages. The first page, the so-called title page, carried a heading which indicated the number and type of shares available, the name of the issuing corporation and below this heading were listed, in smaller type, the names of the transfer agents and the registrars. Next, a statement similar to the following would appear:

> The following information has been summarized by B. L. Worden, Esq. President of the company, from his letter dated March 8, 1928, describing the company and its common stock....

Then, a summary of the highlights of the president's letter would be presented.

At the foot of the title page would appear the names of the counsel(s), if any, hired by the banker and the issuer to examine the legal proceedings related to the offering; the firm of accountants' name, if any, which had audited the issuer's books and accounts; information related to the payment and delivery of the stock certificates; a statement indicating whether application would be made to list the stock of an exchange; and the price of the security.

Inevitably, the second and third pages of the management prospectus reproduced the president's letter. Typically, this letter briefly touched upon the following items related to the issuing corporations: history, business, properties, management, patents, capitalization, earnings, balance sheet, dividends, the securities limitations and restrictions, purpose of the issue, and the issuer's future outlook.

In general, the fourth page of the prospectus presented either an audited or unaudited balance sheet showing anywhere between fifteen and twenty-five items. No income statement was presented.

Reproduced below are two examples of full prospectuses published during the period 1918-1930. The first is a typical example of the form and content of a management prospectus published during this 12-year period. The second prospectus is shown so the reader might better appreciate the range of prospectuses used to offer securities to the public. Just as some corporations issued annual reports and others did not; there was a similar range of disclosure in prospectuses. Seldom was more information presented than shown in the first example but, more often, as little information as contained in the second example was published.

20,000 Shares

The Fyr-Fyter Company

(Incorporated Under the Laws of Ohio)

Class "A" Shares

Transfer Agent	(No-Par-Value)	Registrar
First National Bank of Cincinnati.		The Central Trust Company, Cincinnati.

The Class "A" stock is entitled to receive preferential cumulative dividends at the rate of $2 per share per annum, and after dividends amounting to $2 per share have been paid in any year on all Class "B" stock outstanding any further dividends paid in said year shall be paid to the Class "A" and Class "B" equally, share for share.

On voluntary liquidation, the Class "A" stock shall receive $35 per share, and on involuntary liquidation $30 per share, before any distribution to the Class "B" stock. The Class "A" stock is subject to redemption, in whole or in part, at $35 per share and accumulated dividends, upon any dividend date, on 30 days' notice.

We summarize the letter which we have received from Mr. Roscoe C. Iddings, President of the Company, as follows:

CAPITALIZATION	Authorized	Outstanding
Class "A" stock no-par-value	20,000 shares	20,000 shares
Class "B" stock no-par-value	40,000 shares	40,000 shares

HISTORY AND BUSINESS. The Fyr-Fyter Company, located at Dayton, Ohio, was incorporated under the laws of Ohio on May 2, 1916. The Company is the outgrowth of a selling organization which was a distributor of fire fighting appliances in Ohio, Indiana and Michigan from 1910 until 1916. Early in 1916 the former company's assets were taken over by the present corporation.

The Fyr-Fyter organization produces fire fighting equipment. It has a larger diversified line of Underwriters' Laboratories approved products than any other manufacturer and is the largest exclusive manufacturer of hand portable fire extinguishers.

The Company maintains a staff of expert mechanics and chemists who are constantly at work improving its products and developing new ones. Discoveries and inventions made by this Research Department have placed the Company in an advantageous position.

Its products are sold, assisted by national advertising, through a large selling organization working strictly on a commission basis and covering the United States and foreign countries.

The Company's field is wide. Among the outlets for its products are plants, hotels, stores, restaurants, railroads, filling stations, garages, schools, motor vehicles and boats. Lately the Company is meeting with considerable success in selling fire extinguisher equipment for private residence protection and the increased use of aeroplanes provides still another promising market.

PLANT. The factory, which has 50,000 square feet of floor space, is a modern, two-story, reinforced concrete structure, specially designed to accommodate the machinery used in making its product. A private railroad siding reduces trucking to a minimum.

MANAGEMENT. The management will remain in the hands of the executives who have successfully conducted the business since its organization, who own approximately the entire issue of Class "B" stock. The department heads have won their positions through promotions made possible by the growth of the Company. The majority of the employees have worked for the Company since 1918; many are stockholders.

EARNINGS. An audit by Messrs. Haskins & Sells shows that the earnings of The Fyr-Fyter Company, after giving effect to non-recurring charges (interest on notes and mortgage amounting to $5,188.27 in 1925, $5,231.14 in 1926, $4,878.00 in 1927, and $3,580.00 in the 10 months ended October 31, 1928) and after deducting for Federal Income Taxes at current rates, were as follows:

Year	Earnings as Above	Earnings per Share Class "A"
1925	$ 95,235.89	$4.76
1926	84,007.12	4.20
1927	65,953.22	3.29
1928—10 months	100,517.37	5.02

The above figures show that the average earnings for 1925, 1926 and 1927 were over twice the dividend requirements on the "A" stock, and that for the ten months of 1928 the Company earned more than 2½ times the Class "A" dividend requirements of $2 per share for the entire year.

ASSETS. The balance sheet as of October 31, 1928, giving effect to recapitalization and refinancing, as certified to by Messrs. Haskins & Sells, shows the Company in a strong financial position. The Total Current Assets of $333,730.45, were over 3.84 times Total Current Liabilities of $86,831.14.

REMARKS. The Company has no funded debt, no Preference shares other than these, and no bank loans. Of the 20,000 shares of "A" stock outstanding, 13,000 shares have been acquired from individuals and the remaining 7,000 shares from the Company. The proceeds of the sale of this stock have been used by the Company to call and redeem the 7% Preferred stock, to pay the 6% Mortgage maturing April 1, 1929, and for additional working capital.

The Company has agreed to make application to list the stock on the Cincinnati Stock Exchange.

The legal proceedings have been passed upon by Messrs. Ernst, Cassatt and Cottle for the Bankers and by Messrs D. W. and A. S. Iddings of Dayton, Ohio, and Mr. Lem S. Miller for the Company. The books and accounts of the Company have been audited by Messrs. Haskins & Sells. The appraisal of Fixed Assets as of October 31, 1928, has been made by The Lloyd-Thomas Company.

We offer the Class "A" stock for delivery if, as and when issued and received by us, subject to the approval of counsel.

Price $28.00 a share, to net 7.14%

W. E. HUTTON & CO.

FIRST NATIONAL BANK BUILDING

CINCINNATI

NEW YORK DETROIT TOLEDO DAYTON LEXINGTON

The statements contained herein are not guaranteed, but are taken from sources which we believe to be reliable.

The Fyr-Fyter Company

Dayton, Ohio

December 7, 1928.

MESSRS. W. E. HUTTON & COMPANY,
Cincinnati.

Gentlemen:—

In connection with your purchase of Class "A" stock of The Fyr-Fyter Company, we take pleasure in furnishing you the following information:

HISTORY AND BUSINESS

The Fyr-Fyter Company, located at Dayton, Ohio, was incorporated under the laws of Ohio on May 2, 1916. The Company is the outgrowth of a selling organization which was a distributor of fire fighting appliances in Ohio, Indiana and Michigan from 1910 until 1916. Early in 1916 the former company's assets were taken over by the present corporation.

The Fyr-Fyter organization produces fire fighting equipment. It has a larger diversified line of Underwriters' Laboratories approved products than any other manufacturer and is the largest exclusive manufacturer of hand portable fire extinguishers.

During 1916 and 1917, The Fyr-Fyter Company had its product built for it under contract on a cost plus basis, but late in 1917 the Company engaged in manufacturing on its own behalf. At first the "Super Fyr-Fyter" was the only model built and the basic principles of that first machine are to-day incorporated in the new improved "Super" which is the most universally used of all the products turned out by the Company's large modern factory.

Both mechanical and chemical research laboratories have been created and engineers versed in fire fighting methods placed at the head of them with the result that to-day the Fyr-Fyter line has some 17 different types and sizes of extinguishers ranging in capacities from one-quart to forty-gallons, incorporating many features found in no other line of fire fighting equipment. The latest addition is the 1¾-gallon "Instant Fyr-Fyter" which is covered by United States and foreign patents. This uses entirely new chemicals that extinguish both ordinary wood and inflammable liquid fires with great rapidity. Other sizes of Instants have been prepared and will be put on the market.

The management is progressive and the Company has grown from a very small beginning to one of the largest in the field of fire protection, with a selling organization numbering around 3,000 men selling on a commission basis and covering the United States and foreign countries. The Company's field is wide. Among the outlets for its products are plants, hotels, stores, restaurants, railroads, filling stations, garages, schools, motor vehicles, boats and aeroplanes. Lately the Company has been meeting with considerable success in selling fire extinguisher equipment for private residence protection.

PLANT

The plant, and extra land for expansion are owned by the Company. The factory building has 50,000 square feet of floor space, and is a modern, two-story, reinforced concrete structure, specially designed to accommodate the machinery used in the production of its product. A private railroad siding reduces trucking to a minimum.

EARNINGS

An audit by Messrs. Haskins & Sells shows that the earnings of The Fyr-Fyter Company, after giving effect to non-recurring charges (interest on notes and mortgage amounting to $5,188.27 in 1925, $5,231.14 in 1926, $4,878.00 in 1927, and $3,580.00 in the 10 months ended October 31, 1928) and after deducting for Federal Income Taxes at current rates, were as follows:

Year	Earnings as Above	Earnings per Share Class "A"
1925	$ 95,235.89	$4.76
1926	84,007.12	4.20
1927	65,953.22	3.29
1928—10 months	100,517.37	5.02

The above figures show that the average earnings for 1925, 1926 and 1927 were over twice the dividend requirements on the "A" stock and for the ten months of 1928 the Company earned more than 2½ times the "A" stock dividend requirements of $2 per share for the entire year.

DIVIDENDS

The Class "A" shares are entitled to $2.00 preferential cumulative dividends, accruing from date of issue, payable January 15, April 15, July 15, and October 15. In addition these Class "A" shares participate equally per share in all dividends after payment of $2.00 per share on Class "B" stock in any year.

ASSETS

The balance sheet as of October 31, 1928, giving effect to recapitalization and refinancing, as certified to by Messrs. Haskins & Sells, shows the Company in a strong financial position. The Current Assets of $333,730.45 were over 3.84 times Total Current Liabilities of $86,831.14.

TERMS AND PROVISIONS

The Class "A" stock is entitled to preferential cumulative dividends of $2.00 per share per annum, payable quarterly on the fifteenth days of January, April, July and October in each year out of the surplus or Net Profits of the corporation in preference to Class "B" stockholders. After dividends amounting to $2 per share are paid in any year on all Class "B" stock issued and outstanding, any further dividends paid in said year shall be paid to the Class "A" and Class "B" equally, share for share; payable to the respective shares outstanding, not to classes but to shares.

In the event of voluntary liquidation the Class "A" stock shall receive $35 per share, and on involuntary liquidation $30 a share, before any distribution is made to the Class "B" stock.

The Class "A" is subject to redemption, in whole or in part, at $35 per share and accumulated dividends, upon any dividend date, on 30 days' notice. If part only of said Class "A" stock is to be redeemed, it shall be selected by lot or pro rata, by such method as shall be provided by resolution of the Board of Directors. The Board of Directors may increase or decrease the amount redeemed from any holder so as to avoid fractional shares. On the redemption date fixed by said notice, all rights of such stockholders with respect to said stock, except the right to receive the redemption price, shall cease, and all stock so redeemed shall be surrendered and canceled, and shall not be reissued.

The Company may also purchase Class "A" stock for a price acceptable to the holder not in excess of $35 per share and accumulated dividends, and may re-issue and sell or may retire and cancel same, as the Board of Directors may determine.

Without consent in writing of the holders of at least 75% of the then outstanding Class "A" stock or on the dissent of 25% or more of the outstanding Class "A" stock at a meeting called to consider the same the Company shall not:—

(a) Create any mortgage on its real or personal property to secure the issue of bonds or otherwise; but nothing herein shall affect the right of the Company to mortgage by purchase money mortgage, individual parcels of real estate purchased by it, or to purchase or acquire property subject to mortgage.

(b) Issue any additional stock having right as to dividends or assets equal or prior to this authorized issue, or increase the amount of this authorization.

(c) Sell its entire or substantially entire property and assets.

Class "A" stockholders shall not be entitled to vote at any stockholders' meeting of the Company, nor to receive notice thereof, except such meetings as may be called to consider subjects with respect to which unalterable voting rights are conferred by law upon such stockholders and except as provided above, and except, also when four quarterly dividends upon such stock are in arrears in which case and thereafter said Class "A" stockholders shall be entitled to vote two votes for each share by them held at all stockholders' meetings until payment of preferential dividends have been resumed and all unpaid dividends have been paid in full.

Class "B" stock shall have all of the rights and privileges of common stock generally, subject, however, to the prior rights and interests of the holders of Class "A" stock as hereinbefore stated.

MANAGEMENT

The management will remain in the hands of the executives who have successfully conducted the business since its organization, who own approximately the entire issue of Class "B" stock. The department heads have won their positions through promotions made possible by the growth of the Company. The majority of the employees have worked for the Company since 1918; many are stockholders.

GENERAL

The Company has no funded debt, no Preference shares other than these and no bank loans. Of the 20,000 ~~shares of~~ "A" stock outstanding, ~~13,000 shares have been acquired from individuals and the remaining~~ 7,000 shares from the Company. The proceeds of the sale of this stock have been used by the Company to call and redeem the 7% Preferred stock, to pay the 6% Mortgage maturing April 1, 1929, and for additional working capital.

Application will be made to list the Class "A" stock on the Cincinnati Stock Exchange.

Respectfully submitted,

THE FYR-FYTER COMPANY,
(Signed) **Roscoe C. Iddings**, President.

The Fyr-Fyter Company

(Incorporated in Ohio)

BALANCE SHEET, OCTOBER 31, 1928

Giving effect to the proposed retirement of Preferred stock, and mortgage; to the contemplated recapitalization; to the exchange of Common stock for Gold Notes, and the sale of Class "A" shares held in Treasury.

ASSETS

Current Assets:		
Cash	$ 36,466.61	
Time certificates of deposit	16,000.00	
Notes receivable	3,173.59	
Accounts receivable:		
Customers (less reserve of $5,000.00)	133,937.80	
Miscellaneous	1,933.43	
Accrued interest receivable	266.67	
Inventories (based on physical inventory and priced at cost):		
Materials and supplies	91,465.41	
Goods in process	17,180.24	
Finished goods	33,306.70	
Total current assets		$333,730.45
Property:		
Land (at cost)	$ 10,000.00	
Replacement value, as appraised by The Lloyd-Thomas Company:		
Buildings	150,624.22	
Machinery and equipment	81,152.37	
Jigs and dies	8,123.00	
Automobiles	3,461.00	
Furniture and fixtures	44,383.00	
Tools and patterns, at company's estimate of value	21,596.95	
Total	$319,340.54	
Less reserve for depreciation	40,335.67	
Net book value		279,004.87
Patents		17,535.68
Good-Will		1.00
Deferred Charges:		
Insurance premiums, unexpired portion	$ 1,733.92	
Other expenditures applicable to future operations	802.87	
Total deferred charges		2,536.79
Total		$632,808.79

LIABILITIES

Current Liabilities:		
Accounts payable:		
Trade creditors	$ 25,733.06	
Miscellaneous	2,383.23	
Commissions payable	35,725.58	
Accrued accounts:		
Wages	3,690.75	
Federal income tax	15,618.48	
State and county taxes	3,492.45	
Other	187.59	
Total current liabilities		$ 86,831.14
Class "A", 20,000 shares of no-par-value } Class "B", 40,000 shares of no-par-value }		443,500.00
Surplus from operations		102,477.65
Total		$632,808.79

CERTIFICATE

We have made a general examination of the accounts of The Fyr-Fyter Company for the period from January 1, 1925, to October 31, 1928, and

We hereby certify that in our opinion the above balance sheet, giving effect to the proposed change in capital structure and application of the proceeds from the sale of Class "A" shares held in treasury, is correct.

(Signed) Haskins & Sells,
Certified Public Accountants.

NEW OFFERING

75,000

Shares of no par value

Freed-Eisemann Radio Corporation

CAPITALIZATION

Authorized, 300,000 Shares

To be presently Outstanding, 300,000 Shares

Price $30. per Share

All transactions under this offering of 75,000 shares are made subject to approval of Counsel and are made "when, as and if issued and accepted" by the Bankers. Delivery may be made in either Temporary Certificates or Interim Receipts, exchangeable later for Engraved Certificates.

The statements contained in this memorandum, while not guaranteed, are obtained from sources believed to be reliable.

October 24, 1924.

FREED-EISEMANN RADIO CORPORATION

PRICHITT & CO., Inc., New York, October 23rd, 1924.

60 Broadway,

New York City.

Gentlemen:

Referring to your contract for the purchase of common stock of the above company, I submit herewith the following information:

HISTORY AND BUSINESS

FREED-EISEMANN RADIO CORPORATION was organized in February, 1922, at which time it acquired the business of "Radio Manufacturing Co.", a company engaged exclusively in the manufacture of the crystal type radio receiving set. The Company occupied a plant at No. 251 Fourth Avenue, New York City, and gradually expanded its business in crystal receiving sets until it necessitated the use of two floors in that building. Gross business for the first calendar year amounted to $250,315.64. As radio broadcasting stations multiplied, the field for the Company's product expanded accordingly, and in the Fall of 1923, we began the manufacture of "Neutrodyne", and other multi-tube receiving sets similar to the Company's present product. With this widening field a rapid increase in business took place during the last few months of 1923, and the total business for that year, the second of the Company's existence, amounted to $979,028.69.

In December, 1923, the Company's plant was moved to its present location in the "Sperry Building", in the Borough of Brooklyn, City of New York, where it originally occupied a floor space of approximately 15,000 square feet, which has been gradually extended until at present the Company's personnel and equipment occupy approximately 50,000 square feet of floor space.

Sales for the first nine months of the present calendar year were $2,880,286.07, and based upon orders in hand we estimate that shipments during the months of October, November and December will bring the total volume of business for the year 1924 to an amount in excess of $5,000,000. Orders in hand aggregate $1,250,000., and we are daily in receipt of additional orders which, in our judgment, will cause the aggregate of the year's business to exceed the figures hereinabove stated.

EARNINGS

Operating profits, before taxes and liberal payments to executives, were as follows:

1922	$ 1,981.50
1923	202,638.84
1924..9 months, Jan. 1 to Sept. 30.	1,246,897.06

Based on past experience and orders now in hand, we believe a conservative estimate of our operating profits for the entire year 1924 is approximately the sum of $2,000,000.

According to our experience, the peak months of our business are directly ahead of us, and it is estimated that we will reach a monthly sales total before the year closes of over $1,000,000. for a single month's shipments.

While it is my desire to estimate figures conservatively, I believe that 1925 will show an increase over the figures of 1924. This opinion is based upon the fact that the months of January and February, 1924, showed sales of over $1,600,000., and it is our expectation that the same months in 1925 will greatly exceed these figures. Up to September, 1924, our operations were largely confined to the manufacture of one type of receiving set, while our present production comprises six different models built to meet various price markets and includes the cabinet style of receiver to fill the demand for a high-class ornamental radio receiver installed in decorative console cabinets.

We have never had occasion to undertake any extensive advertising in the Company's behalf, most of the advertising heretofore placed having been done by the Company's dealers at their own expense. Recently, however, we have contracted for an intensive advertising campaign to maintain the dominance of the Company's product.

DISTRIBUTION

The Company's business is carried on with approximately seventy large wholesale distributing houses located in the various centers of population and each serving its contiguous territory.

Losses through bad accounts have been negligible.

CAPITALIZATION

At its inception, the Company operated upon a cash working capital of $12,000. Its present net worth of approximately $900,000. has been attained entirely as the result of profits accruing from operations, after deducting liberal bonuses, salaries and dividends paid to stockholders and executives.

Your contract to purchase a part of the capital stock represents an acquisition by you of a proportionate part of the holdings of individual stockholders of the Company, and no part of the proceeds will go to the Company which has ample working capital, its present cash balances being approximately $500,000.

The same management which has been responsible for the upbuilding of the Company, retains substantial stock control, and will continue to devote its time and efforts to the interests of the business.

At present orders are being received in excess of our ability to ship and we contemplate a substantial increase in our personnel so as to assure the production of a greater volume.

Yours truly,

JOSEPH D. R. FREED,
President.

The balance sheet of the Fyr-Fyter Company shown above was typical of the balance sheets presented in those management prospectuses giving the fullest disclosure of the issuing corporations affairs. Seldom were comparative balance sheets shown in prospectuses.

Not all management prospectuses presented even a condensed balance sheet. The Freed-Eisemann Radio Corporation prospectus was such a case. In this particular prospectus the only balance sheet data revealed was that the company had an authorized and outstanding capitalization of 300,000 shares of no par stock and:

> At its inception, the company operated upon a cash working capital of $12,000. Its present net worth of approximately $900,000 has been attained entirely as the result of profits occurring from operations, after deducting liberal bonuses, salaries and dividends paid to stockholders and executives...the company...has ample working capital, its present cash balances being approximately $500,000.

By 1928, it was a common practice to append an audit certificate of a certified public accountant to the balance sheet. In 1929, on this particular development related to audit certificates Richardson, the editor of <u>The Journal of Accountancy</u>, had this to say:

> If one turns to the published announcements of the offer of securities by industrial or mercantile concerns it is now unusual to find an advertisement which does not contain a statement to the effect that the accounts

> have been audited by certain specified accountants. Only a few years ago the conditions were quite opposite and it was a rarity to find the name of an accountant associated with the published accounts....Many companies which submit to audit submit reluctantly and only because they feel that the chances of selling securities will be slim unless the name of a reputable accountant supports the statements which are to be made....[1]

The use and misuse of the audit certificate will be discussed later under the heading "Reliability and Utility."

Neither of the two above post-1918 prospectuses, it should be noted, presented full income statements. In fact, during the entire 30-year period covered by chapter seven, prospectuses consistently failed to show an income statement relating gross revenue to expenses. After 1918, the following two examples were as elaborate a statement related to income as one was like to find:

> The company's net earnings, available for dividends, as reported by Haskins & Sells, C.P.A., averaged $309,227.78 for the past 6 years, or $7.73 per share, as follows:

	Net Earnings	Per Share on 40,000 Shares Class "A"
1917	$345,202.37	$ 8.63
1918	590,733.64	14.77
1919	151,893.79	3.80
1920	171,165.31	4.28
1921	287,490.07	7.19
1922	308,881.52	7.72
Average	$ 309,227.78	$ 7.73

[1]"Auditor's Responsibility to the Public," _The Journal of Accountancy_, Vol. 47, No. 4, April 1929, p. 297.

These earnings are after depreciation, federal taxes and dividends on the preferred stock, but before amortization of patents and goodwill.

*****

In no year since the founding of the business 50 years ago, has THE FAIR[1] failed to show a profit. Approximately 72½% of the company's sales are for cash. Net sales and earnings for the past 5 years, adjusted for the savings or company charges on non-productive real estate recently sold and for interest payments eliminated by new cash capital, as reported by Messrs. Ernst & Ernst, and as shown by the company's books for previous years, adjusted as to possible additional Federal Tax liability, have been as follows:

Year Ending January 31	Net Sales	Net After Taxes	Per Share Common to be Outstanding
1925	$24,404,632	$1,270,638.61	$2.64
1924	25,790,812	1,367,446.51	2.90
1923	23,894,229	1,827,253.80	4.12
1922	24,570,252	1,444,637.55	3.10
1921	27,725,765	2,134,538.81	4.94
5 year average		1,608,903.05	3.54
10-year average		1,389,696.63	2.95
15-year average		1,274,258.64	2.65
20-year average		1,157,347.51	2.33
25-year average		1,098,567.09	2.18

Records of the company show that in no one of the past 35 years have net profits failed to show a substantial balance available for common stock, based on present capitalization. With present facilities sales can be increased to $35 million or $40,000,000 annually.

The practice of presenting only the average or the most recent earnings and sales figures described earlier also persisted throughout this period. Sometimes, after 1924, the raw earnings figure so presented was converted to an earnings per share basis.

---

[1]A large department store located in Chicago.

Beginning about 1918, an indication of the issuing corporation's dividend payment history was more often included in prospectuses. Prior to this time the common practice had been to state the current dividend rate and imply management would continue to pay the same, or slightly larger, dividends in the future. Dividend histories, when presented, were in either the table or narrative form, the latter being more common than the former. Presented below are three representative samples showing how dividend records were presented in prospectuses:

> The company paid cash dividends on its outstanding preferred and common stock in every year for the past 20 years. It is expected that dividends will be inaugurated on the present common stock at the annual rate of $2 per share.

*****

> The business has paid dividends uninterruptedly since 1882 totaling $4,110,187, comprising $1,082,800 in par value of capital stock and $3,027,387 in cash. Of the cash dividends over $1,586,000, including distribution out of surplus of $625,000 in 1924.

*****

> The Hydraulic Pressed Steel Company has paid cash and stock dividends on its outstanding common stock as follows:

	Cash	Stock		Cash	Stock
1909	*		1915	8%	
1910	8%	100%	1916	8	50%
1911	8		1917	8	125
1912	8		1918	8	
1913	8	100%	1919	8	
1914	8				

*Cash dividends were inaugurated in July 1909, at the rate of 2% quarterly.

Having described the range and extent of the disclosure of financial information, the treatment given in prospectuses to the following non-financial topics will be briefly discussed: purpose of issue, management, business, industry, banker and the security. In general, enough details describing the form of the security, its provisions and restrictions, callable features, voting powers, etc. were presented to satisfy most investors.[1] Information related to the banker was customarily limited to the name of the principal members of the syndicate handling the offering. And data pertaining to the industry to which the issuing corporation belonged was seldom, if ever, presented within the prospectus.

Typically, the information directly related to management was brief, vague, general and complimentary. The following representative statements drawn from president's letters published in prospectuses issued during the period 1900-1930 are illustrative of the total information usually shown under the heading "MANAGEMENT":

---

[1]In 1920, the Industrial Securities Committee of the Investment Bankers Association of America reporting on its examination of current prospectuses concluded the form of the security was "usually covered in considerable detail and in a satisfactory manner." 1920 Industrial Securities Committee Report, op. cit., p. 165.

> The management has been built up by Mr. Samuel Zemumary, the President, who as such will continue to direct the affairs of the company. It is well organized and managed in all its departments -- production, transportation, and selling. The other officers and directors are largely interested in the company and expect to continue their interests and activity.

*****

> The corporation's business will be under the direction of executives who have been instrumental in the growth of predecessor companies. Operations of each department will be in charge of men of practical training and long technical experience. The corporation contemplates the establishment of a research department, which will include chemists who have had particular training in the scientific and technical division of this industry.

Occasionally, more detailed information on the management was presented. For instance:

> Virtually all of the officers of the company, including its president and vice president-general manager have been continuously and successfully engaged for many years in the manufacture and installation of automatic sprinklers for the periods stated in the lists below, and their continuance with the company assures its successful administration.

Name	Office	Years Experience
Powell Evans	President	24
A. M. Lewis	First Vice President & General Manager	23
Thomas Evans	Secretary	10
J. S. Mallory	General Sales Manager	22
W. F. Ritz	Ass. Sec. & Ass. General Manager	16
A. C. Rowley	Mechanical Engineer	24
C. B. Garrett	Ass. Mechanical Engineer	19

*****

> The management of the company will remain unchanged and continue in charge of the members of the Hires family, who are responsible for the successful development of the business and will own approximately 90% of the Class "B" stock and all the management stock of the company. Officers are Charles E. Hires, President; Harrison S. Hires, Secretary; Charles E. Hires, Jr., Treasurer. Directors will include the foregoing and: J. Edgar Hires, W. W. Terry, and representatives of Cassett & Co., and Edward Smith & Co.

The information shown in the Fyr-Fyter Company prospectus under the heading "History and Business" may be considered typical of the amount and character of the data shown in prospectuses on that subject.

In about 50% of those prospectuses examined which were issued after 1918 information related to the "purpose of the issue" was presented. In those cases where such information was shown, the following two actual examples would be representative of the range of disclosure on this matter.

> The proceeds from the sale by its company of 75,000 shares of common stock will be used towards the retirement of all of the outstanding preferred stock of the company, which will be called for redemption on May 1, 1928.

*****

> The proceeds of the sale of this $10,000,000 par value 7% preferred stock will be used in part to defray the cost of installing additional equipment already ordered which will increase the output of plant No. 2 from 10,000 to 16,000 tires per day; in part to enlarge the amount of cord tires in our main plant; to construct a new mechanical building with the most up-to-date equipment and conveniences; to build a new plant for the manufacture

> of steel rims; and to supply additional working capital for the continuous expansion of the company's business.

Prior to 1918, the specific purpose for which the securities were issued was seldom revealed.

Investor's Information Needs

Having discussed the content of prospectuses issued between 1900 and 1930 a brief description of the information needs of "intelligent" investors as represented in contemporary financial literature, including the works of Clinton Collver, will now be presented. In general, these described needs far exceeded the amount and quality of information provided investors.

The prospectus, which was the means whereby securities were introduced to investors, served two principal functions: to advertise a particular offering and to provide investors with the information needed to appraise the investment value of the securities offered. This business instrument--the prospectus--Berle and Means regarded "as the most important document in the early market history of a security... since it appears at a time when the bankers or promoting group are probably the sole possessors of facts permitting an accurate appraisal of the security."[1]

---

[1]Berle and Means, op. cit., p. 301.

This was particularly true about 1900, and between 1914-1918, and 1923-1929, when a number of private companies were being converted to public companies and were, for the first time, offering securities--debt and equity--to the public. Prior to such offerings no information related to the affairs of these particular corporations had been available to the public.

In the case of the private company going "public" or the non-reporting public company previously discussed the prospectus was particularly relevant to two types of investor. It was directly relevant to those who purchased the original securities from the marketing syndicate or their agents and indirectly pertinent to those investors who later bought the securities in the open market. The decision of the original purchaser to acquire the securities from the underwriter might be postulated to have depended, in part, on the representations contained within the prospectus. Those investors who later bought the securities in the open market also bought, indirectly, on the basis of the prospectus since the market appraisal of the security was, in many cases, determined, in part, by the information disclosed in the original prospectus. Thus, what was disclosed by the prospectus was, or <u>should</u> have been, of interest to investors.

The word "should" was used above, as many have argued the average investor neither read the prospectus nor was competent to evaluate or interpret the financial data contained therein. No doubt in many cases this allegation was true. Usually, those who took this position argued the true protection of such investors would come from either government regulation of securities, or through a banker's or some professional investment adviser's investigation of the issuer, or an independent audit of the issuer by certified public accountants: not from more voluminous prospectuses. Unfortunately, in fact, these recommended safeguards, as will be seen, all too often proved illusory.

During the period now under review, the fictions known as the qualified "professional investment advisor" and the "sophisticated investor"--people who did read the prospectus and were capable of understanding its contents--required, according to the contemporary publications related to investment analysis, certain essential data in order to make an informed judgment as to the value of securities as either a speculation or an investment. In general, contemporary experts in the area of finance said for such decisions the investor would need to have readily available adequate information related to the security, the management, the issuing corporation and the underwriter.

Not all experts, however, were agreed as to what weight should be assigned to each of these four factors. For instance, investment bankers argued for many years the underwriter's reputation was the most important of these four factors--the security, management, issuer, and underwriter. In contrast, accountants believed reliable financial data was, for the investment decision, the most relevant material. The relation of each of these four topics to the investment decision, and any perceptible shifts in their relevance to such decisions is discussed below. In addition, the data required to undertake an "intelligent appraisal" of securities along the lines suggested by Clinton Collver, the pioneer industrial security analyst previously mentioned in chapter six, will also be outlined.

<u>The Security</u>

Most contemporary "experts" on the subject of security investment agreed that adequate information on the first point--the provisions, restrictions and type of security--would be essential if the investor was to evaluate intelligently such things as his rights in liquidation and voting, and the limit of his liability.

In addition, the nature of the security was, in part, a determinant of the degree of risk associated with the investment.

However, information related to the type of security, it was said, was not enough--other facts were also needed. For instance, on the importance of the information related to the security the Industrial Securities Committee of The Investment Bankers Association of America had this to say: "It is believed....that neither the banker nor investor base their judgment as to their purchase on the form of security alone...."[1]

Management

A number of people close to the investment market believed information related to management was the most important of the four classes of information mentioned above. In fact, for some, the character and attitude of management were almost as important to the investment decision as management's business ability. The Investment Bankers' Industrial Securities Committee on this matter said:

> Those in control of the operation and policies of the company should not only command a good general reputation but must be experienced in the particular line in which they are engaged and be actually capable of handling what they have under taken. Personality is often a controlling

---

[1]1920 Interim Report Industrial Securities Committee, op. cit., p. 162.

> element of success or failure and the character and ability of the owners and managers of any enterprise can not be too carefully investigated. Much depends also upon the attitude of management....[1]
>
> ...it can not be too strongly emphasized that correct and ample information on management -- the first consideration of the banker in passing on a loan -- should be included in every circular....[2]

One particular guide to management's ability, the Industrial Securities Committee said, was how well it had "handled its financial affairs over a period of years:"

> In addition to the general statement about the experience and capability of a management, a banker or investor can gain a very definite impression of a management's policies and its ability from observation of how it has handled its financial affairs over a period of years. If a company has its equity largely in the form of common stock on which it pays ample dividends and has a good surplus remaining for depreciation, or to be used for the benefit of the property, the impression is very different from that given by a management which carried a large floating debt on which it must pay out most of its earnings in interest, or a management which distributes practically all of its income in dividends, turning back nothing to the property and making no provisions for depreciation. Unless a summary is made on these points, as is occasionally done in offerings, it is very difficult without considerable study to find out what the policy of the management has been in these respects. It is believed that greater attention is given now than in the past to

---

[1] *Ibid.*, p. 159.

[2] *Ibid.*

> questions of depreciation and the maintenance of sound equities, and information bearing on these points seems to be very essential.[1]

At a minimum the careful investor ought, it was often said, to know the names of the issuing firm's principal owners, directors, and management--the men to whom he was entrusting his capital.

<u>The Issuer--Financial Data</u>

In general, information related to the company issuing the securities--the third factor--could be broken down into four subgroups: the issuing firm's place in its industry; the nature of the corporation's business; financial data related to the issuer's operations and financial condition; and the purpose of the issue. Such data were all relevant to predicting the issuer's future direction of expansion and the probability of its success.

Of these four subclasses, it was said, quantitative data pertaining to the issuer's operations and financial position was of particular interest to many investors, for it was from a record of such items as past dividends, earnings, sales, assets and liabilities that a general idea of the issuing firm's dividend policy, stability of earnings, general

---

[1]1920 Interim Report Industrial Securities Committee, <u>op. cit</u>., p. 164.

credit, and return on capital investment could be derived. All these factors ought, it was said, be relevant in some way to any particular investment decision.

The principal source of quantitative data was, in most cases, the balance sheet and the income statement. Historically, there was a shift in the relative importance to the investment decision from the balance sheet to the income statement. This shift, which is discussed below, was closely related to the changing theories of common-stock investment and financial statement analysis which evolved during the period 1900-1933.

Initially, the theoretical value of common stock of investment grade was closely related to its dividend yield and its book value. Later, sometime after 1924, the theoretical value of investment stock was more closely related to the expected rate of change of earnings per share. Graham and Dodd have described the characteristics of a pre-World War I high grade investment stock, which as noted above were usually found among the railroad or utility stocks,[1] thus:

---

[1]The status of the industrial stocks in the hierarchy of investment securities in 1900 is clearly portrayed by the following statement reproduced from a 1900 banker's circular:

"We suggest for investment the following stocks, in what are known as Industrial Enterprises.

They are not to be classed with government, state, municipal, or high-grade railway bonds, nor with the

...the distinction between investment grade and speculative common stocks was quite clear in the minds of experienced investors. The chief characteristic of the former was a stable, and perhaps increasing, dividend rate, maintained in the face of panic, and depression periods, such as 1907-1908. This dividend stability carried with it, as prerequisites, a reasonable stability of earnings, a sound financial structure, and ample working capital....

One of the signs of an investment issue was an average market price close to or exceeding the par value. Most of these stocks were understood to be backed by a real capital investment equal to their par value plus accumulated surplus--as contrasted with the fictitious or 'watered' asset[1] values shown on the balance sheet of many speculative enterprises.[2]

---

best of the railway stocks, the returns on which, however, now range at less than 4%, per annum; but we are of the opinion that money carefully invested among the best located reasonably capitalized, and best managed of this class of corporations, will in the long run not only give larger returns, but will prove to be safely invested."

Banker's circular, Kidder, Peabody & Co., Boston, Massachusetts, April 2, 1900, p. 3.

[1]The principal item used to inflate the value of a firm's stock was "goodwill" and "going concern value." Both of these items were a form of capitalization of earning power and as such represented intangible rather than tangible assets. Among industrial corporations "watered stock" was more prevalent than, say among railroads and as a consequence, industrial stocks were, in general, regarded as "speculations."

[2]Graham and Dodd, op. cit., p. 385.

During the period immediately following World War I the importance of the balance sheet data as a guide to a security's investment worth declined when it became apparent that stock of the more successful industrial and mercantile enterprises such as General Electric and Corn Products were of equal investment standing with the railroad equities of prior years. Both classes of company had paid regular dividends and prospered during the war years.

The traditional measures of security value, such as book value, had less meaning for the new industrials than, say, for the railroads: industrial plants being, "as a rule, not readily marketable."[1] Recognizing the condition, the principal criteria against which investors appraised industrials became their probable future yield. The best guide to that figure, it was said, was the firm's earning power and past dividend record. Now, the characteristics of the high-grade industrial and similar stocks were an "adequate earning power" and an "adequate dividend return." Thus, the income statement, which was more relevant to the new theory of investment value than the balance sheet, began to assume a new importance for a number of investors.

---

[1]1920 Report of Industrial Securities Committee, op. cit., p. 154.

Subsequently, during the bull market of the late 1920's another investment theory, which Graham and Dodd have called "the new-era market investment theory," grew out of a 1924 study by Edgar Lawrence Smith.[1] Smith's study, which was to become the "official 'textbook" of the new-era stock market"[2] (1925-1929), had shown that since the Civil War representative common-stock lists had consistently out performed standard bond investments over any 10-year period, taking into account both income return and price changes.[3] Historically, the accepted investment theories had held common stock were more "risky" than bonds, but on the basis of Smith's study, such theories were apparently incorrect.

The new-era market investment theory consisted of two parts which Graham and Dodd have labelled "historic optimism" and "growth selectivity." Now, in 1925, on the basis of Smith's study, common stocks were regarded as "sure fire bearers of increasing dividends and ultimate price appreciation"[4] and, in view

---

[1]Edgar Lawrence Smith, Common Stocks as Long-Term Investment (New York: The Macmillan Company, 1924).

[2]Graham and Dodd, op. cit., p. 389.

[3]Ibid.

[4]Ibid.

of the projected era of prosperity, were equally attractive to both investors and speculators. This was the historic optimism portion of the theory. The growth selectivity aspect of the new investment theory simply recognized the obvious fact that the stocks of some companies would be better investments than others. Combining the two aspects of the theory, the reasoning of those who adopted this investment theory ran as follows:

> Since we favor common stocks as a whole because of their dynamic growth quality, we should use our intelligence as investors to pick out those individual companies which are most likely to grow rapidly and we must avoid those which stand still or retrogress.[1]

Future growth prospects became the most important factor in the investment decision and, in practice, a company's growth was measured by the rate of change of its earnings per share. The greater the percentage change from the prior comparable period the greater the premium, as expressed by the price-earnings multiplier, the investor was willing to pay for such a stock. Thus, the primary concern of the investor was the future and the most relevant figure in the financial statements was the "net profit": the older indicators related to the determination of asset value, dividend rate and earning power were abandoned. Now, earnings

---

[1] Ibid.

per share assumed a new importance for, it was said, a projection based on historic earnings per share was one of the best indicators of future investment success.[1]

The 1929 stock market crash and the depression years which followed led "many people to believe the whole idea of common-stock investment had been a delusion, and that common stocks by their nature could not be other than speculative."[2] Neither the future nor the past was any help in determining their value: investing in common stocks was gambling and financial data was not relevant to such a decision.[3]

---

[1]Graham and Dodd presented the following example of typical 1929 security valuations in relation to the earnings trend on one hand and the average earnings on the other:

	Earnings Per Share		
Year	Company A (Electric Power & Light	Company B (Bangor & Aroostock R.R.)	Company C (Chicago Yellow Cab)
1925	$1.01	$6.22	$5.52
1926	1.45	8.69	5.60
1927	2.09	8.41	4.54
1928	2.37	6.94	4.58
1929	2.98	8.30	4.47
5-year average	$1.98	$7.71	$4.94
High price 1929	86 5/8	90 3/8	35

[2]*Ibid.*, p. 391.

[3]Later, after 1935, a modified form of the new-era market investment theory was cautiously developed.

The second reason for the shift in emphasis from the balance to the income statement during the period 1900-1933 was related to the development of new theories of financial statement analysis,particularly ratio analysis,for general credit purposes.

Prior to 1900, financial statements were regarded principally as the "proof" of the bookkeeper's work. About this time, however, bankers and other grantors of credit began to develop the notion that financial statements might be used as a basis for determining an applicant's eligibility for credit. In fact, as early as 1895, the New York Bankers Association adopted a resolution "to recommend to the members...that they request borrowers of money from their respective institutions to give them written statements over their signatures of their assets and liabilities, in such form as the Committee on Uniform Statements of the various groups recommended." No indication, however, of how these statements were to be used was given.[1]

Quantitative analysis of financial statement for credit purposes progressed slowly during the years prior to World War I.[2] The principal ratios used during these years were those pertaining to working

---

[1]John N. Myer, Financial Statement Analysis (New York: John N. Myer, 1939), p. 4.

[2]Sistor Isadore Brown, The Historical Development of the Use of Ratios in Financial Statement Analysis to 1933 (Washington: The Catholic University of America Press, 1955), p. 13.

capital analysis, such as the "current" and "quick" ratios. Over the years, the limitations of this type of ratio became apparent and new ratios relating balance sheet items became accepted. Solvency and the "pounce value" of assets were the primary concerns of such theory of credit worth.

Later, about 1914, financial statement analysis for both credit and investment purposes underwent an important change when, as already noted, there developed a greater recognition of the "going concern" value of a business: "the new idea was to be more concerned with the continuance of the business and how it would perform in the future."[1] To get such a picture of a business it was necessary to consider both the balance sheet and the income statement individually and together. Of the two statements, however, the income statement became the more important.

Having digressed somewhat to trace the shift from the balance sheet to the income statement as the financial tabulation more relevant to the investment decision, we now return to discuss the fourth possible factor in the investment decision: the "investment banker."

Investment Banker

During much of the 30 years covered by this chapter it was commonly held that investors bought securities on

---

[1] *Ibid.*

the basis of their confidence in the investment banking house marketing the offer. If an investment banker offered a security that was enough--the investor need only know the type of security, its yield, maturity and interest payable dates. Furthermore, the banker "practically guaranteed the security" and, under these conditions, an elaborate prospectus was hardly needed. This attitude, as already shown, was challenged in the 1920's by some investment bankers who put forth the heretical proposition that securities should be offered on their own merits.

The theory of investment related to "confidence in the banking house" was based on three beliefs. First, it was generally held the investment banker undertook a thorough investigation of the securities and the issuing corporation before offering such securities to his customers. In 1908, Edward Sherwood Meade[1] described the bankers' analysis thus:

> ...This involves a very thorough investigation of the proposition and it involves the covering of every possible point on which any doubt might be expressed. It involves the answering of a large number of questions covering every feature of the proposition; it involves the organization of this material gotten together by engineers, accountants, lawyers, and by businessmen in the different industries affected, in the form of a complete report, sometimes running into hundreds of pages, a regular prize

---

[1]In 1908, Meade was Professor of Finance in the University of Pennsylvania.

> essay on the business proposition, going down to the last intimate detail of it, and then it involves the consideration of that proposition by bankers and others to whom they may be referred.[1]

Second, the banker recognized he had a fiduciary relation to his customers:

> ...[The investment banker's] relation to his customer is now recognized to be a fiduciary relation--not in law but in fact. His main stock in trade, his most valuable asset in pushing his business, is the confidence which his customers have in him; because if he can gain the confidence of a man who has $5,000 a year to invest, he will sell that man $5,000 worth of securities every year for perhaps 20 to 30 years; so simply by selling that man safe investment he will have the investment of $100,000 or more money....This confidence is regarded as so important that in practice though not in law, many private bankers guarantee the securities which they sell to the public.[2]

Third, the banker was concerned with the "safety of the investment":

> ...safety; that is the primary consideration, and you find it running through all the advertising literature,--"This thing is perfectly good." The investor values that more than the income. Since bankers practically guarantee the value of the securities they sell, and since safety is the primary consideration, you see what supreme importance it is to the banker that the propositions he advances should be absolutely sound; and you see that that can be guaranteed only by a careful preliminary investigation which seeks

---

[1]Edward Sherwood Meade, "Initial State of Organization," Corporation Finance Lectures 1908-1909. Copyright, 1908, by President and Fellows of Harvard College, Boston, p. 46.

[2]Ibid., pp. 47-48.

> to go down into the minutest parts of the proposition and produce every unfavorable factor, and to take account of everything which might seem to cast any discredit upon the value of the scheme.[1]

Others who agreed with Professor Meade were Wallace B. Donham and William H. Lough. In 1908 Donham, the future Dean of the Harvard Graduate School of Business Administration,[2] said: "The only way that the public in this country can get the protection given by the English Companies Act is by going to a banking house of high standards and great care."[3] Later, in 1919, William H. Lough[4] said: "The first test of a security is to see that it is sponsored by one or more reliable investment firms." Many a promising corporation, Lough said, had been ruined through having its securities handled by a weak or untrustworthy security house.[5]

Not all were agreed the investor need look no further than the recommendation of the banker. As early

---

[1]*Ibid.*, pp. 48-49.

[2]In 1908, Donham was Vice President of the Old Colony Trust Company, Boston, Massachusetts.

[3]Wallace B. Donham, "Underwriting Securities and the Purchase and Sale of Securities Through Banking Houses," *Corporation Finance Lectures, 1908-1909*. Copyright, 1908 by the President and Fellows of Harvard College, Boston, p. 199.

[4]Author of finance text books.

[5]William H. Lough, *Business Finance* (New York: The Ronald Press, 1919), pp. 37-44.

as 1908, George O. May, speaking to the same group previously addressed by Meade, said:

> I do not, however, find myself altogether in agreement with Professor Meade....I can agree with Professor Meade that...a large number of sound proposals have been accepted by bankers and by them placed before the public. But I cannot agree with Professor Meade that the virtues which he finds in the method of presentation to or through bankers are necessarily inherent in or peculiar to that method....what I have to say is based on actual experience. I have had personal familiarity with matters which were accepted by bankers and by them offered to the public without adequate investigation and on a basis which was essentially unsound....[1]
>
> Now, Professor Meade has told you that banking houses practically guarantee the securities they sell, but I think it would not be safe to put too broad an interpretation on this statement....[2]

May, as we have already seen, argued for disclosure similar to that required under the English Companies Act and in particular independently audited financial statements.

Another who spoke on the need of the investor to possess information related to the members of the marketing syndicate was Louis D. Brandeis. In 1913, it will be recalled, Brandeis said the investor ought to receive information on the underwriter's profit so that the investor could judge the "safety" of the

---

[1]George O. May, "Floatation", Corporation Finance Lectures 1908-1909. Copyright 1908, by President and Fellows of Harvard College, Boston, p. 118.

[2]Ibid., p. 130.

investment and the interest in the security of those who advised him in such matters. In addition, Brandeis said, this information related to the bankers' "spread" would assist the investor to appraise the offered security's value.

Clinton Collver: Investment Analysis Requirements

In 1917, Clinton Collver, as noted above in chapter six, published, through Moody's Investors Service, How to Analyze Industrial Securities. This particular book, and Collver's other publications in the field of industrial security analysis, were important for several reasons: they presented a unified and comprehensive statement of the "best" security analysis techniques of the day; and also influenced future investors and security analysts in their appraisal of security values. Those portions of Collver's book related to investor information needs are discussed below.

According to Collver, profits and dividends---past, present, and prospective---were the main determinants of industrial common stock prices. In most cases, book value, Collver said, was of limited significance:

> ...The book value is at best usually only of real service if the assets are of salable nature or backed by good earning power.... The prices of the common stocks are mostly based upon earnings, past, present and prospective, and dividends past, present, and prospective. Value of assets, particularly "natural resource assets" such as oil and lumber, are usually of value to an industrial

> only as these assets can be turned into finished products, the finished product sold, and profits realized....[1]

Collver, in his book on the analysis of industrial securities, also touched on the relationship of the following major topics to the security investment decision: business factors, management, balance sheet and income statement. The ingredients comprising each one of these areas which, Collver said, should be analyzed, are briefly discussed below. No attempt has been made to critically examine the investment theory suggested by Collver since what is important for the purpose of this study is that the "professional investors" believed they required certain facts pertaining to an offering so as to intelligently appraise it for investment purposes.

In the area of "business factors", according to Collver, an analysis of four major facts was necessary: fluctuations in demand; control over the permanent sources of raw materials; standardization of products and location of plants; and competition. First, with respect to demand characteristics of the issuer's products the investor was advised to examine the nature of the general demand for the products of the issuer's industry; the particular demand for the products of the

---

[1]Clinton Collver, op. cit.

issuer; the trend in the sales of both the issuer and the industry; the extent of any fluctuation in these sales; the degree of product and geographic diversification achieved by the issuer; and the market areas serviced by the issuer.

Second, on the subject of control over raw material supplies the investor should inquire into such matters as the nature of the raw material used by the corporation offering the securities and the general demand for these products; the location, price fluctuation, and reliability of this supply; the amount of the issuer's capital tied up in inventory and raw materials; and the degree of vertical and horizontal integration achieved by the issuer.

Third, the degree of standardization of the issuer's products and the location of his plants were, of course, related to the issuer's ability to produce low cost items and service his markets--both important areas to which Collver said the investor should devote some attention.

Fourth, on the nature of competition within the issuer's industry the investor ought, Collver believed, to analyze such facts as the percentage of the industry under the issuer's control and the changes over recent years in this percentage; the strength of the patents and trade names owned by the issuer; the trend in the issuer's operating margins; the role of technological innovations in the industry; and the ease with which new competitors could enter the industry.

Such an analysis of "business factors" was necessary Collver said since:

> Good business will hide many sins. Sins of promotion, of organization, capitalization, manipulation, and management are well concealed behind the skirts of constantly increasing sales....Will the sales keep up--not only keep up, but consistently expand?--should be the security holder's first mental inquiry.[1]

The second major factor to be considered by investors when analyzing industrial securities, Collver said, was management: "The ability of the managers to increase sales, to lower costs, to improve the quality of the product, to direct the policy, and to master the financial problems, constitutes an important element in maintaining the standing of industrial securities."[2] In fact, Collver believed the importance of the man was much greater in industrial than in railway management where the management had become "standardized."

Consequently, in the area of management, which was "one of the first considerations to the investor or speculator," Collver outlined four aspects to be

---

[1] *Ibid.*, p. 21.

[2] *Ibid.*, p. 48.

examined: the "personal equation"; cooperation and loyalty; financial control; and financial policy. First, of the management, Collver said, investors should know if they were "able," "careful," "farsighted," and "skillful" men who knew the particular problems of their industry and were capable of successfully managing an expanded operation. These facts comprised the personal equation. In addition, how long the current management was likely to remain with the corporation was of particular interest.

Second, in evaluating a corporation's management, Collver claimed, it was "essential...to find whether it has the enthusiastic loyalty of directors, officers, and employees."[1] In particular the existence of such things as profit sharing plans, employee stock purchase plans, bonus systems and management-labor relations should be examined by the intelligent investor.

Under the label management and financial control the careful investor should look at who controlled the corporation and the strength of their control; the banking community's opinion of these people; the control's commercial and financial alliances; and the controlling group's relations with suppliers, competitors and customers. And in the area of financial policy the

---

[1] Ibid., p. 55.

investor should also try to determine whether the issuer had displayed prudence and farsightedness. For example, specific topics such as dividends, cash, and retained earnings should be examined to determine if the issuer had paid excessive unwarranted or unearned dividends.

The third and fourth major topics discussed by Collver--balance sheets and income statements--have already been mentioned in chapter five and will not be again discussed here in detail. The data provided through the adoption of both his recommended balance sheet and supporting schedules and the Federal Reserve Board's proposed income statement would, Collver believed, be useful to the investor. Such forms of financial statement would allow the investor to compute the offered securities' book value and a number of financial ratios related to the issuer. These ratios included the following: current assets to current liabilities; accounts and notes receivable to merchandise; net sales to accounts and notes receivable; sales to merchandise inventory; net worth to fixed assets; sales to net worth; total debt to net worth; sales to fixed assets; "percentage of total expenses of running the business, including manufacturing, selling, and administration, to gross sales; average inventory to annual sales; working capital to total capital; and cash and cash resources to total capital, to gross volume of business, and to current liabilities. Such an analysis based on ratios, he said, was only meaningful if the investor related the various ratios to each other, took into account the particular times of the year covered by the data and compared ratios from year to year.[1]

The reliability of these ratios, Collver warned, was limited when comparing a company's performance from year to year and different companies, since the standards of accounting used by industrial companies varied from year to year and from company to company.

The next topic--the utility and reliability of prospectuses--will show the relationship between the content of prospectuses and the four major areas of interest to investors discussed above--the issue, the management, the firm, and the investment banker. In particular, the discussion will focus on the utility and reliability of the financial data revealed in prospectuses.

Utility and Reliability

A number of the topics related to investment analysis previously discussed in the section of this chapter labelled "Investor Information Needs" were

---

[1]Clinton Collver, Industrial Securities (New York: Doubleday, Page & Company, 1921), pp. 89-95.

covered in one prospectus or another but no one prospectus touched upon them all. In fact, in almost every case examined, there was "almost always something omitted which every intelligent investor would want to know."[1] In addition, there was often a question as to the reliability of the information presented.

Utility

Prospectuses provided the "intelligent investor" and "professional investment analyst" with little of the information required to make informed investment decisions. The most serious and common--perhaps universal--omission from prospectuses was a full income statement showing sales less the major classes of expense. Lacking such a statement it would be difficult to carry out successfully a ratio analysis along the lines suggested by, say, Collver. The substitution of a statement of average sales and earnings would hardly suffice. On the prevailing practice of only presenting average profits Collver said: "to the careful man, the whole record explained, even when containing a lean profit, is more attractive than the always dubious mystery of average profits."[2]

---

[1]"The Full Prospectus is Rare," The Journal of Accountancy, Vol. 45, No. 1, January 1928, p. 30.

[2]Collver, How To Analyze Industrial Securities, p. 188.

In general, after 1914, prospectuses offering industrial securities contained at least a truncated balance sheet. Often, however, those investors more concerned with an analysis of the balance sheet data faired no better than those who looked to the income statement for an indication of a security's worth. This condition was brought about by such common accounting and reporting practices as a failure to show contingent liabilities; the maturity date(s) of debentures, bonds and bank loans; and the valuation basis of inventory and other assets. Other important omissions from balance sheets were: distinction between tangible and intangible assets; comparative data covering two or more years; and mention of consolidated or non consolidated subsidiary companies. Also omitted was information related to depreciation policy; reconciliation of the surplus account and provisions for bad debts. Again, given these practices a satisfactory ratio analysis of balance sheet items and the calculation of such things as tangible book value were difficult, if not impossible.

Two changes in prospectuses between 1900 and 1930 which did reflect similar changes in the current popular theories of investment were the addition, about 1918, of some record of dividend payments in a number of prospectuses and the stating of the earnings figure on a per share basis after 1924. These small concessions, however, were far from enough to satisfy the information needs of the "sophisticated investor."

Two other important ingredients in the investment decision related to "management" and the "investment banker." The information presented to investors on both these topics was meager. Seldom, as noted above, were more than the names of the principal underwriters shown on the prospectuses. Facts pertaining to the banker's "spread" and the net return from the issue to the issuer were absent from every prospectus examined. As will be seen in chapter eight, it was not the "custom" to present such data. And on the topic of management only a short paragraph similar to those presented earlier, which were all written by the management, was shown. Such statements could only be considered as *ex parte* and hence of questionable reliability. In addition, the lack of financial information compounded the problems of those investors seeking to appraise the effectiveness of the issuer's management.

Reliability: Auditor's Certificates

In 1912, as noted earlier, Alexander Smith published an article entitled "The Abuse of the Audit in Selling Securities." Later others, including

George O. May, Clinton Collver and A. P. Richardson, expressed concern, not only over the lack of material provided investors, but also over the reliability of the meager information that was published in prospectuses. The auditor's certificate, as a number of individuals said, was often omitted, misused and abused by management in prospectuses. Used properly, these observers said, the auditor's certificate was a guarantee of the reliability of the financial data; used improperly it could only mislead.

The bulk of the material presented in prospectuses was either the representation of the investment banker or the vendor and as such could not be regarded as being unbiased. In addition, the accountant who audited the vendor's books was usually hired by management and regarded himself as representing management--not the public. The only legal restraint upon the statements which these parties could make was the common law related to deceit and fraud.

Before 1920, in the area of financial data few prospectuses showed certified public accountant's audit certificates but eight years later, by 1928, most balance sheets were accompanied by an audit certificate. Occasionally, this certificate also covered the net profit figures presented. The historical development of the use in prospectuses of the audit certificates is outlined below.

About 1900, when banker's prospectuses were most frequently used, the full prospectus on occasion would contain a letter, similar to the one reproduced below signed by a public accounting firm and addressed to the banker. The auditor in such cases acted as an agent for the underwriter.

Messrs. Baring, Magoun & Co., New York
Gentlemen:

We have examined the accounts of Messrs. P. Lorillard & Co., for the period of five years ending December 31, 1890. After writing off a fair amount to meet depreciation of machinery and plant, but before providing management remuneration of partners we find the profits to be as follows:

Year 1886	$686,703.82
" 1887	788,858.76
" 1888	235,377.07
" 1889	386,252.23
" 1890	558,960.17
	$2,625,852.15

Or an average per annum of $525,170.43

The above profits do not bear charges for rents paid by the vendors, as we understand the real estate will be purchased by the Company.

The decreased profit for the year 1888 is accounted for by failure of the leaf crop in 1887 and extensive alterations and improvements to the Drying House necessitating a reduction in the sales of Tobacco.

We are, Gentlemen,
Yours obediently,
(Signed) DELOITTE, DEVERS, GRIFFITHS & CO.

London and New York, June 22, 1891.

Later, during the period when the banker's prospectus was declining in popularity and the form of the management prospectus for industrial offering was slowly evolving, the practice of including a statement from the auditor directly in the prospectus fell from favor. In fact, before 1918, audit certificates were seldom shown in prospectuses. However, a reference to an independent audit was made in about 25 per cent of the pre-1918 prospectuses examined through statements similar to the two shown below. For instance, in a banker's prospectus the reference by the banker to the audit of the issuer's accounts might read:

> We have had made by [name of audit firm] a very complete audit of the company's books and account....

And in a management prospectus:

> The condensed balance sheet of the Company as of [date] adjusted to give effect to the recapitalization, the acquisition of the [name of firm acquired], and certified by [name of accounting firm].
>
> The books of the firm have been audited for the last five years by [name of accounting firm]....

About 1918 and thereafter, the practice of including an audit certificate along with the balance sheet shown in prospectuses became more frequent and, as noted above, by 1928 the practice of presenting balance sheet audit certificate had become a common one. The typical post-1918 audit certificate read as follows:

> WE HEREBY CERTIFY, that we have audited the books of account and record of [name of company], and affiliated companies as of the close of business [date] and it is our opinion that the above Condensed Balance Sheet correctly shows the financial position of the [name of company] as of [date], after giving effect to certain transactions not yet consummated as stated above.
>
> [date] [signature of accounting firm]

Not all certificates, however, read as above. For instance, in 1925, one well-known nation-wide firm of public accountants issued the following certificate:

> We have practically completed our examination of the books of account and record of [name of company] as of January 31, 1925, and we have prepared therefrom the foregoing Preliminary Balance Sheet after giving effect to transaction to be consummated as above stated.
>
> [signature of accounting firm]

The presence of an audit certificate did not always mean the audited data was reliable. For instance, in 1919, on the subject of audit certificates, Collver, who had worked with a prominent firm of auditors, warned investors not to place too much reliance upon the certification by public accountants of financial statements. In addition, he expressed dissatisfaction over the common method of appointing auditors:

> Too much reliance has been placed upon the indorsement of public accountants of income accounts and balance sheets. Of course an uncertified financial report is like an unsearched real estate title. But

> as there are various grades of skill and reliability in the field of title searching, just so are there various grades of skill and responsibility in public accounting work. Nor does it necessarily avail that the financial report be certified by a public accounting firm of large size and many offices. Two of the largest firms, whose certificates are found on many large corporations' reports, do not enjoy a good reputation among accountants. Firms do exist which will, for a small fee, certify to balance sheets which are entirely if not criminally misleading. It is unfortunate that the public accounting firm is not chosen by the stockholders as is the case abroad. In this country the officers of a corporation choose the auditors and naturally they will find such as will certify to the accounts as the officials present them.[1]

Noteworthy abuses of accounting work, Collver noted, were the bidding system and "partial audits."

> One special abuse in accounting work is the bidding system. Many corporations do not realize the importance of thorough work, and actually solicit bids for the work. Fancy submitting questions of a law involving millions of dollars to the lawyer making the lowest bid for the case! Another source of abuse is the "partial audit," the accountants being employed to audit only part of the accounts or part of the books, while the financial reports, as submitted to the public, appear to the unsuspecting to be founded on books of account entirely vouched for.[2]

In addition, Collver described several specific abuses of the audit. Public accountants had, in many cases, certified, without comment, the balance sheets of parent companies without auditing the books

---

[1]*Ibid.*, pp. 71-72.

[2]*Ibid.*

of the subsidiary companies. And, in other situations, public accountants, because of inadequate audits, had unwittingly certified balance sheets when a large part of the assets listed thereon appeared on the company's books but no place else.

Collver presented three examples in which either the auditor had conducted an unsatisfactory audit or the promoter had misused the auditor's name:

> Early in his business experience the writer had charge of the books of a subsidiary of a corporation whose stocks were listed on the New York Stock Exchange. The subsidiary corporation erected a very large office building. The shell was completed and charged, as it should be, against capital. The building was completed, partitions and fixtures were installed, and this large amount was treated as an expense under the blind of "Fixtures for Tenants." One of the largest firms of public accountants certified to the financial records of the parent corporation, never even touching the subsidiary books, which would have disclosed concealed assets running up into six figures.
>
> The smash in the McCrum-Howell Company is one of many examples of companies ending in a most spectacular failure soon after the publication of a wonderful financial report signed by a firm of public accountants. It transpired that a large part of the assets appeared on the books but no place else.
>
> In certain flotations, for example, Pugh Stores, securities have been sold on the standing of the public accountants which according to the prospectus "audited the books and accounts." Later it would be found that while the books and accounts were duly audited, the certified figures were not those given out. The reliability of the distributor of all information should be beyond question and the accountant's report should be available.[1]

---

[1] *Ibid.*, pp. 72-73.

Another who complained, and complained often, of the "misuse of accountants' reports" was A. P. Richardson, the editor of <u>The Journal of Accountancy</u>. For a number of years this outspoken editor had advocated the adoption of independent balance sheet audits for public reporting and credit purposes. At the same time, he had vehemently denounced those who abused the audit. In 1920, Richardson protested:

> There has been much comment because prospectuses and other literature issued prior to the flotation of securities have so frequently failed to indicate whether or not the affairs of the companies concerned have been subjected to independent investigation. In other cases when audits have been made there have been only incomplete and often misleading summaries of the accountants' figures and findings.
>
> In the interest of all concerned it should be a fixed rule that securities in which the public is asked to invest should be supported by statements showing the results of impartial examination conducted by reputable practitioners.
>
> The ideal condition would be the publication of the accountants' complete certificate, but in no case should there be any condensation which eliminates essential facts.
>
> Often in these days one reads that John Doe, president of the company, supplies the following information. Of course, presumably John Doe is an honest and honorable man, but as an interested party he cannot be completely impartial. The element of self-interest therefore will incline him to magnify the merits of the proposition and to deal gently with its demerits....

Furthermore, Richardson said, action by private groups, such as the New York Stock Exchange and the Accountants, to bring about conditions similar to those imposed by the English Companies Acts--the 1907 Act required independent audits--was desirable.

> Stock exchanges could no much, if they would, to bring about a needed reform following the lines of the English Companies Act or similar legislation in force in Canada and other British possessions.
>
> It is not sufficient, however, that there be an independent audit, unless the public is sure that the accountant's findings are truthfully conveyed to possible investors. It is really worse than no report at all if vital figures are omitted or qualifications in the certificate are suppressed.
>
> Incidentally a duty rests upon accountants to require clients and their bankers to make a fair use of their reports or certificates. Unless they do this they are morally responsible to the public for any misrepresentation in regard to which they do not exhaust every corrective remedy.

Next, Richardson presented an example showing how the improper use by management of their auditors' names in prospectuses misled the public.

> As an illustration of the use of an accountant's name in a way that might mislead the public, it is instructive to consider a recent prospectus, one paragraph of which reads somewhat as follows:
>
> "Our accountants are John Smith & Son of Boston, who have audited our books for the last two years. All statements given, except for the year 1919, of which an audit is about to be made, are supplied by public accountants of high standing employed by us prior to our association with John Smith & Son."
>
> In other words, the company leads the public to believe that its affairs have been audited by John Smith & Son, and that a clean bill of health has been given. As a matter of fact, the paragraph quoted means absolutely

> nothing except that John Smith & Son have conducted an audit -- and it is quite possible that the accounting firm found it necessary to damn the whole financial condition of the company. There is no copy of the certificate, and the figures which are given are apparently in no wise connected with the accountants' investigation.
>
> An unthinking prospective investor glancing over the prospectus to which we refer might be forgiven if he came to the conclusion that the financial affairs of the company had been investigated and their soundness endorsed by the well-known and reputable firm of John Smith & Son.
>
> This is a misuse of the accounting profession against which the entire membership should vehemently protest.[1]

Later, in 1925, Richardson noted prospectus audit certificates showed "evidence of a steadily increasing clarity in report and certificate," but, he also observed, a number of the abuses he described above still persisted. The blame for the misuse of audit reports in prospectuses, Richardson claimed, lay in most cases with either the management of the vendor or the underwriter handling the issue:

> In general, the publication of bare fact of audit is not the fault of the auditors but rather of the investment banker or of the corporation about to issue securities. The auditors are usually more sinned against than sinning in this matter of incomplete information.[2]

---

[1]"Misuse of Accountant's Reports," The Journal of Accountancy, Vol. 29, No. 4, April 1920, pp. 299-300.

[2]"The Accounts Have Been Audited," The Journal of Accountancy, Vol. 29, No. 5, May 1925, p. 394.

Subsequently, in the same 1925 editorial, Richardson said: "The time seemed ripe for definite action by the American Institute of Accountants to discourage, and, if possible prevent certificates of auditors from being indefinite, misleading and full of weasel words." In order to end this undesirable state of affairs Richardson suggested the institute concern itself with those cases of ambiguous certificates issued by accounting firms within the institute's jurisdiction. Those accounting houses which did not belong to the institute were, of course, beyond its control. In addition, he said:

> Rules founded upon the fundamental principles of frankness would probably meet with the instant approval of practically the entire membership of the institute. If the organization were to write such rules it would at least place the public on notice that vagueness is not to be tolerated by the professional body, and this in time would lead to a public demand that there should be definiteness and the clear assumption of responsibility by every accountant giving certificates in regard to financial condition....[1]

Three years later, in 1928, Richardson again returned to the question of audit certificates and prospectuses. By this time, however, despairing of private reform in this area through the efforts of the Institute he called for the enactment of laws

[1] Ibid., p. 397.

governing financial disclosure.

> Many prospectuses appearing from time to time present no evidence of independent verification. The accounts are prepared in the office of the borrowing company and no pretense is made that they have been impartially prepared. These ex parte statements, however, are coming into disrepute or at least into disfavor and it is growing more and more to the customer to call upon independent accountants for examination prior to the issuance of any securities....But there seems to be no legal bar to the publication of the accountant's name without anything more than that, save in the remote possible contingency that an attempt to deceive can be proven.... The cure for the evil can be found in the enactment of laws prohibiting publication of prospectuses without adequate--not necessarily full--information, and the information cannot be adequate unless the accountants' certificate is in its proper place under the statement of accounts whether full or condensed, which is published.[1]

The next topic discusses the responsibility for the conditions previously described in this chapter.

The Disclaimer Clause

Beginning around 1910 prospectuses--full and abridged--frequently contained statements--the so-called disclaimer clause--inserted by the investment banker handling the issue similar to the following:

> The information and statistics contained in this circular are not guaranteed but have been obtained from reliable sources and we believe them to be accurate.

*****

---

[1] "Legal Rules Seem Necessary," The Journal of Accountancy, Vol. 45, No. 1, January 1928, p. 32.

> All statements in this circular are based upon information which we regard as reliable, being in part the data upon which we have acted in our purchase and valuation of the securities offered.
>
> *****
>
> Statements contained herein are in no sense to be construed as representations by us.
>
> *****
>
> We do not guarantee the statements and figures presented herein but they are taken from sources which we believe to be reliable.

These statements disclaiming responsibility on the part of the banker and the use of the president's letter discussed above would indicate it was the intent of investment bankers to place the full responsibility for prospectus disclosure upon the issuing corporation. Such an artifice, according to Berle and Means, "probably fails of its effects. While the corporation may make the statement [contained in the prospectus], the banker assumes the responsibility of repeating it."[1] Discussed below are some aspects of the question related to the responsibility for the nature of the corporate and financial data revealed in prospectuses.

Not all statements contained within the prospectus could be attributed to the officer signing the president's letter. Such a statement as "These securities

---

[1]Berle and Means, op. cit., p. 304.

are legal investment for Massachusetts Savings Banks" would be made by the banker as his own knowledge. This type of statement usually appeared above or below the president's letter and it is doubtful if such comments could be construed to the responsibility of the issuer. The question remains, however, to what extent were the officers of the issuing corporation responsible for the president's letter? The answer lies in an understanding of the process whereby the president's letter was written.

The prospectus, including the president's letter, was commonly prepared under the general supervision of both the officers of the issuer and the underwriting firm. The lawyers of both those parties, however, were the two groups most directly concerned with the preparation of the prospectus. In general, according to Berle and Means, the prospectus was "drawn in the office of the banker or his lawyers; presented for revision to the corporate officials; drafted and redrafted with a view to accuracy, putting the best foot forward, creating a proper market effect, and diminishing, so far as possible, the responsibility of everyone concerned in the flotation."[1]

A similar description of the process whereby

---

[1] Ibid., pp. 301-302.

prospectuses were drawn up was given to the writer by a retired investment banker who had been actively engaged in that industry from 1900-1933. His description, in contrast to Berle and Means, would indicate the lawyers of both parties were equally involved in the affair.

Q. As you know, prospectuses issued during the period 1900-1933, in general, consisted of a letter from a senior officer of the issuing company. What part did the investment banker play in the drawing up of these letters?

A. Well, the lawyers--they usually called all the plays. They worked over these things to see that everything was all right so that there would be no legal problems.

Q. Was this matter principally the concern of the underwriter?

A. No. The lawyers of both parties--the underwriter and the issuer--both worked on it together....

Q. What was their objective in preparing the prospectus?

A. Of course, they would tell about the company. Prospectuses were never negative. They always stressed the good. It was just as if you had

> a house to sell--you never tell people
> that it is built on a swamp....[1]

Thus, the work of preparing the prospectus, including the president's letter, was delegated by management to his and the marketing syndicate's lawyers. The principal concerns of these lawyers were two in number: avoid legal problems; and present an attractive picture of the issuer and the issue. The presentation of full and frank financial information to the investor was seldom, it would seem, the goal of the issuer, the underwriter and their respective lawyers.

Since the prospectus was a joint production of the banker and the issuer, irrespective of the disclaimer clause, it would appear both were in some way responsible legally[2] and morally--for the contents of the president's letter.[3] Later, in 1933, the investment bankers were to avow a complete lack of responsibility for this matter.

*****

---

[1]Field notes.

[2]"The few cases that have gone through the courts regarding dealer responsibility give no clear insight into the strength of the bankers usual disclaimer of legal responsibility."--Arthur Stone Dewing, The Financial Policy of Corporations. Third Revised Edition (New York: The Ronald Press Company, 1934), p. 1017.

[3]The lawyers, of course, acted only as agents under contract in this matter and could not be responsible directly to the investor--only to their respective principals.

In general, the information--particularly financial data--shown in prospectuses failed to meet the minimum standards of financial and corporate disclosure proposed by a number of the groups and individuals previously discussed in chapters one, three and six. For instance, none of the prospectuses examined touched on all the 13 points required under the 1900 British Companies Act discussed in chapter one. Later a number of people, such as George O. May and A. Lowes Dickinson, recommended the adoption in the United States of the minimum disclosure standards for prospectuses set forth in this and later British Companies Acts.

Subsequently in chapter three, the recommendations of the Industrial Commission's 1900 report, which called for the disclosure to investors of the "full details" necessary for making "safe and intelligent" investment decisions, and the Pujo Committee's plea in 1913 for "complete publicity" were discussed.

The proposals of these two committees were vague and, hence, not easy criteria to judge prospectus disclosure against. However, both of these investigatory bodies were dissatisfied with the contemporary level of disclosure and, as shown above, the level of prospectus financial disclosure later achieved, judged by the expressed needs of the "professional" users of such data, could hardly have been regarded as "full" nor "complete."

In chapter six starting with the Federal Reserve Board's publication Uniform Accounting more specific proposals related to financial disclosure were made by a number of groups and individuals including the Federal Trade Commission, Clinton Collver and the Investment Bankers Association of America.

In 1917, the Federal Reserve Board in conjunction with the Federal Trade Commission and the American Institute of Accountants had, it will be recalled, published a pamphlet called Uniform Accounting which sought to promote balance sheet audits for credit purposes. Included in this document were suggested "proper" forms for auditor's certificates, balance sheets and profit and loss accounts. Not one prospectus among those surveyed contained certificates or financial statements similar to the standard forms proposed by the Federal Reserve Board. In the area of prospectus financial disclosure the impact of Uniform Accounting was "almost nil."

Next, again in 1917 and for a number of years thereafter, Clinton Collver, recommended the adoption of the Federal Reserve Board's proposed format for income statements by industrial concerns for public reporting purposes. In addition, Collver proposed the adoption of his suggested balance sheet form with supporting schedules. Such financial statements, he said, would provide investors with the type of financial data required to make "intelligent" investment decisions. None of the balance sheets examined showed information in the detail or form suggested by Collver.

Later, in 1919, the Federal Trade Commission, for a brief time, required promoters to file a questionnaire related to their promotions and the securities they planned to issue. Again, on the basis of the prospectuses surveyed, the influence of this attempt by a federal agency to indicate some preferred corporate disclosure practices appeared to have had little influence on the content of prospectuses.

Subsequently, between 1920 and 1925 several committees of the Investment Bankers Association of America presented to the Association's annual convention reports which contained recommendations related to prospectus financial disclosure. In all instances, the reports were unanimously approved by the convention. The 1920 report of the Industrial Securities Committee, among other things, condemned the use of average earnings figures and proposed all prospectuses show an "adequate balance sheet" and "correct and ample information on management." Subsequently, the 1925 report of the Special Committee on Circulars recommended every prospectus present information on a number of specific items, including a description of the industry and an "understandable balance sheet."

Two years later, in 1927, the Industrial Securities saw evidence of an "endeavor...to follow the suggestions of previous Industrial Securities Committees." Unlike the 1927 committee I could not comment of the intent of those preparing prospectuses, but, as shown above, as late as 1930 the use of averages continued; a number of balance sheets, by standards of the 1925 report, were still neither "adequate" nor "understandable"; and, as shown above, correct and ample information on management was not always presented.

Yet, between 1918 and 1930, the average investor was apparently unconcerned with the inadequacies related to prospectuses described above "simply because, unfortunately, investors wish generalities and do not welcome 'statistics'...."[1] The careful investor and the professional security analyst, however, could not be so complacent as "investment and intelligent speculation are possible only as frequent and complete information as to income and financial condition are available."[2]

---

[1]Collver, Industrial Securities, p. 85.

[2]Ibid., p. 33.

All too often the public when purchasing securities was gambling--"the staking of money on the unknown."[1] In fact, the critics of big business claimed this was an unfair gamble, because "insiders" possessed full financial information and the financial statements presented to the public were frequently incomplete or misleading. Such inadequate financial disclosure practices, the critics said, must not persist, but few before the economic débâcle of 1930 took the critics' demands seriously.

---

[1] *Ibid.*

CHAPTER EIGHT

THE SECURITIES ACT OF 1933

The long standing requests for more honest and complete corporate disclosure were partially satisfied with the passage of the 1933 Securities Act. The enactment of this reform measure, which some said was inevitable, was without doubt sped by the 1929 stock market crash and the economic depression which followed soon after.

Beginning in October 1929 the market price of securities rapidly declined from their previous September peak and the "indian summer of the old order" suddenly drew to a close. Within a few weeks the aggregate value of listed securities declined by as much as thirty billion dollars[1]--the public's confidence in Wall Street was destroyed. Next, in early 1930 the economy too began to show definite signs of a decline[2] and before long the nation was experiencing all the horrors, chaos and fear of a major economic depression.

---

[1]Allen, op. cit., p. 145.

[2]The actual downturn, as measured by most of the accepted indices of economic activity, occurred during the second half of 1929 and "by autumn of 1929 the economy was well into a depression." John Kenneth Galbraith, The Great Crash of 1929 (Boston: Houghton Mifflin Company, 1955), p. 93.

DOI: 10.4324/9781003169420-8

As the "new era of prosperity" became the "great depression", the attack on big business and its attendant demand for greater corporate publicity was reopened with new vigor. The misery of the depression, and the financial chicanery revealed at the hearings on stock exchange practices conducted by the Senate Committee on Banking and Currency during 1932 and 1933, led to a widespread public desire for economic and social reform; the critics knew what reforms were necessary and the public were again sympathetic to the critics' proposals. Others, such as the New York Stock exchange and the Institute of Accountants, were also bestirred by the débâcle of the early 1930's and once again attempted to exert their influence over corporate executives in an attempt to improve corporate financial disclosure practices through private rather than government action. However, by 1930, the promise of such private reform was too late.

Beginning with the congressional elections of 1930, the political pendulum swung to the left and on March 4, 1933, Franklin Delano Roosevelt was installed as the nation's thirty-second president. Subsequently, in May 1933, Congress for the protection of investors passed the Securities Act:-

An Act to provide full and fair disclosure of the character of securities sold in interstate and foreign commerce and through the mails, and to prevent frauds in the sale thereof, and for other purposes.[1]

The Economic, Political and Social Environment 1929-1933

During the period 1929 to 1933 the immediate events which were most relevant to the passage of the 1933 Securities Act were: the stock market crash; the economic collapse of the nation; the renewed attack on big business; the 1932-1933 Senate investigation of stock exchange practices; the publication of Berle and Means's book *The Modern Corporation and Private Property*; and the 1932 presidential campaign. Each of these topics, which have been well covered by other authors and are familiar to most of us, are briefly discussed below.

The 1929-1933 Stock Market Decline

During the late 1920's it was widely believed that the United States had entered an era of never-ending prosperity and permanent high levels of stock prices. Such was not to be the case. The first signs that all was not well came in October 1929 when securities prices began to decline---slowly at first but then faster, and, despite a few rallies, the long-run trend was ever-downwards.

---

[1]Public Law No. 22, 73rd Congress, 1st Session.

By September 1929 there were about 10 million stockholders in the United States and the dollar value--on paper--of their holdings was at an all-time high. Then, throughout October, the market began to decline and on Tuesday, October 29, 1929, the earlier so-called "technical readjustment" turned into a "crash"--

> The big gong had hardly sounded in the great hall of the Exchange at ten o'clock Tuesday morning before the storm broke in full force. Huge blocks of stock were thrown upon the market for what they would bring. Five thousand shares, ten thousand shares appeared at a time on the laboring ticker at fearful recessions in price. Not only were innumerable small traders being sold out, but big ones, too, protagonists of the new economic era who a few weeks before had counted themselves millionaires. Again and again the specialist in a stock would find himself surrounded by brokers fighting to sell--and nobody at all even thinking of buying....Within half an hour of the opening the volume of trading had passed three million shares, by twelve o'clock it had passed eight million, by half-past one it had passed twelve million, and when the closing gong brought the day's madness to an end the gigantic record of 16,410,030 shares had been set. Toward the close there was a rally, but by that time the average prices of fifty leading stocks, as compiled by the New York Times, had fallen nearly forty points. Meanwhile there was a near-panic in other markets--the foreign stock exchanges, the lesser American exchanges, the grain market.[1]

Between September 1929 and July 1932--the low point of the market--a number of the recognized indices

---

[1]Frederick Lewis Allen, Only Yesterday (New York: Harper & Brothers, 1931), pp. 333-334.

which measure stock market price levels recorded the decline thus: the Dow-Jones industrial stock average fell from 386.10 to 40.56; the Dow-Jones railroad stock average sank from 190.60 to 13.16; the Dow-Jones utility stock average went from 144.61 to 15.78; and the New York Times average for 25 industrials fell from 469.49 to 57.62. By July 1932 the aggregate value of securities listed on the New York Stock Exchange stood at $15 billion---some $74 billion less than in September 1929.

The enormity of the decline called for some kind of government action to prevent a reoccurrence of such a disaster. By 1932, the year of the presidential elections, a substantial majority favored this proposal.

The Economic Collapse

Shortly after the stock market crash the economy too began to show signs of a major depression which, as events progressed, was to hit bottom during the early spring of 1933. For example, between 1929 and 1933 the nation's gross national product fell from $104 billion to $56 billion; national income sank from $87 billion to $40 billion; and per capita disposable personable income declined from $678 to $360. Unemployment rose from 1.5 million to 12.8 million; aggregate corporate profits fell from $10.3

billion to a net loss of $2 billion; and the farm product price index sank from 105 to 51 (1926=100). In addition, of the country's 24,000 banks in 1929 over 6,000 had failed by 1933.

The bubble had burst and by 1933

> There was....a kind of crowding hysteria in the air which no one could escape....Thrifty families in every locality of rural America were being torn from the acres they had cultivated and turned loose in communities which had no further use for them. And even those who remained on their farms awoke each morning to a little more rust on their machinery, a little more flaking of the paint on their barns. In the cities...bread lines were lengthening. The streets were crowded with idle men. Many a businessman had seen his occupation disappear; and the stock market's magic had reduced everyone's security to the vanishing point....[1]

Thus did the new era prosperity become the great depression of the thirties.

Big Business Under Attack

The liberals, progressives, socialists and communists all gained new strength from the depression and once again renewed their attacks on big business. The economic defense of big business which had for so long seemed impregnable was now shattered. Most obviously, the critics said, big business was inefficient and, in face of the facts, businessman had no answer.

---

[1]Tugwell, *op. cit.*, p. 20.

> ...in the Depression pent up hostility toward big business was unleashed in a torment...many big corporations looked pretty feeble. Some, especially among the railroads and utilities, had gotten mixed up in pretty curious, not to say odorous, kinds of deals. In the minds of many, these situations reflected discredit on all big business....Giving big business a back-handed sort of credit for being a key instrumentality in the American economy, critics said it was responsible for the depression. The operation of the economy, all too obviously, was far from the ideal.... the whole issue /of big business/ was fully reopened on a grand scale.[1]

The nation was in chaos; businessmen and investment bankers were discredited; and the public were sympathetic to the--by now almost traditional--demands for corporate and social reform advocated by the critics of big business. In 1932, in contrast to the years prior to 1918, the demands of the critics now included adequate protection for investors as well as consumers, employees and independent small businessmen from the abuses of corporate power.

<u>Senate Committee on Banking and Currency, 1932-33</u>

In March 1932 the Republicans,dominant in the Senate, at the urging of those Republican Senators from the western farm states, adopted Senate Resolution 84, which authorized the Senate's Committee on Banking and Currency to make "a thorough and complete invest-

---

[1]Glover, <u>op. cit.</u>, pp. 304-305.

igation of the practices with respect to the buying and selling and the borrowing and lending of listed securities upon the various stock exchanges, [and] the value of such securities...."[1]

Later, much of the testimony heard at the hearings pursuant to this Senate Resolution revealed laxity on the part of the New York Stock Exchange in overseeing the publication of "honest, complete, and correct information" related to the affairs of listed companies.[2] In addition, numerous cases of misrepresentations and concealments in prospectuses which were purported to incorporate all the "authentic and pertinent facts regarding the issue"[3] were discovered. Also, several instances were uncovered of the "flagrant betrayal" by corporate directors and officers "who used their positions of trust and the confidential information which came to them in such positions, to aid them in their market activities. Closely allied to this type of abuse was the unscrupulous employment of inside information by large stockholders who, while not directors and officers, exercised sufficient

---

[1]Senate Resolution 84, 72nd Congress, 2nd Session.

[2]See, for example, Stock Exchange Practices, Report Of The Committee On Banking And Currency Pursuant To S. Res. 84 (72nd Congress) and S. Res. 56 and S. Res. 97 (73rd Congress), 73rd Congress, 2nd Session, Senate Report No. 1455, p. 68ff.

[3]*Ibid.*, p. 100ff.

control over the destinies of their companies to enable them to acquire and profit by information not available to others."[1]

Initially, during 1932, the hearings focused on the practices of the New York Stock Exchange, but in early 1933, soon after Ferdinand Pecora was hired by the Committee as its special counsel, the scope of the hearings was broadened to include the financial activities of certain holding companies, banks and investment banking houses. Outlined below is a brief history of Senate Resolution 84 and the subsequent much publicized hearings held prior to the passage of the 1933 Securities Act. Selected samples of the testimony related to prospectus disclosure heard at these hearings are also presented.

As early as December 1929 Senator King of Utah, as the spokesman for the Republican Senators from the western farm states, had asked for a senate resolution to authorize the investigation of stock exchange and banking practices. This proposal had the support of most of the Democrats and the Western Republicans then in the Senate.[2] King's proposal had appealed particularly to those from the western farm states for

---

[1]*Ibid*., p. 55 ff.

[2]*New York Times*, December 19, 1929, p. 39.

at least two reasons: bank failures had been heaviest in the West; and among farmers stock brokerage operations were regarded as "crap shooting on a large scale." Later, in March 1932, the Senate passed Senate Resolution 84 which embodied several of the proposals suggested earlier by King.

Of this particular resolution, and the motives behind those who proposed such action Galbraith has said:

> Our political tradition sets great store by the generalized symbol of evil. This is the wrongdoer whose wrongdoing will be taken by the public to be the secret propensity of a whole community or class. We search avidly for such people, not so much because we wish to see them exposed and punished as individuals, but because we cherish the resulting political discomfort of their friends. To uncover an evil man among the friends of one's foes had long been a recognized method of advancing one's political fortunes. However, in recent times the technique has been greatly improved and refined by the added firmness with which the evil of the evildoer is now attributed to friends, acquaintances, and all who share his way of life.
>
> In the nineteen-thirties Wall Street was exceptionally well endowed with enemies. There were some socialists and communists who believed that capitalism should be abolished and obviously did not seek to have its citadel preserved. There were some people who merely thought that Wall Street was bad. There were yet others who did not seek to have Wall Street abolished or who did not care much about its allegedly evil ways but who enjoyed as a matter of course the discomfiture of the rich and the powerful and the proud. There were those who had lost money in Wall Street....Wall Street's crime, in the eyes of its classical enemies, was less its power than its morals. And the center of immorality

> was not the banks but the stock market. It was on the stock market that men gambled not alone with their own money, but with the wealth of the country. The stock market, with its promise of easy riches, was what led good if not very wise men to perdition--like the cashier of the local bank who was also a vestryman. The senseless gyrations of the stock market affected farm prices and land values and the renewal of notes and mortgages. Though to the sophisticated radical the banks might be the real menace, sound populist attitudes pointed the finger of suspicion at the New York Stock Exchange. There, accordingly, was the place, if possible, to find the symbol of evil, for there was the institution about which people were ready to believe the worst.[1]

The Senate investigation of the New York Stock Exchange began on April 11, 1932 and, in general, the results were disappointing--no sensational wrongdoings were revealed. Initially, the Committee interrogated Richard Whitney, the President of the New York Stock Exchange, and after three days of "unproductive" testimony he was excused. Next, the Committee questioned several "famous market operators," including Harry F. Sinclair, Percy A. Rockefeller and Bernard E. Smith. The testimony of these men too was disappointing--"all that could be proved was what everyone knew, namely, that...[these men] and others had engaged in large-scale efforts to rig the market....Moreover, reprehensible as these activities were, it remained that only three short years before they had been regarded with breathless admiration."[2] Political

---

[1]Galbraith, op. cit., pp. 159-161.

[2]Ibid., p. 163.

reputations would not be made by such "revelations" which were already known to all.

In addition to attempting to reveal rascality in the Stock Exchange the Committee also sought advice as to how such miscreant practices might be prevented in the future. On June 14, 1932, William Z. Ripley, perhaps the era's most articulate critic of corporate machinations, appeared before the Committee and in his testimony repeated sentiments similar to those previously published in his book Main Street and Wall Street. He told the Committee:

> Many of these abuses and evils which have been exposed at your public hearings--failure of the Bank of the United States; the Gillette Razor scandal; and the collapse of the Insull properties--all of these thrive on secrecy. You would better stop short selling and speculation if everyone knew just what was going on among those companies in any other way. Therefore, I urge once again that you exercise the Federal power as appurtenant to the taxing power, to require that all means by which the Federal Income Taxes are computed, should be disclosed upon standardized, accepted forms prescribed by the United States Government.[1]

Given such information, Ripley claimed, the professional analysts and the research departments of reliable bankers would be better able to advise the "widow and the orphan" who were unable themselves to analyze corporate accounts.

---

[1]Hearings S. R. 84, p. 857.

In addition, Ripley said, it was not infrequent that when a business was operated "honestly and decently conducted," but without making full disclosure of its affairs, others, such as stock dealers in New York, would manufacture information related to the corporation so as to speculate in its stocks. Such speculation, Ripley declared, robbed "the common people, school-teachers and white-collar workers... out of the product of their thrift and industry."[1]

Compulsory publicity, Ripley said, had first been applied to railroad and later extended to telephone and telegraph companies doing an interstate business. Now, he said, "there is no reason in the world---and I have asked the advice of good constitutional lawyers...why this same requirement might not be extended to industrial corporations which are of a sufficient size and public importance to warrant the procedure."[2] The Committee, and much of the financial press,[3] seemed to agree with Ripley.

---

[1] _Ibid._, p. 878.

[2] _Ibid._

[3] For instance, on May 23, 1932, the editorial of the _Journal of Commerce_ discussed a similar proposal made by Ripley to the Savings Bank Association. The editorial said: "The recent collapse of two great holding company systems, one in the United States and one in Sweden, has afforded startling evidences of the dense ignorance of supposed experts and financial advisors regarding the involved accounting practices and

Next, the Committee began to investigate the collapse of two giant holding companies--Kreuger & Toll, and the Insull empires. On January 11 and 12, 1933, the Hearings were devoted to the flotation and distribution of the security issues of the Kreuger and Toll Co. The testimony of these two days again repeated what everyone else knew by now--the audits of Kreuger & Toll's subsidiaries had been inadequate; in America it was the practice of accountants to regard themselves as answerable to management; and the responsibility of accountants, accountants claimed, was limited by the technical language contained within their audit certificates. Such other well known facts related to the Kreuger episode also revealed included: Kreuger's earlier protests that secrecy on his part was essential in regard to some of his "secret agreements", which he claimed he could not disclose without bringing disastrous consequences to the company, were false; Kreuger's secret was that he was paying dividends out of capital; and the Kreuger prospectuses, which included a "rather enthusiastic endorsement by Ivor Kreuger himself," issued in

---

mispractices of organizations whose bonds and debentures have been widely recommended as sound investments to the people of this country. These revelations emphasize the need for full and authentic information to throw light in dark corners, where dishonest manipulators work, and to give facts about concealed operations which, even when legitimate, ought to be known to prospective investors." Ibid., p. 883.

support of the several Kreuger and Toll offerings were incomplete and misleading as were the company's other representations to shareholders and investors.

Subsequently, on January 24, 1933, Ferdinand Pecora was appointed special counsel to the committee. As a consequence of this addition, the scope of the investigation was broadened and under Pecora's guidance the Committee "became the scourge of commercial, investment, and private bankers."[1]

On February 15, 16 and 17, 1933, the Committee, now under Pecora's able direction, heard testimony related to the Insull Utility Investments (Inc.) failure. This testimony disclosed that Halsey, Stuart & Co., the investment banking firm which had offered the Insull securities to the public, held substantial financial interests in Insull Utility Investments, and certain members of Halsey, Stuart, as directors of the Insull holding company, had approved the sale of securities to Halsey, Stuart at a substantial discount. These transactions had not been revealed in the prospectuses and other advertising matter which offered Insull securities to the public.

The following testimony of Harold L. Stuart, President of Halsey Stuart & Co., relates to a pres-

---

[1]Galbraith, _op cit_. p. 141.

pectus offering Insull Utility Investments (Inc.) bonds issued in January 1929. The prospectus consisted of the usual president's letter and carried a disclaimer clause:

Pecora: Mr. Stuart, do you think it is sound of an investment house offering investments to the public to disclose to the investing public any and all things in connection with its issues and allied securities?

Stuart: I think it should be done.

Pecora: You think it should be done?

Stuart: Yes, sir.

Pecora: Was it done when your company put out the circular which has already been called to your attention and in which it offered the 5 per cent gold debenture bonds to the public in the Insull Utility Investments (Inc.)?

Stuart: It was not done.

Pecora: It was not done?

Stuart: It was not the custom in the profession to do it at that time.

Pecora: You mean it is not the custom to disclose it to the public?

Stuart: It is not customary when offering securities of corporations or affiliates, and whether they ---

Pecora: (interposing) It was not then fair to the public?

Stuart: Excuse me. I think it should be in the future.

Pecora: It was not done in the past?

Stuart: No.

Senator Norbeck: It may have to be done in the future.

Senator Walcott: I was going to say that the law in England prohibits this sort of thing.

Pecora: The British Companies Act is based upon full disclosure.

Senator Walcott: Yes.

Pecora: Now, Mr. Stuart, when your company put out this circular...instead of consulting the public, it was concealing its own profit interest in the Insull Utility Investments (Inc.)?

Stuart: No.

Pecora: It concealed it in not putting it out?

Stuart: It was not the customary thing to do.

Pecora: The fact is, it was concealed?

Stuart: We did not state it, that is true.

Pecora: Whether it was customary or not.

Stuart: Yes, sir.[1]

---

[1]Hearings S. R. 84, pp. 1615-1616.

Later, between February 21 and March 2, 1933, the Committee heard testimony related to the affairs of the National City Bank and the National City Company. On February 21, 1933, Charles E. Mitchell, chairman of the board, National City Bank of New York and National City Company appeared before the Committee. Mr. Pecora on this occasion questioned Mitchell on the failure of bankers to disclose their "spread" to the public---a failure Brandeis had commented on twenty years before. Mitchell in reply said it was not customary to reveal such data; the public would not understand if it was published; and, anyway, he could not see how it was in the interest of the investor to have data related to the banker's "spread" published in prospectuses.

Subsequently, the Committee questioned Mitchell on the desirability of presenting "fuller information" in prospectuses than was the current practice. The chairman of the Committee pointed out to Mitchell the British Companies Act required "full information"--

Mitchell: I am heartily in favor of fuller information. I wish we could regulate it all through the investment banking business.

Pecora: The National City Co. is the biggest investment house in the country isn't it? Do you know of any bigger?

Mitchell: Well, I think that it has a very large producing organization; that is, as an issuing house its own originations are large. I do not think they are as large perhaps in dollars as some others.

Senator Norbeck: He has previously testified to this committee that his bank is the largest bank in the world.

Pecora: Yes; but isn't the National City Co. the largest investment company selling securities to the public?

Mitchell: I should think probably; but I would not want to make any boast about that, Mr. Pecora.

Pecora: It would not have been unbecoming for the National City Co. to have taken the lead in bringing about a change in custom with regard to putting out fuller information to the public?

Mitchell: We are doing it every day. We are issuing to the public today more complete information regarding the condition of the companies that we finance than we ever have in our history, and we are trying to go a very long way. We are trying to blaze a trail with respect to that.

Pecora: When did you commence to blaze that trail?

Mitchell: I should say a year and a half ago. We have learned much. We have all made mistakes, and a man that can not profit by it certainly is not very worthy. We are trying to blaze the way for investment finance into a higher ground than it has been.

Pecora: But you have not yet blazed the trail to the point where you are giving the investing public information concerning the price at which the company acquires these securities that it offers to the public?

Mitchell: And I have told you why.

Pecora: I mean you have not yet reached that stage in the blazing of the trail?

Mitchell: No.[1]

Subsequently, on February 27, 1933, Pecora asked Hugh B. Baker, president of the National City Company, a number of questions related to certain bond issues of Peru, Chile and the State of Minas Geraes in Brazil which National City had sold to the American public during 1927 and 1928. In 1933 all of these bond issues were in default.

Baker's testimony showed that the original prospectuses issued for these bonds failed to disclose

---

[1]Hearings S. Res. 84, p. 1808.

a number of facts related to the offering which may well have been of interest to investors. For instance, in 1927 and 1928 the officers of National City were in possession of reports from their local representatives in Peru which described Peru as an "adverse moral and political risk" and told of the country's past unsatisfactory debt record and current "bad internal debt situation." In addition, J. H. Durrell, the vice president and overseas manager of the National City Bank said in a 1927 memoranda to Charles Mitchell that there were "two factors which will long retard the economic importance of Peru": the large indian population; and the high probability of revolution following the death or retirement of the current president of Peru. None of this information was ever included in prospectuses offering Peruvian bonds. When asked by Pecora if he, Baker, thought it was fair to the investing public to withhold this information related to Peru which National City possessed, the following testimony was heard:

Pecora: ...Do you think that the public here would have subscribed at 91½ for these bonds if they have been given the information that was given to your company by its overseas manager and vice president, that "there are two factors that will long retard the economic importance of Peru"?

Baker: You say, Would the public have subscribed with those statements?

Pecora: Yes.

Baker: I doubt if they would.

Pecora: And do you think that the public would have subscribed to these bonds at 91½ if they had been told in the circular that Mr. Durrell in July, 1927, advised the company that "Peru's political situation is equally uncertain. I have no great faith in any material betterment of Peru's economic condition in the near future?"

Baker: I doubt if they would.

Pecora: Do you know why that information was not embodied in this circular?

Baker: I do not. We did not write the circular, but evidently we did not altogether agree with some of the things.

Pecora: You say you did not write the circular---but your name appears on it.

Baker: Yes: it was approved by us.

Pecora: And it was approved by your company?

Baker: That is right.

Pecora: Which makes your company just as responsible as though it had itself prepared the text of that circular?

Baker: We were responsible for those statements, subject to those conditions; yes. We believed them to be correct.

Pecora: Do you know why this information was not given to the investing public in the circular?

Baker: No, sir.

Pecora: Do you know upon whose judgement it was withheld from the investing public?

Baker: No, sir.

Pecora: Do you think that it was fair to the investing public to withhold this information that your company had about Peru?

Baker: Well, I think it is fair to present the facts in reference to Peru, as we tried to do. I do not see any occasion to go into--going over all of these long studies that have been made in which the people were not altogether in accord, and in which generally there were changes taking place, and, as some of them said, the economic trend was improving and all that. You could write, of course, a whole book on the subject, giving various people's opinions, but when we arrive at a conclusion it seems to me that a statement of the important facts connected with it is what is necessary and proper.[1]

---

[1]Hearings S. Res. 84, p. 2076.

On April 4, 1933, the Senate of the seventy-third Congress approved Senate Resolution 56 which materially expanded the earlier Senate Resolution 84. The new resolution, which was further supplemented by Senate Resolution 97 on June 8, 1933, authorized the Committee on Banking and Currency to

> investigate the matter of banking operations and practices, transaction relating to any sale, exchange, purchase, acquisition, borrowing, lending, financing, issuing, distributing, or other disposition of, or dealing in, securities or credit by any person or firm, partnership, company, association, corporation, or other entity with a view to recommending necessary legislation, under the taxing power or other federal powers.

Since the bulk of the hearing conducted under the authority of Senate Resolutions 84 and 97 of the seventy-third Congress were held after the passage of the 1933 Securities Act, those hearings will not be discussed---they had no influence on the nature of the 1933 Act.

The Committee's report was not issued until 1934 but throughout the hearings conducted prior to the passage of the Securities Act,into the question as to why the stock market was allowed to reach such dizzy heights and then collapse, there were several assumptions related to financial disclosure which seemed to underlie the questions posed by members of the Committee and their special counsel. These beliefs were, in general, similar to those held by critics of business and finance.

First, the Committee appeared to adopt the assumption businessmen were reluctant for a variety of reasons, including stock market manipulation, to disclose information pertaining to their corporation's affairs. Such a corporate practice the Committee seemed to believe was outmoded.

Other important assumptions related to financial disclosure included: auditors ought to be responsible to the public---not management---for the financial statements they audited and this responsibility extended beyond the audit certificate to the financial statements themselves; the New York Stock Exchange had a responsibility to investors to prevent the price of listed securities from rising too high above their "intrinsic value"---a responsibility, in the absence of fraud, the Exchange categorically denied was its; and, finally, investment bankers were responsible to the public and, despite the bankers' avowals to the contrary, such a responsibility extended to the representations included in prospectuses including the president's letter.

Three groups---accountants, New York Stock Exchange and investment bankers---had a responsibility in the minds of the Committee to force management to present to the investing public more complete financial data and in this respect they had failed. Clearly, as the testimony before the Committee showed, public accountants had served management and considered themselves responsible only for the opinions expressed in their audit certificate--not the audited financial statements which they said were the representations of management alone; the New York Stock Exchange had both failed and denied its duty to halt the bull market of the late 1920's and, in addition, had not effectively enforced listing agreements; and the investment banker had violated the public's confidence--investment bankers had joined with corporate executives to suppress financial data for personal profit. Such actions and attitudes, given the Committee's assumptions, were not desirable and could hardly lead to the now popular concept of the "social corporation" advocated by Berle and Means--the next topic discussed.

Reform was needed and the Committee's preference for an alternative to private reform seemed to lie with the passage on the federal level of a securities act setting forth minimum standards of prospectus disclosure and based on the disclosure philosophy underlying the British Companies Act.

"The Modern Corporation and Private Property"

In the midst of the ugly revelations of fiduciary irresponsibility brought to light by the Senate

Committee on Banking and Currency Hearings, there appeared a new book, written by Adolf A. Berle and Gardner C. Means, The Modern Corporation and Private Property, in which it was argued that the basic responsibility of management ought to be to society and the need of the times was for management to develop a social conscience. As noted in chapter five the dispersion of the ownership of American industry had resulted in a growing disparity between the ownership and control of a number of the nation's leading corporations. The passing of the control over corporate affairs from the stockholders to management aroused much concern among the so-called liberals, including A. A. Berle Jr.,--perhaps their most prominent spokesman on this issue.[1]

Initially, during the period of economic prosperity from 1924-1929 the primary concern of such critics as Berle was that management through its ability to control the affairs of corporations might seek to deprive the puny stockholder of his property rights--control and dividends. The sole responsibility of management, the critics then argued, was to earn profits for their stockholders. If management abused

---

[1]Berle had been a student and associate of both William Z. Ripley and Felix Frankfurter--two well known critics of the power and abuses of big business. Later, Berle was a member of Franklin D. Roosevelt's so-called "Brain Trust."

this responsibility, public opinion, the courts and, as a last resort, the government must establish some sort of control over management's actions.

Later, under the pressure of the Great Depression, Berle and his co-author Means in their book expressed an important modification to Berle's earlier concep of the basic responsibility of management. Now, no longer was it feasible for management to regard the stockholder as its sole concern. The basic responsibility of management was to develop "a system of community obligations...that would guide them in their relations with employees and the general public, as well as the stockholders."[1]

Henceforth, the modern corporation must serve not alone the owners or the control but all society.[2] If management would not voluntarily accept <u>their</u> new social responsibilities, the government would have to find the means to encourage management to do so. Thus, the changes in the scope and composition of the investing public brought forth new demands for corporate reform based on the peculiar nature of the modern corporation; the campaign oratory of Roosevelt and the Securities Act of 1933 were both to reflect

---

[1]Richard S. Kirkendall, "A. A. Berle Jr.: Student of The Corporation, 1917-1932," <u>Business History Review</u>, Vol. XXXV, No. 1, Spring 1961, p. 54.

[2]Berle and Means, <u>op. cit</u>., p. 356.

this new concept of corporate responsibility.

The 1932 Presidential Campaign

The promise of a federal securities statute was an important plank in the 1932 Democratic Presidential Platform. The Republican Presidential Platform contained no such promise.[1]

In 1932 the Chicago Convention of the Democratic Party adopted the following as an integral part of their party's platform:

> We advocate protection of the investing public by requiring to be filed with the government and carried in advertisements of all offerings of foreign and domestic stocks and bonds true information as to bonuses, commissions, principal invested, and interests of the sellers.

The Democratic party's candidate, Franklin D. Roosevelt,[2] faithfully embraced his party's platform and in his first major speech of the campaign delivered at Columbus on August 24, 1932, denounced the preceeding four years as having been "the heyday of promoters, sloganeers, mushroom millionaires, opportunists, [and] adventurers of all kinds."[3]

---

[1]The Platform of American Industry for 1932 drawn up under the auspices of the National Association of Manufacturers did not mention the topics of securities regulation and investor protection.

[2]While a student at Harvard College, Roosevelt had William Z. Ripley as one of his teachers. Later, both Daniel Fusfeld (The Economic Thought of Franklin D. Roosevelt and the Origins of the New Deal) and Rexford G. Tugwell (The Democratic Roosevelt) believed Ripley more than anyone else had dominated Roosevelt's Harvard educational experience.

Speaking of 1932 conditions he said:

> We find two-thirds of American industry concentrated in a few hundred corporations, and actually managed by not more than five hundred individuals.
>
> We find more than half of the savings of the country invested in corporate stocks and bonds, and made the sport of the American stock market.
>
> We find fewer than three dozen private banking houses, and stock-selling adjuncts of commercial banks, directing the flow of American capital....
>
> We find a great part of our working population with no chance of earning a living except by grace of this concentrated industrial machine; and we find that millions of Americans are out of work, throwing upon the already burdened Government the necessity of relief....[1]

The nation's economic life was "a seamless web," he said, and "we cannot have independence....unless we take full account of our interdependence in order to provide a balanced well-being for every citizen."[2] None could live in isolation--all were interdependent. It was the duty of Government--not private enterprise--to see that the public interest was protected. The maintenance of fairness in dealings between individuals and groups required the government to intervene to prohibit and punish any exploitation of the public.

The Columbus speech gave notice to the nation that

---

[1] *Ibid.*, p. 679.

[2] *Ibid.*, p. 697.

the progressives and liberals were returning to finish the work left undone in 1916. By 1932, for these people the passage of a federal securities act was imperative.

To Roosevelt's promise of a federal securities bill Herbert Hoover, the Republican candidate, simply replied he was "advised that this is not within the constitutional authority of the Federal Government."[1]

In November 1932, the American public, encouraged by Roosevelt's pledge to help the American people "gain a larger social justice" and a "New Deal" for the "forgotten man at the bottom of the economic pyramid," overwhelmingly elected Roosevelt President. And as one observer has remarked, it seemed as if there was a widespread "mutual appreciation of the fact that rich and poor, those with jobs and those without, were in the same boat and that their only hope of salvation depended upon mutual faith and cooperation under the leadership" of Roosevelt.[2] Once Roosevelt assumed the mantle of president the "old order" was never to be again revived--government intervention in commercial life, for good or bad, was to be for the benefit of all

---

[1]The St. Louis Address; Boston Evening Transcript, November 5, 1932, p. 6.

[2]Cleveland Rodgers, The Roosevelt Program (New York: G. P. Putnam's Sons, 1933), pp. 204-205.

people and not just for the business interests.

Cooperation Between Accountants and the Stock Exchange

While the pressure for federal legislation related to prospectus disclosure was mounting, two groups---the New York Stock Exchange and the American Institute of Accountants---made one last desperate effort to seek reform through private action.

Between 1930 and 1933, as in the earlier periods, a number of people associated with the New York Stock Exchange and the accounting profession spoke on the subject of corporate financial disclosure. Never before, however, had there been such a sense of urgency and importance in this matter. Better disclosure, it was said by both the critics and those sympathetic to big business, was needed to protect investors and restor confidence in the securities market.

The first positive action in this regard was taken by the New York Stock Exchange and the American Institute of Accountants, who together belatedly attempted to impose standards of financial disclosure upon management so that investors and stockholders might be better protected. First, in 1930, at the suggestion of J.H.B. Hoxsey, the executive assistant on stock list of the New York Stock Exchange, the

American Institute of Accountants appointed a committee to cooperate with the New York Stock Exchange "in the consideration of all problems which are of common interest to investors, exchanges and accountants."[1] Later, on January 6, 1933, Richard Whitney, president of the New York Stock Exchange, announced that after July 1, 1933, all listing applications from corporations must contain the certificate of independent public accountants. Subsequently, on March 31, 1933 the Chicago Stock Exchange, the nation's second largest exchange, also issued a similar statement.

In the spring of 1930, J. M. B. Hoxsey addressed the annual meeting of the American Institute of Accountants. "Accounting," Hoxsey said, "is a matter of conventions but it is questionable whether these conventions have kept pace with the changes in modern business conditions."[2] To date, accounting had evolved, he said, with primary emphasis on two objects: 1) to supply management with accurate information essential for the conduct of business; and 2) to pro-

---

[1]"Cooperation Between Accountants and Stock Exchanges," The Journal of Accountancy. Vol. L, No. 4, October 1930, p. 242.

[2]J.M.B. Hoxsey, "Accounting for Investors," The Journal of Accountancy, Vol. L, No. 4, October 1930, p. 251.

vide prospective creditors with accurate information essential to the determination of credit capacity. The widespread ownership of corporations, however, had created a new need for "sound accounting practices" and, while the need of management for reliable information was paramount:

> ...under conditions of today, the next order of importance has become to give to stockholders, in understandable form, such information in regard to the business as will avoid misleading them in any respect and will put them in possession of all information needed, and which can be supplied in financial statements, to determine the true value of their investments.

To achieve this end, Hoxsey suggested the American Institute appoint a committee to cooperate with the New York Stock Exchange to consider the accounting problems related to depreciation,[1] consolidated statements,[2]

---

[1]"There are so many different theories of depreciation that an exact understanding of the actual policy pursued is essential to any just appreciation of values or comparison of earnings of different companies."--*Ibid.*, p. 254.

[2]The most pronounced step forward in the direction of adapting accounting to the needs of investors is the introduction of consolidated financial statements. The question is to whether they are as inclusive as they should be. There appears to be no consensus of opinion as to the degree of ownership which warrants consolidation."--*Ibid.*, p. 259.

gross revenue,[1] other income,[2] surplus and surplus entries,[3] stock dividends paid and received, and the accountant's tradition of "over-conservatism."[4] In all these areas Hoxsey saw either a multiplicity of accounting practices which tended to confuse investors or a lack of disclosure which prohibited the proper

---

[1]"...in the matter of showing the amount of net sales, more and more corporations are abandoning the practice....Next only to net profits, the amount of sales (or gross revenue) is probably the most significant figure in financial statements. It is the key upon which almost every item of analysis of the competence of the manggement depends. You [the Institute] could help its public interest by using your influence to secure the dissemination of this needed information." --Ibid., p. 260.

[2]"...there is frequently no distinction made between operating income and other income."--Ibid., p. 261.

[3]"Except for the fact that it is omitted so frequently, it would be unnecessary to say that reports are never complete nor fully informative unless both the earned surplus and the capital surplus (if any) at the end of the preceeding period are tied in with the corresponding items at the end of the reporting period and any large debits or credits directly to surplus account itemized."--Ibid., p. 264.

[4]"To those of you...particularly to those of you who pride yourselves upon your high sense of professional ethics I have only one more suggestion to make--drop some of your over-conservatism!...there is the investor to consider....It is almost, if not quite, as harmful to publish inaccurate accounts leading him to believe that his investment is less valuable and profitable than it actually is as it is to delude him in the opposite direction....It is the business of the management, not the accountant, to stand up against pressure to pay too large a proportion of the real earnings in dividends." Ibid., pp. 276-277.

analysis of financial data.

Subsequently, the Institute appointed a Special Committee on Cooperation with Stock Exchanges and nominated George O. May as its chairman.[1] An appropriate choice as May, it will be recalled, four years earlier in 1926, had advocated such cooperative ventures.

The results of the Special Committee and the Stock List Committee's joint efforts were first expressed in a letter, dated January 12, 1932, from the Stock List Committee of the New York Stock Exchange to the chief executives of all listed companies. This letter read, in part, as follows:

> Dear Sir: In line with our constant efforts to secure reasonable uniformity in annual reports for the benefit of listed companies, their share-holders, accountants, and the investing public, this committee is herewith advising you of its general attitude as to the following features of such reports:
>
> (1) When the books and accounts have been audited by public accountants, the text of their auditor's certificate should be given.
>
> (2) The number of shares of capital stock, both common and preferred, authorized by the charter and the amount outstanding should be shown in the balance-sheet.
>
> (3) The number of shares and the amount of holdings of own unretired stock and bonds should be separately disclosed, with indication of the valuation and the basis at which carried.

---

[1]Other members of the committee were Archibald Bowman, Arthur H. Carter, Charles B. Couchman, Samuel D. Lerdesdorf, and William M. Lybrand.

(4) Surplus should be separated at least into capital surplus and earned surplus. If all surplus is earned surplus (representing realized profits) it should be so designated.

(5) Any changes for the period covered in either capital surplus or earned surplus should be indicated by adjustments thereto.

(6) Differences between cost and subsequent retirement or resale of the company's own stock should be fully disclosed. This committee prefers that such differences be reflected directly to the capital surplus account, especially where common stock, and preferred stock without compulsory retirement features are involved....

(7) Full disclosure should be given of any change since the previous annual report in the basis of valuation in investments, inventories, or property account.

(8) Full disclosure of any change in the depreciation policy should be given.

(9) If other income represents a substantial part of the total income, the principal component items of other income should be disclosed.

(10) This committee does not deem it advisable to establish at this time requirements as to the method by which revised or fluctuating rates of foreign exchange should be reflected in the consolidated balance-sheets or earnings statements of listed American companies having foreign subsidiaries subject to these factors, or in the parent company statements of listed American companies themselves having assets, liabilities, or earnings similarly affected. Irrespective of the method followed, disclosure should be given of the basis on which such items are reported.

(11) A list of officers and directors should be included in the report....[1]

Subsequently, sometime before February, 1932, Richard Whitney, the president of the New York Stock

---

[1] The Journal of Accountancy, Vol. 53, No. 2, February 1932, pp. 146-147.

Exchange, addressed a letter to a number of the listed corporations urging them to issue quarterly financial statements in the comparative form. Of these developments the editor of The Journal of Accountancy said:

> ...the stock exchange is encouraging increasing candor on the part of its listed corporations. There must be a wide departure from past practice in order to meet the just demands of the investing public....The public now demands information and everything which can bring about more comprehensive statements should receive hearty support....American custom has a little reformation to undertake--and there is evidence that it will be undertaken.[1]

And on August 24, 1932, Richard Whitney told the Senate Banking and Currency Committee that the New York Stock Exchange was "more insistent today upon publicity than we have been in the past and public opinion, which for some years seemed indifferent, is now strongly back of this movement."[2]

Next, on September 22, 1932, the Institute's Special Committee submitted its report to the Committee on Stock List of the New York Stock Exchange. This report was later made public in January 1934 and given

---

[1]"Stock Exchange Calls for Comparative Statements," The Journal of Accountancy, Vol. 53, No. 2, February 1932, p. 83.

[2]Statement by Richard Whitney, President of the New York Stock Exchange, Made to the Governing Committee and the Membership in regard to the investigation of stock exchange practices by the Committee on Banking and Currency of the United States Senate, August 24, 1932, p. 31.

"warm" approval by the Controllers Institute, Investment Bankers Association and the New York Stock Exchange.[1]

The report of the Special Committee listed four principal objects which its members thought the Exchange should "keep constantly in mind and do its best to gradually achieve." These goals were to bring about a better recognition by the public that balance sheets did not show present values of the assets and liabilities of corporations; encourage the adoption of balance sheets which would more clearly show on what basis assets were valued; to emphasize the cardinal importance of the income account; and to make universal the acceptance by listed corporations of certain broad principles of accounting which had won fairly general acceptance. On this last point the report warned the Exchange against attempting "to restrict the right of corporations to select detailed methods of accounting deemed by them to be best adapted to the requirements of their business."[2]

In addition, the report suggested it might be desirable to formulate the statement laying down the "broad principles" only after consultation with a small

---

[1]George O. May, _Financial Accounting: A Distillation of Experience_ (New York: The Macmillan Company, 1943), p. 57.

[2]Report of the Special Committee on Cooperation with Stock Exchanges of the American Institute of Accountants. September 22, 1932.

group of qualified persons including corporate officials, lawyers and accountants.

The report also suggested the Exchange might ask each listed corporation to submit a clear and detailed statement of the principles it observed when classifying charges and credits as between (a) balance sheet accounts, (b) income account and (c) surplus account. Any deviation from these principles was to be reported to the Exchange and noted in the audit certificate accompanying the annual report to shareholders. In addition, the report listed several "broad principles" and a number of the details to be covered in the statement of accounting methods.

To date, this document was the most specific statement formulated on just how financial reports could be made "more informative and authoritative." The Institute, for the first time, had issued a statement on accounting principles designed to afford investors and shareholders greater protection. Officially, the promotion by the Institute of balance sheet audits for credit purposes was a thing of the past.

Later, on January 6, 1933, the New York Stock Exchange announced henceforth corporations seeking listing must submit financial statements audited by independent public accountants and agree to have all future annual reports to stockholders similarly audited.

Richard Whitney's announcement said:

> Since April of 1932 all corporations applying for listing of their securities upon the New York stock exchange have been asked to enter into an agreement to the effect that future annual statements published...shall be audited by independent public accountants....
>
> The New York stock exchange now announces that its present policy in this respect will be continued until July 1, 1933, after which date all listing applications from corporations must contain the certificate of independent public accountants...certifying to the correctness of the balance-sheet, income statements and surplus statement for the most recent fiscal year. In general, the audit or audits must cover all subsidiaries, and the scope of the audit must be not less than that indicated in a pamphlet entitled Verification of Financial Statements....All applications must include an agreement to the effect that future reports published or sent to stockholders will be similarly audited and accompanied by a similar certificate....
>
> Representative houses and banks of issue have been advised of the foregoing program and have expressed themselves as in accord with the plan outlined above, which they believe is sound and consistent with the importance of affording to the public the most complete and accurate information in regard to the financial condition of corporations whose securities are publicly dealt in.[1]

Gone were the days when the Exchange would simply request corporate executives to furnish adequate financial statements. Now the Exchange could set the standards and the discredited businessman was unable to resist without fear of public censure.

---

[1]Announcement of Richard Whitney, January 6, 1933 as reproduced in "Stock Exchange Demands Audit of Listed Companies," The Journal of Accountancy. Vol. 55, No. 2, February 1933, pp. 81-82.

The accountants read Whitney's announcement with "a feeling of hearty gratification." Richardson, who had campaigned long and vigorously for such a listing requirement, hailed the announcement as probably the "most important forward step in the history of accounting within recent years."[1]

Such joy was to be short lived, for within six months the role of the Committee on Stock Lists and the Institute's Special Committee in effect passed to a federal agency--first to the Federal Trade Commission and then to the newly created Securities and Exchange Commission in 1934.

Ironically, the "great depression" which had provided the incentive for the American Institute of Accountants and the New York Stock Exchange to privately formulate minimum standards of financial disclosure as well as the power to enforce these standards, also forced the government to intervene at the very time when effective private reform in the area of corporate disclosure was, perhaps for the first time, possible. Unfortunately by 1930, the New York Stock Exchange and the Institute's efforts in this matter were too late.

---

[1] *Ibid.*, p. 82.

The Securities Act of 1933

On March 29, 1933, within one month of his inauguration, President Roosevelt fulfilled one of the promises of his party's platform by sending to Congress a special message which called for the enactment of a federal securities statute. His message read as follows:

> I recommend to the Congress legislation for Federal supervision of traffic in investment securities in interstate commerce.
>
> In spite of many State statutes the public in the past has sustained severe losses through practices neither ethical nor honest on the part of many persons and corporations selling securities.
>
> Of course, the Federal Government cannot and should not take any action which might be construed as approving or guaranteeing that newly issued securities are sound in the sense that their value will be maintained or that the properties which they represent will earn profit.
>
> There is, however, an obligation upon us to insist that every issue of new securities to be sold in interstate commerce shall be accompanied by full publicity and information, and that no essentially important element attending the issue shall be concealed from the buying public.
>
> This proposal adds to the ancient rule of caveat emptor, the further doctrine "let the seller also beware." It puts the burden of telling the whole truth on the seller. It should give impetus to honest dealing in securities and thereby bring back public confidence.
>
> The purpose of the legislation I suggest is to protect the public with the least possible interference to honest business.
>
> This is but one step in our broad purpose of protecting investors and depositors. It should be followed by legislation relating to the better supervision of the purchase and sale

> of all property dealt in on exchanges, and by legislation to correct unethical and unsafe practices on the part of officers and directors of banks and other corporations.
>
> What we seek is a return to a clearer understanding of the ancient truths that those who manage banks, corporations and other agencies handling or using other people's money are trustees acting for others.[1]

Earlier the same day, identical copies of a proposed security bill had been placed in the hands of the Senate and the House. This bill, which was modeled on the regulatory and anti-fraud type state blue sky laws, the English Companies Acts, and the previously rejected Volstead and Denison bills, had been drawn up at the direction of Roosevelt by Huston Thompson, a former chairman of the Federal Trade Commission.[2] Thompson's draft bill required all securities--both outstanding and new issues--to be registered through the filing of certain information related to the issuer with the Federal Trade Commission; and granted to the Federal Trade Commission the authority to forbid the sale of any security in interstate commerce on the basis that it was either an unsound or fraudulent investment, or the information contained in the filing statement was in some way unsatisfactory. In addition, the signatories to the registration statement were

---

[1]Special Presidential Message, March 29, 1933.

[2]Thompson, it will be recalled, was one of the two Federal Trade Commissioners who in 1926 believed Ripley's proposal that the Federal Trade Commission regulate corporate reporting practices was within the Commission's authority.

liable to civil suit for any misstatement in the registration; and, despite a satisfactory registration with the Federal Trade Commission, it was a federal offense to offer for sale through the mails a security in a state in violation of that state's blue sky law.[1]

The President's message and the draft bill were, according to the New York Times, "enthusiastically received on Capitol Hill by Republicans as well as Democrats." The Investment Bankers, the strong opponents of most of the earlier securities acts, were "with the principle of full publicity generally agreed." In fact, in its "present chastened mood banking and the brokerage business....was not prepared to challenge" the proposed legislation.[2]

Subsequently, the Thompson draft was referred by the Senate to its Committee on Banking and Currency, which held public hearings from March 31 to April 6,[3] and by the House to its Committee on Interstate and Foreign Commerce, which held its public hearings on

---

[1]James M. Landis, "The Legislative History of The Securities Act Of 1933," The George Washington Law Review. Vol. 28, No. 1, October 1959, p. 29.

[2]New York Times, March 30, 1933, p. 25.

[3]Hearings on S. 875, Committee On Banking And Currency. Senate. 73rd Congress, 1st Session.

the bill between April 1 and April 6.[1] In general, those who appeared before these two Congressional committees were in favor of some federal measure to protect investors. For instance, Mr. Frank Gordon, the president of the Investment Bankers Association, said:

> I wish to assure you that the President's message to Congress outlining the need for the objectives to be accomplished by a Federal securities law has the entire approval of our association, and I am sure, also, that it has the approval of the country at large.
>
> Our association tenders its full co-operation without reservation toward a detailed consideration of the provisions of the act to carry out the purposes of the President's message to the end that practicable and workable legislation may result.
>
> I know of no responsible security dealer who is not eager to see effective laws to prevent and punish fraud and misrepresentation in the sale of securities.
>
> Such laws are not only in the interest of the public, but also in the interest of those who deal in legitimate securities, and we are therefore thoroughly in accord with the intent of the bill now under consideration.[2]

Other prominent witnesses who approved the principal objective of the bill were the representative of the Comptrollers Institute of America, the United States Building and Loan League, Kuhn Loeb and

---

[1]Hearings on H. R. 4314. Committee on Interstate and Foreign Commerce. House. 73rd Congress, 1st Session.

[2]Hearings on H. R. 4314, p. 159.

Co., and the New York State Society of Certified Public Accountants.

As the House Committee on Interstate and Foreign Commerce hearings progressed, it soon became apparent to Representative S. Rayburn of Texas, the chairman of the committee, that the Thompson bill did not meet the specifications for a securities bill as set forth in Roosevelt's March 29 message. The President, as noted above, had called for a securities bill based on three requirements: full publicity; the federal government was not to take upon itself the task of approving or disapproving the issue; and protection of the public was to be achieved with the least possible interference with honest business. The Thompson Bill was poorly drafted; imposed an undue responsibility on the government; and would not have prevented the sale of fraudulent securities since the filing of the registration statement automatically qualified the security for sale to the public. Accordingly, Representative Rayburn of Texas, as Chairman of the House Committee on Interstate and Foreign Commerce, informed the President "that the Thompson bill provided no basis for sound federal securities legislation."[1]

Hastily, the White House staff looked to a new source for the needed securities bill. Professor

---

[1]Landis, op. cit., p. 33.

Raymond S. Moley, the reputed head of Roosevelt's "Brain Trust", turned to Professor Felix Frankfurter of Harvard Law School for assistance in this matter. Frankfurter in turn asked three other men to assist him in the preparation of a new securities act: James M. Landis, a fellow Harvard Law School professor; Benjamin V. Cohen, a practising lawyer; and Thomas G. Corcoran, the counsel to the Reconstruction Finance Corporation.

At their first meeting the new drafting team decided to base their work on the English philosophy of disclosure. Later, in 1959, Landis recalled the thinking of the group with respect to the construction of their first draft bill:

> After a brief session with Frankfurter, where we determined to take as the base of our work the English Companies Act....We had to work under certain limitations imposed upon us by the fact of the Thompson bill. Tactically it seemed wise to shape our proposals as "perfecting" amendments to that bill, with the result that our original bill embodied a number of proposals contained in the Thompson bill that were subsequently happily discarded. The core of the Securities Act of 1933 is, however, to be found in that hurried draft of ours.
>
> Our draft remained true to the conception voiced by the President in his message of March 29, 1933 to the Congress, namely that its requirements should be limited to full and fair disclosure of the nature of the security being offered and that there should be no authority to pass upon the investment quality of the security. This, of course, is the theory of the English Companies Act, but to the sanctions of that act we added the right of the Commission to suspend the regis-

> tration of any security if inadequate compliance with the stated requirements for disclosure or misrepresentations of fact were found to exist in its registration statement....
>
> The registration requirements with respect to the scope and extent of disclosure, which as amended now comprise Schedules A and B of the Securities Act, were both tightened and expanded....The civil liabilities of the registrant, its officers, directors and experts, drawn generally from the English Companies Act, were carefully revised. We were particularly anxious through the imposition of adequate civil liabilities to assure the performance by corporate directors and officers of their fiduciary obligations and to impress upon accountants the necessity for independence and a thorough professional approach.[1]

The new draft, which was presented in the guise of "perfecting" amendments to the original Thompson bill, was approved by the House Committee on Interstate and Foreign Commerce. Subsequently, on May 3, the bill was reported to the House and two days later it was passed as reported. On May 8, 1933, the House bill was sent to the Senate.

Meanwhile the Senate, independently of the Frankfurter group, was still working with the original Thompson bill. On April 27, 1933 the Senate Committee on Banking and Currency recommended the Senate version of the Thompson Bill be passed and on May 8, after a brief discussion, it was approved by the Senate.

Since there were differences between the Senate and House bills, it was necessary to send them to the House and Senate Conference Committee for reconcilia-

---

[1]*Ibid.*, pp. 34-35.

tion. Later, the Conference Committee's compromise bill, which was based largely on the House bill, was adopted by the Senate on May 22. The next day, May 23, the House approved the Conference Committee's bill and, on May 27, 1933, President Roosevelt signed it.

From the time of the Presidential Message to Congress calling for the passage of a securities law to the eventual passage of such an Act by Congress, few voices were raised in opposition to the principle of protecting investors through full and frank disclosure of corporate affairs. On October 30, 1933, Landis said:

> The President's message calling for federal security legislation and outlining the basic principles that should be embodied in such legislation has yet to find any critic. No opposition to the President's aims was voiced at the hearings of the Bill, which were wholly devoid of any sensationalism....With one exception, its passage through the House as well as the passage of the companion bill through the Senate evoked no dramatic speeches, no threat of retaliation against a class. No member of either House at any time voted against the passage of the bill, nor took occasion to criticize any provision that the bill contained.[1]

---

[1]James M. Landis, "The Federal Securities Act and Regulations Relating to the Work and Responsibility of the C.P.A." Address and Discussions Relating to the Federal Securities Act And Accounting Requirements Under The National Industrial Recovery Act. Presented before the Eleventh Annual Fall Conference of The New York State Society of Certified Public Accountants, October 30, 1933, p. 6.

The Securities Act of 1933 required all corporations, subject to certain exemptions and limitations,[1] when offering securities to the public to file a registration statement with the Federal Trade Commission.[2]

The function of the Federal Trade Commission in this matter was to see that all of the information which might be relevant to a "prudent" investor was contained within the registration statement and any prospectuses subsequently issued by the registrant. The Commission did not pass on the soundness of the securities offered.

In addition, the Act prescribed minimum standards of corporate and financial disclosure for those prospectuses issued by registered companies. The inclusion of untrue or misleading statements or

---

[1]Securities of the following were exempted from the provisions of the Act: securities guaranteed by the United States, State or political subdivisions; government corporations; national banks; federal reserve obligations; religious and other non profit organizations; building and loan associations whose business was substantially confined to members; farmers cooperatives; and common carriers subject to Interstate Commerce Commission jurisdiction. In addition, receivers certificates and annuity contracts were excluded.

[2]In 1934, the Securities and Exchange Act created the Securities and Exchange Commission. Subsequently, this body took over from the Federal Trade Commission the regulation of security issues. The 1934 Act also provided for the control of the stock exchange practices by the Securities and Exchange Commission and amended the Securities Act of 1933.

omission of material facts from either the registration or the prospectus were grounds for any person purchasing securities on the basis of such false or incomplete information to sue, at law or in equity, every person who had signed the registration statement; every person who had been a director or named as about to become a director of the issuing corporation at the time the registration statement was filed; every accountant or other "expert" who had allowed his name or certificate to be used in the prospectus; and every underwriter wtih respect to the offering. The liability of these people ended ten years after the date of the original issue and the maximum amount recoverable under such action, which was based on the assumption that the buyer had relied on the statements contained in the registration statement and prospectus, was the total price paid for the securities.[1]

All corporations, except for several specified exemptions, offering securities the aggregate amount of which exceeded $100,000, were required to file registration statements with the Federal Trade Commission prior to offering the securities described therein to the public. Twenty days after the filing

---

[1]Opposition to this section of the Act among those potentially liable under the Act soon developed and in 1934 the liability of these groups was modified.

of the registration statement, unless notified otherwise by the Commission, the registrant was free to offer the securities to the public.

The information and documents required to be filed was set forth in the Act in the so-called Schedule A. The same information shown in the registration statement and most of the documents attached thereto were also required to be reproduced in any prospectuses issued by the registrant.

Briefly, Schedule A called for detailed information related to the corporation issuing the securities, its directors and principal shareholders, and the underwriters handling the offering. In particular Schedule A required the filing of data pertaining to the issuing corporations's name, location and charter; the amount of securities held by the principal stockholders, directors and underwriters associated with the offering; and the amount of the offering these people intended to purchase. Other information required included the character of the issuer's business; its capitalization, outstanding options, capital stock and funded debt; the purpose of the issue; and the remuneration paid by the issuer to its directors and officers.

In addition, Schedule A required information on such topics as: the estimated net proceeds from the issue; the price the securities were to be offered to the public; any commissions or discounts paid by the issuer to the underwriters; all expenses of the offering; and the net proceeds of previous issues within the last two years. Other information to be filed included: the names, addresses of the vendors and the purchase price of any property, or good will, acquired or to be acquired with the funds raised by the offering; the interests of any of the issuer's principal stockholders in such property or good will; the name and address of the counsel engaged to pass upon the legality of the issue; and any material contracts made by the issuer in the ordinary conduct of his business including management bonus or profit sharing schemes.

In addition, the following documents were required to be filed: copies of a recent balance sheet and income statement "in such detail and form as the Commission shall prescribe;"[1] the certificate of the

---

[1]Section 12(25)(26) and (27) of the 1933 Securities Act related to financial statements:

> (25) a balance sheet as of a date not more than ninety days prior to the date of the filing of the registration statement showing all of the assets of the issuer, the nature and cost thereof, whenever determinable, in such detail and in such form as the Commission shall prescribe (with intangible items segregated), including any loan in excess of $20,000 to any officers, director, stockholder or person directly or indirectly controlling

certifying public accountant; the underwriting

---

or controlled by the issuer, or person under direct or indirect common control with the issuer. All the liabilities of the issuer in such detail and such form as the Commission shall prescribe, including surplus of the issuer showing how and from what sources such surplus was created, all as of a date not more than ninety days prior to the filing of the registration statement. If such statement be not certified by an independent public or certified accountant, in addition to the balance sheet required to be submitted under this schedule, a similar detailed balance sheet of the assets and liabilities of the issuer, certified by an independent public or certified accountant, of a date not more than one year prior to the filing of the registration statement, shall be submitted;

(26) a profit and loss statement of the issuer showing earnings and income, the nature and source thereof, and the expenses and fixed charges in such detail and such form as the Commission shall prescribe for the latest fiscal year for which such statement is available and for the two preceding fiscal years, year by year, or, if such issuer has been in actual business for less than three years, then for such time as the issuer has been in actual business, year by year. If the date of the filing of the registration statement is more than six months after the close of the last fiscal year, a statement from such closing date to the latest practicable date. Such statement shall show what the practice of the issuer has been during the three years or lesser period as to the character of the charges, dividends or other distributions made against its various surplus accounts, and as to depreciation, depletion, and maintenance charges, in such detail and form as the Commission shall prescribe, and if stock dividends or avails from the sale of rights have been credited to income, they shall be shown separately with a statement of the basis upon which the credit is computed. Such statement shall also differentiate between any recurring and nonrecurring income and between any investment and operating income. Such

agreements; the legal counsel's opinion; and material contracts; the articles of incorporation; and any agreements or indentures affecting any stock, bonds, or debentures offered or to be offered by the registrant. These documents as well as the other registration material were to be available for public inspection.

All of the information, and several of the documents[1] required to be filed with the Federal Trade Commission, was, as noted above, also required to be shown in any prospectuses issued subsequent to the filing. This information was to be placed in a conspicuous part of the prospectus and in type as large

---

> statement shall be certified by an independent public or certified accountant;
>
> (27) if the proceeds, or any part of the proceeds, of the security to be issued is to be applied directly or indirectly to the purchase of any business, a profit and loss statement of such business certified by an independent public or certified accountant, meeting the requirements of paragraph (26) of this schedule, for the three preceding fiscal years, together with a balance sheet, similarly certified, of such business, meeting the requirements of paragraph (25) of this schedule of a date not more than ninety days prior to the filing of the registration statement or at the date such business was acquired by the issuer if the business was acquired by the issuer more than ninety days prior to the filing of the registration statement.

[1]Prospectuses of the registrant "need not include" the documents related to the underwriting agreement, legal counsel's opinion, material contracts, articles of incorporation, and agreements and indentures affecting stock, bonds, or debentures offered or to be offered.

as that used generally in the body of the prospectus.

In addition, the Commission had the authority "to classify prospectuses according to the nature and circumstances of their use, and, by rules and regulations subject to such terms and conditions as it shall specify therein, to prescribe as to each class the form and contents which it may find appropriate to such use and consistent with the public interest and the protection of investors."[1]

The impact of the Securities Act upon the disclosure practices of management was striking as the illustration presented below will show. This illustration, which is a comparison in column form of the contents of prospectuses issued before and after 1933, was prepared by Rudolph L. Weissman, a former financial editor of the American Mercury. Of this comparison Weissman said:

> To illustrate concretely the differences in the information because of the disclosures now required and the responsibilities fixed by law, comparison has been made of two stock underwritings of small corporations of similar size and engaged in a kindred business. These were offered by the prospectus of Philip A. Singer & Bros., Inc., dated September 8, 1937, and an offering circular of Federal Fur Dyeing Corporation, whose stock was offered in 1928. In choosing these as illustrations, no reflection on the corporations is intended. More informative prospectuses and less informative circulars could have been used for purposes of

---

[1]1933 Securities Act, Sec. 10(4).

illustration. The issues represent a fair example of the financing of the small corporation at present and before the Securities Act of 1933. It is a coincidence that the pro forma balance sheet of one showed total assets of $769,911 and of the other $786,465. The earlier offering was made by a circular containing four pages, of which the first was solely a title page and the fourth contained the pro forma balance sheet. The 1937 offering was made by a 22-page prospectus. Although information is not to be measured by the number of words used, the reader will be able to judge for himself the value of the prospectus in making an intelligent appraisal of the value of a security as either a speculation or an investment.[1]

---

[1]Rudolph L. Weissman, The New Wall Street (New York: Harper & Brothers, 1939), p. 211.

PROSPECTUS DISCLOSURE: BEFORE AND AFTER 1933 SECURITIES ACT

Present: Securities Act of 1933 and Rules of Securities and Exchange Commission	Before Securities Act of 1933
Business and History	
General statement of origin and development	General statement of origin and development
Peak production and lowest activity stated	No statement
Average number of employees	No statement
Details of terms, option as to price, etc., details of business, connection if any, of owners of business optioned and officers and directors of issuer, or leading stockholders; financial statements of optioned business	Option to purchase stock of two corporations, business of which is peculiarly adapted to and will fit in with business of issuer
Plants	
Details of leases, rentals, renewals, contracts, etc.	Premises are occupied under long-term leases, with provisions of renewal
Construction of plants	No statement
Statement of pending suits for infringement of trademarks, royalties, etc.	No statement
Statement that issuer knows of no proceedings contemplated by governmental authorities	No statement
Capitalization	
Present capitalization and previous changes, especially changes leading to capitalization after new financing	Present capitalization
Underwriting and Offering	
Statement as to:	
Net Proceeds to company	No statement except offering of 20,000 shares of common stock
Provisions of underwriting agreement as to price paid corporation, underwriting discounts or commissions; proceeds to issues, proceeds to stockholders; options to underwriters and officials and terms of options	
Agreement to make application to list within 12 months, and statement as to payment of expenses, etc.	Agreement to list—no time limit
Concessions to be allowed selling group	No statement
Statement that underwriter may buy and sell for long or short account and description of limitations	
Purpose of Financing	
Details:	
Payment of bank indebtedness	
Payment to other creditors	Only statement: "and the proceeds of the issuance thereof will be used for general corporate purposes"
Payment of mortgages	
Payment for redemption of preferred stock or bonds	

Source: Ibid., pp. 212-215.

Present: Securities Act of 1933 and Rules of Securities and Exchange Commission	Before Securities Act of 1933
Payment for improvements or additions to plant or for purchase of machinery (in detail) Balance for working capital	
Earnings	
Complete year to year statement of income, profit and loss statements, Details as follows: Gross income or sales Less discounts and allowances Cost of production Selling and shipping expenses Administrative expenses other income other deductions	Net profits only for nine months; Estimated net profits for year— Net profit after eliminating certain nonrecurring changes and other income items, and after giving effect to service contracts now to be in effect
Balance Sheet	
Over 60 separate items	Approximately 25 separate items
Balance sheet as of May 31, 1937 Pro forma balance sheet as of May 31, 1937, after giving effect to proposed financing and acquisition of the assets and liabilities of corporation and the liquidation of certain liabilities	Only pro forma balance sheet after recapitalization and new financing
Inventories (as taken and valued by the company) Chemicals Work in progress Finished work	Inventories of merchandise, supplies, and work in process No breakdown or basis of valuation
Note to balance sheet: "The inventories were certified by the officers of .... No check was made of this item"	
Fixed Assets: Land and building Machinery and equipment Furniture and fixtures Automobile trucks	Fixed Assets: Machinery and equipment, less reserve for depreciation Delivery equipment, less reserve for depreciation
Total Less reserves for depreciation an appraisal dated July 1, 1937 made by the American Appraisal Company shows:	

Assets	Reproduction Cost New	Sound Value

Present: Securities Act of 1933 and Rules of Securities and Exchange Commission	Before Securities Act of 1933
Land	Not broken down
Improvement to leased buildings	
Building construction and fixtures	
Machinery and equipment	
Office furniture and fixtures	
Automobiles	
Notes payable	Notes payable
Banks	
Creditors	Not broken down
Notes to balance sheet:	
"We have made an examination of the Balance Sheet of Philip A. Singer & Bros. Inc., as at May 31, 1937, and the Statement of Operations and the Surplus Account for the five months ended May 31, 1937. In connection therewith we have examined or tested accounting records of the Company and other supporting evidence and obtained information and explanations from the officers and employees of the Company; we also made a general review of the accounting methods and of the Operating Statements for the years 1934, 1935, 1936, but we did not make a detailed audit of the transactions. We did not verify the quantities and conditions of the inventories, which quantities and conditions were certified to us by responsible officials of the company. "In our opinion, based upon such examination, the accompanying financial statements fairly present, in accordance with accepted principles of accounting consistently maintained by the Company during the period under review, the financial position of the Company as at May 31, 1937, and the results of operations for the five months ended May 31, 1937."	"We have examined the books of account and records of the Federal Fur Dyeing Corporation, a New York Corporation, as at September 30, 1928. We have also examined the agreement dated October 23, 1928, providing among other things for: (a) amendment of charter of Federal Fur Dyeing Corporation, changing the authorized capital stock to 150,000 shares without par value and the issuance of 80,000 shares in exchange for presently outstanding capital stocks of said company: (b) the sale of 20,000 additional shares for cash: and (c) the reduction of value of processes and formula to $1.00. "We hereby certify that the above pro forma balance sheet correctly sets forth the consolidated financial condition at the date stated as it would have appeared had the above mentioned transaction been consummated at that date and after giving effect to the retirement of bank loans to cash received in a part liquidation of a certain account receivable and the subsequent acquisition by the Federal Fur Dyeing Corporation of the entire capital stock of David Goldberg, Inc."

Management

Names and Addresses	Names
Salaries—agreement to limit for 3-year period	No statement
Persons owning 10 per cent or more of stock	No statement
Names	
Amounts	
Per cent of class of stock	
Reference to further information in registration statement	
(18 items), including:	
Remuneration paid to officers, directors, employees, and others	No statement
Revaluation of investments	
Consents of experts	
Names of certified public accountants who have certified financial statements since February 1, 1932	

****

The 1929 stock market crash and the 1930 depression shocked the nation. Such disasters, it was said, must be prevented from ever occurring again. One of the ways suggested to prevent,or at least limit, such disasters was full disclosure of corporate affairs to investors. This particular suggestion was also related to the older, but once again popular, demands for "corporate democracy" and the regulation of big business.

During the presidential election of 1932 Roosevelt promised, if elected, to recommend to Congress the passage of some form of securities act. The need for such legislation had been clearly revealed during the Pecora hearings. In 1933, after Roosevelt's election, Congress and the nation were receptive to Roosevelt's request for a federal securities statute. Accordingly, despite the last minute efforts by the New York Stock Exchange and the American Institute of Accountants to bring about private reform in the general area of corporate disclosure, the Securities Act, which was modified along the lines of the existing British Companies Acts, was signed into law on May 27, 1933.

Thus, in 1933, in the public interest and for the protection of investors minimum financial and corporate disclosure standards, at least for prospectus purposes, were created through federal legislation. The old doctrine governing security transactions of *caveat emptor* was replaced by a new concept, namely, *caveat vendor*.

Why it was necessary to pass the Securities Act of 1933 and the lessons today's corporate executives can draw from this historical study are discussed in the next chapter -- chapter nine.

CHAPTER NINE

CONCLUSIONS

All the preceeding has been a description of how the control over an instrument of corporate finance---the prospectus and its contents---passed from management to the federal government. The outcome of the events and attitudes recorded---the Securities Act of 1933---was the first attempt by the federal government to throw open to the scrutiny of a government commission, and those of the public who were able to use and understand it, a full statement of the financial position and the results of operations of corporations, other than public service corporations, approaching the public money markets. In addition, the Act---again for the first time---prescribed some compulsory minimum standards of financial disclosure for such companies.

Much of the credit for the enactment of this required legislation can be taken by the critics of big business.[1] And, in 1933, if corporate management, investment bankers and public accountants collectively disliked such regulation, they had only themselves to blame.

---

[1]Glover, op. cit., pp. 304-305.

DOI: 10.4324/9781003169420-9

Chapter nine--the concluding chapter of the study--has been broken down into four parts labelled: "historical summary and analysis," which deals principally with the events, needs and practices which made necessary the passage of the 1933 Securities Act; "historical observations," which focuses more directly on the previously discussed practices and reform attempts related to corporate financial disclosure; "a general theory," which presents a conceptual framework incorporating the matters related to financial disclosure practices and standards discussed in parts one and two; and "administrative implications," which discusses the relevance to today's administrator of the study's conclusions pertaining to financial disclosure.

Part I: Historical Summary and Analysis

By 1933 the enactment of some form of federal securities legislation setting forth compulsory financial disclosure standards to be observed by management was necessary for at least two reasons: the repeated unwillingness since 1900 of corporate executives to improve significantly their financial disclosure practices to investors; and the public's loss of confidence, in 1933, in the ability and enthusiasm of several non-government groups such as the Investment Bankers Association to bring about through private efforts voluntary managerial reform in the area of corporate financial disclosure.

The chief obstacle to voluntary reform--either as the result of the efforts of private groups external to the firm or managerial self-regulation--was the continual unwillingness or inability of a number of corporate executives, aided and abetted by several segments of the financial community, to correctly perceive and respond to those changes within the socio-economic environment which created a long-run need for a new attitude on the part of management toward financial disclosure and management-investor relations. More directly stated, too many managements observed the principle of caveat emptor in their dealing with the public (including investors) long after this pre-twentieth century concept became incompatible with the realities of a modern industrial society.

By 1933, it was too late for private reform. The 1929 stock market crash, the subsequent economic collapse and the 1932-33 Senate revelations of corporate and financial chicanery all led to a loss of public confidence in those who had promised private reform--management and its commercial and financial associates. In addition, these same factors created an urgent and widespread public demand for the realization of a number of the overdue corporate reform measures, including more adequate corporate financial disclosure, persistently advocated during the prior thirty years by the critics of big business. By 1932 the promise of private reform was unacceptable: government intervention was necessary.

The Securities Act: Its Origins

The Securities Act of 1933 was the outcome of an historical process which started during the late nineteenth century with the rise of big business. The decline of the importance of the owner manager and the rise in public ownership of the nation's productive resources created a new need for management to report upon its activities to its public shareholders. Previously no such need had existed. Thus the rise of big business, and its attendant diversification of ownership, set in motion the forces which, in the absence of management's recognition of its new reporting obligations, contributed to the social and economic justification for this 1933 legislation.

The Securities Act had a long legislative history: the Act was not solely the product of the Seventy-third Congress. The 1933 Act's underlying philosophy and many of its provisions were based on the earlier English Companies Acts; the experiences of the various types of blue sky legislation--antifraud and regulatory--had guided its drafters; and the discarded Taylor, Denison and Volstead bills were legislative pioneers in this area.

The contents of the 1933 Act itself had historical counterparts; the Act's provisions were the products of earlier draftsmen refined to meet more modern needs. For instance, the Securities Act's underlying philosophy of disclosure, its antifraud and liability sections, the concept of a registration statement requiring specific items to be disclosed and the provision for the review by a government commission of all filed and published data pertaining to security offerings--all had been either tried or recommended long before their incorporation in the Securities Act.

In addition, the Act reflected a number of the recommendations and conclusions stated as early as 1895 in the reports of several much publicized government investigations and the writings of a number of prominent private individuals: the Act represented more than the social philosophy of the few people who drafted it. For example, the character of the Act was influenced by the reports of such government bodies as the Davey Commission, the Industrial Commission and the two previously discussed anti-big business congressional investigations conducted under the direction of Arsène Pujo and Ferdinand Pecora, respectively. In addition, the publications over the years of such critics of big business as Louis Brandeis, William Ripley and Adolph Berle, Jr.,--all of whom spoke with much prestige and authority--greatly influenced those who drafted and approved the 1933 Act.

These particular government reports and influential men contributed a number of specific suggestions related to financial disclosure and security regulation which were later to be embodied in the various provisions of the Act. But, perhaps more important, these reports and men formulated and extended to management-public relations two new notions--the "social corporation" and caveat vendor. These new concepts were offered as replacements for the older and by now inappropriate concepts of the "private corporation" and caveat emptor. In 1933, it was the popular endorsement of these two new social philosophies which led to the widespread demand for a securities act to regulate the recalcitrant management-underwriter-public accountant group.

Much of the nature, contents and character of the 1933 Securities Act were determined by the behavior of management with respect to the public since at least 1900. The corporate machinations just prior to the emergency of 1930 only increased, rather than created, the need for reform. In particular, the comprehensive financial disclosure standards--"all material information"--and the harsh liability provision provided for in the Securities Act were made necessary by the past actions of certain corporate managements, investment bankers and public accountants. Since at least 1900 the membership comprising each of these groups, with a few individual exceptions, had repeatedly denied or abused their public responsibility; failed to bring about the needed improvements in corporate financial disclosure standards; and, in the case of corporate management and investment bankers, shamelessly used "inside information" for private profit at the expense of either uniformed or misinformed investors. It was these past practices and attitudes which the Act sought to eliminate and, therefore, in a back-handed sort of way, management and some of their corporate friends were not only responsible for the Act but determined the nature of its contents and coverage.

Thus, the genealogy of the Securities Act can be traced back to at least 1900--if not earlier. And, from 1900 to 1933, the character of the genes which were to determine finally the characteristics of the Securities Act were not only influenced in part by the changes in the environment occasioned by the rise of giant corporations but also by the actions of the critics of big business and the practices of the business sector.

The Changing Environment: Big Business and Small Investors

The need to achieve the reforms ultimately brought about by the Securities Act were caused by two prior changes within the American socio-economic environment: the rise of big business about 1900 and the growth of a large class of small investors, particularly after 1918. It was in such a changing environment that a number of the things previously discussed occurred: the continued failure of corporate executives to bring about significant changes in their financial and corporate disclosure practices; the spasmodic and half-hearted efforts of such groups as the Investment Bankers Association, the New York Stock Exchange and the American Institute of Accountants to establish some standards of financial disclosure for the guidance of their members and corporate officers; and the persistent demands of the critics of big business for greater corporate financial disclosure. Between 1900 and 1933 the behavior of each of these several groups influenced and in turn was influenced by the changing social, political, economic and moral aspects of their environment--internal and external.

Both these factors---big business and small investors---were relevant to management financial disclosure practices and the standards against which such practices were judged by society. First, the rise of big business created conditions which made the long honored common law doctrine of caveat emptor incompatible with the realities of a modern industrial society such as the one which arose in the United States after 1900. In addition, the emerging of the giant corporations created a new power center within the American social structure which either destroyed, or threatened to destroy, some popular laissez-faire concepts related to how the economy of a democratic society ought to operate.

Second, after 1918, the growth of a nation-wide class of small investors led to the end of another long revered nineteenth century image, namely, the independent small businessman who was the owner-manager of his own enterprise. After 1918, however, there existed a large stock-owning class which was not directly in control of those enterprises employing their capital. Management and control in many companies became divorced. Few investors, however, appeared to object to this arrangement. Later, a number of these small investors, sometimes under "unfair" conditions, enthusiastically participated in the 1926-29 bull market. But when the stock market collapsed in 1929 the faith of these small investors in the virtues of big business evaporated.

The rise of big business and the growth in the number of small investors created for management new needs and new opportunities. One of the new needs was for a more appropriate concept than caveat emptor to govern management's relations with those with whom it had commercial intercourse. Unfortunately, the one opportunity a significant number of managements saw in these new conditions was the opportunity to enlarge their private fortunes at the expense of the public. The new conditions and some managers' questionable commercial and financial practices gave rise to a movement to achieve through political action either the regulation or dissolution of big business. Later, particularly after 1918, the protection of small investors from those corporate officers and stock market operators who sold fraudulent or unsound securities and manipulated security prices became an objective of reformers.

Before 1900: In general, before 1900 the American public, including some businessmen and many who were later to become their critics, subscribed to a number of the simple principles of laissez-faire economics related to marketing. In particular, the public recognized the common law tenet of caveat emptor as governing commercial transactions. The only general exception to these two articles of belief were public service corporations which were "clothed with public interest" and hence subject to regulation by the state. Furthermore, in keeping with the general economic and commercial philosophy, there were few legal restraints upon management's public reporting practices. For instance, the incorporation laws varied greatly from state to state and required little or no public reports from corporations; and the common law related to fraud and deceit was vague, inadequate and difficult to enforce against those who made false statements with respect to corporate promotions. Few sellers and apparentely fewer buyers, it would seem, were disturbed by this absence of legal restraints.

1900-1918: About 1900, however, it became evident to many that the rise of big business through numerous mergers and consolidations was clearly in conflict with the traditional laissez-faire economic model and that the existence of these industrial giants could even threaten the fundamental civil liberties and morality of the American society. Clearly, the rise of big business also rendered the rule of caveat emptor, which was based on the assumption that both the seller and the buyer were of equal strength and capable of knowing all the facts surrounding any transaction, incongruous with the times.

Simply, the fact of the matter was that the giant corporations on one hand and the puny individual employees, customers, small businessmen and--later--the investors on the other, were not of equal strength and not equally capable of knowing all the facts related to any transaction between these two classes.

To many social critics, such as Louis Brandeis, and their public following this imbalance of power, and its potential social, economic and moral consequences, was intolerable. Accordingly, these people set in motion a strong, vigorous and popular demand for a political solution to redress the balance. In addition, and for much the same reasons, these critics agitated for the strengthening of the lax state incorporation laws; the passage of a federal incorporation law to regulate better the giant interstate companies; and some legislative action to supplement the inadequate common law doctrines related to deceit and fraud. Later, after the entry of the United States into World War I, the popular appeal of these various demands subsided, the nation's attention being devoted to the pursuit of its war aim--victory.

<u>1918 Onwards</u>: Next, about 1918, as a result of the impact of the Liberty Loans upon investor habits and the growing need of corporations for more capital, corporate ownership became dispersed and a large

nationwide class of small investors came into existence. This development was significant for two reasons. First, the dispersion of ownership resulted in an acceleration of the breakdown of the traditional concept of the individual who was both owner and manager of the enterprise in which his capital was invested. Now, the ownership and the control were tending to be represented by different persons and the balance of power in this relationship lay with management rather than the stockholders. Later, during the early 1920's it was this apparent inability of stockholders to control their management which led to a demand by a number of people, such as Berle, for some form of "corporate democracy" as a means whereby the control of corporate activity would be placed back in the hands of the owners who had abdicated their power. Management, such people as young Berle said, had a responsibility to its stockholders. Subsequently, after 1930, this belief was restated--management, Berle and his fellow critics now said, had a public responsibility which went beyond its obligations to the control or the ownership. Management had a public responsibility. If management would not accept this responsibility, then, the critics said, political action (legislation) in this area was necessary.

The second consequence of the appearance of a large class of investors of moderate means was the development of a belief that it was the duty of the government to protect small investors from security frauds, swindles, speculations and unfair gambles. Unfortunately, a number of the new members of the investor class were unsophisticated in the mysteries of finance and all too readily became the victims of nefarious security schemes. As a consequence, beginning with Kansas in 1911, a number of the states to protect the "common man" and his savings from the seductive false promises of promoters of fraudulent enterprises enacted "blue sky laws" which sought to regulate directly security issues and dealers. About the same time, on the federal level, the Progressive Party's platform pointed out that the public was being swindled out of millions of dollars by investing in stocks offered by "highly colored prospectuses" and declared federal government action was necessary to halt this practice.

Later, the unrestrained security speculation--some said gambling--of the late 1920's further disturbed such men as Ripley and his fellow critics, since such speculation was considered by these people to be basically unfair--management possessed "inside information" which was denied to the small investor.

However, during the 1920's the vast majority of the public, including most investors, were indifferent to these calls for reform, apathetic to the few corporate and political abuses revealed and ignorant of the numerous undetected abuses. And, corporate executives, subject to some individual exceptions, continued to practice the philosophy of caveat emptor when dealing with investors. In fact, most corporate executives, the public and the nation's political leaders were either unconcerned with or unable to see the potential consequences of the economic, political and social shenanigans of the decade.

Subsequently, the 1930 débâcle brought the American public, including the chastened business community and the poorer but, hopefully, wiser investors, face to face with the tragic results of their previous follies. And, in the process, all effective opposition to corporate reform was swept aside.

The Critics: Persistent Agitation for Reform

Much of the credit for the passage of the 1933 Securities Act belongs to those commonly labelled "the critics of big business." Initially, between 1900 and 1916, these critics--for economic, social, and moral reasons--sought primarily to curb the power of the "trusts" for the protection of employees, customers and independent businessmen. One of the prerequisites for such action was greater publicity of corporate affairs. At the time, it will be recalled, it was not customary for corporations--both large and small--to publish in detail either their financial position or the results of operations. Greater publicity of corporate activities, the critics believed, would demonstrate to all the economic inefficiencies of big business: the unjust monopoly profits enjoyed by the giant corporations and the dangerous extent to which the trusts had control over the nation's resources---economic, human and social. Given such information, it was argued, the public would be better able to deal with the abuses of corporate power.

Later, particularly after 1918, following the rapid increase in the number of small investors, the critics of big business lengthened their list of wards and became the self-appointed guardians of the small investor who, they said, were "the sport" of those dishonest promoters, greedy corporate officers and unscrupulous members of the financial community who rigged the stock market for personal gain. These "wicked" promoters, it was said, operated in the "darkness"--let there be "light," the reformers claimed, and both the manipulation of the stock prices and sale of fraudulent securities would cease.

More specifically, the critics, particularly Ripley, demanded full and honest corporate disclosure to investors. But, during the 1920's, unlike their earlier general call for corporate publicity, the critics, now joined by such security analysts as Clinton Collver, were more specific with respect to the type of information which they believed should be disclosed. In addition, those critical of management's corporate disclosure habits---particularly financial disclosure---also expressed dissatisfaction with the accounting principles and practices underlying existing corporate reporting practices. It was necessary, the critics said, that either a federal law similar to those sections of the British Companies Act related to "full disclosure" be enacted or, that corporate executives voluntary adopt standards of disclosure similar to those suggested by Clinton Collver and William Ripley. If voluntary reform could not be achieved, then, the critics constantly said, the government must intervene to bring about the needed reform.

Accountants, Bankers and the Exchange: Ineffectual Reformers

Throughout the period from 1900 to 1933, a number of private groups sought with limited success to bring about voluntary reform in the area of corporate financial disclosure. These groups, which included the New York Stock Exchange, the Investment Bankers Association and the American Institute of Accountants, from time to time, declared themselves in favor of fuller corporate publicity and (individually and severally) outlined some minimum standards of financial disclosure for prospectus, annual report and credit purposes.

Each one of these bodies, or at least their leadership, at one time or another recognized and publicly stated that the inevitable alternative to a failure to achieve voluntary reform in the area of corporate publicity was government regulation. Yet, despite the general dislike for government regulation among corporate executives, none of these private groups succeeded in gaining general acceptance by management, or even their own membership, of these suggested standards.

These three private bodies were unable to bring about substantial reform in the area of financial disclosure for a variety of reasons other than the unwillingness on management's part to change its public reporting practices. The leadership of each one of these three groups either lacked the desire or the ability to force the adoption of their recommended disclosure standards by their unenthusiastic members and those reluctant managements with whom they came in contact. For instance, the American

Institute, while promoting balance sheet audits, did not take disciplinary action against those of its members who allowed management to abuse the audit certificate. The New York Stock Exchange publicly advocated better corporate disclosure but privately was lackadaisical in enforcing its existing listing agreements related to corporate annual reports to stockholders. And the Investment Bankers Association after setting forth some minimum prospectus disclosure standards then refused to put pressure upon its members and those managements making public security offerings to observe these standards--compliance was "voluntary".

Lacking the ability directly to enforce their suggestions related to financial disclosure, the only readily available tool for those who belonged to these three groups and who truly sought private reform was moral suasion. This was almost bound to be ineffective because the bulk of the members of each of these three private groups were in some way dependent of management for their livelihood. Despite the much publicized "independence" of public accountants and the much feared power of the "money trust", only a few public accountants and investment bankers had established an existence independent of management's beneficence. (Perhaps one can infer for such people strongly to oppose management was to endanger one's own short-term interests).

There was another, and perhaps more damaging, reason for the failure of private reform in the area of financial disclosure to investors. A number of those who belonged to the investment banking fraternity, which publicly advocated greater corporate financial disclosure, were in fact using the "custom" of corporate secrecy to promote personal profits at the expense of investors. For instance, as the Pecora hearings revealed, a number of respected investment bankers and members of the various exchanges, individually, or in conspiracy with corporate officers, concealed information from investors so as to make "insider's profits" in stock market transactions or unload questionable securities which might not have been purchased by investors had the full truth surrounding such offerings been known to the public.

Such short-sighted practices were related to another phenomena: the lack of public responsibility of a number of those actively engaged in business and finance. In fact, in addition to corporate management, each one of these three private groups--investment bankers, public accountants and stock exchange members--denied rather than sought the larger public responsibility demanded of them by the changing times. The investment banker tried to avoid such a responsibility through the "disclaimer clause;" the public accountant limited his public responsibility to the technical language of his certificate; and the New York Stock Exchange denied it was responsible in any way, except in the case of fraud, for the regulation of the price behavior of listed stocks. Finally, of course, in addition to being concerned with the financial disclosure standards of management, the leadership of these three groups were also concerned with a number of other, and perhaps more pressing, problems---organizational and personnel.

Thus, given the conditions, practices and attitudes described above, the efforts of these three private groups to bring about voluntary reforms in the area of corporate financial disclosure were doomed to failure for the "sins and omissions" pertaining to financial disclosure of corporate executives were also shared, if not supported, by the membership, including some of the so-called leaders, of the various stock exchanges, the investment banking fraternity and the then "non-independent" accounting profession.

Later, the events of 1932 and 1933, including the testimony related to stock exchange practices before the Senate Banking and Currency Committee, resulted in a sharp decline in the public's confidence in the integrity of those who comprised the membership of these three groups. This, in turn, led to serious doubts on the public's part as to the ability or willingness of such private bodies to bring about those reforms in the area of corporate publicity they had long publicly advocated. Consequently, by 1933, when it was obvious some form of reform was needed, there was really no publicly acceptable alternative to federal government regulation of securities and security markets.

Corporate Management

By 1933 passage of a federal securities statute was necessary primarily because of the repeated failure of many corporate executives to perceive, interpret and respond in a responsible fashion to the long-run social, political and ethical implications arising from the development of big business and the growth of a large nation-wide class of small investors. The failure of corporate managements fully to appreciate these changes--partially brought about by these same executives--led in turn to an underestimation of the long-term import of the previously discussed public demands of those articulate users of accounting data and the critics of big business for more honest and adequate corporate disclosure--particularly financial disclosure. In short, management, for some of the reasons suggested below, continued to base its relations with the public (including investors) too much upon the doctrine of caveat emptor long after this concept became incompatible with modern industrial life.

In addition to the critics, a number of management's corporate friends--accountants, investment bankers and stock exchange officials--published calls for improved corporate disclosure and even suggested minimum financial disclosure standards. Without management's cooperation, these efforts, as noted, were doomed to failure because of the dependent nature of these groups' relationship to management and the negative attitude of their membership toward their own public responsibility.

It is difficult to say why management failed to adjust its disclosure practices to satisfy its critics and the changing needs of the times. Perhaps, as a number of the economic and business histories covering this 33-year period have already shown, management was more concerned with short-run rather than long-run operating results; preoccupied with tactical rather than strategic goals; and personal rather than corporate profit. Whatever the answer, the sad fact remains that management because of its own blindness, and the attitudes of its friends, failed to respond in a positive, forthright and responsible fashion to the demands of its critics and the challenges of the environment.

The rise of big business and the dispersion of corporate ownership among people of moderate means called for a new philosophy to govern management--public (including investors) relations--the old doctrine of caveat emptor was outmoded. And it was the critics rather than management who developed the more appropriate and lasting concept to govern such relationships, namely, caveat vendor, which, among other things, called for improved corporate financial disclosure practices.

In contrast, management failed in its relations with investors to develop and accept a philosophy to replace caveat emptor that would in the long run, under the new conditions, be acceptable to the public and to management's critics. It was this failure of management, as well as the reasons for it, which in the end led to federal intervention.

Part II: Historical Observations, 1900-1933[1]

This section of chapter eight presents some historical observations related to the practices and attitudes pertaining to financial disclosure of the critics of big business, the users of accounting data,

---

[1]To each one of these general observations there were, of course, individual exceptions. A number have been noted earlier.

the public and corporate executives between 1900 and 1933. These observations, several of which already have been briefly mentioned under the heading "Historical Summary and Analysis", have been segregated because of their particular pertinance to subsequent parts of this chapter. At least nine major observations are presented below.

Financial Disclosure: A Political, Social and Moral Issue

During the period 1900-1933, the adequacy (or inadequacy) of corporate financial disclosure, thanks to the agitation of the critics of big business, became a political issue with social, economic and ethical overtones. Subsequently, in 1933, in the absence of private reform, the controversy was partially resolved through legislation (political action). Henceforth, corporate financial disclosure practices were to be a concern of the government (a political instrument) as well as the ever-present articulate and vigilant critics of big business whose demands for more stringent legislation were still unsatisfied.

From about 1900 onwards, aroused by the rise of big business and the consequences for weaker groups and individuals who were touched by this development, those who wished to regulate or destroy big business through legislative action generated a sub-demand for greater corporate publicity, including more honest and adequate financial disclosure. Compulsory corporate publicity was envisioned by the critics of big business as but a stepping-stone to more stringent government actions. Until such a final goal was achieved, however, fuller corporate disclosure would for the time being aid employees, independent businessmen, customers and investors in their economic dealings with the giant corporations. Other critics, as we have seen, viewed compulsory corporate publicity as but one of several methods whereby some of the existing undesirable social and moral conditions attributed to the existence of big business would be eradicated.

Later, in 1933, through the Securities Act, the federal government was also drawn into the controversy related to management financial disclosure practices.

Thus, at the end of the thirty-three years just reviewed, there was promise that as long as the critics of big business continued to act out their historical role and the Securities Act remained on the statute books, those in the future who would attempt to change management's financial disclosure practices, or those managements who resisted or ignored the need to change such practices, would be obliged to consider the broad social and political implications of their actions.

Critics' Standards Govern Long-Run Public Evaluation

The standards of financial disclosure and the underlying attitude toward management-investor relations ultimately embodied in the Securities Act of 1933 were drawn from among those offered by management's critics rather than from the practices and attitudes in this area of management.

The critics of big business, as indicated in chapter two, were a heteregeneous body of individuals with a common enemy---big business. The numbers, composition and influence of this articulate and dedicated group, which was an ever present influence throughout the thirty-three years studied, changed from time to time but never the ultimate goal---the containment or orderly destruction of big business through government action, including, as a preliminary, compulsory financial disclosure.

The critics' progress toward the satisfaction of their goal--which was only partially realized in 1933--was slow but persistent, and, finally, when government action became necessary, it was the standards and attitudes of the critics which were enacted into law rather than those of the discredited corporate executive and his corporate friends. Hence, at the time of crisis, it was the critics' proposed disclosure standards--not management's actual standards and practices--by which management was finally judged.

Changing Environment and User Needs Create New Disclosure Needs

Between 1930 and 1933, the standards of financial disclosure advocated by the critics and sophisticated users of accounting data were ever-changing in response to certain changes in the nature of the environment and needs of the users of financial statements. For instance, the increasing attractiveness of industrial securities for investment purposes led to a new need on the part of investors and those who advised investors for more adequate income statements; and the rise of a large class of small investors created a new demand on the part of the critics for greater and different types of corporate financial disclosure to investors. In contrast, during the period 1900-1933, management's financial disclosure practices underwent few significant changes. It was, as noted earlier, the failure of management to perceive correctly and respond to these changes which led to federal intervention.

Persistent Demand by Users for Standardization

Throughout the thirty-three years studied the critics of big business and the articulate users of financial data persistently demanded "standardization" and "uniformity" of corporate accounting procedures, practices and principles. In support of this plea the compulsory uniform system of accounts of the

Interstate Commerce Commission was often credited with having facilitated the comparison of one railroad with another for purposes of railroad security analysis. A similar scheme for public reporting, such people as Ripley and Collver said, should be imposed on the large publicly held industrial corporations by either government or private action. The Securities Act of 1933, while it did not create such a system of uniform accounts, did leave with the Federal Trade Commission, and later the Securities and Exchange Commission, the power to regulate the accounting practices of registered companies.

Public's Current Attitude No Guide to Long-Run Acceptability of Financial Disclosure Practices

During the years 1900 to 1933 the general public's feelings toward big business and the related question of corporate financial disclosure ran "hot and cold" and proved to be a poor indicator of the long-run acceptability of management's financial disclosure practices. In the long run, it was the values and standards of the critics rather than those of management which shaped the nature of the public's reaction to the traumatic events of 1930-33. But, during the decade prior to 1930, management, encouraged by the apparent apathy of the public toward the inadequacies of corporate financial disclosure, ignored the critics' repeated demands and warnings related to financial disclosure. This temporary response on the part of the public, it should be noted, was in part the product of management's own public relations work. Unfortunately, the attitude of the fickle public was to prove no indication as to how management's past perfommances would be judged in the long run. For, with the end of prosperity the public's love affair with management also came to an end.

Management Delegated Responsibility for Financial Non-Disclosure to Others

From 1900 to 1933, at least in the case of prospectus disclosure, management, either explicitly or implicitly, allowed others to determine the extent of management's disclosure of financial and corporate information to the public. For instance, it was the lawyers for the investment banking syndicate and the issuing corporation who were the principal parties charged with preparing the prospectuses to accompany new public security offerings. The lawyers undertaking this task had two principal concerns: to reduce as far as possible the legal liability of all those concerned with the issue for the contents of the prospectus and to make the offering as attractive as possible to potential buyers. Both of these considerations were selfish and short-run in character and had the tendency in practice to discourage more adequate financial disclosure.

The consequences of this practice of delegating the responsibility for corporate disclosure to others were, at least in the case of prospectuses, twofold. First, after 1918, the desire to reduce the legal liability led, in part, to the increasing use of what has previously been described as the standard form of management prospectus. A form of prospectus which was so deficient with respect to financial disclosure that fraudulent promoters could, in the absence of common law and statutory restraints, adopt with impunity the same prospectus format used by legitimate promoters. Hence, the public, on the basis of the prospectus, was unable to distinguish the sound from the unsound investment and the honest from the dishonest promoter. Second, the need to present an attractive picture to the public, the second concern of the lawyers and underwriters, led to the concealment of all the unfavorable aspects of the offering. Such practices and goals, it should be noted, were in line with management's belief in "corporate secrecy" and hence acceptable to management.

However, in the long run financial disclosure dictated by such considerations was to prove unacceptable to the public which was, by 1933, highly critical of any management maneuvers which appeared to avoid management's public responsibility or manipulate stock prices. Unfortunately, the prospectuses created by the motives described above presented such an image. Management, in practice, had delegated the responsibility for financial non-disclosure to others but in the eyes of those external to the firm it was management which was ultimately held responsible for this matter.

<u>Private Reform Without Management Cooperation</u>

Between 1900-1933, those private groups--investment bankers and accountants--who attempted to establish some minimum financial disclosure standards to be observed by management, in general, excluded management from the process whereby these standards were established. Management was neither invited, nor, apparently, sought to be included in such discussions. Whatever the reasons for this absence of management, the failure to attract or seek management participation in these discussions contributed, in part, to the inability of these groups to impose their standards upon management. Surely, without management participation voluntary acceptance by management of these standards was made more unlikely, given management's existing disposition to not change its financial disclosure practices.

If, in fact, these private groups who publicly sought private reform by not including management in their efforts made private reform less likely, and if the alternative to private reform was government regulation, these poorly conceived efforts to seek private reform may, by the very act of failing, have added, in part, to the apparent need for government intervention--the very outcome the accountants and bankers wished to avoid.[1]

Henceforth, Management, Accountants, Underwriters All Responsible

Following the passage of the Securities Act of 1933, corporate financial disclosure standards became the joint concern of management, accountants and underwriters. The Securities Act held the management, underwriters and public accountants associated with any public security offering responsible for the contents of prospectuses. The liability section of the Act recognized that these three groups had a community of interest and were jointly responsible for the level of financial disclosure achieved in any prospectus. Thus, in the future, despite past attitudes and practices, these three parties--and later the stock exchanges--could not afford, without fear of punishment, to let any one of their numbers either develop lax habits in the area of financial reporting or preempt the role of arbiter in this matter.

---

[1]Management was also excluded by the framers of the Securities Act of 1933 from the deliberations leading up to the passage of the Act.

A Top Management Responsibility: In Retrospect

During the period 1900-1933 the improvement of corporate financial disclosure to investors and shareholders was not considered a top management problem. In general, during much of this period, top management's sole concern in the matter, for competitive or other reasons, had been the suppression of corporate information. This practice resulted, in part, from the inheritance by management after 1900 of a number of the attitudes of the owner-managers of the past when there had been few or no outside investors, so there had been little need for thinking about the problem of financial disclosure. Under these conditions, corporations' financial statements had been considered private.

However, looking backwards from our present vantage point and applying modern theories of management to the period 1900 to 1933, one might well conclude corporate financial disclosure practices _should_ have been the concern of top management--as distinct from the middle or operating levels. This conclusion is valid, not only because the critics, public accountants and investment bankers said financial disclosure was a management responsibility, but because of two other more basic factors: the historical characteristics of the top management function--as distinct from practices--and the characteristics of the administrative implications which did in fact arise from management's attitude toward financial disclosure. Again, it should be emphasized that the concept of top management being applied is of recent origin in so far as management theory based on empirical research is concerned. During the period reviewed while top management in practice carried out this function, the standard was not articulated.

Today, it is becoming more generally recognized that the function of top management is the "strategic guidance of organizations in a rapidly changing world."[1] More specifically, the function of top management in any corporation is to relate effectively--currently and in the long run--the enterprise to its socio-economic environment by being able effectively to "perceive, evaluate, and respond to the advent of all sorts of new opportunities and needs" which may be "brought about by new popular aspirations, new knowledge, and new ways of thinking, new techniques, new applications of all sorts, new ideas of all kinds, and new pressures and problems."[2] Such processes

> ...are fundamental to the management of the innovation, evolution, adaptation, survival, and growth of enterprise in a well-nigh

---

[1]John M. Baitsell, John D. Glover and David F. Hawkins, "Introduction", McGraw-Hill Publishing Company, Inc. (Boston: Harvard Graduate School of Business Administration, 1961), p. 1. Note: The "Introduction" to this particular case series was written by John D. Glover with the assistance of John M. Baitsell and David F. Hawkins.

[2]Ibid., p. 4.

incomprehensibly complext environment....

> New opportunities and needs for devising new ways of relating a corporation more effectively to important and powerful entities about it may be found in any direction: for instance, in user markets, money markets, labor markets....
>
> The entities with which it may be necessary or profitable to relate the company in new ways include individuals, corporations, associations, unions, and government instrumentalities.[1]

In short, it is the function of top management to examine the environment and decide what is both relevant and significant to the organization as an on-going system and in the light of these findings set appropriate strategic goals for the enterprise, and reserve for itself the management of those relationships which it deems to be of greatest importance to the attainment of these goals.

Between 1900 and 1930 a number of the external and internal influences which conceivably could have materially affected corporate life and development underwent many important changes. These changes, in turn, placed, according to our modern theory, the obligation upon top management to devise new ways of relating itself and the corporations under its direction to the existing or rapidly developing entities

---

[1] *Ibid.*

of importance within this environment. In the areas of marketing and production top management was able to successfully meet these challenges of the new environment. But in the area of financial disclosure to investors management failed.

From 1900 to 1933 two noteworthy and significant changes within the environment related to corporate financial disclosure, as previously noted, were the rise of big business and the dispersion of corporate ownership. These two developments led in turn to the emergence of three entities as new and important factors--the critic of big business, the federal government and its agencies, and the small investor. The formation of such groups--and their potential influence, directly or indirectly, upon the evolution, survival and growth of the corporate form of business called, as modern management theory and hindsight now indicate, for top management attention. Clearly, these developments, as later events clearly showed, were particularly relevant and significant to corporate life since in the end the failure of management to effectively relate itself to these emerging groups led, in part, to uninvited government regulation of a number of business instruments including prospectuses and a new and larger role for the federal government in the nation's economic affairs vis a vis the private sector.

One of the major reasons why management failed to relate itself effectively to its critics and stockholders--potential and actual--was the neglect by management of one of its principal means of communicating with those external to the firm, namely, financial reports. After 1900, the same conditions which led to a growing significance of the critic, investor and government to corporate management also gave rise to a need to develop a new attitude on the part of management toward financial disclosure. In fact, the critics and investors--or at least those who advised investors--repeatedly asked for more honest and adequate corporate financial disclosure. Under the new social and economic conditions these people felt a genuine need for more complete financial reports: their reasons were not capricious. Management failed to meet these requests. The inappropriate--and often dishonest--management practices related to financial disclosure created constant conflict and antagonism between management and a number of those external to the firm. Surely, if the critic, government and investor were important enough to be a top management concern--and admittedly the full significance of the rise of these groups may have been difficult to appreciate between 1900 and 1930--then the appropriateness of the principal means including financial reports whereby management communicated with these groups should also have been a top management concern.

Historically, top management's concern with financial disclosure was one of limiting disclosure: an inappropriate objective. Therefore, in 1933, because the management class either could not or would not readjust its financial reporting practices to conform to the conditions of modern industrial life the government intervened. This intervention was justified when the public, under the influence of the critics of big business, judged both the dishonest and the inadequate but otherwise honest management financial disclosure practices to have adversely affected the "public interest."

Part III: A General Theory

Chapters one through eight described the economic, social and political events and trends which resulted in the passage of the 1933 Securities Act. The last two parts of chapter nine--"historical summary and analysis" and "historical observations"--identified, analyzed and discussed a number of the factors which led to this need to create minimum standards of corporate financial disclosure, particularly prospectus disclosure, through federal legislation prior to 1933. Below, based on the material previously covered, the discussion moves to a higher level of abstraction with the presentation of a "general theory" relating the top management function to the nature of the standards governing corporate financial disclosure practices to the public.

Corporate financial disclosure practices to investors are a top management responsibility. The standards, from the point of view of the public, by which these financial reporting practices are evaluated in the long run, are set by persons external to the firm. When management's financial disclosure practices persistently lag behind these externally set standards government regulation will result. These three broad notions--the reasonableness of which is derived from the prior description, analysis and interpretation of the material covered to date--are the essence of a series of hypotheses related to corporate financial reporting presented below. In particular, these thoughts apply to annual reports to stockholders as well as prospectuses.

The "general theory" runs as follows: The issue as to what financial, economic and accounting data ought to be revealed by corporate officers, and the means by which this information is to be communicated to the stockholders and the general public, in the absence of complete government regulation, possess characteristics of a problem calling for a top management decision. Irrespective of how management in fact views its responsibility with respect to corporate disclosure, ultimately the public holds top management responsible for the adequacy of its disclosure practices.

In practice, the nature, extent and form of the financial information disclosed by corporate managers is determined, within the broad limitations of "generally accepted accounting principles", by management's concept of its obligation to report the results of its stewardship to the public; the customary disclosure practices of other managements; the importance and priority management assigns to financial reporting problems; and management's interest and comprehension of the technical aspects of reporting which management assigns, implicitly or explicitly, to others. The financial disclosure decision is, in part, also effected by management's judgement as to the relevance to the user of such information and the advantages, competitive and personal, arising from disclosure as well as nondisclosure.

The standards for judging the long-run adequacy, from the point of view of the public, of management's financial disclosure practices are set, explicitly and implicitly, by the needs--past, present and anticipated--of the numerous and diverse articulate users of financial statements including the so-called critics of big business. These groups, of course, exist externally to the firm. In general, these standards are shaped primarily by the user's objectives, social values, and expectations---rational and irrational---as well as the general political, economic and social environment.

The external standards governing financial disclosure are ever changing as new needs and opportunities are created by new economic relations, new popular aspirations, new knowledge and new ways of thinking, new applications of all sorts, new ideas of all kinds, and new pressures and problems. Similarly, management's financial disclosure practices, which are also related to the changing environment as well as the changing needs of the users of financial reports, should also change to reflect the new conditions.

When the financial disclosure practices of management persistently over a number of years fail to meet the ever changing requirements---stated and unstated---of the users of financial data, the probability of government intervention to correct the deficient reporting practices of management increases. Such a discrepancy inviting government regulation is most likely to occur if top management---as a class---minimizes, neglects or delegates to others the decision as to what constitutes a "full and fair" disclosure of a particular corporation's activities.

In addition, perhaps with the view to removing the need for government intervention, any efforts without the support and cooperation of management by private groups external to the firm to improve corporate financial disclosure through voluntary managerial reform are not likely to be successful. The failure of these non management participating reform efforts, in turn, increases the probability of government intervention. Therefore, as a corollary, it would seem to behoove top management to seek a major role in such private reform efforts related to corporate disclosure. Especially, if management wishes to retain, in the long run, its control over corporate financial reporting practices--one of the principal methods by which management relates itself to those external to the firm.

Hopefully, the reasonableness of the above "general theory" has been demonstrated by the earlier material presented and, therefore, there is no need to elaborate upon this matter any further.

The next portion of chapter eight, labelled "administrative implications", will use this general theory as a guide to identify, examine and appraise some present trends and conditions which, unless checked or modified, may well lead to further limitations upon the flexibility now enjoyed by management in the preparation of its periodic financial reports to the public including stockholders.

Part IV: Administrative Implications

A sense of historical forces, events and time can often aid administrators to conceive of more useful and timely responses to the changing world about them. Hopefully, the historical survey just concluded will assist top managers--today's and tomorrow's--to grasp better the significance and importance of their financial disclosure practices and the factors--personal and environmental--which create the ever-changing standards against which such practices in the long run are evaluated by the public.

Today, the Securities and Exchange Commission, while specifically holding management responsible for financial representations to investors, has in effect deprived management of much of its freedom to determine its own financial disclosure practices for prospectus purposes. However, in the case of annual reports to stockholders, management still continues to enjoy nearly unrestrained freedom, within the broad limits of "generally accepted accounting principles" and management's own conscience, to choose between alternative financial disclosure practices.[1] Never-

---

[1]The Securities Exchange Commission requires the filing by registered companies of detailed periodic statements, the so-called 8K, 9K and 10K reports. The material presented in these reports is not subject to

theless, some people--accountants, "professional" investors and politicians--wish to limit further management's prerogatives in the area of financial reporting to stockholders. In particular, the American Institute of Certified Public Accountants is now undertaking a program to review "generally accepted accounting principles" and a number of other aspects of corporate financial statements. To date, management has not participated in these efforts of the Institute. In addition, others who use financial data, especially security analysts, have expressed a need for more adequate financial reports.

Perhaps the present study may awaken management to the possible consequences which could arise from these reform efforts and calls for more adequate financial disclosure and, at the same time, provide some clues as to how management might retain the remaining flexibility it now possesses with respect to financial reporting. The final outcome, however, rests with management--individually and collectively.

Three questions come to mind: Will the misfortunes,

---

the rules covering Proxy Statements, except in the case of a contest for control of a corporation, and hence need not be reproduced in annual reports. In the case of a "proxy battle" much of the 10K material must be presented to the stockholders.

State law pertaining to financial disclosure has not progressed much beyond the level described earlier. See, for example, page 138.

oversights and attitudes similar to those just described which led to the need to pass the Securities Act of 1933 and its companion legislation--particularly The Securities and Exchange Act--overtake management again? How might such an occurrence effect management? How might it be prevented? To provide meaningful answers to these three questions the "general theory" derived from the preceeding historical study will be used as a guide to identify, analyze, and appraise those aspects of the current environment which may influence future financial disclosure standards and practices. Only the future, of course, will demonstrate the validity of the theory.

Conditions, Needs, Reformers--1962

The 1962 American scene--social, political and economic--in so far as it touches financial disclosure standards and practices is pregnant with new needs, opportunities and dangers. Some of these factors are analogous to past conditions, others are peculiar to recent times.

For the last ten years the United States has experienced a relatively high level of economic prosperity. Partly as a consequence, in 1962, there are more stockholders than ever before. Stock market activity has pushed security prices to new peaks. And those who advise investors--security analysts--

are seeking more adequate and useful corporate financial statements. In addition, the stock exchanges are now under government investigation. Big business is bigger and the critics of big business are still active. Corporate ownership is more widely dispersed; and there are many who are seeking to place the control of corporate activity back in the hands of stockholders. And, among these critics greater corporate publicity is a common demand. Also, driven in part by a fear of government intervention, the American Institute of Certified Public Accountants is currently attempting to review and revise "generally accepted accounting principles"--the conventions which govern the compilation of published financial statements. Again, as in the past, management is neither actively participating in these reform efforts of the accountants nor readily adopting those recommendations related to financial disclosure of the security analysts and the critics. In fact, there is some evidence which suggests a number of top managements either still do not regard financial reports as a top management responsibility or seek to avoid more disclosure of corporate affairs.

A larger number of small investors than ever before hold securities. In 1962, there was upwards of 15,000,000 stockholders in the United States--

about one-half of whom have incomes of less than $7,500. As late as 1958, these people were described thus: "for the most part, [they] are doctors, lawyers, executives, school teachers first, and stockholders second. They are investors who for the most part, do not wish to be bothered---except by dividends."[1] However, the recent bull market has also led to an avid interest by a number of these part-time investors in capital appreciation. In fact, encouraged by the belief that the current high level of stock prices---the Dow-Jones average now stands above 710---is permanent, speculation by these investors of moderate means is prevalent. As to what these people's reaction will be when---not if---stock prices decline we can only guess. In 1849 Lord Overstone is reported to have said:

> Whenever the fingers are burned, a cure is always lustily called for by those who have been burned the most severely, and their object in this, as in the diversion that has hurt them is always the same---they call for the appointment of a government officer, who shall from time to time regulate how they shall hold their hands to the fire without being burned.[2]

And subsequent history has not shown him to be wrong.

Investors may only be superficially concerned with the fortunes of those companies in which they

---

[1]J. A. Livingston, The American Stockholder (Philadelphia and New York: J. B. Lippincott Company, 1958), p. 38.

[2]George O. May, Financial Accounting, p. 57.

invest but security analysts—those who advise or at least profess to advise such investors—are beset and frustrated by a number of problems associated with financial statement analysis. Faced with an ever increasing need to compare more intelligently one company with another, security analysts have expressed a wish that conventional financial statements be recast in order to meet today's analytical needs.[1] Such "improvements" in financial reports as the following have been requested: a more widespread presentation of funds flow statements; adjustments for changing price levels; five or ten-year tabulations of relevant statistics; uniform grouping of accounts by industries; segregation of sales and earnings by divisions; estimates of future cash flow needs; a breakdown of depreciation into normal and emergency categories; and a division of the inventory account by methods of valuation.[2]

In 1962, security analysts, in so far as financial disclosure is concerned, are an important group, far greater than before the passage of the Securities Act.

---

[1]Charles T. Horngren, "Increasing the Utility of Financial Statements," The Journal of Accountancy. Vol. 108, No. 1, July 1959, p. 39.

[2]Nicholas E. Crane, "A Security Analyst Looks at Annual Reports," The Journal of Accountancy. Vol. 105, No. 3, March 1958, p. 31ff.

Those who have advocated security regulation based on the disclosure philosophy--the basis of the Securities Act--have always recognized that the average investor would, in all probability, not use the material published under the requirements of such acts. The protection of investors, it has been argued ever since the Gladstone report, would come from the expert use of the required published material by those men who professionally advised investors. Today, security analysts perform, in part, that function. Therefore, given the existence of the Securities Act and its underlying philosophy of disclosure, security analysts are indeed an important group and their demands for greater corporate disclosure deserve the attention of top management.

To date, a few managements have adopted several of the analyst's requests: none, as a recent study by Alan Cerf clearly shows, have adopted all.[1] When asked why, management has usually replied: such information would help competitors.[2] A number of persons, however, believe such an excuse is rarely

---

[1]See, for example, Alan Robert Cerf, Corporate Reporting And Investment Decisions (Berkeley: Institute of Business and Economic Research, University of California, 1961). Cerf's study involved the comparison with the annual reports of 527 companies with the expressed needs related to financial reporting of security analysts.

[2]*Ibid.*, pp. 66-67.

valid. For instance, Robert H. Hay has pointed out:

> Competitors get information, once considered secret, by various means. Since much of the same information is reported to the Securities Exchange Commission, the secret information argument is a threadbare excuse for not reporting full information in the annual report.[1]

The attack on big business and its demand for greater corporate publicity continues. Today, the giant corporations dominate the American economy. For instance, in 1959 Carl Kaysen reported the 202 corporations in the largest size class--each with assets of $250 million or more--owned 40 per cent of the assets of all active nonfinancial corporations.[2] A number of people still fear the power which goes with such "bigness" and are actively seeking to curb any further unrestrained expansion of large corporate enterprizes. In Washington, for example, these people include Estes Kefauver in the Senate; Emanuel Celler in the House; and Lee Loevinger, the new assistant attorney general in charge of the Antitrust Division.

In fact, since World War II, according to Glover, "the attack on big business has been twice renewed in

---

[1]Robert D. Hay, "Management Thinking Concerning Corporate Annual Reports," Accounting Review, Vol. XXX, No. 3, July 1955, p. 445.

[2]Carl Kaysen, "The Corporation. How Much Power? What Scope?" The Corporation in Modern Society, ed. Edward S. Mason (Cambridge: Harvard University Press, 1959), p. 85.

full measure. In 1949 by the 'Celler Committee' of the House of Representatives. In 1952 by the Subcommittee of the Senate Select Committee on Small Business."[1] To Glover's tally, which was made in 1955, the 1960-61 Kefauver investigations of the drug industry and the 1962 anti-trust suits of Loevinger must be added. Each of these investigations touched upon corporate publicity, including financial disclosure. Despite the fact each of these hearings revealed questionable business practices hidden by inadequate public reporting, the public--including corporate executives--stupefied perhaps by the narcotic "prosperity"--have not responded in a positive fashion to the critics' demands for reform.

Corporate ownership is more widely dispersed than ever before and the gap between the ownership and the control has widened. Such corporate giants as General Motors, United States Steel and General Electric were, in 1962, "owned" by over 848 thousand, 417 thousand and 275 thousand persons respectively.[2] This dispersion of ownership has created "a virtually omnipotent management and an impotent shareholdership."[3] And, today, as

---

[1]Glover, op. cit., pp. 12-13.

[2]Moody's Industrial Manual: American and Foreign (New York: Moody's Investors Service, 1961).

[3]Bayless Manning, "The American Stockholder," Yale Law Journal. Vol. 67, No. 8, July 1956, pp. 1477-1496.

in the past, a number of prominent persons including A. A. Berle, Jr., Edward S. Mason and those "professional minority stockholders" the Gilbert Brothers and Wilma Soss, are actively seeking to improve management's concept of its social responsibility, including shareholder responsibility, and to devise new schemes for achieving more effective stockholder control over management.

Those people seeking to strengthen the control of stockholders over management, irrespective of their suggested formula for achieving "corporate democracy", almost without exception see more adequate corporate financial disclosure as one means whereby their goals might be at least partially achieved. The Gilberts, for instance, have indicated they would like to see the following improvements in published annual financial statements: more audit certificates addressed to the stockholders; more reports showing comparative data; disclosure of sales, profits and losses by divisions; publication of investment portfolios; more disclosure of advertising and research expenditures; a clearer distinction between operating and non-operating profits; and, in the case where a corporation controls another corporation, the publication of the statements of the controlled company in the controlling company's annual report. In addition, the Gilberts complain of the failure of management to correct false, unreasonable or doubtful reports and opinions related to their corporations which are expressed in brokerage letters.[1]

Today, the people who make these demands for more honest and complete corporate publicity are serious and dedicated individuals. Their efforts are noted in the press and commented on widely in academic and financial circles. Yet, despite management's publicly expressed concern for management-investor relations, few managements have taken these calls for financial reporting reform seriously. In fact, almost universally, management disclosure practices lag far behind the general standards proposed by those numerous individuals and groups who seek either "corporate democracy", the regulation of big business, or simply more useful data for investment analysis purposes.

In the absence of managerial self regulation, and the ominous threat of government regulation, the American Institute of Certified Public Accountants has been for the last three years attempting to review and, where necessary, revise "generally accepted accounting principles" so as to lessen the existing areas of con-

---

[1]Lewis D. Gilbert and John J. Gilbert, Twenty-First Annual Report of Stockholder Activities at Corporation Meetings During 1960, pp. 83-100.

flict between such "principles" in theory and their application in practice. In this endeavor the Institute has the blessing of the Securities Exchange Commission and the New York Stock Exchange.

The Securities and Exchange Commission is, however, more than a spectator; it is already an arbiter and through its administrative control a possible dictator in this matter. Impressed with the growing need for uniform, objective and well-defined accounting standards, the Securities and Exchange Commission has from time to time expressed concern over the lack of such standards. In fact, failure by the accounting profession to develop and gain acceptance of more adequate accounting practices and principles might well force the Commission to exercise its latent authority to prescribe accounting rules. Hitherto, the Securities and Exchange Commission has used its power to impose accounting practices directly on registered companies judiciously and with restraint. But repeatedly the Commission has warned the accounting profession that the failure of private reform would lead to intervention by the Commission. To date the Commission has been patient in this matter. There is no guarantee, however, that its patience is unlimited.

To date, the Institute as a result of its new study and reform program has issued two studies, one related to "accounting postulates"[1] and the other to "funds flow."[2] In both cases, the Institute has jealously excluded non-members, including top management, from the planning, deliberations and publications related to these two studies. Management, rather than complaining of its exclusion from the top councils of the Accounting Principles Board[3] and the accountants' dangerous attempt to pre-empt the responsibility for financial accounting, has remained silent: management has not asked to be included in this program and the accountants have not sought management participation.

The question arises: Should the Institute see the need to change radically conventional reporting practices and standards, how will it impose its wishes on management?

The Institute has no direct power over management and the 70,000-odd certified public accountants who do not choose to belong to the Institute. As Herman Bevis has said:

> ...it is appropriate to take note here of the ideas that the resources of the American Institute of CPAs should be utilized to deter-

---

[1]Maurice Moonitz, The Basic Postulates of Accounting. Accounting Research Study No. 1. American Institute of Certified Public Accountants, 1961.

[2]Perry Mason, "Cash Flow" Analysis and The Funds Statement. Accounting Research Study No. 2. American Institute of Certified Public Accountants, 1961.

[3]The Institute's committee charged with the responsibility of overseeing this program.

> mine what are acceptable accounting standards and that the weight of its authority should be invoked in enforcing them....any illusions as to the extent of authority of the Institute to impose them upon issuers should be quickly dispelled. The Institute's direct authority runs only to those CPAs who voluntarily choose to take membership in it, and this does not even include all CPAs. It has no authority which runs directly to the issuers of accounting data, although its influence is increased to the extent of reliance placed by the SEC on Institute bulletins.[1]

Clearly, in the absence of government intervention, the success achieved by the Institute's efforts will be determined largely by management's reaction to the whole program.[2] Historically, such private reform programs failed as a consequence of the absence of management participation and enthusiasm for change. Today, there is little evidence to suggest the future

---

[1]Herman W. Bevis, "Riding Herd on Accounting Standards," Paper delivered at the Annual Meeting of the American Accounting Association, Columbus, Ohio. August 31, 1960.

[2]In the past, the Institute has issued a number of Accounting Research Bulletins which make "authoritative" pronouncements pertaining to troublesome accounting and financial reporting problems. In 1959, L. Vann Seawell reported a survey of 255 1956-annual reports in which he sought to measure the degree of management's compliance with the Institute's Accounting Research Bulletins. In such areas he found unsatisfactory compliance (less than a 90 per cent level of compliance): net income, retained earnings, and income taxes; long-term leases; working capital; contingency reserves; comparative statements; and amortization of emergency facilities. In two areas only had management complied with the Institute's recommendations: depreciation and high costs; and inventories.--L. Vann Seawell, "Corporate Reports: Financial Fantasy," Business Horizons. Vol. 2, No. 3, Fall 1959, p. 95.

will differ from the past in this respect.

Management, despite its outward show of interest and concern with stockholder, investor and public relations, still in all too many cases prefers to avoid publicity of corporate affairs. For instance, Gordon Donaldson, following a study of management attitudes and practices in the area of debt financing, concluded one of the reasons managements sought debt financing, particularly from private sources, was the avoidance of the necessary disclosure associated with stock issues. Donaldson said:

> /A/ related consideration is that of privacy. An issue of stock by a publicly held company involves the annoyance of public explanations to government agencies, stock exchanges, shareholders, and the industry at large. In the light of the information which must be disclosed, the objection is more apparent than real but to some businessmen it is a significant consideration. Privately placed debt, on the other hand, involves only the management and the lender at the time the decision is made and at the year end a brief word of explanation to the shareholders in the annual report if management considers it necessary.[1]

Thus, just as before 1933, a number of managers are still today reluctant to disclose information related to corporate activities.

In addition, there is some evidence which suggests that corporate financial reporting is still not regarded

---

[1]Gordon Donaldson, Corporate Debt Capacity (Boston: Division of Research Graduate School of Business Administration, Harvard University, 1961), p. 78.

among managers as a top management function. For instance, in 1955 Robert D. Hay conducted a survey of 205[1] corporations to determine management thinking concerning corporate annual reports. He reported the following statistics.

Who prescribes the form and arrangement of your financial statements in your annual reports:

	No. of replies	%
Your company	143	69.8%
Public accountants	22	10.7
Combination of company and public accountants	40	19.5
Total	205	100.0%

Of the 143 who answered that the company prescribed the form of the statements, the following breakdown of those who have this responsibility is shown:

Controller	39
Treasurer	28
Combination of officers	17
President	9
Other	12
Did not say	38
Total	143[2]

Finally, despite the many improvements in corporate disclosure since 1933, survey after survey of management financial disclosure practices during the last sixteen years from the point of view of the investor have shown indications of a need to improve

---

[1]These companies had 5,078,755 <u>book</u> shareholders--Robert D. Hay, *op. cit.*, p. 444.

[2]*Ibid.*, p. 450.

corporate reporting practices.[1] In fact, in 1959, after a two-year study of nearly 800 published annual reports of American industrial corporations, L. Vann Seawell concluded: "It is impossible for me to avoid a conclusion that corporate reporting to shareholders is in some respects a financial fantasy."[2]

Implications

Given existing conditions, there is a high probability that government regulation of corporate financial disclosure practices will be extended to annual reports to stockholders sometime in the not too far distant future. Such a prophesy is based on the previously discussed "general theory" which held government intervention in financial reporting practices was most likely when (a) the adequacy of corporate financial disclosure, from the point of view of the public, was not regarded by management as a top management responsibility; (b) corporate financial disclosure practices lagged far behind the proposed disclosure standards of certain groups external to the firm, for example, critics of big business and security analysts; and (c) the existence of private efforts to

---

[1]For a complete catalogue of these surveys and reports, particularly those conducted by Thomas Sanders (1949), the Securities and Exchange Commission (1946, 1950 and 1956) and the National Federation of Financial Analysts Societies (1950-56), see Cerf, op. cit., pp. 174-177.

[2]L. Vann Seawell, op. cit., p. 92.

reform corporate financial disclosure practices which lacked the support or participation of management. Today, all three conditions are present. In addition, unlike in 1930, a government agency--the Securities and Exchange Commission--stands ready and authorized to intervene.

A drastic extension of government control, if the past is any indication of future events, would most probably come soon after some traumatic event affecting investors directly, such as a significant decline in the general level of stock prices, or some other similar event involving corporate financial disclosure. At that time the proposed standards of those external to the firm would, in all probability, be the basis for the new laws related to corporate financial disclosure to investors. These standards, it should be noted, may not be undesirable standards for management to observe, but such standards need not be the most useful for all users and practical for every issuer.

At the present a stock market decline is perhaps the most likely event which could bring about government action related to corporate financial disclosure. The author, perhaps by disposition rather than logic, is not so sanguine as to believe the present dizzy heights reached by the general level of stock prices will persist forever. Certainly, the experiences of the South Sea bubble and the more recent speculative boom--the 1926-29 bull market--would indicate otherwise. The present speculative mania may last for one, five, ten or even fifteen years but the chances are that it will not last forever!

Today the 70 per cent margin requirement and the other untried restraints imposed upon investors to limit the scope and impact of security speculation might prevent another collapse similar to the 1929 catastrophe. But, will they prevent a decline over a year's period in the Dow-Jones average of, say, 300 points? Each of us has his opinions on this much debated topic: its probability, timing and impact. Hence, because of the difficulties associated with predicting the occurrence of such a traumatic event as a stock market collapse, the author prefers to leave it up to the reader to answer the questions related to the timing of any future government intervention in corporate financial disclosure practices. Instead, the author will be content to point out to management the present dangers related to financial disclosure and their possible implications.

When (if) the federal government does take it upon itself to regulate corporate financial disclosure practices, the standards the government will impose on management and the accounting profession will be those of the critics and that new and significant group, the security analysts: not the prevailing practices of management (this assumes the above three conditions plus the presence of big business and many small investors will continue to exist for some years to come.) On this point the "general theory" is quite clear.

Today, at least, the standards of those external to the firm not only call for more complete corporate financial disclosure but also for more uniform reporting practices and accounting principles. The changing environment will probably increase the need for these reforms as well as, of course, create new and as yet unspecified needs. In short, any future government regulation related to financial disclosure will most probably have the effect of limiting management's freedom to choose from alternative accounting practices for public reporting purposes. Perhaps, a system of uniform account analogous to that now used by the Interstate Commerce Commission might be imposed, for good or for evil, upon large publicly owned corporations such as General Motors. Anyway, given management's present attitude toward uninvited government regulation, it is doubtful if management would welcome further regulation of its financial reporting practices. On the other hand, a number of people external to the firm would welcome any improvement in present reporting practices.

Unfortunately, as in the past, when the time for direct government regulation arrives, any promises by management related to financial disclosure reform would be too late. The time to seek to avoid regulation through the satisfactory fulfillment of managements' social obligation to present complete, fair and honest corporate financial reports is now--not tomorrow--for even today may be too late.

Recommendations

The recommendations are few in number and leave the responsibility for action with management--where it belongs.

First, the adequacy of corporate financial disclosure must become a genuine, important and continuing concern of top management. If management wishes to lessen the probability of government regulation of its annual reports to stockholders and, at the same time, better perform its now widely recognized social role, each management group must review its present disclosure practices and wherever possible, consistent with its other obligations, adopt the recommendations related to financial disclosure of the critics and principal users. Shibboleths such as the "competitor argument" must, for most businessmen, be assigned to the past where they belong. Once management has accomplished the needed improvements in its financial reporting practices, top management, in line with the nature of its function, must continually be alert to the emergence of new user needs for financial data brought about by changes within the environment. These new needs will, of course, demand a positive and sympathetic response by management. Therefore, current reform and future vigilance are necessary if management is to effectively perform its social function with respect to public financial reports.

Second, top management must demand, irrespective of the accountants' protests,[1] active representation on the top councils of the Accounting Principles Board. And, once there, management must further insist upon the membership of the Board being enlarged to include prominent and interested representatives of the principal user groups--security analysts, critics of big business, trade unions--and the principal stock exchanges. Financial disclosure standards are not the exclusive jurisdiction of the accounting profession and management and to regard them as such would be to invite government regulation. Perhaps, as others have pointed out, such management

---

[1]The accounting profession, of course, by refusing to incorporate management in its reform program is courting government regulation in the area of "generally accepted accounting principles"--the very outcome the accountants are now seeking to avoid.

and user participation could produce financial disclosure reforms which are truly of use to the user and practical for the issuer--management.[1]

These recommendations raise, of course, a number of practical questions: How is top management (and the accountants for that matter) to be persuaded to change its present attitudes and practices related to corporate financial disclosure? What authority would the reconstituted Accounting Principles Board have? If management slavishly adopts the critics' proposed standards, might not all the alleged undesired effects of government regulation be imposed upon management without such regulation? These three questions will be briefly answered below. Other questions related to financial disclosure, such as "What specific items ought to be disclosed to investors?", are beyond the scope of this study and will not be considered. The critics and security analysts, of course, have already given their answers to this very important question and some of their suggestions have been mentioned above.

The relevant group of top managers to which the

---

[1]The present study, of course, can give no indication of the outcome of such cooperative reform efforts. There is no historical evidence related to this matter. The existing data only show that private non-cooperative reform efforts related to financial disclosure have repeatedly failed and by failing have increased the probability of government regulation.

above recommendations are addressed are those who control the nation's 500 or so largest public corporations. These companies' stockholders comprise by far the largest percentage of the entire stockholder group--perhaps as high as 80 per cent. Any reform by these companies would, of course, be significant and of wide impact. Hopefully, these top managements by being exposed to studies which carry a message similar to the one presented here will become more aware of the nature of financial disclosure and the consequences of their neglect of it. Unfortunately, to date much of the available literature on this subject has been published in such professional journals as The Analysts Journal and The Journal of Accountancy--journals which seldom come to the attention of top management.

Once management is aware of its current shortcomings in the area of financial disclosure and significantly impressed by the value of unregulated financial reports to take action along the lines suggested above, perhaps such an institution as the Harvard Graduate School of Business Administration, which has established and respected relations with the accounting and commercial worlds and, surprisingly, with also the critics of big business, might act as a catalyst or marriage broker to bring together the representatives of the accounting profession, top management and the principal user groups. But first, more studies, more publications, more speeches and more courses related to financial accounting which stress the need for management responsibility and participation---and its benefits---will be needed. Then, the rest is up to management.

A reconstituted Accounting Principles Board would have as its source of authority only the reputations of those who comprise its membership---much the same as now exists. However, the wider representation would, hopefully, add more prestige and produce recommendations which, while satisfying the user's needs, would be more palatable to management. The relevant issue, however, is not the Board's authority but the usefulness and acceptability of its recommendations to management and the user groups.

And, finally, the answer to the question "might not the effect of regulation be achieved without regulation?" is "yes". This is precisely the goal of the above recommendations. They were not offered to preserve the present reporting practices which the author too believes are inadequate and often misleading. Yet regulation through non-regulation might well preserve some flexibility for management and the user---something which is conspicuously absent from the Interstate Commerce Commission system of accounts---and make possible the continual discussion and revision of existing generally accepted practices as well as the evolution of new standards. The alternative--strict government regulation--has many limitations:

> ...where any of the standards deriving from government sources have been sweeping, even for issuers presumably rather homogeneous, three lessons have been learned: first, the standards always fail to provide comparability in many important details; second, the more extensive and detailed the prescribed standards, the more exceptions and loopholes and the more difficult the enforcement; and third, inflexible standards which are continued after change in the conditions for which they were once suitable can commence to hide a state of affairs, rather than fairly reflect it.[1]

*****

It has been said: those who do not know history are doomed to repeat it. Hopefully, the study by treating the topic of "financial disclosure" historically will help management, accountants and others to avoid repeating the errors of those who went before them. In addition, the study, perhaps because it is so obviously incomplete, indicates a need for a more widespread discussion, analysis and recognition by management, accountants and teachers of business administration of the significance of financial disclosure practices and standards to top management, the accounting profession and the various users of accounting information. This study is but a small contribution

---

[1]Bevis, <u>op. cit</u>.

to that movement.

Today, the existence of a larger number of small investors than ever before, the numerous unsatisfied demands for improved corporate publicity, the dominent role of the giant publicly owned corporation in the nation's economic life and the widespread acceptance--both in and out of government--that such corporations have a social responsibility--all call for a reappraisal by management of its attitudes and practices related to corporate financial disclosure. The need and a possible solution have been shown. The primary responsibility for this matter now rests--as it always has--with top management for, in the long run, it will be management, above all, who will be held responsible by society for any failure to develop and adopt more acceptable financial reporting practices.

APPENDIX A

The F. T. C. questionnaire is reproduced below:

Date.............

Name of Company...

Principal place of Business.............................

Organization:

1. Date of incorporation?
2. State of incorporation? Statutory office?
3. Places other than principal office where company maintains office or does business?
4. In what States other than the State of incorporation is the company authorized to do business? To sell stock?
5. Amount of preferred and common stock authorized; state the par value of each.
6. Amount of preferred and common stock issued, or agreed to be issued.
7. What bonds, debentures and secured obligations have been issued, agreed to be issued or are about to be issued; describe each?
8. Is the company the result of any consolidation, merger, or reorganization; if so, give details?
9. What subsidiary companies are controlled by stock ownership or otherwise, with the amount and percentage held in each?
10. Give the names, address, then and now, of each officer, director, promoter and organizer, who has been, is now, or is proposed to be connected with or interested in your company, with their experience and qualifications.
11. State the compensation, benefit, advantage, stock, securities, cash or otherwise, promised or paid for their activities, services or properties transferred, as to each?
12. Give the names and addresses of the seven largest stockholders, and the amount held or issued to each, consideration in moneys, services or property paid or agreed to be paid by each.

Business:

13 Describe briefly the business purposes and objects of your company; where it is to be conducted; the facilities and plant available therefor.

14. When did or will your company commence business? The amount of capital paid up at the commencement of business?
15. Have you or will you take over any existing business. Describe It?

Plans:

16 What is your immediate plan of action; what amount of money will be necessary to accomplish it; how is it proposed to raise this money; what stocks or securities are to be sold therefore or have been sold, and on what basis?
17. Do you propose or are you selling your stock direct or through others; state who?
18. Give the names and addresses of all stock or securities sales agents or representatives now in the field?
19, Describe accurately the compensation paid or to be paid; discounts allowed and benefits promised or agreed to be given to each?
20. At what price are your stocks or securities to be sold?
21. What percentage of the gross proceeds thereof are to be paid to your company?
22. Have the stocks or securities which you propose to sell been underwritten and on what basis, or are you otherwise assured that all of the funds needed will be obtained?
23. To what extent are subscriptions to be made conditional upon your obtaining total subscriptions or a given amount and what amount?
24. Annex copies of all literature, advertisements, prospectuses and circulars used in furtherance of the sale of your stocks and securities by yourself or others, and any instructions, to your stock salesmen?

Properties:

25. Describe accurately, but briefly, the properties acquired or to be acquired, real and personal, with all improvements or plant now or to be placed thereon, the amounts paid or to be paid in money, stocks, bonds, securities or otherwise, therefor and the actual value of each portion or parcel thereof.

Financial Condition:

26. Annex a copy of a trial balance sheet and profit and loss statement, prepared for the purpose of your report hereunder or made up within thirty days prior to the date of this notice.

27. Attach a copy of the last annual and last quarterly balance sheet and profit and loss statement.
28 As to the assets enumerated therein, describe briefly each item and state the actual cost and the present estimated value thereof.
29 State the book value of each class of stock per share and the estimated actual value thereof eliminating all doubtful, contingent, speculative or excessively valued assets, stating what is eliminated and why?
30. State any existing facts or probable developments concerning your company, its officers, directors, managers, brokers, or representatives, properties, business or prospects, which have not been covered by preceding questions, but which should be made known to an investor.
31. Do you offer to accept, exchange or dispose of Thrift Stamps, War Saving's Stamps, or Liberty Bonds in order to sell your own stock or securities?
32. If your answer to question 31 or any part thereof is yes, will you voluntarily cease and desist from such practices in the future?

Clinton Collver, <u>How To Analyze Industrial Securities</u>, 2nd edition (New York: Moody's Investors Service, 1919), pp. 206-208.

A SELECTED BIBLIOGRAPHY[1]

The Accountant. Vol. 20, New Series. No. 1028. August 18, 1894

The Accountant. Vol. 25, New Series. No. 1280. June 17, 1899.

Allen, Frederick Lewis. *Only Yesterday*. New York: Harper and Brothers, 1931.

Allen, Frederick Lewis. *The Big Change: America Transforms Itself 1900-1950*. New York: Harper and Brothers, 1952.

American Association of Public Accountants. *The Influence of Accountant's Certificates on Commercial Credit*. Copyright, 1913.

American Association of Public Accountants. "Protection of Investors," *The Journal of Accountancy*. Vol. 21, No. 1. January 1916. Pp. 52-53.

American Institute of Accountants. Report of the Special Committee on Cooperation with Stock Exchanges. September 22, 1932.

Ashby, Forrest Bee. *The Economic Effect of Blue Sky Laws*. Philadelphia, 1926.

Ayres, Arthur V. "Governmental Regulation of Securities Issues," *Political Science Quarterly*. Vol. XXVII, No. 4. December 1913. Pp. 586-592.

Baitsell, John M., Glover, John D., and Hawkins, David F. *McGraw-Hill Publishing Company Inc*. Boston: Harvard Graduate School of Business Administration, 1961.

The Bankers' Magazine. Vol. 27. September 1867.

The Bankers' Magazine. Vol. 58. July 1894.

The Bankers' Magazine. Vol. 60. September 1895.

Barnes, Irston R. *Public Utility Control in Massachusetts*. New Haven: Yale University Press, 1930.

---

[1]Includes books, articles, reports and government documents cited.

Berle, Adolf A. Jr. and Means, Gardiner C. The Modern Corporation and Private Property. New York: The Macmillan Company, 1933.

Bevis, Herman. "Riding Herd on Accounting Standards." Paper delivered at the Annual Meeting of the American Accounting Association. Columbus, Ohio, August 31, 1960.

Boston Evening Transcript. November 5, 1932.

Brandeis, Louis D. Other People's Money. New York: Frederick A. Stokes Company, 1913.

Brown, Sistor Isadore. The Historical Development of the Use of Ratios in Financial Statement Analysis to 1933. Washington: The Catholic University of America Press, 1955.

Campbell, William B. "Cooperation Between Accountants and Bankers," The Journal of Accountancy. Vol. 45, No. 1. January 1928. Pp. 1-13.

Capital Issues Committee. Rules and Regulations. Washington: Government Printing Office, 1918.

Cerf, Alan Robert. Corporate Reporting And Investment Decision. Berkeley: Institute of Business and Economic Research, University of California, 1961.

Cherington, Homer V. The Investor and the Securities Act. Washington: American Council on Public Affairs, 1942.

Collver, Clinton. How To Analyze Industrial Securities. 2d ed. New York: Moody's Investors Service, 1919.

Collver, Clinton. Industrial Securities. New York: Doubleday, Page & Company, 1921.

The Commercial and Financial Chronicle. August 28, 1926.

The Commercial and Financial Chronicle. September 4, 1926.

Connell, A.C. Companies and Company Law. London: Pitman & Sons, 1924.

Connelly, William E. A Standard History of Kansas and Kansans. Chicago: Lewis Publishing Company, 1918.

Corporation Finance Lectures 1908-1909. Copyright, 1908, by President and Fellows of Harvard College.

Cowles, Virginia. The Great Swindle. New York: Harper and Brothers, 1960.

Crafts, William A. State Railroad Commissions. New York: The Railroad Gazette, 1883.

Dewing, Arthur Stone. The Financial Policy of Corporations. 2 vols. 3d ed. revised. New York: The Ronald Press Company, 1934.

Dickenson, A. Lowes. "Duties and Responsibilities of the Public Accountant with regard to New Issues of Stocks and Bonds," The Journal of Accountancy. Vol. 1, No. 1. November 1905. Pp. 16-27.

Donaldson, Gordon. Corporate Debt Capacity. Boston: Division of Research Graduate School of Business Administration Harvard University, 1961.

DuBois, Armand Budington. The English Business Company after the Bubble Act 1720-1800. New York: The Commonwealth Fund, 1938.

Edelman, Jacob Murray. Securities Regulation in the 48 States. Chicago: The Journal of State Governments, 1942.

Faulkner, Harold Underwood. The Quest for Social Justice, 1898-1914. New York: The Macmillan Company, 1931.

Federal Reserve Bank of Boston. "A History of Investment Banking in New England," Annual Report for 1960.

Federal Reserve Board. "Uniform Accounting," Federal Reserve Bulletin. Vol. III. April 1917. Pp. 270-284.

Federal Reserve Board. Uniform Accounting. Washington: Government Printing Office, 1917.

Federal Reserve Board. Approved Methods for the Preparation of Balance Sheet Statements. Washington: Government Printing Office, 1918.

Federal Reserve Board. Verification of Financial Statements (Revised). Washington: Government Printing Office, 1929.

Fixel, Arthur E. False Financial Statements. New York: Mathew Bender & Company, 1924.

Flowers, William Baker. Criteria for Disclosure of Post-Statement Events. Austin: Bureau of Business Research The University of Texas, 1960.

Frankfurter, Felix. "The Federal Securities Act," Fortune. Vol. 8, No. 2. August 1933. P. 53 ff.

Galbraith, John Kenneth. The Great Crash 1929. Boston: Houghton Mifflin Company, 1955.

Gilbert, Lewis D., and Gilbert, John J. Twenty-First Annual Report of Stockholder Activities at Corporation Meetings During 1960.

Glover, John D. The Attack on Big Business. Boston: Division of Research Graduate School of Business Administration Harvard University, 1954.

Graham, Benjamin, and Dodd, David L. Security Analysis: Principles and Techniques. New York: The McGraw-Hill Book Company, Inc., 1951.

Great Britain. Parliamentary Papers. Vol. VII (1844).

Great Britain. Report of the Departmental Committee Appointed By The Board Of Trade To Inquire What Amendments Are Necessary In The Acts Relating To Joint Stock Companies Incorporated With Limited Liability Under The Companies Acts, 1862 to 1890, British Parliamentary Papers. Vol. LXXXVIII (1895).

Great Britain. Seventh General Annual Report by the Board of Trade under Section 29 of the Companies Act, 1890. London: Her Majesty's Stationery Office, 1898.

Griffith, William (ed.). The Roosevelt Policy. 2 vols. New York: 1919.

Hay, Robert D. "Management Thinking Concerning Corporate Annual Reports," Accounting Review. Vol. XXX, No. 3. July 1955. Pp. 444-450.

Hicks, John D. The Populist Revolt. Minneapolis: The University of Minnesota Press, 1931.

Hidy, Ralph W., and Hidy, Muriel E. Pioneering in Big Business 1882-1911. New York: Harper & Brothers, 1955.

Hill, Julien H. "Information Desired by the Banker," The Journal of Accountancy. Vol. 30, No. 5. November 1920. Pp. 338-343.

Horack, Frank Edward. The Organization and Control of Industrial Corporations. Philadelphia: C. F. Taylor, 1903.

Horngren, Charles T. "Increasing the Utility of Financial Statements," The Journal of Accountancy. Vol. 108, No. 1. July 1959. Pp. 39-46.

Hoxsey, J.M.B. "Accounting for Investors," The Journal of Accountancy. Vol. 50, No. 4. October 1930. Pp. 251-284.

Investment Bankers Association of America. Proceedings of the Organization Meeting. August 8, 1912.

Investment Bankers Association of America. Proceedings of the Annual Convention. 1912-1933.

Johnson, Arthur M. "Theodore Roosevelt and the Bureau of Corporations," The Mississippi Valley Historical Review. Vol. XLV, No. 4. March 1959. Pp. 571-590.

Journal of Accountancy. Vols. 1-56. November 1905-December 1933.

Kansas State Bank Commission. Biennial Reports. 1896 and 1910.

Key, V.O.,Jr. Politics, Parties and Pressure Groups. New York: Thomas Y. Crowell Company, 1952.

Kirkendall, Richard S. "A. A. Berle Jr.: Student of the Corporation, 1917-1932," Business History Review. Vol. XXXV, No. 1. Spring 1961. Pp. 43-58.

Kirkland, Edward C. Men, Cities and Transportation. 2 vols. Cambridge: Harvard University Press, 1948.

Landis, James M. "The Federal Securities Act and Regulations Relating to the Work and Responsibility of the C.P.A." Address presented before the Eleventh Annual Fall Conference of the New York State Society of Certified Public Accountants. October 30, 1933.

Landis, James M. "The Legislative History of the Securities Act of 1933," The George Washington Law Review. Vol. 28, No. 1. October 1959. Pp. 29-49.

Littleton, A. C., and Yamey, B. S. Studies in the History of Accounting. Homewood: Richard D. Irwin, Inc., 1956.

Livingston, J. A. The American Stockholder. Philadelphia: J. B. Lippincott Company, 1958.

Loss, Louis. Security Regulation. Boston: Little, Brown and Company, 1951.

Loss, Louis, and Cowett, Edward M. Blue Sky Law. Boston: Little, Brown and Company, 1958.

Lough, William H. Business Finance. New York: The Ronald Press, 1919.

McCormick, Edward T. Understanding the Securities Act and the S.E.C. New York: American Book Company, 1948.

McLaren, N. Loyall. Annual Reports to Stockholders. New York: The Ronald Press Company, 1947.

Magazine of Wall Street. September 11, 1926.

Manning, Bayless. "The American Stockholder by J. A. Livingston," Yale Law Journal. Vol. 67, No. 8. July 1958 Pp. 1477-96.

Marquis, Albert Nelson. Who's Who in America: 1930-1931. Chicago: The A. N. Marquis Co., 1930.

Martin, H. S. The New York Stock Exchange and the "Money Trust." Copyright 1913 by H. S. Martin.

Mason, Edward (ed.). The Corporation in Modern Society. Cambridge: Harvard University Press, 1959.

Mason, Perry. "Cash Flow" Analysis and The Funds Statement. Accounting Research Study No. 2. American Institute of Certified Public Accountants, 1961.

Massachusetts General Court. Report. Special Commission to Investigate the Sale of Corporate Securities and Related Matters. House No. 1175. January, 1921.

May, George O. "Corporate Publicity and the Auditor," The Journal of Accountancy. Vol. 42, No. 5. November 1926. Pp. 321-326.

May, George O. Financial Accounting: A Distillation of Experience. New York: The Macmillan Company, 1943.

Means, Gardiner C. "The Diffusion of Stock Ownership in the United States," The Quarterly Journal of Economics. Vol. XLIV, No. 4. August 1930. Pp. 561-600.

Meeker, James Edward. The Work of the Stock Exchange. New York: The Ronald Press Company, 1922.

Montgomery, Robert H. "Federal Control of Corporations," The Journal of Accountancy. Vol. 14, No. 4. October 1912, Pp. 272-290.

Moody's Industrial Manual: American and Foreign. New York: Moody's Investors Service, 1961.

Moonitz, Maurice. The Basic Postulates of Accounting. Accounting Research Study No. 1. American Institute of Certified Public Accountants, 1961.

Mulvey, Thomas. Report Upon Existing Registration In Canada And Elsewhere Prepared By The Under Secretary Of State. Ottawa: Government Printing Bureau, 1913.

Myer, John N. Financial Statement Analysis. New York: John N. Myer, 1939.

Neill, Humphrey B. The Inside Story Of The Stock Exchange. New York: B. C. Forbes & Sons Publishing Co., Inc., 1950.

The New Republic. September 18, 1926.

New York Times. March 30, 1933.

New York Times. December 19, 1929.

Pillsbury, Albert E. Arguments of Ex-Att'y Gen'l. In Behalf Of The Boston Associated Board Of Trade, Massachusetts State Board of Trade, And Boston Merchants' Association In Support Of The Bills To Prevent Stock And Debt Watering And To Provide For Supervision Of The Issue Of Securities By Railroad, Street Railway, Gas, Electric Light, Telegraph, Telephone, Aqueduct, And Water Companies. And To

Provide Further Supervision of Railroad and Street Railway Leases And Consolidations Before The Joint Special Committee On Revision Of Corporation Laws, April 9, 1844. Boston: Geo. H. Ellis, 1894.

Reed, Dougherty & Hoyt. Blue Sky Laws. Prepared for the Investment Bankers Association of America. November, 1920.

Ripley, William Z. Railroad Finance and Organization. New York: Longman's, Green and Co., 1920.

Ripley, William Z. "Stop, Look, Listen!" The Atlantic Monthly. Vol. 138, No. 3. September 1926. Pp. 380-399.

Ripley, William Z. Main Street and Wall Street. Boston: Little, Brown & Co., 1927.

Rodgers, Cleveland. The Roosevelt Program. New York: G. P. Putnam's Sons, 1933.

Saloutos, Theodore and Hicks, John D. Agricultural Discontent in the Midwest, 1900-1939. Madison: University of Wisconsin Press, 1951.

Seawell, L. Vann. "Corporate Annual Reports: Financial Fantasy," Business Horizons. Vol. 2, No. 3. Fall 1959. Pp. 92-101.

Sells, Elijah W. "The Accounting Profession: Its Demands and Its Future," The Journal of Accountancy. Vol. 20, No. 5. November 1915. Pp. 325-333.

Shultz, Birl E. Stock Exchange Procedure. New York: New York Stock Exchange Institute, 1936.

Simmons, E. H. H. Cooperation Against Security Frauds. New York: Committee on Publicity New York Stock Exchange, 1925.

Smith, Alexander. "The Abuse of The Audit in Selling Securities," The Journal of Accountancy. Vol. 14, No. 4. October 1912. Pp. 243-253.

Smith, Edgar Lawrence. Common Stocks as Long-Term Investment. New York: The Macmillan Company, 1924.

Stacey, Nicholas A. English Accountancy 1800-1954. London: Gee and Company, 1954.

Sterrett, J. E. "Legislation for the Control of Corporations," The Journal of Accountancy. Vol. 9, No. 4. February 1910. Pp. 241-247.

Times. November 10, 1898.

Topham, Alfred F. Principles of Company Law. 2d ed. London: Butterworth & Co., 1908.

Tugwell, Rexford G. "The Progressive Orthodoxy of Franklin D. Roosevelt," Ethics. Vol. 64, No. 1. October 1953. Pp. 1-23.

U. S. Congress, House. Money Trust Investigation. Report of the Committee appointed Pursuant to House Resolutions 429 and 504 to Investigate the concentration of control of Money and Credit. H. R. Report No. 1593, 62nd Congress, 3rd Session.

U. S. Congress, House. Report of Capital Issues Committee. H. R. Doc. No. 1485. 65th Congress, 3rd Session.

U. S. Congress, House. Proposed Federal "Blue-Sky" Law. Committee On The Judiciary Hearings on H. R. 188. 66th Congress, 1st Session.

U. S. Congress, House. "Blue Sky" Bill. Committee on Interstate and Foreign Commerce. Hearings on H. R. 7215. 67th Congress, 1st Session.

U. S. Congress, House. Securities Act. Committee on Interstate and Foreign Commerce. Hearings on H. R. 4314. 73rd Congress, 1st Session.

U. S. Industrial Commission. Preliminary Report on Trusts and Industrial Combinations. Vol. I. Washington: Government Printing Office, 1900.

U. S. Industrial Commission. Final Report. Vol. XIX. Washington: Government Printing Office, 1902.

U. S. Congress, Senate. Stock Exchange Practices. Hearings Before The Committee on Banking and Currency On S. Res. 84. Parts 1-6. 72nd Congress, 1st Session.

U. S. Congress, Senate. Securities Act. Hearings Before The Committee On Banking And Currency on S. 875. 73rd Congress, 1st Session.

U. S. Congress, Senate. Stock Exchange Practices. Report Of The Committee on Banking and Currency Pursuant to S. Res. 84 (72nd Congress) and S. Res. 56 and S. Res. 97. (73rd Congress.) Senate Report No. 1455. 73rd Congress, 2nd Session.

Weissman, Rudolph L. The New Wall Street. New York: Harper & Brothers, 1939.

Whitney, Richard. "Business Honesty." An address before the Philadelphia Chamber of Commerce. April 24, 1933.

Whitney, Richard. Statement by Richard Whitney, President New York Stock Exchange. Made to the Governing Committee and the Membership in regard to the investigation of stock exchange practices by the Committee on Banking and Currency of the United States Senate. August 24, 1932.

Wilson, Woodrow. The New Freedom. New York: Doubleday, Page & Company, 1913.

Woytinsky, W. S., and Woytinsky, E. S. World Population and Production. New York: The Twentieth Century Fund, 1953.

Zornow, William Frank. Kansas. A History of the Jayhawk State. Norman: University of Oklahoma Press, 1957.

For Product Safety Concerns and Information please contact our
EU representative GPSR@taylorandfrancis.com Taylor & Francis
Verlag GmbH, Kaufingerstraße 24, 80331 München, Germany